A·N·N·U·A·L E·D·I·T·I·O·N·S

Accounting

99/00

Second Edition

EDITOR

Aileen Ormiston
Mesa Community College

Professor Aileen Ormiston is chairperson of the Business Department and teaches accounting at Mesa Community College in Mesa, Arizona. She received her bachelor's degree in accounting from Michigan State University and a master's degree in finance from Texas A&M University. She is a Certified Public Accountant and a member of the American Institute of Certified Public Accountants, the American Accounting Association, and the Institute of Management Accountants. Mesa Community College was one of the 13 universities and colleges that received a grant from the Accounting Education Change Commission and Professor Ormiston was actively involved in developing the new accounting curriculum.

Dushkin/McGraw-Hill
Sluice Dock, Guilford, Connecticut 06437

Visit us on the Internet
http://www.dushkin.com/annualeditions/

Credits

1. Financial Accounting
Facing overview—© 1998 by PhotoDisc, Inc.
2. Managerial Accounting
Facing overview—© 1998 by PhotoDisc, Inc.
3. Accounting Issues of Government
Facing overview—© 1998 by PhotoDisc, Inc.

Copyright

Cataloging in Publication Data
Main entry under title: Annual editions: accounting. 1999/2000.
1. Accounting. I. Ormiston, Aileen, *comp.* II. Title: Accounting.
ISBN 0–07–030578–1 657 ISSN 1096–4282

Second Edition

Cover image © 1999 PhotoDisc, Inc.

Printed in the United States of America 1234567890BAHBAH54321098 Printed on Recycled Paper

Editors/Advisory Board

Members of the Advisory Board are instrumental in the final selection of articles for each edition of ANNUAL EDITIONS. Their review of articles for content, level, currentness, and appropriateness provides critical direction to the editor and staff. We think that you will find their careful consideration well reflected in this volume.

To the Reader

In publishing ANNUAL EDITIONS we recognize the enormous role played by the magazines, newspapers, and journals of the public press in providing current, first-rate educational information in a broad spectrum of interest areas. Many of these articles are appropriate for students, researchers, and professionals seeking accurate, current material to help bridge the gap between principles and theories and the real world. These articles, however, become more useful for study when those of lasting value are carefully collected, organized, indexed, and reproduced in a low-cost format, which provides easy and permanent access when the material is needed. That is the role played by ANNUAL EDITIONS.

New to ANNUAL EDITIONS is the inclusion of related World Wide Web sites. These sites have been selected by our editorial staff to represent some of the best resources found on the World Wide Web today. Through our carefully developed topic guide, we have linked these Web resources to the articles covered in this ANNUAL EDITIONS reader. We think that you will find this volume useful, and we hope that you will take a moment to visit us on the Web at ***http://www.dushkin.com/*** to tell us what you think.

Annual Editions: Accounting 99/00 is the second edition of a collection of articles that will, it is hoped, become a part of many introductory accounting courses. The goal of this anthology is to provide relevant reading material that students will find informative, interesting, and complementary to their textbook readings.

In 1989, the creation of the Accounting Education Change Commission (AECC) was a significant step that was taken to promote change in accounting education. Grants were given by the AECC to 13 universities and colleges willing to make curricular changes to better meet the needs of the accounting profession. Rapid changes in the 1980s and 1990s had altered the skills that students will need to be successful in the twenty-first century's business environment. The AECC's first formal position paper, "Objectives of Education for Accountants," discussed the need for educational programs to change from a focus on rote knowledge acquisition to a focus of helping students learn how to learn.

The 1990s has been a decade of change for accounting educators. While not all universities and colleges have embarked on change, the success of the AECC grant program has been a catalyst for continuous improvement and change in numerous accounting programs nationwide. The traditional and false perception of accounting has been that the subject matter is dull and boring, and that accountants are number crunchers performing repetitive tasks. Changes in the way accounting is taught are now finally allowing students to see that accounting is a constantly evolving, controversial, and interesting subject, and that accountants need many skills other than math. One of those skills is learning to learn. Reading is a key component of becoming a proficient learner. This collection of articles can help students learn the value of reading. Students will also recognize that what they are learning in their accounting courses has relevance to actual events in the real world.

To date, changes that have occurred in accounting education have resulted in multiple approaches to teaching accounting courses. With this in mind, the articles have been organized into three key topical areas: financial accounting, managerial accounting, and accounting issues of government. The first unit includes articles about financial accounting topics that relate to cash flows, profits, and financial statements analysis and their components, as well as coverage of history, current changes in the accounting profession, accounting organizations and accounting standards, information technology, internal control, ethics, and fraud, assets, liabilities, and revenue recognition, and international accounting. Unit 2 focuses on management accounting topics including cost accounting systems, activity-based costing, cost-volume profit analysis, information technology and the year 2000, budgeting, quality, and cost control. A short, but diverse, collection of articles related to the accounting system in the federal government is offered in the final unit.

Several features are included in this edition for easier use. Abstracts in the *table of contents* briefly describe the content of each article. A *topic guide* lists accounting topics and articles related to those topics for quick location of specific articles. With the vast amount of information now available on the Internet, *Annual Editions* has made it easier than ever to locate *Web sites* related to accounting. A list of accounting Web sites is included in this edition, and all Web sites are hot-linked through the *Annual Editions: Accounting 99/00* home page at *http://www.dushkin.com/annualeditions*.

We believe that this *Annual Editions: Accounting 99/00* volume is unique. Although other anthologies of accounting articles exist, we are unaware of any that have been developed specifically for the introductory level of accounting. We hope you find this edition useful. Please let us know what you think by completing and returning the postpaid *article rating form* on the last page of the book. Your thoughts and suggestions will allow us to improve this collection so it better meets your needs.

Aileen Ormiston

Aileen Ormiston
Editor

Contents

Financial Accounting

The 26 articles in this section examine the history of accounting and current changes in the profession, national and international financial reporting issues, internal control, fraud, concepts related to specific assets, liabilities, revenue recognition, profits and cash flows in companies, and financial statement analysis.

The concepts in bold italics are developed in the article. For further expansion please refer to the Topic Guide and the Index.

The concepts in bold italics are developed in the article. For further expansion please refer to the Topic Guide and the Index.

The concepts in bold italics are developed in the article. For further expansion please refer to the Topic Guide and the Index.

Managerial Accounting

The 19 selections in this unit examine issues important to decision making within an organization. Topics include cost-accounting systems, information technology, activity-based costing, cost-volume-profit analysis, budgeting, standard costing systems, and behavioral and quality issues.

The concepts in bold italics are developed in the article. For further expansion please refer to the Topic Guide and the Index.

The concepts in bold italics are developed in the article. For further expansion please refer to the Topic Guide and the Index.

Accounting Issues of Government

The three articles in this section examine the history of accounting in the federal government, the improvements currently being implemented in the federal government, and the role of the accounting profession now and into the future.

Topic Guide

This topic guide suggests how the selections and World Wide Web sites found in the next section of this book relate to topics of traditional concern to accounting students and professionals. It is useful for locating interrelated articles and Web sites for reading and research. The guide is arranged alphabetically according to topic.

The relevant Web sites, which are numbered and annotated on pages 4 and 5, are easily identified by the Web icon (◎) under the topic articles. By linking the articles and the Web sites by topic, this ANNUAL EDITIONS reader becomes a powerful learning and research tool.

TOPIC AREA	TREATED IN
Accounting Profession	1. First Century of the CPA 2. Are You Ready for New Assurance Services? 3. Prescription for Change 4. How the Andersens Turned into the Bickersons 8. Beresford Looks Forward 28. It's Not Your Father's Management Accounting! 46. Federal Financial Management ◎ ***2, 7, 12, 14, 15, 20, 24, 26***
Accounting Rules/Standards	1. First Century of the CPA 5. FASB under Siege 6. How Should the FASB Be Judged? 7. Corporate America Is Fed Up with FASB 9. Challenges to the Current Accounting Model 22. New Accounting Standards and the Small Business 24. How Companies Report Income 25. Understanding Global Standards 26. IAS Express Gains Steam 29. Managerial Accounting Needs a Philosophical Base ◎ ***9, 10, 12, 15, 19, 33, 34***
Accounts Receivable and Doubtful Accounts	11. 12 Tips to Make Financial Operations More Efficient 15. High-Tech Sales 16. Numbers Game at Bausch & Lomb? 21. Dangers of Creative Accounting 23. Surviving Explosive Growth ◎ ***16, 27***
Activity-Based Costing	30. Cost/Management Accounting: 21st Century Paradigm 33. Using ABC to Determine the Cost of Servicing Customers 34. How ABC Changed the Post Office 35. ABC: Why It's Tried and How It Succeeds ◎ ***16, 21***
Analysis	15. High-Tech Sales 19. Cash Flows, Ratio Analysis and the W. T. Grant Company Bankruptcy 20. Cash Flows: Another Approach to Ratio Analysis 21. Dangers of Creative Accounting 31. Updating Standard Cost Systems 33. Using ABC to Determine the Cost of Servicing Customers 36. Multidimensional Break-Even Analysis 37. Planning for Profit 40. Measuring the Costs of Quality ◎ ***6, 14, 16, 18, 21, 22, 26, 27***
Assets	9. Challenges to the Current Accounting Model 15. High-Tech Sales 16. Numbers Game at Bausch & Lomb? 17. First In, First Out 18. Inventory Chicanery Tempts More Firms, Fools More Auditors 21. Dangers of Creative Accounting ◎ ***6, 9, 10, 12, 13, 14, 16, 18***
Audits/Auditors	1. First Century of the CPA 2. Are You Ready for New Assurance Services? 18. Inventory Chicanery Tempts More Firms, Fools More Auditors 41. We Need Better Financial Reporting 48. Government Issues First Consolidated Financial Report ◎ ***6, 7, 9, 10, 12, 13, 14, 24, 25, 33, 34, 36***
Break-Even Analysis	36. Multidimensional Break-Even Analysis 37. Planning for Profit ◎ ***22***
Budgets	38. Is It Time to Replace Traditional Budgeting? 39. How to Set Up a Budgeting and Planning System ◎ ***11, 14, 16, 18, 27***
Cash Flows	19. Cash Flows, Ratio Analysis and the W. T. Grant Company Bankruptcy 20. Cash Flows: Another Approach to Ratio Analysis 21. Dangers of Creative Accounting ◎ ***6, 11, 14, 16, 18, 27***
Cost-Volume-Profit Analysis	30. Cost/Management Accounting: 21st Century Paradigm
Costs/Operating Expenses	32. Are We Making Money Yet? 33. Using ABC to Determine the Cost of Servicing Customers 34. How ABC Changed the Post Office 35. ABC: Why It's Tried and How It Succeeds 40. Measuring the Costs of Quality 42. How Nonfinancial Performance Measures Are Used 45. Year 2000 Problem ◎ ***16, 21, 23, 24***
FASB (Financial Accounting Standards Board)	1. First Century of the CPA 5. FASB under Siege 6. How Should the FASB Be Judged?

World Wide Web Sites

DUSHKINONLINE

Annual Editions: Accounting

The following World Wide Web sites have been carefully researched and selected to support the articles found in this reader. If you are interested in learning more about specific topics found in this book, these Web sites are a good place to start. The sites are cross-referenced by number and appear in the topic guide on the previous two pages. Also, you can link to these Web sites through our DUSHKIN ONLINE support site at *http://www.dushkin.com/online/*.

The following sites were available at the time of publication. Visit our Web site—we update DUSHKIN ONLINE regularly to reflect any changes.

General Sources

1. FedWorld

http://www.fedworld.gov/

A comprehensive central access point for locating and acquiring government information is available on this Web site.

2. The List of CPA Firms

http://www.cpafirms.com/

This directory links to over 1,00 CPA firms worldwide and includes a Web Placement System for accountants. The five largest U.S. accounting firms can be reached through this site: Arthur Andersen, Deloitte & Touche, Ernst & Young, KPMG Peat Marwick, and PricewaterhouseCoopers.

3. Standard & Poors

http://www.advisorinsight.com/pub/indexes/idx_contents.html

The S&P indices, guidelines, and FAQs are at this site.

4. Stock Exchanges

http://www.rutgers.edu/Accounting/raw/resources/stexchg.htm

Nineteen stock exchanges, from the American Stock Exchange alphabetically through the one in Zagreb (Croatia), can be accessed from this site.

5. StockMaster

http://stockmaster.com/newbody.html

Serving individual investors, this Web site allows rapid stock and mutual fund quotes along with historic charts.

Financial Accounting

6. Activity-Based Risk Evaluation Model of Auditing

http://www.efs.mq.edu.au/accg/resources/abrema/index.html

This Web site presents the underlying concept stages in a risk model of auditing.

7. AICPA Assurance Services

http://www.aicpa.org/assurance/index.htm

This Web site, developed by the Special Committee on Assurance Services, will tell you what you need to know about this new addition to CPA services.

8. Academy of Accounting Historians

http://weatherhead.cwru.edu/Accounting/page/

A series of abstracts about accounting history is offered at this Web site.

9. Business Ethics Resources on WWW

http://www.ethics.ubc.ca/resources/business/

Here is an excellent resource for ethical business questions. It covers codes of ethics, public sector ethics, institutions and organizations, and other topics.

10. Corporate Social Responsibility Principles & Codes

http://www.goodmoney.com/directry_codes.htm

This group of resources will help global businesses understand the business practices of other countries.

11. The Credit Process: A Guide for Small Business Owners

http://www.ny.frb.org/pihome/addpub/credit.html

This booklet on the Web was produced by the Federal Reserve Bank of New York to help first-time entrepreneurs. It covers everything from borrowing to business plan making.

12. Financial Accounting Standards Board (FASB)

http://www.rutgers.edu/Accounting/raw/fasb/

Dedicated to improving standards of financial accounting and reporting, the FASB offers this excellent Web site for the guidance and education of the public.

13. Internal Auditing World Wide Web

http://www.bitwise.net/iawww/

Information and knowledge pertaining to internal auditing professions and functions across all associations, industries, and countries can be found on this Web site.

14. International Accounting Network (IAN)

http://www.csu.edu.au/anet/

IAN consists of six members that provide a networked, electronic forum for the exchange of information and the discussion of accounting and auditing issues. They also provide extensive links to professional associations and home pages of professionals and academics active on the Web. The six sites are: ANet—Australia; Nordic Accounting Network—Finland/Sweden; Rutgers Accounting Web—United States; Summa Project—United Kingdom; University of Hawaii—United States, and The CAARNET—Singapore.

15. International Accounting Standards Committee (IASC)

http://www.iasc.org.uk/frame/cen0.htm

The aim of the IASC is to achieve uniformity in the accounting principles that are used for financial reporting around the world, and thus to improve the ability of investors, creditors, and governments to make informed resource allocation and policy decisions. Visit all 13 sections of this site.

16. Palo Alto Software:bplans.com

http://www.bplans.com/start.cfm/

This site is dedicated to supplying information about real, implementable plans for small- and medium-sized businesses. It contains a list of sample plans representing many different kinds of businesses. There is also a section on start-ups.

17. The Public Register

http://www.publicregister.com/

Billed as the information source for investors, this page links to individual company pages, financial profiles, contacts for investor relations, annual reports, and research reports.

18. Small Business Exchange

http://www6.americanexpress.com/smallbusiness/

This page is a computer community for entrepreneurs. It offers 10 ways to increase small business cash flow, buying/selling a business, day-to-day management, finding money, and customers, franchising, and expanding internationally.

Managerial Accounting

19. American Bar Association (ABA)
http://www.abanet.org/
This entry site for the ABA has hyperlinks to a wealth of business law at *lawlink/home.html.*

20. American Institute of CPAs (AICPA)
http://www.aicpa.org/
This home page of the AICPA can be accessed for information on current accounting topics, a membership directory, and a detailed series of hyperlinks to a wide range of publications, relevant state news, and tax information.

21. Activity-Based Costing (ABC)
http://www.pitt.edu/~narst8/Welcome.html
Narcyz Roztocki, at the University of Pittsburgh, has put together an excellent group of papers on ABC and EVA (Economic Value Added) systems at this site.

22. Break-Even Analysis
http://web.miep.org/bus_plan/break.html
Break-even analysis concepts and an excellent description of a business plan (with templates) are offered at this site.

23. Information Technology Association of America (ITAA)
http://www.itaa.org/
Information about the IT industry is available at this rich site, including Internet Policy Issues, Year 2000 problems, and ITAA Public Policy and Government Affairs positions.

24. International Federation of Accountants (IFAC)
http://ifac.org/StandardsAndGuidance/InformationTechnology.html
The Information Technology Committee of IFAC presents here a guideline text, Managing Security of Information, which seeks to promote executive understanding of the key issues affecting the management of information and communications as it affects security.

25. MFR Assurance Services
http://www.mfrgroup.com/fraud.htm
MFR's forensic auditing and accounting experts offer Fraud Prevention, Detection, and Investigation services.

26. TAPNet
http://www.tapnet.com/nav.htm
From this home page of the Tax & Accounting Professional Network, you can access accounting software solutions, Management Accounting Magazine article abstracts, and discussion lists for accounting and tax professionals.

27. World Wide Web University
http://www.csun.edu/~vcact00g/acct.html
A complete course in Management Accounting is offered on the Internet by Professor Donald L. Raun of California State University, Northridge.

Accounting Issues of Government

28. Bureau of Economic Analysis
http://www.bea.doc.gov/
The BEA, an agency of the U.S. Department of Commerce, is the country's economic accountant.

29. CCH Federal and State Tax News
http://www.cch.com/f_s_tax/master.htm
Highlights of daily tax news items, such as IRS rulings, court opinions, and legislative updates can be found here.

30. Consumer Price Index (CPI)
http://www.stls.frb.org/fred/data/cpi.html
This Web site offers the CPI for the past several years as well as current data figures.

31. FinanceNet
http://www.financenet.gov/
This is the home page for public financial management worldwide. This site links government financial management administrators, educators, and taxpayers across geopolitical boundaries to improve government accountability.

32. FindLaw
http://findlaw.com/
This is an extensive legal directory that provides whole text on U.S. Supreme Court cases, U.S. federal government resources, state law resources, and international resources.

33. Government Auditor's Resource Page
http://www.trib.infi.net/~zsudiak/GARP.html
This Web site provides access to government resources, government documents, audit resources, links for auditors of state and local governments, and Internet search tools.

34. Governmental Accounting Standards Board
http://www.rutgers.edu/Accounting/raw/gasb/gasbhome.html
Accounting and financial standards for all U.S. state and local governmental entities are established on this Web site.

35. House of Representatives Internet Law Library
http://www.house.gov/
This Web site provides free access to basic documents of U.S. law as well as access to other law resources. There are currently over 8,900 Internet law references available.

36. Internal Review Service
http://www.irs.ustreas.gov/prod/cover.html
This site has the latest federal tax information, updated daily. Download tax forms and instructions.

37. SEC EDGAR Database
http://www.sec.gov/edgarhp.htm
This Securities and Exchange Commission Web site allows users to download (at no charge) publicly available electronic filings submitted to the SEC from 1994 to the present.

38. Tax Resources
http://www.taxresources.com/#contents/
A comprehensive list of tax resources, this site includes federal and state tax forms; legislative, judicial, and administrative U.S. laws; state and foreign tax laws; news groups; newsletters; and discussion forums.

39. TaxWeb
http://www.taxweb.com/
This Web site is a collection of hyperlinks to nearly all state tax sites, plus a wide range of tax resources—tax forms, federal and state legislation, tax publishers, discussion groups, and professional organizations.

40. Thomas Legislative Information
http://thomas.loc.gov/
The full text of recent legislation, as well as the *Congressional Record,* is offered on this Web site.

We highly recommend that you review our Web site for expanded information and our other product lines. We are continually updating and adding links to our Web site in order to offer you the most usable and useful information that will support and expand the value of your Annual Editions. You can reach us at: *http://www.dushkin.com/annualeditions/*.

Unit 1

Unit Selections

Key Points to Consider

- Will the accounting profession be able to make the needed changes quickly enough to enter the twenty-first century? Industry is demanding more skilled and qualified accountants than ever before. Will small CPA firms survive in the next century? How rapidly will change occur due to advances in information technology?
- As the Financial Accounting Standards Board (FASB) continues to require more controversial disclosures on financial statements, they no doubt will acquire more enemies. Will the FASB continue to exist in the next century or will it be replaced by a new organization?
- Questionable accounting practices and fraud have resulted in a negative image for accountants as well as serious litigation problems. Will the accounting profession be able to reverse this image and minimize fraud in the future? What could be done to eliminate these ethical dilemmas? Will auditors and accountants find better ways to enforce internal control procedures?
- The business environment is now a global environment. Will the accounting profession be able to fulfill the needs of management and diverse users of accounting information? Defend your answer.

DUSHKINONLINE Links www.dushkin.com/online/

6. **Activity-Based Risk Evaluation Model of Auditing**
   http://www.efs.mq.edu.au/accg/resources/abrema/index.html
7. **AICPA Assurance Services**
   http://www.aicpa.org/assurance/index.htm
8. **Academy of Accounting Historians**
   http://weatherhead.cwru.edu/Accounting/page/
9. **Business Ethics Resources on WWW**
   http://www.ethics.ubc.ca/resources/business/
10. **Corporate Social Responsibility Principles & Codes**
    http://www.goodmoney.com/directry_codes.htm
11. **The Credit Process: A Guide for Small Business Owners**
    http://www.ny.frb.org/pihome/addpub/credit.html
12. **Financial Accounting Standards Board (FASB)**
    http://www.rutgers.edu/Accounting/raw/fasb/
13. **Internal Auditing World Wide Web**
    http://www.bitwise.net/iawww/
14. **International Accounting Network (IAN)**
    http://www.csu.edu.au/anet/
15. **International Accounting Standards Committee (IASC)**
    http://www.iasc.org.uk/frame/cen0.htm
16. **Palo Alto Software:bplans.com**
    http://www.bplans.com/start.cfm/
17. **The Public Register**
    http://www.publicregister.com/
18. **Small Business Exchange**
    http://www6.americanexpress.com/smallbusiness/

These sites are annotated on pages 4 and 5.

Financial Accounting

Significant changes have taken place in the accounting profession and accounting education in the past 10 years. The Financial Accounting Standards Board (FASB) issues new rules each year that affect how companies report financial information. The Accounting Education Change Commission (AECC) served as a catalyst in the 1990s to change accounting education. Poor accounting practices and fraud in companies have created litigation problems for accounting firms. Advances in information technology have drastically changed the role of the accountant. As a result of all the changes, accounting firms are discovering that continued profitability means meeting new needs of clients. A global economy has offered opportunities and challenges to accountants working in an international environment.

This unit offers insights into the changes affecting the accounting profession and the controversies that are part of the financial accounting area. The first article in this section offers a historical overview of the accounting profession. Three additional articles offer insights into the effects of change on the accounting profession in both large international firms as well as small CPA firms.

The FASB, created in 1973, has recently been criticized because of controversial issues it has chosen to tackle. This accounting board has had a life longer than any of its predecessors. The articles "FASB under Siege," "How Should the FASB Be Judged?" and "Corporate America Is Fed Up with FASB" offer the reader information on how the FASB operates and why it may or may not continue to exist in its current form. Then, two forward-looking articles discuss the challenges that lie ahead for accounting standard-setting bodies.

The advent of computers is a key reason why the accounting profession is experiencing change. How businesses are using technology to cut costs and increase profits is outlined in the next two articles in this unit.

With increased costs of litigation negatively impacting public accounting firms, auditors must implement changes to be better prepared to detect fraud. Internal control structures are critical in preventing fraud. Three selections in this unit address the connections between good internal control and fraud prevention.

In the next subsection, five articles that discuss the concept of revenue recognition as well as specific assets and liabilities are included. Examples of manipulation of accounts receivable and inventory to achieve higher revenue numbers are offered in articles about the high-tech industry and Bausch & Lomb. The many ways inventory fraud has been committed in companies is explored in the article "Inventory Chicanery Tempts More Firms, Fools More Auditors."

The differences between the FIFO and LIFO inventory valuation methods and why management would choose one over the other are addressed in two classic *Wall Street Journal* editorials.

Although it has been quite a few years since the FASB required companies to prepare a statement of cash flows, to date no single approach for analyzing this statement exists. Two selections address this important financial statement in the next subsection. The classic case of the W. T. Grant Company is outlined in the article "Cash Flows, Ratio Analysis, and the W. T. Grant Company Bankruptcy." This article illustrates the value of the cash flow statement. This is followed by a selection that offers innovative ways to assess the statement of cash flows using ratio analysis.

Earnings quality and financial statement analysis are addressed in the next two articles of the subsection. Although the articles cover different companies and different topics, a common thread throughout the selections is that users of financial statements can uncover potential problems of firms if they know where to look and how to analyze the financial statements. "The Dangers of Creative Accounting" offers users a concise list of warning signs that can easily be found on a set of financial statements. In the article "New Accounting Standards and the Small Business," the authors analyze the impact of accounting method choices on lending decisions and are surprised by what they find.

Many small firms experience huge sales but often are not profitable. The selection "Surviving Explosive Growth" addresses why this occurs and offers recommendations on how a business could avoid this problem.

The FASB has changed the reporting format required for the income statement. "How Companies Report Income" explains this new change and illustrates the way comprehensive income should be displayed in a set of financial statements.

The final unit area covers international accounting. Although the International Accounting Standards Committee was formed in 1973, the most impressive developments in this area have just recently occurred in the 1990s. Two subsection articles offer a history and the progress made in developing a single set of accounting rules for the world.

The First Century of the CPA

BY DALE L. FLESHER, PAUL J. MIRANTI AND GARY JOHN PREVITS

Public accounting was one product of the forces that transformed the United States in the late 19th century. The country moved from a primarily rural and agricultural society to one that was urban and industrial. Although the increased importance of Wall Street was a new force, the Main Street bankers in every town and hamlet were equally important as small businesses turned to their bankers for credit. These changes created a more complex social order, requiring the specialized knowledge of new professions.

One emerging profession was public accounting, whose members, like the characters in Frank Baum's contemporary classic, *The Wizard of Oz*, were in search of the yellow brick road to personal fulfillment. But in the accountants' case, the search involved the acquisition of income and status by winning acceptance for their auditing, management consulting, and, later, taxation services.

THE PIONEERING PERIOD

The focal point of the efforts to organize the profession of public accounting was in New York City. Here, two rival organizations competed to create a framework for professional governance. First, there was the Institute of Accounts, an organization founded in 1882 that brought together public accountants, bookkeepers and businessmen interested in accounting. The membership was further unified by a nationalistic outlook supporting the post-Civil War reconciliation of the North and the South. Its leaders included Union Colonel Charles E. Sprague, an accounting theoretician and president of the Union Dime Savings Bank, and Major Henry Harney, formerly of Baltimore, who had served in Robert E. Lee's Army of Northern Virginia.

The rival American Association of Public Accountants (AAPA), founded in 1887, emulated the traditions of the British profession of chartered accountancy. Its founders included Edwin Guthrie, a chartered accountant, Frank Broaker, a correspondent for several British accounting firms, and Richard Stevens, whose family had founded the Stevens Institute of Technology in Hoboken, New Jersey.

Both organizations issued certificates of proficiency to their members. As early as 1884, the Institute of Accounts issued certificates based on passing an examination. The AAPA, the forerunner of the American Institute of CPAs, began issuing certificates in 1887 on the basis of experience. However, this early certification was limited because the organizations could not restrict practice by non-members. Legislation was needed to control the growing ranks of practitioners.

It was Henry Harney and Charles Sprague who wrote the original CPA bill that was submitted to the New York legislature. It was introduced in February 1895 but failed to emerge from a House committee and was defeated in the Senate. At the same time, another bill was being circulated by the AAPA. In March 1895, members of the rival organizations met to negotiate the differences between the two bills; the nationalistic bill from the Institute of Accounts was selected with one alteration: The provision requiring CPAs to be U.S. citizens was changed to allow individuals who *planned* to become citizens to be CPAs. Thus the British-dominated AAPA supported the Institute bill. In 1896, Frank Broaker led the profession's lobbying interests, and the bill passed by almost unanimous vote. It was signed by the governor on April 17, 1896. This law had a grandfathering provision allowing experienced practitioners to become CPAs without taking an examination.

In 1897, the first state CPA society was established in New York under the charismatic leadership of Charles Waldo Haskins, a descendant of poet Ralph Waldo Emerson.

Within four years of the New York CPA law, Pennsylvania, Maryland and California passed similar legislation. By 1921, with passage of the New Mexico law, the professionalization of public accounting had spread throughout the nation.

In 1905, the AAPA merged with the Federation of Societies of Public Accountants in the United States (a loose connection of state accounting organizations) and kept the AAPA name; many CPAs viewed the merger as the first step in obtaining uniform national standards for the profession. But it soon became apparent the AAPA did not have the authority to enforce meaningful standards. The merger had failed to heal bitter regional and ethnic divisions among practitioners. By 1916, a decade of frustration had convinced association leaders that the national body had to be reorganized to still criticism of the profession. Following a reorganization, a new name, the American Institute of Accountants, or AIA, displaced the AAPA—ending the nexus that had bound together state and national bodies.

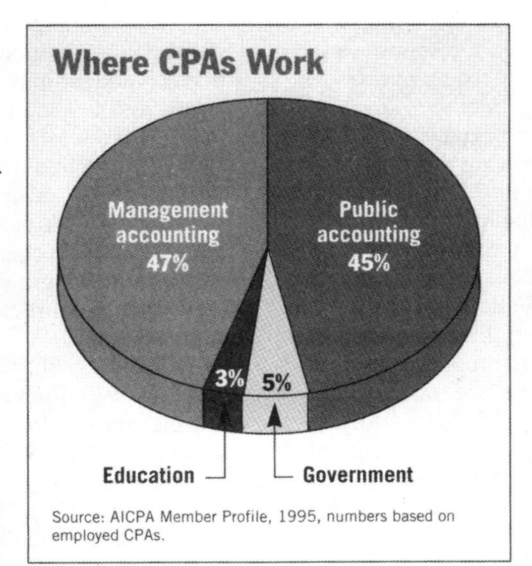

Source: AICPA Member Profile, 1995, numbers based on employed CPAs.

The AIA initiated a program to raise the quality of practice by establishing an extensive professional library, publishing a bibliography, the *Accountants' Index,* and developing its own Uniform CPA Examination, which it offered to share with any state licensing board.

Moreover, beginning in 1917, the AIA's prestige was enhanced by its contribution to the U.S. victory in World War I. Many CPAs served critical roles in a variety of wartime government agencies. A zenith was reached in 1921, when the AIA's annual meeting delegates were invited by President Warren Harding to the White House.

PERIOD OF CRISIS

Unfortunately, the centralization of control within the AIA eventually led to sharp conflicts between dissident elements. Practitioners' opinions split between the differences in business practices and the socioeconomic backgrounds of members. Many had become incensed by the passage in 1921 of ethical rules prohibiting advertising and client solicitation, believing them to be subtle devices to preserve the market power of the larger firms. Consequently, many dissatisfied CPAs formed their own national organization in Washington, D.C., in 1921, the American Society of CPAs, which Durand W. Springer of Michigan led for nearly 16 years.

The splintering of the AIA seriously weakened the profession, because it created confusion in the public

EXECUTIVE SUMMARY

■ IN THE LATE 1800s, post-Civil War America moved from an agricultural to an industrial society, creating a complex society requiring the knowledge of new professions, among them accounting.

■ EFFORTS TO ORGANIZE THE PROFESSION began in New York City, where, in 1896, the first state accounting law was passed. In 1921, the passage of the New Mexico law marked the spread of public accounting as a profession to every state in the nation.

■ THE TWENTIES WERE YEARS OF turmoil that saw a splintering of the profession when dissatisfied CPAs formed their own national organization, a criticism of the shortcomings of financial reporting practices and the encroachment by outside groups during the years of crisis following the stock market crash of 1929.

■ THE 1933-34 SECURITIES LAWS, a result of a stock pyramid scam, called for audits of all companies with listed securities. Soon after, CPAs united to stave off federal regulatory authority, which led to the government's acceptance of some self-governance.

■ THE POST-WORLD WAR II ERA WAS A maturation time, with the focus on education, standard setting and accounting methods.

■ THE FORMATION OF CONTEMPORARY important bodies began in the 1970s: the Financial Accounting Foundation, the Financial Accounting Standards Board and the AICPA auditing standards board, the accounting and review services committee and the division for CPA firms as well as the independent Public Oversight Board.

■ JUST AS IN THE PAST, CPAs today also confront a round of challenges: litigation, the technology explosion, the 150-hour education requirement and the scrutiny of lawmakers, to name only a few.

DALE L. FLESHER, CPA, CIA, CMA, CGFM, is the Arthur Andersen Alumni Professor and associate dean in the School of Accountancy at the University of Mississippi, University. A prolific writer, he is a former editor of the *Accounting Historians Journal.* In 1990, he received the Leon Radde Award from the Institute of Internal Auditors as the outstanding auditing educator worldwide. PAUL J. MIRANTI, CPA, PhD, is an associate professor of accounting at Rutgers University, New Brunswick, New Jersey. In addition to writing many articles, he is the author of a forthcoming book entitled *A History of Corporate Finance* (Cambridge University Press). GARY JOHN PREVITS, CPA, PhD, is professor of accountancy and associate dean in the Weatherhead School of Management at Case Western Reserve University, Cleveland, Ohio. He was the founding president of the Academy of Accounting Historians and is a coauthor of *A History of Accountancy in the U.S.A.* to be published in 1997 (Ohio State University Press). Dr. Previts received the AICPA 1996 Lifetime Achievement in Accounting Education Award.

mind about whose authority prevailed in accounting matters. Disunity made it difficult to mount a response to the rising criticism of the shortcomings of contemporary financial reporting practices. Making matters worse, the profession became vulnerable to encroachment by outside groups during the years of crisis following the stock market crash of 1929.

Most worrisome from the standpoint of professional autonomy were the securities laws passed in 1933 and 1934. The 1933 law was the direct result of the largest financial statement scam in history. Following World War I, Swedish businessman Ivan Kreuger, the "Match King," issued stocks and bonds to gain match monopolies from foreign governments. Kreuger's were the most widely held securities in the United States and the world. Unfortunately, Kreuger operated a huge pyramid scheme involving 400 subsidiary corporations. He was able to hide his operations from the investing public by insisting the financial statements not be audited. The bankruptcy that followed Kreuger's suicide in 1932 led to numerous changes in financial reporting. The media coverage made it politically expedient to pass laws to prevent such schemes. The result was mandatory audits, by CPAs, of all companies with listed securities.

Some say that it was Colonel Arthur H. Carter, the senior partner of Haskins & Sells, who persuaded Congress to limit the mandated audits, at least for all practical purposes, to CPAs. Just as income tax laws in 1909 and 1913 had created new demands for the work of CPAs, the Kreuger fraud led to more laws benefiting the accounting profession.

Despite new work for CPAs, a worrisome professional autonomy problem emerged when the 1934 act established the Securities and Exchange Commission, empowering it to promulgate standards for financial accounting and auditing. These circumstances underscored the need for a united profession. A consensus among practitioners would give their representatives greater leverage in negotiating with political leaders to countervail the undesired extension of federal regulatory authority. One champion of this view was Robert H. Montgomery, who as president of the AIA in 1936 called for a merger with the American Society of CPAs and a closer association with the state CPA societies. The recombining of the rival bodies helped strengthen the profession and led to the SEC's acceptance of the AIA as promulgator of standards for financial accounting and auditing. This was an important precedent, because it reflected the government's willingness to accept a degree of professional self-governance, provided the public interest was protected. This legacy of government-professional relationships continues to shape the governance of CPAs today.

The new, united American Institute formed the committee on accounting procedure (CAP). The accounting research bulletins issued by it were soon a source of "substantial authoritative support," which the SEC demanded all public companies employ in their financial reporting.

The second initiative in practice standardization established the committee on auditing procedure in 1939, which issued pronouncements addressing the auditing problems revealed in the 1939 McKesson & Robbins case. (The case showed in the yearend 1937 financial statements that the lack of two then-not-required audit procedures—observation of inventories and confirmation of receivables—had helped cover up $19 million in fictitious assets out of total assets of over $87 million.) These pronouncements later served as the nucleus of the statements on auditing procedure.

After a half-century of debate, CPAs had discovered the yellow brick road to professional advancement—a road they would continue to traverse in the years of explosive practice growth that emerged after World War II. The years of conflict were followed by consensus.

THE TAKE-OFF PERIOD

As World War II ended, American society was changing. The income tax base had broadened to encompass much of the populace, and the accounting profession was ready to expand as well. Though there were only 9,000 practitioners at this time, the growth in the economy presaged a growth in the number of CPAs.

Just as in World War I, many CPAs made major contributions to the national war effort during World War II. As a result, government became more aware of the value of the CPA's specialized skills. In 1945, on the recommendation of John L. Carey of the American Institute, T. Coleman Andrews, a Virginia CPA, was appointed to head the Corporation Audits Division of the General Accounting Office. Andrews professionalized the GAO by installing an audit style in the federal government similar to that used by CPA firms. Andrews received the Institute's 1947 Gold Medal Award for Distinguished Service to the Profession. In 1947, Andrews chaired the Institute's committee on federal government accounting that assisted the first Hoover Commission on the Organization of the Executive Branch of Government. In 1954, he became the first CPA to be appointed commissioner of internal revenue. Subsequently, Andrews was to run for president in 1956; he finished third in the balloting. He remained the only CPA to run for U.S. president until the 1996 campaign of former Colorado Governor Dick Lamm, who challenged Ross Perot for the Reform Party nomination.

The postwar period brought significant changes in accounting education, which took on greater importance as many state licensing boards required prospective CPAs to have a college education. In the 1960s, questions raised about the rigor of business education induced the AICPA to form a committee to support research defining the basic body of knowledge that CPAs should acquire in college. The committee, chaired by Elmer Beamer of Haskins & Sells, issued a report in 1969, following *Horizons for a Profession,* the 1967 Carnegie Corporation–AICPA study of the common body of knowledge for CPAs. The Beamer committee report concluded that a five-year collegiate program was needed to acquire the knowledge necessary to begin a career in public accounting. Nearly a third of a century later, the profession is just now beginning to achieve this goal.

The AIA changed its name to the American Institute of Certified Public Accountants in 1957. Its focus in the 1950s on financial accounting and the need for greater research in standard setting led to the 1959 formation of the Accounting Principles Board. In its 14-year tenure, the APB promulgated 31 opinions. However, the APB disappointed practitioners because of its failure to define an underlying conceptual framework for accounting and its allowance of flexibility in applying accounting procedures. Also, questionable accounting methods employed by several conglomerates in the 1960s did not help the APB, nor did the SEC's disregard of the APB's authority when it overrode the guidance set forth in Opinion no. 2, which prescribed the method of accounting for the investment tax credit. SEC Chief Accountant Andrew Barr believed the opinion did not meet the needs of the economy as visualized by Congress when it passed the bill creating the investment tax credit. Since the APB essentially was defeating the intent of Congress, Barr said the SEC could not support the opinion.

The response to these concerns prompted the formation of two exploratory AICPA committees, the first of which was chaired by Robert M. Trueblood of Touche, Ross & Co. The 1973 Trueblood report, *Objectives of Financial Statements,* stressed the need for underlying concepts that would be helpful to financial statement users.

Another committee recommended in 1972 that standard-setting activities remain in the private sector but be broadened by involving both users and issuers of financial statements. Those recommendations led to the establishment of the Financial Accounting Foundation, whose main subsidiary, the seven-member Financial Accounting Standards Board, replaced the APB.

The practice of auditing also changed following World War II. First, practice was enriched by the introduction in 1948 of the first of 13 specialized industry audit guides. In 1972, standard setting was revamped by the establishment of the auditing standards executive committee, whose new statements on auditing standards specified minimum levels of practice quality rather than define particular rules of practice, as had been the case earlier.

Further changes came from recommendations made by the Commission on Auditors' Responsibilities, headed by former SEC Commissioner Manuel F. Cohen, responding to investigations of the profession in the 1970s by congressional committees. These investigations questioned whether the auditing standard-setting process was too narrowly focused on public companies. The Cohen commission did find that an expectations gap existed between what auditors thought they were providing and what investors thought they were getting from CPAs.

In 1978, a new body, the auditing standards board, replaced the auditing standards executive committee. At the same time, a parallel entity—the accounting and review services committee—was formed to provide guidance for compilation and review services for nonpublic companies.

This period also witnessed a rising sensitivity to the need for effective practice management in the delivery of high-quality professional services that led ultimately to the establishment of the AICPA division for CPA firms in 1978. The division required adherence to quality control standards for membership in either the SEC practice section or the private companies practice section.

Also in 1978, the Public Oversight Board was formed, under the chairmanship of John J. McCloy, to monitor the peer review system that was used to gain compliance with quality control standards. The POB reports annually whether the public interest is being protected.

The three decades following World War II saw the profession of public accounting reach maturity. Of course, there were still conflicts, for example, whether the CPA's providing of tax services was an infringement on the rights of attorneys, but the conflicts were less obvious and were more often with external parties than within the profession.

RENAISSANCE AND SOPHISTICATION

The period since the mid-1970s has been one of renaissance and increasing sophistication for the profession. Whereas there were only about 9,000 CPAs in 1945, the number had increased to over 95,000 by 1973. By 1996 that number had grown to over 350,000. While most members in 1945 and 1973 were male, today's new entrants to the profession are predominantly female.

Indeed, the past two decades of the CPA movement have been decades of demographic change. As important as the influx of women is to the AICPA, the change in membership from a mostly public accounting orientation to a predominantly managerial accounting background is equally important.

The CPA's primary preoccupation in the late 1970s was with federal government activities. The passage of the Foreign Corrupt Practices Act in 1977 put a great new responsibility on accountants, particularly those in industry. In 1978, the Federal Trade Commission became concerned that the AICPA's ethical rule prohibiting advertising was a restraint of trade.

Much of the accounting news of the 1980s related to the congressional investigation of the profession, which was chaired by Congressman John Dingell (D-Mich.). Bankruptcies during the early 1980s, many occurring just days after the auditor had rendered a clean opinion, raised a hue and cry from taxpayers for new laws to regulate the profession. Leaders of the profession testified before Congress, with many of the messages emphasizing that the accountants themselves were victims of the frauds, not the perpetrators.

One of the accounting profession's responses to this outcry was the creation of the National Commission on Fraudulent Financial Reporting (the Treadway commission) to investigate the causes of financial reporting frauds. Although the Treadway commission report, issued in 1987, gave many recommendations for limiting such frauds, the main points were that effective internal auditors were needed and corporate audit committees should be more active.

Accompanying the bankruptcies of the 1980s came lawsuits. Plaintiffs believed CPA firms had deep pockets, and the number of lawsuits filed was much greater than in previous decades. It is hoped the joint and several liability that caused many firms to pay out large judgments despite little or no wrongdoing will be countered by the 1995 federal law—the Securities Litigation Reform Act—limiting judgments in such cases.

Other newsworthy events of the 1980s included the 1984 establishment of the Governmental Accounting Standards Board and the late 1980s mergers of several large CPA firms. At the same time, the emergence of the personal computer was changing the way audits were conducted and the type of information that was audited.

Important Dates, People, Events

1887—Formation of the American Association of Public Accountants (AAPA), the direct lineal ancestor of the American Institute of CPAs

1896—First CPA law passed on April 17 in New York

1896—First CPA by waiver of exam: Frank Broaker (alphabetical order)

1896—First CPA exam given; first to pass: Joseph Hardcastle, age 69

1897—First state CPA society founded in New York

1898—First woman to pass CPA exam: Christine Ross

1904—First Congress of Accountants, held in St. Louis

1905—First issue of *Journal of Accountancy*

1905—First rules of professional conduct

1909—Corporation excise tax law enacted

1913—Passage of the Sixteenth Amendment to the U.S. Constitution. Enlarged scope of services: taxes and management services

1916—AAPA changes name to American Institute of Accountants (AIA)

1917—Publication of "Uniform Accounts," the first set of auditing standards published in the *Federal Reserve Bulletin*

1917—First Uniform CPA Examination given

1921—American Society of CPAs established in Washington, D.C.

1921—First CPA in Congress: William E. Wilson, Evansville, Indiana

1921—Entire country has CPA laws with passage of New Mexico law

1928—New York passes law (to take effect in 1938) requiring CPA candidates to hold a college degree

1931—*Ultramares Corp.* v. *Touche;* CPAs held to be liable to third parties for gross negligence

1932—Ivan Kreuger dies, his swindle uncovered; CPAs, led by George O. May, support federal securities legislation, which is passed in 1933

1932—New York Stock Exchange requires audits

1934—Securities Exchange Act; first SEC chief accountant: Carman G. Blough

1936—Committee on accounting procedure (CAP) established

1936—The term "generally accepted accounting principles" used in AIA report

1936—Merger of AIA and American Society of CPAs

1938—New York requires CPA candidates to be college graduates

1939—McKesson & Robbins case

1939—CAP begins publishing accounting research bulletins

1939—Committee on auditing procedure established

1943—Income tax withholding begins

1944—First year of AIA/AICPA Gold Medal Award for Distinguished Service to the Profession; some recipients: George O. May, William A. Paton, Arthur H. Carter, T. Coleman Andrews, Robert H. Montgomery, Carman G. Blough, Maurice H. Stans, Lloyd Morey

1945—GAO Corporation Audits Division formed; head: T. Coleman Andrews

1945—World War II ends; continuing professional education starts; Thomas Leland of Texas A&M writes first AIA CPE course

1948—First specialized industry audit guide issued

1949—Conflict with tax lawyers

1953—First CPA IRS commissioner: T. Coleman Andrews

1957—AIA name changed to AICPA

1959—Accounting Principles Board formed

1961—First APB opinion issued

1962—APB Opinion no. 2 unpopular; SEC Chief Accountant Andrew Barr does not support APB

1967—Joint Carnegie Corporation-AICPA education project studying the common body of knowledge for CPAs; publication of *Horizons for a Profession*

1972—Retirement of Andrew Barr, longest-serving chief accountant of the SEC

1973—Financial Accounting Standards Board formed

1973—*Equity Funding* fraud; auditing around computer not sufficient

1974—Cohen commission report reveals expectations gap exists

1974—Committees chaired by Senator Lee Metcalf and Congressman John Moss complete their investigations into the profession

1977—Creation of the AICPA division for CPA firms

1977—Foreign Corrupt Practices Act important to accountants in industry

1978—Government forces CPAs to allow advertising; Congress passes Inspector General Act

1980s—Committee chaired by Congressman John Dingell; 150-hour education movement; public interest becomes part of AICPA mission statement (indicating maturity)

1984—Congress passes Single Audit Act

1984—Governmental Accounting Standards Board established

1987—Treadway commission report

1989—Mergers of several large CPA firms

One of the most controversial issues of the 1980s related to education. The knowledge needed to practice public accounting had broadened and deepened since 1896 and even since 1938, when New York implemented the first requirement for CPAs to be college graduates. Consequently, many leaders in the profession began to recognize that a baccalaureate degree was not sufficient to allow a person to pass the Uniform CPA Examination; more education was needed.

Beginning in the late 1970s, several universities established professional schools of accountancy, which grant master's degrees. This led to accreditation of accountancy programs in 1982, when the American Assembly of Collegiate Schools of Business agreed to provide special accreditation for accounting after the AICPA threatened to start its own accreditation agency. Subsequently, the AICPA passed a rule limiting membership after the year 2000 to CPAs who have at least 150 semester hours of college education.

As CPAs start their second century, they do so as highly educated, respected professionals. In many respects, they have accomplished the goals of their forebears.

The history of the CPA is rich in its variety. There has been conflict, and there has been consensus, and always there has been the legal framework. From the original 1896 New York law to the 1995 federal securities legislation, CPAs have benefited from changing laws, but because of the CPA's responsibility to the public, the profession has constantly been under the scrutiny of lawmakers.

Perhaps Dennis Beresford best summed up the profession when he made the following statement at the 1989 American Accounting Association annual meeting:

"I firmly believe that accounting improvement in the United States has come about not merely as a matter of nature taking its course. Improvement has occurred as a result of sustained, committed, cooperative effort. Every step of accounting evolution has been helped along by a good firm push."

Such a statement should give CPAs hope for the future. With sustained, cooperative effort, individuals can help accomplish the goals of the profession. The profession has reached a level of maturity, but the CPA is still traveling down that yellow brick road. While today's CPAs do not face the problems of the pioneer CPAs, they still have to reach out to find fulfillment.

It's time for CPAs to look beyond their traditional role.

Are You Ready for New Assurance Services?

BY ROBERT K. ELLIOTT AND DON M. PALLAIS

The growth opportunities for CPAs are much larger than anyone imagined. The profession's current accounting and auditing income—about $7 billion annually—could double or triple through the introduction of new assurance services. And the opportunities are open to CPA firms of all sizes.

But change will not come without effort. New services must be identified, new competencies must be developed, a customer-focused mind-set will be needed and competition and other barriers must be overcome. Nevertheless, great opportunities are available for all CPAs.

That was the conclusion of the American Institute of CPAs special committee on assurance services, which began studying the economics of the audit–assurance function more than two years ago and recently reported its findings and recommendations. The report is available on the Internet—as part of the AICPA Web site (www.aicpa.org).

This article is the first in a series that will highlight findings and suggestions from the special committee's report. The article describes the extent of the new opportunities and the concept of assurance services.

LOOKING BEYOND THE TRADITIONAL ROLE

The opportunities are both impressive and timely. The special committee found clear evidence that financial statement audits are a mature product. Accounting and auditing revenue, adjusted for inflation, has remained flat for the last seven years. The traditional audit of financial statements adds value to both users and clients, is widely appreciated for its effect on the integrity of the capital markets, contributes to the CPA's reputation for objectivity and integrity and will continue to be in demand in the future. But the greatest opportunity for growth lies in assurance services. A close look at potential customers and the trends changing the practice environment shows why. The need for information services is exploding and in those needs lie opportunities for the CPA profession. The core benefit of the audit–attest tradition—information improvement—provides a foundation for new value-added services.

The quality of the information that organizations and individuals use will increasingly influence their fates.

- Decision makers' needs are influenced by the headlong pace of economic change, the intensity of competition and heightened levels of interdependency—both global and domestic. A higher proportion of economic inputs to corporate operations is "knowledge work," a term coined by business writer Peter Drucker to describe the activities of workers who manipulate knowledge. By definition, knowledge work is information-dependent.
- Information technology is transforming the way data are created, stored, transmitted, accessed and interpreted, making possible measurements and reports with timeliness, breadth, accuracy and analytical features that are a quantum jump from the best of paper-and-pencil days. Information can be part of a modern business problem—when essential facts are available but can't be located amid virtual mountains of data. But brought to bear on decisions, it also can be a huge part of the solution.
- Accountability is playing an increasing role in social, economic and political life. All sorts of stakeholders in groups, political units and organizations want those who affect their lives to be accountable for the

Assurance Services: Implications for Academia

Accounting students need to prepare for a practice world that includes the new assurance services. This means professors should both revise the curriculum and perform the research that will accelerate the move to assurance services. If adaptation progresses ideally, greater synergy will develop between college campuses and public practitioners than ever before, strengthening accounting as an academic discipline.

CURRICULUM CHANGES

The reforms championed by the Accounting Education Change Commission are under way and will serve emerging assurance services very well. But more still needs to be done. For example

■ Student communications skills should be enhanced, and the enhancement should dovetail with an emphasis on customer needs. Students should better understand users' decision-making processes.

■ Students should learn the strategic implications of information technology. What does it mean, for example, for the conduct of transactions, future markets, business structure, teamwork, cost control and building intellectual assets? Students should have access to the specific information technology knowledge needed to provide new services.

■ Students need skills in model building and measurement theory they can adapt to specific service needs.

■ A solid understanding of a reliable, comprehensive business model (such as business strategist Michael Porter's value-chain model) can substantially empower practitioners to analyze business circumstances and processes, identify needs for information services and explain those needs.

RESEARCH NEEDS

A great variety of research also would help the profession's expansion into new assurance services. Here are some examples of the kind of research that would serve practitioner and classroom needs as well as expand the frontiers of the accounting profession:

■ Decision makers' information and assurance needs.

■ Measurement criteria needed to perform specific services.

■ Relevance enhancement services (services to assure that decision makers have the right information).

■ Assurance methods and reporting (such as the concept of "assurance risk").

■ Criteria for identifying risks and assessing their likelihoods.

■ Criteria for assessing the integrity and security of electronic commerce.

■ Systems design reliability and continuous systems assurance.

The special committee's action plan for academics is located at www.aicpa.org/assurance/scas/howaffct/academ/apa/index.htm.vs/elderpl/index.htm.

responsibilities they have assumed. Effective judgments about whether or not economic and other responsibilities have been met depend on sound information.

THE CONCEPT OF ASSURANCE SERVICES

To pursue service expansion under these conditions, a service concept was needed that was in the audit–attest tradition but more comprehensive. The special committee defined assurance services as "independent professional services that improve the quality of information, or its context, for decision makers." This broad concept includes audit and attestation services and is distinct from consult-

EXECUTIVE SUMMARY

■ THE INTRODUCTION OF NEW ASSURANCE services could double or even triple the CPA profession's $7 billion accounting and auditing income. But the new opportunities will not come easily. New services must be identified, new competencies developed and barriers will have to be overcome.

■ THE REPORT OF THE AICPA SPECIAL committee on assurance services is available on the Internet as part of the AICPA Web site (www.aicpa.org). In the report the committee defined *assurance services* as "independent professional services that improve the quality of information, or its context, for decision makers."

■ WITH ACCOUNTING AND AUDITING income flat for the last seven years, the CPA profession's greatest opportunity for growth lies in new assurance services. The special committee developed business plans for six services covering diverse areas such as elder care, electronic commerce, performance measurement, the delivery of health care services, risk information for internal decision makers and information systems design and operation.

■ THE SPECIAL COMMITTEE recommended that CPA firms identify assurance services for their own markets and that the AICPA identify services for the profession as a whole. The newly formed assurance services committee will continue the Institute's service development efforts.

■ THE ASSURANCE SERVICES WEB SITE is designed to support two of the special committee's conclusions—that the profession must focus on its customers and that facility with information technology is essential to the profession's future. Web site visitors can select from one of several perspectives that highlight the findings most important to their segment of the profession.

ROBERT K. ELLIOTT, CPA, is a partner of KPMG Peat Marwick, LLP, in New York City. He was chairman of the AICPA special committee on assurance services. DON M. PALLAIS, CPA, has his own practice in Richmond, Virginia. He was executive director of the AICPA special committee on assurance services and now is a member of the assurance services committee.

ing (although similarities exist) because it focuses primarily on improving information rather than on providing advice or installing systems.

The assurance services concept is broad in other ways because there is no limit to the type of information. It can be financial or nonfinancial. It can be about past events or conditions or about ongoing processes or systems (such as internal controls). It can be direct (information about a product) or indirect (information about someone else's assertion about a product). It can be internal or external to the decision maker. There also is no limit to the type of improvement. The assurer can improve the information's reliability, relevance or context.

Thus, if CPAs are going to take advantage of assurance service opportunities, they must stretch their perspective beyond financial statements. Decision makers' information needs will guide the range of services CPAs provide.

IDENTIFIED SERVICES

CPAs can get some idea of that range, at least at this early stage of service expansion, from the services the special committee already has identified. The committee developed business plans for 6 services, explored several others in abbreviated form and identified over 200 more through a survey of services already provided. These are the business-plan services:

1. Provide assurance to concerned parties about whether care delivery goals for elderly individuals are being met (see the sidebar at right for more information).

2. Assess whether the information features of electronic commerce function in accordance with accepted criteria. The service would provide assurance with respect to the integrity and security of electronic transactions, electronic documents and supporting systems.

3. Assess the relevance and reliability of an entity's performance measures. Potential engagements include assessing the reliability of the information reported from an organization's performance measurement system, assessing the relevance of an organizations' performance measures, identifying performance measures for organizations that need them and helping to design and implement a performance measurement system.

4. Assess health care provider's performance for the decision-making benefit of care recipients and their representatives (such as corporate employers and unions).

5. Improve the quality of risk information for internal decision makers through independent assessments of the likelihood of significant, adverse events and quantify the possible magnitudes of the effects.

ElderCare-Plus

The elderly—an increasing proportion of the population—need services to cope with the effects of the aging process and can afford to pay for them. The wealth controlled by persons over age 65 is estimated to be $11 trillion to $13 trillion. ElderCare-Plus—as the AICPA special committee on assurance services has dubbed it—helps the elderly and concerned family members. In this situation, the basic assurance service CPAs can provide is to obtain evidence and report whether specified goals are being met by various caregivers—including providers of medical, household and financial services. The specified goals would be established in discussions with the elderly person and his or her adult children or other family members.

Adult children who live too far away from an elderly parent to personally monitor the care the parent receives are candidates for this service. The CPA can report on care received and also help by providing some services directly to the elderly parent and by providing some consulting or facilitating services for the older person and his or her loved ones.

A mix of ancillary services would be integral to the typical engagement. The CPA might, for example, oversee investments (though not invest funds) and account for the client's income and expenses. Other potential services include help in selecting care providers and making arrangements for needed care and services (for example, arranging for in-home sitters and cooks, for transportation or for placement in a retirement care facility).

MARKET POSITIONING

The CPA's reputation as an independent, honest, objective and reliable professional will be a market advantage in competing for this kind of work. Many CPA firms provide tax or financial planning to clients who are or could become candidates for ElderCare-Plus. These market advantages will be helpful because a variety of competitors already deliver portions of the service. They include welfare agencies, geriatric specialists, bank trust officers and lawyers.

CPAs appear well positioned to take advantage of this market. Market research commissioned by the AICPA confirms that elder care is an opportunity for CPAs and that trustworthiness is important to potential customers. According to Yankelovich Partners, 89% of higher income Americans age 40 to 64 would be "extremely," "very" or "somewhat" likely to use services in the ElderCare-Plus package if the need arose.

CPA QUALIFICATIONS

CPAs already have the measurement and reporting skills needed for the job, although they would need additional training. The AICPA has developed an elder care self-study course. (The course can be ordered on-line at www.aicpa.org/store/products/732022.htm.) In addition, Practitioners Publishing Co., in conjunction with the special committee, has developed relevant practice aids, including material on communicating with older persons, Social Security, Medicare and Medicaid, long-term care and planning for contingencies (CPAs can download a sample at www.ppcinfo.com/scas/scas.htm).

The special committee's complete report on ElderCare-Plus is located at www.aicpa.org/assurance/scas/newsvs/elderpl/index.htm.

How to Read the Web Site Report

The Internet is a resource for pursuing assurance and other services. CPAs can keep up with professional news, do research and conduct business by establishing a Web site and making contacts with potential clients. They also can join a group and interact with their peers, exchanging practical, money-making ideas. The assurance services Web site links to the group page called "CPAs Discuss Assurance Services" as well as to the "Report of the AICPA Special Committee on Assurance Services" page.

INTERNET ACCESS

To get started, you need a modem, an Internet service provider and a Web browser (that is, a program for locating and viewing Web sites)—along with a computer. The AICPA recommends you use either Microsoft Internet Explorer or Netscape Navigator to view its site, preferably the most recent versions. A 14.4Kbps modem or higher will be sufficient. The Institute's affinity program with NETCOM, an Internet service provider, gives participating AICPA members unlimited access and comes with Microsoft Internet Explorer.

FUNDAMENTALS OF NAVIGATION

Basic procedures to navigate the Web site are given below. Users of the special committee's CD-ROM will navigate the same way.

Every Web page (a separate location within a site)—and the site's home page—has an address (technically known as an URL) and can be reached directly by typing the address in the Web browser. To reach the special committee's report, for example, you would type www.aicpa.org/assurance/scas/index.htm.

Once you find a page of interest on the AICPA Web site, you have options about what to visit next. You can return to the prior page (the "back" button on the browser) or to the home page ("home" in the path at the top left of the page). By clicking on underlined terms (links), you reach the Web page dealing with the subject indicated by that term. Graphics other than buttons also may be used as links by site designers.

You can "bookmark" sites by selecting "Add Bookmark" from the bookmarks menu for Netscape Navigator or "Add to Favorites" from the favorites menu for Microsoft Internet Explorer. A bookmark makes a later visit easier, and can be made simply by selecting from the list in the bookmarks (favorites) menu.

Forgotten anything? Don't worry. The AICPA site tutorial is at www.aicpa.org/tutor/index.htm. Visit the tutorial to review these fundamentals and to learn more.

SITE MAP

At the assurance services Web site (www.aicpa.org/assurance/sitemap/index.htm) is a map of the site (see illustration below). You can reach specific locations directly by clicking on the graphic element containing the subject name you've chosen. The site map can take you to the special committee's report and all its major sections and to "Ongoing Assurance Services Development," which will keep you up-to-date on the assurance services committee and its task forces.

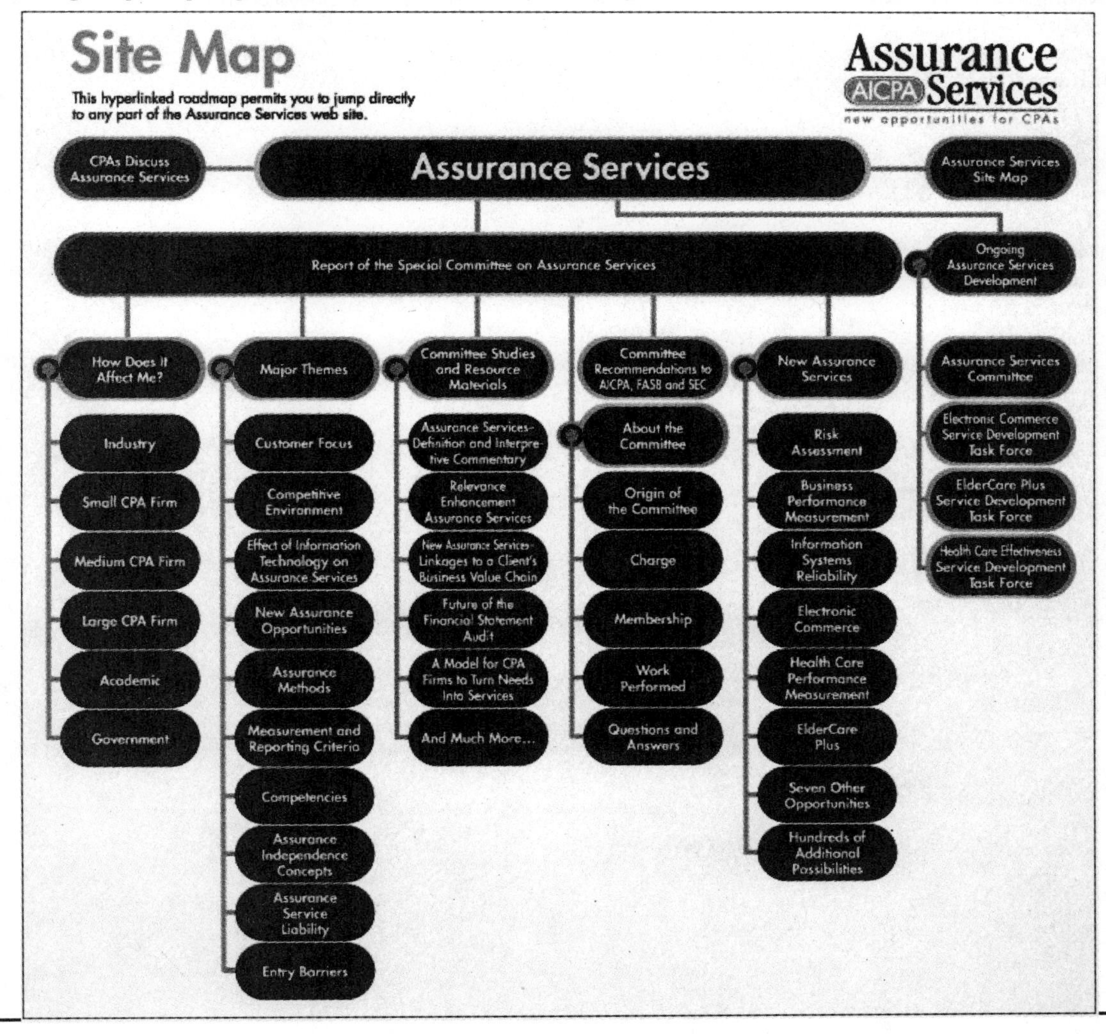

6. Provide assurance that systems are designed and operate in a manner that provides reliable information or operate according to accepted criteria.

The estimated market for electronic commerce assurance services alone is between $1 billion and $11 billion; for elder care, between $2 billion and $7 billion. Information systems reliability also is a market estimated in the billions of dollars, and risk assessment is estimated at 10% to 20% of annual audit fees.

Systems and information technology naturally play a prominent role in the new assurance services. They are part of how information for decision making is gathered and deployed and used in transactions. More opportunities will open up as the information technology revolution continues. Practitioners' information technology knowledge and skills will affect not only the range of new assurance services they can avail themselves of but also the way they adapt their traditional services to changing circumstances.

IDENTIFYING NEW ASSURANCE SERVICES

The special committee recommended that CPA firms identify services for their own markets and that the AICPA identify services for the profession as a whole. The newly formed assurance services committee will continue the Institute's service-development efforts. Its task forces already are developing the services identified by the special committee. Customer focus will play an important role in the move to new assurance services. Effective service identification depends on understanding customers' needs.

The traditional audit, with its standard report and measurement criteria designed to enhance comparability across all reporting entities, is a general purpose service. The specific information needs of individuals and groups will dictate new assurance services. To identify these needs, practitioners will require a new mind-set, communications skills, business knowledge and the capacity to make inferences from relationships between business circumstances and economic and industrial trends. The special committee's report includes information on how firms and individual CPAs can identify customer needs and turn them into services. It can be found at www.aicpa.org/assurance/scas/comstud/amodel/index.htm.

THE WEB SITE REPORT

The Web site report is designed to be consistent with two of the special committee's main conclusions—that the professional role, such as member in a small firm, a member in business or industry or a member from academia. (See the sidebar "Assurance Services: Implications for Academia" for the academic perspective.) It's also possible to go a level deeper to explore the themes that underlie the findings and recommendations, or a level deeper still to the papers and research that were the basis for the report's conclusions. Visitors also are free to read every word from every file at every location on the Web site. Even first-time Web visitors should find it easy to find what they want to read. (See the box on page 17 for more information on visiting the assurance services Web site.)

A small firm advocate reveals what it takes to succeed in a rapidly evolving environment.

A Prescription for Change

BY ANITA DENNIS

Many people have predicted that small CPA firms will not be able to survive into the next century because of competitive and cost pressures. David Schlotzhauer, a partner of the six-person, Kansas-based Mills & Schlotzhauer firm, has spoken to numerous small practitioners across the country in the last several years, and he strongly disagrees with such predictions. He believes, however, that firms must face up to one major challenge: the need for monumental change in the way they will practice.

CHUCK KNEYSE/BLACK STAR

David Schlotzhauer thinks small firms have a bright future if they can creatively adapt to changes in the profession.

A NEW APPROACH

Schlotzhauer, the chairman of the American Institute of CPAs small firm advocacy committee, has developed a deep understanding of the issues facing local practitioners from his experience in his own firm and from the small firm roundtables the committee sponsors around the country. Here are some of the ways he believes the practice environment will differ in the future:

1. ***The type of work firms do will have to change.*** "There will be more movement away from compliance work and into consulting," Schlotzhauer predicts. His own firm performs all the traditional services for its closely held small business clients, but it has expanded its business consulting to the point where it now makes up 25% of revenues. Involvement in projects such as mergers and acquisitions "is much more fun," he says. "Although compliance is important, the client does not easily perceive the value." Offering consulting services enhances the firm–client relationship, Schlotzhauer believes. "You become very personally involved with clients; they come to rely on you totally. You become their strategic business adviser. Small firms have done this for years, but it's really mushrooming now."

One reason for this new trend is because of threats to long-standing CPA services, such as recurring discussions of flat or consumption taxes. "Tax work is a huge part of the practice of small firms. One practitioner I spoke with recently said 90% of his practice was tax compliance. If that goes away, what do you do? CPAs are asking themselves that question."

2. ***Firms will have to change their hiring approaches.*** Practitioners must have more than number-crunching skills. This fact has long been accepted in the profession, but Schlotzhauer says clients' attitudes have changed and they now expect all firm members to offer analytical skills. "The computer hardware and software are there to crunch the numbers. You have more numbers than you know what to do with. Now clients want to know how to interpret them and what you can do to help them run their businesses better."

In his own firm, Schlotzhauer has committed to alter his hiring methods to find staff who will meet clients' expanded expectations. He has done this by changing what he's looking for in recruits. "We seek not only technology skill but also thinking skills and maybe even an entrepreneurial outlook." It's not always possible to find the right match in a very subjective process, he admits. One of his regrets is hiring someone who wasn't right and trying to make the arrangement work despite obvious problems. "Small firms become like families. If you get the wrong person, it can really create problems." In terms of hiring, he has found no scientific method to finding the right person, but he no longer attempts to keep on an employee who is not working out.

3. ***New "practice alliances" will form.*** Many firms fail to enter specialized niches because of the risks of narrowing their client bases. "It's hard to make that transition," he says. "How do you give up a $10,000 audit or one that is 20% of your practice?" Schlotzhauer foresees a time when even the smallest of firms will associate in local, national or even international referral networks that allow them the flexibility to specialize in one area while referring work to and receiving referrals from other practitioners in the group. Each associated firm would have its own specialty, including everything from traditional services to business valuation or M&A work. "It would be similar to a loose partnership, but with the freedom to remain independent," he says.

Firm Profile

Name: Mills & Schlotzhauer.
Year opened: 1988.
Locations: Leawood, Kansas.
Total personnel: Six.
Number of partners: Two.
Number of CPAs: Two.
Areas of concentration: Tax; auditing and accounting; consulting.
Gross fees: Over $575,000.
Percentage of fees in
Accounting: 10%.
Auditing: 10%.
Tax: 55%.
Consulting: 25%.
Types of clients: Closely held small businesses.
Advertising and marketing programs: Referrals.
Best thing we did in the last five years: Made a commitment to keep up with technology.
Worst thing we did in the last five years: Hired the wrong person and tried to make it work.
How the practice will change in the near future: Greater emphasis on consulting; move into practice alliances.

THE HUMAN TOUCH

Another constant factor for small firms is new developments in information systems. When Schlotzhauer and his partner, Charles Mills, started their firm in 1988, they decided that keeping pace with technology was crucial. "We make a significant, continuing investment, not only in hardware and software but also in training," he says, adding that the firm devotes between 2% and 5% of fees to technology costs annually. While that is below the 6% to 8% many recommend, "it's a huge figure for small firms," he observes. And while technology can make a practice more productive and efficient, it also means doing more work in a shorter period.

But he has found that small business clients are willing to spend money on technology, and their advisers must follow suit. And he believes that advances in technology benefit small firms in two ways. "The information explosion is affecting small businesses as well as small firms," he observes. "They want help in coping with all of that data and CPAs have unique abilities to handle complex sets of information."

At the same time, small firms' major advantage is the personal touch—and technology will only reinforce that asset. "Our engagements are based on relationships with individuals. As technology explodes and we become disconnected, personal contact will be key. That's where small firms will shine."

MAKING CONTACT

Although he sees a bright future for local practitioners, Schlotzhauer doesn't believe any practitioner will prosper if he or she works entirely alone. He has found that learning about other firms' challenges and solutions has been an important advantage. "It's key for small firms to be tied into other small firms, through professional events or more informally." At his committee's roundtables, "the participants say, 'I thought I was the only one having these problems. I'm not out here by myself.'" He urges fellow practitioners to stay in touch with their peers. "There are people out there willing to listen, to answer a question, to help."

EXECUTIVE SUMMARY

■ ONE OBSERVER of the small firm practice environment believes that local firms have a bright future—if they are willing to change. David Schlotzhauer, a partner of a six-person Kansas firm, says firms must place greater emphasis on consulting services and change their hiring approaches to find staff who can help clients interpret data and run their businesses better.

■ PRACTICE ALLIANCES, loose referral networks that allow firms greater flexibility to specialize, could be another key advantage for small firms.

■ TECHNOLOGY CAN BENEFIT small firms because small businesses will need help understanding the mountains of data available to them. And, as technology creates greater distances between people, the personal attention small firms offer will become an even greater competitive advantage.

■ SMALL PRACTITIONERS SHOULD STAY IN touch with their peers in similar firms, either through professional events or informally, to understand their common challenges.

ANITA DENNIS is a *Journal* contributing editor.

How the Andersens Turned Into the Bickersons

By MELODY PETERSEN

ON a recent Wednesday evening, white stretch limousines crowded the parking lot at Andersen Consulting's headquarters in Palo Alto, Calif. The drivers waited to take the firm's top partners and their counterparts at Arthur Andersen, the accounting firm, to dinner at Spago, an elegant restaurant downtown.

Even though the sister firms had been feuding for months, George T. Shaheen, managing partner of Andersen Consulting, had planned for the top partners on both sides of the Andersen Worldwide family to dine together.

But the limo drivers never saw their expected passengers. The first official meeting between the Andersens since December, when Mr. Shaheen told the world that Andersen Consulting wanted to go its own way, had quickly gone sour.

Like most family feuds, this one is about money. Lately, the consultants have begun to earn more than their peers on the accounting side, and they don't want to hand over any of that money to the accountants. Moreover, they are furious that the accountants have followed them into the lucrative business of giving advice.

In recent days, the bad blood has boiled over, creating an all-out brawl. Divorce, both insiders and outsiders say, is almost inevitable. Little more remains than a division of the spoils and deciding who keeps the Andersen name.

It's a perilous business being the largest professional partnership in the world. And the startling thing is that the feud involves experts whose trade is advising executives on how to run their businesses. "They should all be embarrassed," said Tom Rodenhauser, president of Consulting Information Services in Keene, N.H. "People are saying: 'Can't they figure this out? Isn't that what they are paid to do?' "

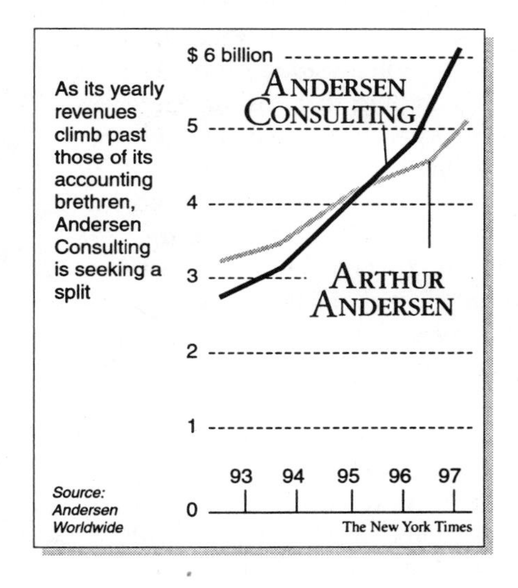

Even though it may be years before the feud is settled, the two sides already act as separate firms and fierce rivals, with top partners snarling at one another over clients like lions eyeing the same gazelle.

At Andersen's offices around the world, Andersen Consulting employees are making plans to separate themselves from the accountants—if they have not already done so.

In New York, at joint offices at 54th Street and the Avenue of the Americas, Mr. Shaheen and Jim Wadia, Arthur Andersen's top managing partner, had sat in adjoining offices whenever they were in the city on the same day—a situation that employees said grew more and more tense. When Andersen Consulting remodeled the 18th floor in January, Mr. Wadia's office was moved to the 12th.

In Chicago, while the two sides still share space at 33 West Monroe Street, the security card of an Arthur Andersen employee will not open the doors leading to Andersen Consulting.

Even the two units' Web sites are not linked.

"They are beyond the point of no return," Gresham T. Brebach, a former senior consulting partner, said recently. "There is no way they can reconcile. They have lost the partnership spirit."

Inside Andersen Worldwide, the umbrella organization for the two businesses, partners have grown concerned that they may be losing clients and hurting their chances of hiring top graduates. Andersen Consulting, which hired 12,000 people last year, many of them M.B.A.'s, recently sent letters to top business schools, trying to reassure students that the firm's future was bright and giving them a phone number to call if they had concerns.

THE feud comes at a precarious time for Andersen Worldwide. The firm is on the brink of losing its place as the world's largest accounting and consulting firm to Price Waterhouse and Coopers & Lybrand, which received Justice Department approval for their merger Thursday. (They will need European regulators to sign off.)

Analysts say they know of no clients that the Andersens may have lost as a result of their bickering. But one competitor, the Deloitte & Touche Consulting Group, recently began running newspaper ads saying that while Deloitte was "focused" on clients, Andersen Consulting was "distracted by in-fighting."

The two sides of Andersen do agree, however, that their brawl cannot be good for business. They agreed last month to no longer talk publicly about their troubles. Instead, they are arguing behind closed doors before an independent arbitrator at the International Chamber of Commerce in Paris, following Mr. Shaheen's request in December for binding arbitration to settle the Andersens' future.

But more details of this private war leaked out late last month at a court hearing in New York. Andersen Consulting had filed a lawsuit to try to blunt a resolution, passed by the accountants who comprise a majority of the 27-member board that manages Andersen World wide, asserting their control. The resolution was passed on Feb. 12, the day after the dinner plans at Spago were abandoned, with the Arthur Andersen partners deciding to dine separately.

At the hearing, Barry R. Ostrager, a lawyer for Andersen Consulting, told Judge John G. Koeltl of the Federal District Court in Manhattan that the resolution created a "protection committee," made up only of Arthur Andersen partners, that would essentially take over Andersen Worldwide.

"What we have here is hardball tactics of the most naked and unreasonable and unlawful manner," Mr. Ostrager said.

While Mr. Ostrager said that Arthur Andersen was trying to put its consulting brothers and sisters "out of business," James Quinn, a lawyer for Arthur Andersen, told the judge that the contention was "absurd." The two sides are tied together financially, Mr. Quinn said, and any attempt by Arthur Andersen to hurt Andersen Consulting would be "self-destructive."

Addressing the judge, Mr. Quinn referred to Dec. 17 as "a day that will live in infamy in the history of Arthur Andersen." For that was the day Andersen Consulting fired off press releases to newsrooms around the world contending that Arthur Andersen had breached its agreement with the consultants by going after the same clients—a contention that the accountants say is "false and misleading."

Partners on both sides refuse to talk publicly about the fracas. They do say, however, that business has never been better, with Arthur Andersen's revenues growing at a 17 percent clip and Andersen Consulting's revenues up 25 percent last year. "I have received no calls from clients who say they are nervous," Mr. Shaheen said. "We have not lost a stride in the marketplace."

Matthew P. Gonring, Arthur Andersen's managing partner for communications, added: "This filing has not changed Arthur Andersen. Our view is that the interests of clients, partners and employees come first. Our business is fundamentally sound."

IF he were alive, the firm's founder might well be breaking his pencils. In 1913, when Arthur E. Andersen, an accounting professor at Northwestern University, founded what was then called Andersen, Delany & Company in Chicago, his motto was that every accountant should work not for himself (they were all men in those days), but for "one firm."

Later, the firm would install the same style of wooden doors in every Andersen office around the world to give clients and employees the impression of walking into a unified organization.

Two months before he died, in January 1947, Mr. Andersen wrote, "We must have, as we have never had before, a united family." A half-century later, the firm is anything but.

A matter at the heart of the dispute is who created Andersen Consulting: Did it grow out of the accounting firm or did it spring forth fully formed, a decade ago? The accountants say the consulting business goes back at least to 1952, when the accountants helped install General Electric's first computer system.

Privately, the Arthur Andersen partners say that they have invested millions of dollars and more than three decades into building the consulting practice, adding that they are not about to let the consultants get away without collecting a hefty return.

The accountants say the partnership agreements—which are read by each side in a different way—require Andersen Consulting to pay 150 percent of its annual revenues, or nearly $10 billion, to the accountants if it wants to separate. In addition, the accountants say, the agreements require the consultants to drop the Andersen name and to return any technology they have developed.

But Andersen Consulting's partners prefer to tell their history by beginning with 1989, the year the firm was split into Arthur Andersen, which would offer traditional accounting services, and Andersen Consulting.

The Andersen Consulting partners say that they have since built their side into the world's largest consulting firm. They owe no money to the accountants, they say, because Arthur Andersen breached the partners' agreement by jumping into consulting, too. The consultants point to papers the firm filed with the Securities and Exchange Commission in 1990 that said that Andersen Consulting, and not Arthur Andersen, would do computer consulting, which makes up the bulk of the consulting work.

The consultants are most frustrated by a term in the agreement that requires the more profitable side to transfer money to the other. While the accountants once paid the consultants money, in recent years the consultants have started writing ever bigger checks to the accountants.

Last year, Andersen Consulting paid Arthur Andersen $173 million—an average contribution of more than $150,000 from each of Andersen Consulting's 1,100 partners. That was a windfall of about $100,000 to each of Arthur Andersen's 1,700 partners. Larry Levitan, a senior Andersen Consulting partner who retired six months ago, explained how he felt about the payments he had made: "I pick out a partner at Arthur Andersen that I know and I say, 'I'm buying you a new Mercedes Benz every single year.' This year I bought him a down payment on a very nice home."

The consultants contend that the accountants are using the money to build a rival consulting practice.

"Our partners say, 'Why are we sending our money to a competitor?' " Mr. Shaheen said on Dec. 17 after he had filed the request for arbitration, arguing that the two sides should separate because of "irreconcilable differences."

The accountants say the Andersens never agreed that the accountants had to remain accountants and could not consult. Indeed, the accountants have ventured so far from their traditional role in auditing corporate financial statements and preparing tax returns that Arthur Andersen now ranks as the world's No. 6 consulting firm. Andersen Consulting is No. 1.

ARTHUR ANDERSEN'S consulting ranges from installing software to training employees for overseas assignments to managing a company's spending on environmental concerns. The firm has even irritated lawyers recently by offering legal services overseas. So it rankles the accountants whenever someone calls Arthur Andersen an "accounting firm."

"Calling us an accounting firm is like calling Disney a cartoon maker or G.E. an appliance manufacturer," John S. Vita, a spokesman for Arthur Andersen, said recently. "While we were founded on accounting, as Disney was on cartoons and G.E. on appliances, we have outgrown that." Arthur Andersen should be called, he said, a "multidisciplinary professional services firm."

Some former partners and industry analysts say the hard feelings might have been soothed long ago if it had not been for the egos of the men leading the two sides. "The battle seems to be a battle of wills," said Mr. Rodenhauser, the New Hampshire analyst.

Indeed, the Andersens' longtime troubles burst into public view last summer when Mr. Shaheen, outspoken and hard-driving, and Mr. Wadia, a soft-spoken lawyer and accountant, each campaigned to become chief executive of Andersen Worldwide. (Andersen Worldwide, with about 1,600 employees, oversees the administrative affairs of Arthur Andersen and Andersen Consulting and officially ties the two together.)

The top post opened up after Lawrence A. Weinbach resigned to become chief executive of the Unisys Corporation. In eight years as chief executive, Mr. Weinbach tried, but failed, to bring the Andersens together. He declined to comment last week on the schism.

But neither Mr. Shaheen nor Mr. Wadia received the necessary two-thirds vote of all Andersen partners, and the board elected an interim chief, W. Robert Grafton, an Arthur Andersen partner who was then chairman of Andersen Worldwide's board.

The rift has been growing wider ever since. Some observers say Mr. Shaheen made a mistake when, six months after losing his bid for chief executive, he filed for arbitration. One former partner, who spoke on condition of anonymity, predicted that if the Paris arbitrator decided that the consultants must pay a hefty price to leave, "some partners could choose to stay, and some could leave, and Andersen Consulting could be no more."

MR. BREBACH, who was managing partner of the firm's North American consulting business until 1988 and worked with Mr. Shaheen, said the Andersen rift would probably be settled peacefully if it were not for Mr. Shaheen.

At first, Mr. Shaheen had seemed to be a "mild-mannered guy" from central Illinois, Mr. Brebach said. "He was not one you would say had an ego problem," he said. "But things change with power."

In an interview, Mr. Shaheen defended his actions, saying he had not acted recklessly by filing for arbitration. He said he had acted in the best interests of all Andersen Consulting partners, not out of his own ambitions. "How could this be reckless?" he asked. "What would be reckless would be to let it go on."

At the court hearing on Feb. 20 in New York, Andersen Consulting's lawyers placed the blame on Mr. Wadia, with Mr. Ostrager portraying him as a man who was "full of himself." Mr. Wadia, who was born in Bombay and now lives in London, is the firm's first managing partner who has never worked as an auditor—making his promotion consistent with Arthur Andersen's move away from auditing and into consulting.

Mr. Ostrager, a lawyer with Simpson Thacher & Bartlett, which is handling the matter for Andersen Consulting, recounted what happened in Palo Alto on Feb. 11 and 12, during a meeting of the board of partners.

Mr. Ostrager said he had confirmed the meetings' events by taking sworn depositions from Mr. Wadia and Mr. Grafton, who has found himself in the middle.

Near midnight on Feb. 11, after the dinner that wasn't, Mr. Wadia and one other Arthur Andersen partner met privately with Mr. Grafton, Mr. Ostrager said at the hearing. Mr. Wadia showed Mr. Grafton a draft of the resolution creating a "protection committee" and said he planned to present it to the board the next day.

But Mr. Grafton told Mr. Wadia that he believed the resolution was inconsistent with advice he had received from the firm's lawyers, Mr. Ostrager said. Mr. Grafton said board members could not vote on any matter related to the arbitration proceeding in Paris because each member was a party to that divorce filing and, therefore, had a conflict of interest.

The next day, though, Mr. Wadia ignored Mr. Grafton's warning and put the resolution before the board. It passed, even though Mr. Grafton and all the Andersen Consulting partners voted against it. The resolution states that the arbitration request was a "scheme" by the consultants "to avoid all duties and obligations they owe to their fellow partners."

The next day, Feb. 13, Mr. Wadia sent a memo to Arthur Andersen's partners saying the board had "put on record their intention to pursue and investigate Andersen Consulting's behavior."

Mr. Wadia also sent the memo to the Andersen Consulting partners, with an attached letter that said the consultants were trying to "inflict pain" on Arthur Andersen in December when they publicized the feud. "Was it really worth it?" Mr. Wadia wrote. "That misconduct, more than anything else, has galvanized Arthur Andersen and has made it more resolute than ever before."

Mr. Wadia declined to comment on the events, citing the continuing litigation.

While it may be years before the Andersens settle their differences, it is clear that life at Andersen Worldwide—where most partners were hired as college graduates—will never be the same.

One former consulting partner remembers the anxiety he felt years ago, when there had been talk of the consultants' going their own way.

"I had spent a lot of time and effort becoming partner, and I was thinking that all that hard work and my future were over," he said. "There must be a lot of that same anxiety now."

How They Stack Up

The Andersens' feud pits players at the top of their fields.

Leading accounting firms*
1997 U.S. revenues, in billions

Ernst & Young	$2.60
Deloitte & Touche	1.96
Arthur Andersen	1.83

*Accounting, auditing and tax services

Leading consulting firms
1996 worldwide revenues, in billions

Andersen Consulting	$3.12
McKinsey & Company	2.10
Ernst & Young	2.10
Coopers & Lybrand	1.92
KPMG Peat Marwick	1.38
Arthur Andersen	1.38

Ernst & Young's fiscal year ended Oct. 31, Coopers & Lybrand's on Sept. 30.

Sources: Public Accounting Report: Consultants News

FASB UNDER SIEGE

The fight over stock options has set the board against its constituents and turned CFOs into lobbyists. Rulemaking may never be the same.

STEPHEN BARR

Stephen Barr is a contributing editor of CFO.

On June 8, the news from Norwalk, Connecticut, was greeted with whoops and hollers in executive suites nationwide. By a unanimous vote, the seven-member Financial Accounting Standards Board decided not to require new information about the value of employee stock options on 1994 financial statements. Furthermore, said board chairman Dennis Beresford in a prepared statement, "All provisions of the exposure draft, including expense recognition and measurement, will be reconsidered."

For the hundreds of executives who had mobilized against the exposure draft, "Accounting for Stock-based Compensation," the news offered the first real hint that they might beat back the FASB proposal. But cracking open bottles of champagne would have been premature. Beresford wasn't making a concession speech.

"There are signs that momentum is shifting, but no, we haven't won," says Douglas Maine, CFO of MCI Communications Corp., in Washington, D.C. "In my view, FASB still has its heels dug in. I see no sign that they are considering killing the proposal."

Nevertheless, the June vote marks a critical juncture in one of the most raucous debates the world of accounting has ever seen. It is a debate whose impact extends way beyond the accounting issues themselves and includes the threat of congressional intervention. When it's over, the furor could irrevocably damage the board and the way accounting standards are made.

The uproar was unleashed a year ago, in June 1993, when FASB formally laid out new stock option accounting rules. The board asked for comments, and comments it got—receiving more than 1,700 letters and taking the testimony of 72 witnesses during six days of public hearings in March.

The tally: For the first time ever on a FASB proposal, all Big Six accounting firms were opposed. So were the American Institute of Certified Public Accountants (AICAP), the Financial Executives Institute, and various shareholder and institutional investor groups. (One of the few defenders was billionaire investor Warren Buffett, who called the current treatment of stock options "the most egregious case of let's-not-face-up-to-reality behavior by executives and accountants.")

"This is the most bitter confrontation with the business community over a standard [I've ever seen]," says Patricia McConnell, a managing director at Bear Stearns Co. Inc., in New York, and a former member of FASB's Advisory Council. "There has been dissension over almost every new rule, but they were just mild disagreements compared with the histrionics over employee stock options."

At the heart of the issue is FASB's contention that stock options are compensation whose value should be accounted for on financial statements. Critics dispute this and argue passionately that the proposal will cripple American business. But they have been most effective in pointing out flaws in FASB's formula for measuring the value of the options—a modification of the Black-Scholes pricing model for traded options.

Since June, board members have focused on how to fix the problems with its measurement formula. "FASB now recognizes that its exposure draft overvalues the options," says Brad Goodwin, vice president and controller of Genentech Corp., in South San Francisco, California. "But even academics can't agree on the right approach,

The stakes are so high there was even a rumor that Beresford had received [false] death threats. Still Beresford takes deadly seriously the threats that the project will kill FASB.

and I don't think FASB should be in the business of arbitrating economic valuation."

Yet FASB won't find it easy to back down. The stakes are so high that there was even a rumor circulating this spring that Beresford had received death threats. (A reporter took a joking comment of his as serious.) Still, Beresford himself takes deadly seriously the threats that the project will kill FASB.

"People say we'll lose all support from the business community and die a natural death," he told *CFO* in an interview in July. "Others say Congress will take over the standards-setting process, and we'll go out of business that way." Either way, FASB's future is on the mind of one critic, who flashed a slide with two tombstones at a recent meeting of like-minded executives. One read "R.I.P. Stock Options," the other "R.I.P. FASB."

Whether the death of FASB will come to pass, no one can say now. But the intensity of the debate—and the recalcitrance displayed on both sides—has created a situation in which the accounting board is in desperate need of a graceful exit. "A big prize to the guy who figures that out," jokes one CFO.

Can FASB drop its proposal and not appear to be bending to outside influence? Can FASB push ahead with a revised proposal and persuade its critics that this one is sound and appropriate? Or can a compromise be struck that pleases the critics and safeguards FASB's long-term effectiveness in setting objective and neutral accounting standards?

Beresford says that FASB won't finish its redeliberations until early 1995, if then, and in the months ahead, each peep by the board will be carefully scrutinized for hidden meanings and messages. This is the story of what has happened so far and how it turned so ugly. It's a tale of dramatic twists and turns, of enmities and recriminations more often associated with soap opera than with rule-making for accountants.

But the real story can't be written yet. That depends on what FASB does next.

TEN YEARS AGO

When FASB first put the stock option project on its agenda, in 1984, it had general support among accounting professionals. "A lot of people told us the whole area of accounting for stock options was messed up," observes FASB vice chairman James Leisenring, who was the board's director of research and technical activities 10 years ago. "Now they tell us they *like* it all messed up."

The apparent mess stems from inconsistencies in APB 25, passed by FASB's predecessor, the Accounting Principles Board, in October 1972. Under those rules, a company that wants to grant true performance-based stock options is penalized, because such an arrangement results in a compensation expense, while fixed stock options, which have no performance contingencies, do not require an earnings charge.

This accounting quirk, the board contends, has resulted in misleading financial statements, because a company paying its employees more in cash shows a bigger compensation expense than a comparable company paying more in stock options. "The new rule is aimed at leveling the playing field," says Robert H. Northcutt, a board member since 1992. "Two companies could compensate employees the same, but the financial reports don't reflect the different mix of instruments. That's ill-serving."

At one time, accountants by and large agreed. The AICPA, one of today's most vocal opponents, was among those that initially urged FASB to look into discrepancies in stock option accounting. And seven of the then–Big Eight accounting firms advocated new rules.

So what's changed in 10 years? Walter Schuetze, chief accountant for the Securities and Exchange Commission, asked just that in January, in a speech that marks one of the most incendiary moments in the clash over stock option accounting. "Such a change in position, without a corresponding change in the underlying concepts and issues," Schuetze stated, referring to reversals by the AICPA and the Big Six accounting firms, "has left some with the impression that the switch was in response to the fear of losing clients or other forms of retaliation."

At a public hearing in March, AICPA representative Norman Strauss denied Schuetze's charge. Rather, he insisted, accountants changed their view because the value of the options cannot be "reasonably estimated." As for one of the Big Six, Arthur Andersen & Co. partner Benjamin Neuhausen says that his firm still believes, as it did 10 years ago, that current accounting is flawed. But, he adds, "given the amount of controversy this project has generated and the time FASB needs to spend on it, we feel that they are better off spending time on other projects."

Schuetze refused to comment on whether these explanations satisfy him. What's clear, however, is that FASB's excruciatingly slow pace gave its supporters a chance to change their minds.

THE SUPREME COURT OF ACCOUNTING

The seven-member accounting board has been seen as a kind of Supreme Court of the profession, strong-willed and intelligent, with members willing to nitpick over seemingly minor points and often putting forth elaborate dissents that do little more than display how smart they are. Most major projects take over five years to complete.

"There's plenty of time for mischief-making by the business community," says McConnell of Bear Stearns.

And with stock options, nothing has come easy. For more than two years, FASB was fixated on whether an employee stock option was an equity instrument or a liability. Depending on the board's answer, the value would be measured at the grant date or at the exercise date, respectively.

Then in 1988, still uncertain of the right answer, FASB put the stock option project on hold by inserting the equity/liability question into another of its projects. But debate on that project didn't begin until 1990, and it wasn't until early 1992 that the board came to the conclusion that stock options are equity instruments. Only then did the board get back to working on stock option accounting.

During that four-year hiatus, excessive executive pay became a white-hot issue. Multimillion-dollar paychecks, the bulk of which came from CEOs cashing in generous stock option grants, proved ready fodder for scandal-hungry reporters, outspoken institutional investors, and shareholder-rights groups. Drives to deflate these rewards came from the SEC and from Congress.

Calling options "stealth compensation," Sen. Carl Levin (D-Mich.) introduced a bill in June 1991 requiring enhanced proxy disclosure of granted options and a mandatory charge against earnings. The following February, at a hearing on his bill, Levin chided Leisenring for FASB's failure to move on its proposed rule change. Four weeks later, the stock option project was back on track.

"We have no doubt there's a causal relationship," says attorney Ken Hagerty, director of the Coalition for American Equity Expansion (CAEE), the Washington lobbying group formed by opponents of FASB's new rule. Hagerty contends that then-SEC chairman Richard Breeden told him directly that Levin could have garnered as many as 80 votes if he took his bill to the Senate floor. The only way to head off congressional action, Hagerty sensed was for Breeden to get FASB to jump-start its project. (Breeden could not be reached for comment.)

Levin himself, when asked whether he is responsible for politi-

WASHINGTON WEIGHS IN

May 31, 1984: FASB formally requests comments on requiring a compensation expense charge against earnings for stock options.

June 4, 1991: Sen. Carl Levin introduces a bill requiring greater proxy disclosure of executive compensation and a mandatory charge against earnings for stock options.

January 31, 1992: Levin holds a hearing on his bill at which he browbeats FASB vice chairman James Leisenring for the board's failure to impose a charge against earnings.

February 26, 1992: FASB votes to revive its stock option project.

June 4, 1992: SEC chairman **Richard Breeden** announces new proposed proxy guidelines for executive compensation, but does not require valuing options in the footnotes.

November 1992: The Coalition for American Equity Expansion (CAEE), which will become the chief lobbying group against FASB, is formed and begins drafting a legislative response.

January 28, 1993: Levin introduces a bill mandating a charge against earnings for stock options and threatens to bring it to a vote if FASB does not act before April 1.

February 19, 1993: The Council of Institutional Investors (CII), Big Six accounting firms, and Treasury Secretary **Lloyd Bentsen** call for enhanced disclosure rather than an earnings charge.

April 7, 1993: FASB votes to reject the CII disclosure proposal and proceed with a charge against earnings.

June 29, 1993: Sen. Joseph Lieberman introduces a bill that has its roots in the CAEE lobbying effort that would head off action by FASB and create a new kind of employee stock option.

June 30, 1993: FASB formally releases the exposure draft on its stock option project and calls for comments by December 31.

August 11, 1993: FASB chairman Dennis Beresford and Leisenring meet with more than 300 Silicon Valley executives and say they are firm in their view that options must be expensed.

October 14, 1993: Levin writes to **President Clinton** complaining that the Lieberman bill will rob FASB of its independence, politicize accounting rules, and damage the credibility of corporate financial statements.

October 21, 1993: At oversight hearing held by Senate Securities Subcommittee, senators criticize FASB's stock option proposal. Says **Sen. Phil Gramm:** "This is a stupid proposal."

December 31, 1993: The comment period of FASB's exposure draft ends, with the board having received more than 1,700 letters.

January 19, 1994: In a major reversal, the Accounting Standards Executive Committee of the AICPA announces that it opposes FASB's project.

March, 1994: FASB holds a series of field hearings in three cities; of the 72 groups and individuals who testify, only 5 agree that options should be expensed.

April 18, 1994: FASB holds a roundtable to discuss various ways of measuring the value of stock options; no agreement is reached.

May 3, 1994: The Senate votes 88-9 on a nonbinding resolution asking FASB not to change current accounting treatment of stock options; an amendment by Levin saying Congress should not legislate accounting standards is then passed 92-2.

June 8, 1994: Beresford announces that FASB will not require disclosure of the value of employee stock options in 1994 financial statements; the board will reconsider all provisions of its exposure draft, and a final vote will not take place before early 1995.

cizing the stock option controversy, readily acknowledges that his bill was "to prod FASB to do what it said should be done." Yet board members insist that the two events were coincidental. "If you look at the record, each step is part of a very predictable process," says Leisenring. "If you want to believe that Levin put his foot on the accelerator, I can't disprove that. I can tell you in good conscience that he did not."

Although the CEO pay issue is a red herring when it comes to what's good accounting, Levin's bill gave the appearance of political interference in the standard-setting process. And that was enough to spark a massive retaliatory effort. "We believe we were dealing with politically cooked accounting standards," says Hagerty, "and we believe it was appropriate to respond with political counterpressure."

A lot of people told us the whole area of accounting for stock options was messed up. Now they tell us they like it all messed up," says FASB's Leisenring.

LAUNCHING THE LOBBYING EFFORT

By June 1993, when FASB, by unanimous vote, finally released its new stock option accounting rules, opponents were ready for a fight.

Eight months earlier, in November 1992, Ken Hagerty had recruited a group of companies to launch the CAEE. ShareData Inc., a Sunnyvale, California, supplier of software for managing employee stock plans, was one of the companies that provided seed money for the launch. More than 55 firms joined the coalition, with groups like the American Electronics Association and the National Venture Capital Association falling in line.

The CAEE's first order of business was to draft a bill that would counter Levin's legislation and create a new kind of performance-based stock option. In May 1993, the CAEE held the first of seven "fly-ins" for CEOs and CFOs to lobby Congress and the Clinton Administration, and the day before FASB's exposure draft was voted on, Sen. Joseph Lieberman (D–Conn.) announced that he would sponsor the CAEE's bill.

While the bill, says ShareData president Cheryl Breetwor, reflected an effort by FASB's foes "to create a positive image for stock options," the debate between the board and the business community generally took place on another level. FASB saw its critics as waging a popularity contest among executives and amassing political firepower in Washington through a well-oiled lobbying campaign. The critics saw FASB as unyielding, no matter what the argument.

There was the accounting argument—that the calculation of earnings per share already captures the dilutive impact of the stock options. "This fictitious expense would be a second hit to EPS," says Douglas Maine, who became involved because MCI gives stock options to about 10 percent of its nearly 40,000 employees.

Robert Northcutt points out, however, that simply adding the shares outstanding to the EPS denominator doesn't accurately reflect the transaction as a form of compensation. "If I issue stock in the market, take the cash, and give it to an employee, nobody would argue that that wasn't an expense and that I didn't have more shares outstanding," says Northcutt. "The substance of the transaction is the same, and therefore it ought to get the same answer."

Then there was the "who benefits?" argument—that investors aren't crying out that financial statements are distorted because the cost of stock options is missing. FASB concedes that it has no evidence of accounting abuses, but the inconsistencies allow one company to appear more profitable than a comparable one. Investors have no way of detecting that.

Finally, there is the public policy argument—that the economy will be stunted because new, cash-poor companies won't be able to use stock options to attract top talent. "A tragedy for capitalism" is how Bernard Marcus, CEO of Home Depot Inc., of Atlanta, put it at a public hearing. To which Beresford responds: "When people say this will hurt emerging companies, we say we're not anti-American; we just look at what's good accounting."

Having failed to budge the board with these arguments, FASB's critics also turned to criticizing the process. "They prejudged the issue," charges Hagerty. "Asking for comments was a sham."

Yet once again, they made no headway. "If you don't have merit to your substantive arguments, arguing process is a strategy, too," counters Leisenring, noting that the purpose of an exposure draft is to state the board's position on an issue. "To say we should have no conclusions defies the issuance of an exposure draft. Seven people voted for that conclusion. We didn't just lob it out as a trial balloon to see if anyone would yell about this. That's not the way we do things."

WILL WALL STREET REACT?

As FASB's defenders see it, the critics' sound and fury signifies nothing. While the current debate is certainly louder and more emotional, past rule-making has been controversial—as far back as 1972, when FAS 2 required companies to expense their research costs, and as recently as 1990, when FAS 106 required balance-sheet recognition of the liability for retiree health care benefits.

"The financial markets yawned," says Bear Stearns's McConnell about the effects of FAS 106. "Wall Street didn't penalize companies, and the whole thing blew over. This will blow over, too."

Marcus of Home Depot disagrees. "You are trying to confuse me with logic here," he said in one of the hearings' more memorable exchanges. "I deal with the emotional side of the Street. You will see the stock prices go down on those companies who reward their employees [with stock options] and have to take it away from the bottom line. There is no question in my mind."

As it turns out, the strongest support for FASB's proposal comes from stock analyst groups, including the Association for Investment Management and Research and The Boston Security Analysts Society Inc. Appearing right after Marcus, Jack Cieselski, an AIMR representative, said that stock options have value and that financial statements ought to "tell it like it is." Expected cash flows determine stock price, he stated, and "those cash flows are not going to be any different before the adoption of this standard [than] after."

But the question remains, can FASB come up with a formula that provides analysts and investors with a reliable measure of the value of stock options?

MEASURE FOR MEASURE

In late March, FASB released a field test of its new stock option rules. It applied the accounting formula in its exposure draft to current company situations, as did ShareData, Coopers & Lybrand, and The Wyatt Co. The four sets of data made visibly apparent, for the first time, that the board's proposal had serious measurement problems.

"There were aspects [of the field test] that were so hard to interpret, and the charge fluctuated so dramatically, that no one knows how accurate the numbers are," says ShareData's Cheryl Breetwor. "This is not something where you just plug numbers into a model."

As a result, the measurement issue moved front and center. "What we're doing at this point is seeing if we can come up with a revised approach to determining the value of the options," Beresford said in an interview this past summer. "All the board members believe that the approach in our exposure draft has some faults."

One possible tweak is to change the date from which the options are valued. The formula in the exposure draft used the grant date, and several comment letters, in particular one from the American Bar Association, suggested that the vesting date might work better.

I'm not ready to say we do away with FASB. But I will look harder than in the past at their proposals," says MCI's Douglas Maine.

At a meeting on July 6, the board agreed to explore such a revision, even though, as FASB's critics see it, that puts them back at square one. "They're so determined to prevail," says the CAEE's Hagerty, "that they're willing to throw out years of work."

But FASB may have no choice. Even its defenders say that the board blundered with the valuation formula it initially proposed. "FASB did acknowledge that it embarrassed itself in saying that it would be easy to measure the cost using the standard Black-Scholes measure," says Roman Weil, a professor of accounting at the University of Chicago, who nevertheless believes that a charge for stock options needs to be recognized.

And while the board redeliberates, FASB's critics are standing by, secure in their belief that the exercise will be futile. Valuing employee stock options is just too complicated, they contend, and eventually the board will be forced to throw up its hands.

DAMAGE CONTROL

Although FASB is answerable to the SEC and Congress, it makes decisions with some assurance that its rules won't be overturned. But any action on stock options will almost surely provoke some kind of challenge.

Already, on May 3, the Senate voted 88–9 on a nonbinding resolu-

THE PROCESS

1. **Prospectus.** Staff sketches out issues and possible solutions.
2. **Task force.** Major projects require a panel of experts from public accounting, industry, government, academia, and securities firms.
3. **Research report.** Sometimes used as the basis for the discussion memorandum or exposure draft, but more often results in no further action.
4. **Discussion memorandum.** Theoretically a neutral paper on the issue, but experts can often get a taste of the board's sentiment.
5. **Public hearings.** People who responded to the discussion memorandum in writing are quizzed by the board.
6. **Preliminary views.** Rarely used and often subject to change, this stage is used by the board when it realizes it may be on thin ice.
7. **Exposure draft.** Invites public comment, but its so-called tentative conclusions rarely change.
8. **Field test.** Used infrequently, it's a chance for real companies to apply the exposure draft to read data to ensure that the proposal is feasible and not too costly.
9. **Final statement.** Supposedly the culmination of the process, but if the public continues to complain the board reopens the subject.

FASB'S AGENDA

	TOPIC
1982	Consolidations and Related Matters • Policy and Procedures • New Basis • Unconsolidated Entities • Disaggregated Disclosures
1984	Stock-based Compensation Plans
1986	Financial Instruments • Liabilities and Equities • Disclosure of Derivatives • Not-for-profit Organizations
1988	Present Value-based Measurements • Impairment of Assets
1993	Mortgage Servicing Rights
1994	Mutual Life Insurance • Earnings per Share

tion sponsored by Joseph Lieberman asking FASB to drop its stock option project. At the same session, the senators voted 94–2 on a resolution introduced by Carl Levin that Congress should not intervene in the rule-making process.

Given these apparently conflicting votes, the real question becomes: How can FASB get out of this bind? "We've entered a phase of damage control," says the CAEE's Hagerty. "How do we get out without damaging FASB, this very useful tool, and the credibility of the accounting standards?"

If FASB comes up with a revised proposal, Senator Lieberman could push for a bill that would overrule the board. "The exposure draft has been soundly rejected as bad accounting," says Ken Glueck, a legislative assistant to Lieberman. "Should FASB move forward with another proposal that does not pass the test of good accounting, clearly there will be a legislative reaction."

Then again, if FASB decides that it can't reliably measure the value of employee stock options and drops its proposal, Senator Levin could act. In an interview, he told *CFO* that he would not, though he would be displeased: "If it now did nothing, I think FASB would be abdicating its judgment."

As for the SEC, chairman Arthur Levitt has written to Congress saying that he respects FASB's process, however long it takes. So, short of SEC intervention, one commissioner, J. Carter Beese, has strongly advocated "an interim step." If FASB truly believes that investors are being misled by current accounting, he argues, it should immediately require greater disclosure of stock options and take its time exploring the measurement issue.

We're here to do difficult things. If we failed to deal with the difficult things because of outside threats, then we would really have a crisis of confidence."

This solution, as Beese stated in a June speech, would "allow FASB to protect and safeguard its independence," as well as consider an earnings charge in a less heated environment. Beresford told *CFO* that "anything's possible," but added, "that's not the thrust of what we're doing right now."

And would even this apparent face-saving solution allow FASB to move ahead on other matters as it always has? "They've given themselves a black eye," says MCI's Maine, who supports Beese's compromise. "I personally think FASB has a purpose and a long history of good work, so I'm not ready to say we do away with FASB. But I will look harder than in the past at their proposals as far as whether they're meaningful, objective, and the right thing to do."

Already FASB has reported reductions in donations from the more than 8,800 contributors who fund it, while 100 CFOs queried by *Bowman's Accounting Report* in July rated FASB's performance 4.1 on a scale of 1 to 10. And things could get worse, considering the number of potentially divisive projects on the board's agenda—especially hedge accounting and derivatives. "Depending on what position they take on how to account for different uses of derivatives, the business community could go bonkers," says McConnell of Bear Stearns.

It's impossible now to predict the future of FASB, but perhaps tellingly, board members are in concert about an internal crisis of confidence—there is none. "The board is in a constant state of crisis, because we're here to do difficult things," says Robert Northcutt. "If we failed to deal with the difficult things because of outside threats, then we would really have a crisis of confidence."

To some that view is self-deluding. To others it's arrogant. To others still, it's honest. Which is correct may ultimately depend on whether the bottles of champagne are ever cracked open.

How Should the FASB Be Judged?

Dennis R. Beresford

Dennis R. Beresford is Chairman of the Financial Accounting Standards Board

How should the success or failure of the FASB be judged? The challenges to the FASB over the past several years, including an unprecedented lobbying campaign as a result of our proposal on accounting for stock options, suggest that many of our constituents hold the FASB accountable for producing accounting standards that they find acceptable.

Some seem willing to go to almost any length to get their preferred solution, even to the point of supporting a government override or takeover if private-sector standard setting produces unacceptable answers. It's no secret that many businesses supported a Sense-of-the-Senate resolution on accounting for stock options that was passed in May 1994. Citing widespread opposition, the resolution said that

> the FASB should not at this time change the current generally accepted accounting treatment of stock options and stock purchase plans contained in APB Decision 25.

Washington interest in the FASB's stock compensation project was not limited to the Sense-of-the-Senate resolution. We received dozens of letters from individual Senators and Representatives asking us to explain and defend our proposal, our field test, our neutrality with regard to "economic consequences," and even our existence. Most were prompted by letters from angry constituents.

The Secretaries of Treasury and Commerce and the chairman of the National Economic Council spoke out against our proposal. The Senate Banking Committee conducted hearings on it. And one SEC Commissioner condemned the proposal publicly, criticizing the FASB for adopting an attitude of "the truth will set investors free"—an attitude, incidentally, for which I find it hard to apologize.

Even President Clinton could not avoid the controversy. In a letter to several members of Congress, he acknowledged that stock options are a "corporate transfer of something of value." But he carefully straddled the political fence by agreeing "that it would be better to avoid legislation on this issue" while also noting that "it would be unfortunate if FASB's proposal inadvertently undermined the competitiveness of some of America's most promising high-tech companies."

Leaders of a number of professional organizations, including the AAA, AICPA, and FEI, publicly opposed legislating accounting standards, as did the Chief Accountant of the SEC. However, most individual companies and accounting firms were noticeably silent on the legislation, although Arthur Andersen's Public Review Board said:

> We strongly disagree ... with those who believe that the Congress should step in to resolve the [stock options] dispute through legislation .... While proponents of particular accounting standards might be pleased by the outcome of particular legislation, turning ac-

Expressions of individual views by members of the FASB and its staff are encouraged. The views expressed in this article are those of Mr. Beresford. Official positions of the FASB are determined only after extensive due process and deliberation. These remarks were presented at the AICPA's Twenty-Second Annual National Conference on Current SEC Developments, January 10, 1995.

counting standards into subjects of political debate would, in the long run, benefit no one.

Not all corporate executives were silent. In a speech at a Bank Administration Institute conference in June 1994, Citicorp Chairman John Reed seemed to support governmentalization of the process when he said:

> We have taken some very intelligent, highly qualified individuals, we've put them up in the jungles of Connecticut, and we've said, "Change accounting rules." Not surprisingly, they have nothing else to do but to do that .... The real question is do we need the changes? I believe we do not .... I do believe that I'd rather have a regulatory agency that has other things to do include standard setting within their portfolio of responsibilities, as opposed to having a single purpose organization that has nothing to do but make accounting changes.

It's hard to say how many others embrace John Reed's philosophy. But it's a point of view that the FASB, and the Trustees who oversee our operation, cannot afford to ignore, particularly in light of events of the past few months.

Because the FASB did not abandon its stock option project in response to the Sense-of-the-Senate resolution, certain members of Congress increased the pressure in October 1994 when they introduced the Accounting Standards Reform Act of 1994. That proposal would amend federal securities law as follows:

> ... any new accounting standard or principle, and any modification to an existing accounting standard or principle, to be used in the preparation of financial statements required to be filed pursuant to this title shall become effective only following an affirmative vote of a majority of a quorum of the members of the [Securities and Exchange] Commission.

At a minimum, that law would require Commission approval of FASB Statements, Interpretations, and Technical Bulletins, as well as all AcSEC pronouncements, EITF consensuses, and SEC Staff Accounting Bulletins. Moreover, because the formal hierarchy of authoritative sources of GAAP includes auditing standards, textbooks, and individual company practices, the legislation *could* extend to them as well.

Whether our recent decision not to require expense recognition for stock options will affect the potential legislation remains to be seen. Nevertheless, I think it is critical that all of us take time, now, to ask how important to our profession is private-sector standard setting.

IMPLICATIONS OF LEGISLATED ACCOUNTING PRINCIPLES

First, we should consider what are the implications of explicit SEC approval of accounting answers or some other form of legislated accounting? Certainly, the ramifications extend well beyond the stock compensation project.

If interested parties found that they could routinely go around the FASB by lobbying in Washington, they certainly would lobby on other issues. The SEC would become a sort of appellate accounting court. And if those parties didn't like the answer they got from the SEC, Congress could easily step in to set accounting standards. Congress would quickly see that it could use accounting as its own economic, political, and regulatory tool, as it did during the S&L crisis. It is not likely that all of their future answers would be widely palatable.

Moving the accounting standards-setting process into the political arena would likely lead to less consistency and conceptual underpinning in accounting standards. That, to me, would be the most significant reversal of the progress that the FASB has made in the past two decades.

It's hard to predict whether the SEC, if it had to explicitly act on everything, would endorse the FASB's and AICPA's answers in all, most, or just some cases. Because accounting standards are conventions rather than natural laws, it is not unreasonable to expect different groups of people to reach different decisions, particularly groups with different constituencies and different missions.

I also believe that, after being overruled a few times by the SEC, the FASB would lose support and motivation, and its constituents would concentrate their efforts on influencing the SEC. As a result, there would be a strong temptation to eliminate the "middleman" and just have the SEC or another federal agency replace the FASB entirely. The next step might be a government takeover of auditing standards and procedures as well, especially in light of recent concerns about auditor independence and some widely publicized audit failures.

SOME HISTORY

Let me put these current events in perspective by providing a little history. The FASB is the third incarnation of the private sector's approach to setting accounting standards over the past six decades. Both of our predecessors were replaced when they seemed to be making significant accomplishments, primarily because some people thought there was a better way to set accounting standards, and not just because the boards weren't doing the job they were established to do.

The Committee on Accounting Procedure, which existed from the late 1930s to the late 1950s, was criticized for reaching ad hoc decisions. The Accounting Principles Board was intended to correct that. The original blueprint for the APB called for research to "find accounting truth" and for the APB to adopt it.

Unfortunately, people quickly disagreed with the APB's view of the truth and sought government relief. Remember the investment credit fiasco? Another criticism was that the truth didn't come quickly. It took the APB five years to issue its first major pronouncement.

The APB lasted 14 years. Ironically, it was replaced by the FASB during its most productive period. The charge to the Wheat Committee, in fact, was how the APB itself could do a better job. In 1972, the Wheat Committee concluded a better job could be done by replacing the APB with a full-time, independent FASB with adequate staff support. Both of our predecessors were replaced through the efforts of a relatively few determined and vocal individuals who concluded that greener grass grew elsewhere.

When the FASB was launched in 1973, Reginald H. Jones, Chairman of General Electric, spoke at an inaugural dinner in New York. He said:

> We must recognize that the new Board will not be a cure-all for every ailment. We must recognize that with its *first* decision the new Board is going to gore somebody's ox—and *that* will be the time for us to pull together—not to splinter apart .... Let's not lose sight of the public and professional momentum that has brought us this far; and let's not forget that if we falter, government stands ready to do for us what we can't do for ourselves.

The FASB got off to a fairly quick start, issuing important standards on R&D, contingencies, leases, and segment reporting in its first four years. And it got going on a conceptual framework that had proved elusive to its predecessors.

Unfortunately, during those same years, highly publicized cases of bankruptcy, fraud, and illegal payments by business corporations caused a deterioration of public confidence in both public and private sector institutions. Shortcomings in accounting standards and corporate disclosure were often alleged to have contributed to business failures and investor losses. And in that atmosphere of disillusionment and distrust, the ability of the private sector to establish standards for its own accountability was questioned at the highest levels, including the Congress.

A 1976 House subcommittee report concluded: "The FASB has accomplished virtually nothing toward resolving fundamental accounting problems .... Considering the FASB's record, the SEC's continued reliance on the private accounting profession [for establishment of financial accounting standards] is questionable." A 1977 Senate subcommittee report titled *The Accounting Establishment* concluded that Congress should assume responsibility for establishing financial accounting standards either directly or through the General Accounting Office or a new body that Congress would create.

In 1978, a comprehensive inquiry about the FASB was conducted by the Senate Subcommittee on Governmental Efficiency. And a bill was introduced in the House, though never enacted, that would have required that the SEC issue certain accounting standards if FASB progress was slow or unsatisfactory.

Although none of the Congressional inquiries led to an SEC takeover of FASB responsibilities, the issues they raised have not gone away. One result has been that the FASB may have become one of the most intensively reviewed organizations in history, with numerous resulting improvements to our process. In 1977, the trustees of our Foundation undertook the first of several comprehensive periodic reviews of the FASB's structure and operating procedures. Among the most important changes that resulted were sunshine operations, independence of the Board's Advisory Council, and no longer requiring a public accounting majority on the Board.

In 1980, the trustees commissioned a Harris Survey of constituents' assessments of the FASB. In 1982, the trustees undertook a second comprehensive review, and a second Harris Survey was conducted in 1985. Also in 1985, a special review committee of the trustees was appointed to examine and respond to criticisms of the FASB by the Business Roundtable. That committee published reports in July and December 1985, and December 1986. And another major structure review was done in 1989.

In addition to all those major reviews, the trustees' structure committee has conducted more limited interim reviews. Further, at my suggestion, in 1989 the trustees formed a standing oversight committee that monitors and reports periodically on the Board's agenda activities from the perspective of adhering to its due process and fulfilling its stated mission.

Several common threads can be identified in the reports of these reviews and constituent surveys:

Almost unanimously across all segments of the FASB's constituency, the sentiment consistently has been to keep accounting standard setting in the private sector. At the same time, the reviews acknowledged that the FASB cannot please everyone. Every new accounting standard is likely to please some and displease others. And some new standards are likely to displease many, if not a majority, of the Board's constituents. But most agree that setting accounting standards should not merely be a popularity contest.

Among the keys to successful accounting standard setting are:

- Sound due process.
- Confidence of constituents that their views are given careful consideration.
- Decision usefulness of the resulting information.
- Neutrality of the standards.
- And reasonable balancing of costs and benefits.

But do those qualities continue to be enough in light of recent assaults on the FASB, particularly in connection with stock options? Does the private sector continue to be the proper place in which accounting standards should be established? And even if it is, is the current structure the right one?

ARGUMENTS FOR SETTING STANDARDS IN THE PRIVATE SECTOR

To stimulate your thinking about those questions, I have made a list of what I perceive as the arguments for keeping accounting standard setting in the private sector rather than having a government takeover of the process. In that regard, I would define a requirement that the SEC review and adopt each FASB pronouncement through rule making as governmental, rather than private sector, standard setting.

I believe that a private-sector board brings greater expertise to the table. It can attract board members and staff with the requisite practical experience, compensate them appropriately, retain them for a sufficient period, and provide the support services necessary for them to do their jobs.

Related to that is the need to reasonably insulate the standard setter from self-serving objectives of special-interest lobbying groups and from government itself. A private-sector board offers a better hope of achieving that objective.

A private-sector board is more likely to develop a body of standards that is consistent with an agreed-on set of underlying concepts.

All of these points, of course, recognize that the SEC already is the ultimate watchdog, safeguard, and enforcer, not just with its statutory "veto" power but also with its powers of persuasion during the development of accounting standards. And, in the long run, FASB standards have been reasonably well accepted by the business community, accounting profession, and users, even when preceded by strong objection. Our standard on retiree medical obligations is a particularly good example.

ARGUMENTS FOR GOVERNMENT STANDARD SETTING

Here are the principal arguments that I have heard in favor of a government takeover of accounting standard setting.

First, the FASB's critics argue that the public interest is at stake. They say that protecting the public is an obligation too important to be left to a body not directly responsible to Congress.

Second, the critics argue that a government board is more likely to be free from conflicts of interest. A private-sector board depends on business for its funding, is overseen by trustees with conflicting private interests, and has members who come from and cannot completely sever their ties to private organizations.

Third, the FASB's critics argue that government is likely to ensure a greater concern for "economic consequences" of accounting standards. They are concerned that the FASB worships at the altar of neutrality without paying sufficient attention to the consequences of its standards on competition or the capital-raising abilities of corporations and similar economic or social objectives.

And, fourth, the critics believe that government would have a greater obligation to make a cost-benefit analysis of potential standards. Some feel that the FASB does not do that adequately.

SELF EXAMINATION—WHAT'S WRONG WITH THE FASB?

Naturally, I am a believer in keeping accounting standards setting a private-sector responsibility. That does not mean that the FASB ought to close its eyes to the recent criticism and assaults and tough it out. Indeed, in announcing its decision on stock compensation last month, the Board acknowledged that "there simply isn't enough support for the basic notion of requiring expense recognition," even though it remains convinced that options have value and are compensation.

It seems to me that this is an appropriate time for all of us to consider what's wrong and what's right with the FASB—completely apart from stock compensation or other controversial topics. Let me begin by identifying and commenting on some of the shortcomings I've heard expressed about the FASB.

Our critics say that the Board is not dealing with the right issues or that it spends too much time on relatively unimportant issues. In thinking about the concerns about our agenda, the following questions seem relevant:

- What are the appropriate roles of the FASB, the AICPA, the EITF, and the SEC in issuing accounting guidance?
- Is the Board sufficiently proactive or too reactive in setting its agenda?
- And is the FASB involved with too many small issues because practicing CPAs are unwilling to take hard lines with their clients on accounting questions?

An independent review of the EITF currently under way should help shed light on whether the Board is dealing with the right issues.

Another criticism is that our process takes too long. While I, too, am often frustrated by the time it takes us, work on many of our projects is often like "R&D"—we're breaking new ground. For example, some of our general discussions on present value concepts, future events, and new basis of accounting will be useful in providing consistent direction for many other specific issues.

And while some say we take too long, others would have us take even longer, in part because they feel we're issuing too many standards. Also, some critics say that our standards are too complex and detailed. On the other hand, we also are told that our standards don't provide enough practical guidance.

We often hear that the Board isn't listening to its customers. Existing practices that the Board has changed or proposed to change are perceived as satisfactory or even beneficial, particularly to preparers who do not want to give them up.

Critics say the Board is not accountable, that there are no checks and balances. But our whole due process is a system of accountability. And, as previously mentioned, the SEC certainly is a major check and balance.

Some critics say the Board has gotten too far out front and has lost the support of the public accounting profession. They feel that the Board needs to strike a better balance between its perceptions of needed improvements to financial reporting and the need to have its standards accepted in the marketplace. After all, they ask, isn't the operative term "generally accepted accounting principles"?

A final criticism is that the Board does not have a vision for future financial reporting. The critics say our conceptual framework is more a description of what *is* rather than a chart for future directions, though my own experience and observation is that the concepts *do* provide important guidance and direction. The Board is, of course, giving careful consideration to the report of the AICPA's Jenkins committee and the position paper on financial reporting in the 1990s and beyond published by the Association for Investment Management and Research.

SELF EXAMINATION—WHAT'S RIGHT WITH THE FASB?

Despite the criticisms, there's a lot that's right with the FASB.

First of all, our standards, and those of our predecessors and others who provide accounting guidance, have produced the finest financial reporting system in the world.

The independence of the standard setter and the neutrality of the standards are critical to the credibility and reliability of reported information. Without independence and neutrality, financial reporting can become propaganda.

I think that our investor/creditor focus is a big plus. We have identified the primary audience and we evaluate the relevance of the information produced by each standard in that context.

We pay attention to our conceptual framework. In every agenda project, we are guided by agreed-on definitions of assets, liabilities, revenues, and expenses and by clear objectives of financial reporting. Our objectives and concepts have resulted in a relatively consistent body of standards, not ad hoc rules decided on a case-by-case basis.

We follow a due process that is widely respected, and we are not afraid to take on tough or unpopular issues.

And, while we are occasionally swayed by politics, for the most part the Board has been guided, above all, by the information needs of investors and creditors.

Perhaps the best validation of our relative success is that standard setters in most other major countries have emulated our process, our concepts, and many of our standards.

WHAT TO DO?

So, in this environment, what should the Board do? And, more important, what should others do?

Yes, the Board's structure and procedures can be studied again and tinkered with some more. We can find ways to speed up or slow down our process, globally or issue by issue. We can further improve our agenda selection criteria in response to constituent concerns. And we can work harder to build a consensus for proposed solutions among our constituents.

But in the final analysis, I believe that the success or failure of the Board must be measured in relation to how well it is achieving its mission. The FASB's stated mission is to improve financial reporting by issuing standards that enhance the relevance and reliability of information used in investment and credit decisions. Stakeholders in the financial reporting process—and that includes investors, creditors, auditors, corporate managers, boards of directors, and accounting academicians—must give more than lip service to that mission.

At the Board, we understand, and are continually reminded, that we must ultimately be accountable to our constituents. But our constituents also have an important responsibility. All accounting professionals must decide what kind of financial reporting system you want. You either must buy into the Board's stated mission or agree on an alternative mission for us or our successor. If you want neutrality and objectivity, you have to stand up for them, and for the standards they produce.

In summary, we cannot give you an accounting system better than you want or deserve. And without your support the FASB cannot succeed or survive.

I sincerely hope that you will join us in cultivating the grass on this side of the fence rather than letting others force a move to perceived greener pastures.

CORPORATE AMERICA IS FED UP WITH FASB

A new chief of the accounting-rules board will face a storm

Wanted: top CPA from Big Six accounting firm to head nonprofit maker of accounting rules in Norwalk, Conn. Annual salary: $425,000. Ivory Tower atmosphere. Must have superb combat skills and skin like a rhino.

That organization, of course, is the Financial Accounting Standards Board (FASB), established in 1973 at the behest of Corporate America to strengthen private-sector control over rulemaking. On Apr. 14, trustees of the Financial Accounting Foundation, which oversees FASB, will meet to deliberate, and possibly decide, on a replacement for 58-year-old Chairman Dennis R. Beresford, who will retire June 30 after serving in the post for the maximum ten-year period. Trustees have managed to keep names of any front-runners a tight secret.

Pity Beresford's successor. By most accounts, the winning candidate will take over the office at a time when FASB's relations with its corporate constituency have deteriorated so sharply that its future as an independent body is in question. Critics, including accounting firms and big corporations such as Citicorp, General Electric, and Motorola, complain that FASB of late has departed from its mission of devising rules that reflect marketplace realities. Instead, FASB is formulating rules that critics find burdensome, incomprehensible, and unnecessary. At the same time that FASB permits big, expensive projects to drag on for years, it overwhelms companies and their accountants with rule and proposal changes faster than they can keep up with them. Philip D. Ameen, vice-president and comptroller at General Electric Co., says that FASB "tends to start with the idea that current accounting has to be overturned. The wholesale dismissal of well-understood practices doesn't seem to be the most effective or productive means of setting standards." Vice-Chairman James J. Leisenring shrugs this off. "The criticism has been issue-specific," not criticism of the institution per se.

FASB should be scrapped altogether, even if that means government regulations, says Citicorp's John Reed

Although corporations have griped about FASB for years, some are going further. Citicorp Chairman and CEO John S. Reed has called for scrapping FASB altogether and has even told Chairman Arthur Levitt Jr. of the Securities & Exchange Commission, which enforces the rules FASB makes, that he'd rather the government made the rules. Citicorp, for one, now steers clear of "wash sale" transactions that would entail compliance with newly effective FASB 125. That rule, which Citicorp Controller Roger W. Trupin describes as "ridiculous" though its financial impact is relatively small, requires gains on asset sales to be reported even if the asset is immediately reacquired. Adds Trupin: "More than ever, they're circling the wagons. They're not listening anymore."

A LOT OF FLAK. Some companies have even quietly discussed simply ignoring some FASB provisions. Asked about such a move, Levitt emphatically responds: "The financial statements would not be acceptable for filing." As for FASB's future, he adds: "I shall do everything in my power to protect the FASB and to nurture the process of

Critics say FASB produces costly, hard-to-understand rules that often represent solutions in search of a problem

independent standard-setting. The alternatives are too onerous. Politicization of the standard-setting process would be an economic catastrophe."

Several recent FASB moves account for much of the dissatisfaction. In 1995, FASB caught so much flak for proposing to require that employee stock options be expensed that the board effectively backed down. Now, companies are fuming over other FASB proposals calling for major changes in accounting treatment, presentation, and disclosure, notably a change that would require current market valuation rather than historical cost treatment for derivatives transactions. Big banks like Citicorp contend that the change will severely erode the value of instruments such as swaps as risk-management tools.

Companies also fault FASB's "comprehensive income" proposal, which would require items such as unrealized gains and losses to be reported separately from net income. Companies say that would make financial statements even more confusing. FASB's so-called segment reporting proposal, which would call for more detailed data on lines of business, would be excessively burdensome, say companies. And they oppose as simply unnecessary a proposal that would require consolidation into the parent of certain units controlled by the company in addition to those in which it holds majority stakes.

FASB: THE RAP FROM BIG BUSINESS

ISSUES

- Too many costly rule changes
- Rules are unrealistic and incomprehensible
- Bias toward investors, not companies
- Resistance to global standards

PROPOSED RULES

- Fair-market valuation for derivatives—Impedes risk management
- Segment reporting—Too detailed
- Comprehensive income—Confusing for users
- Company unit consolidation—Superfluous

DATA: BUSINESS WEEK

To some, the most contentious issue is FASB's dogged resistance to international accounting standards and its demand that foreign companies seeking to raise capital in the U.S. play by its rules. Its resistance, though, could pose the more serious long-term threat to FASB. The New York Stock Exchange, along with an ad hoc organization of financial executives known as the International Accounting Standards Committee (IASC), is pushing for "international harmonization." Officials of the IASC and the NYSE, which seeks foreign company listings, declined to comment. Vice-Chairman Leisenring says that FASB favors global standards but not weaker ones. Right now, he says, FASB and IASC are "miles apart. There are an infinite number of differences."

For his part, Beresford concedes that FASB's consensus culture may be partly to blame for the board's unpopularity. "The chairman has limited authority in terms of forcing things to get done," he says. Personalities play a role, too, FASB-watchers say. In debates over proposed rules, Leisenring, described as a brilliant but strong-willed theoretician, typically outflanks the courtly, more pragmatic Beresford. Without naming Leisenring, Beresford says: "Some people want to study things to death and look for ideal solutions."

To FASB's harshest critics, the accounting body's demise would be the most ideal solution.

By Phillip L. Zweig in New York, with Dean Foust in Washington

The recently retired FASB chairman looks into his crystal ball.

Beresford Looks Forward

BY RICHARD J. KORETO

Old habits die hard. Dennis Beresford retired on June 30 as chairman of the Financial Accounting Standards Board after 10 productive years. He might be expected to look back on his administration, but he is still thinking about the future: Where is financial accounting going? What issues will the FASB have to wrestle with over the next 10 years? Will the FASB even be necessary in an increasingly global economy? Recently, he drew on his years of experience to talk with the *Journal* about where the FASB and financial reporting generally are heading and the whys and wherefores of the FASB's approach.

BROAD TRENDS

"From time to time," said Beresford, "someone asks, 'Haven't you resolved all the issues yet? Is there really a need to have standard setting continue indefinitely?' I always say 'yes.' " New transactions and new ways of processing old transactions are always cropping up, he said, citing derivatives as an example: They've been around for decades as simple commodities futures contracts but have exploded in the last few years, calling for additional guidance. "You will see companies searching for even more ways to deal with complexities and different kinds of risks that are part of doing business today."

In addition, the financial accounting community will have to deal with the increasing importance of intangible assets. "Financial statements do not do a particularly good job of capturing these assets, and this is a problem as we move from a manufacturing economy to an information economy. You can easily see how much money Microsoft has in the bank, but how do you find out the value of its intellectual capital? We may need to consider additional disclosures on training or on developing new products, for example."

Beresford also discussed the continued need to address the comprehensive business reporting model presented in the final report of the American Institute of CPAs special committee on financial reporting (the Jenkins committee). "The FASB hasn't made much progress with this model," said Beresford. He questioned whether there was sufficient support in the accounting community for expanding into a business reporting model, for requirements beyond the basic financial statements. "The FASB will move on this model, but slowly. I suspect the results may be voluntary disclosures, at least in the beginning. So many of the recommendations may apply only to specific industries. Nevertheless," he concluded, "you will see more and more attention given to issues related to the model over the next decade." (See "What's Next for the Business Reporting Model," JofA, Dec. 96, page 14.)

Beresford does not believe in an absolute status quo, but he emphasizes the need to build on what is solid and recognized. "In the end, despite the influence of technology and the Internet, I don't see the traditional financial statements—balance sheets, income statements, cash flow statements—becoming less relevant. The basic statements still provide a bedrock on which other information is supported." For example, if the investing community has some comfort with financial reporting over the Internet, it will be in part because of the credibility of traditional financial reporting. "Other reporting methods may become more relevant than they are now, but traditional reporting will not become less relevant as a result."

AcSEC AND THE SEC: COOPERATION AND CONTROVERSY

"Creative tension" is Beresford's phrase to describe the relationship between the FASB and the Securities and Ex-

From *Journal of Accountancy,* July 1997, pp. 67-69.

change Commission. "Although the SEC relies on the FASB, it has the legal responsibility to establish standards for public companies. However, we have had an absolutely outstanding working relationship with the commission. SEC Chairman Arthur Levitt has been in our offices a half dozen times—he has shown his interest and given advice without trying to control."

Last year, however, the Financial Accounting Foundation locked horns with the SEC over the composition of the FAF board, which chooses FASB members. "The FAF trustees were concerned that this was too much SEC pressure, which was leading to too much SEC control. They pushed back a bit, and in the end the FAF—and the FASB—maintained its independence," although there were some changes in FAF composition. And although Beresford was quick to note that he's felt the FAF has supported the FASB since the beginning of his tenure, he was especially pleased with the changes that resulted from the SEC-FAF debate: "I think the change in the composition of the trustees was the single most important institutional change in the last 10 years—it ultimately confirmed our independence. The SEC supports us but does not control us." The addition of John H. Biggs, Charles A. Bowsher, Manuel H. Johnson and David S. Ruder, he said, "makes it even clearer that the public interest is represented by the FAF, not just the accounting profession and corporate officers. It's left us well positioned for the future." These four are public, or at-large, members (see Highlights, JofA, Aug. 96, page 4).

Beresford also sees a continuing good relationship with another partner in financial accounting, the AICPA accounting standards executive committee. "There has been criticism over the years that the FASB should be the sole creator of standards, but I said 10 years ago and I say again that there is a place for AcSEC, especially with narrower, more specialized issues than the FASB normally handles." He emphasized that the FASB always has the right to prevent AcSEC from impinging on FASB's territory, and, of course, the FASB always must clear all AcSEC pronouncements. The relationship was further solidified, he said, when long-time FASB staff member Jane Adams became the AICPA director of accounting standards.

U.S. vs. THE WORLD

"International accounting standards are probably the biggest challenge we face right now, and it's hard to envision how it will turn out over the next few years." As the International Accounting Standards Committee (IASC) develops its standards, a few people on one side, said Beresford, predict the FASB will become redundant and disappear, while some on the other side say international standards are of limited relevance in the United States. "I think the answer is somewhere in the middle. I do envision a viable FASB, with no loss of power or responsibility, continuing to set U.S. standards and with the ability to strongly influence international standards."

However, he said the FASB also will continue to look outward at how other countries are developing their generally accepted accounting principles and become an importer, as well as an exporter, of accounting theory. He cited the recent harmonization between the IASC and the FASB on earnings per share, which resulted in two nearly identical standards (see "FASB, IASC Finalize Earnings per Share," JofA, Mar.97, page 14). He expects the United States and Canada to issue virtually the same standards on segment reporting as a result of close collaboration. Still, he believes the IASC has some procedural shortcomings. "It doesn't hold open meetings or have a large staff that can ensure consistency from project to project. FASB standards are the result of vigorous debate among accountants, analysts and the business community—this isn't yet true of the IASC. Its standards do not compare favorably with ours right now. Over time, maybe they will."

Finally, Beresford countered the notion that a "kinder, gentler" international GAAP would ultimately win out over a more rigorous U.S. GAAP. "Big companies realize that U.S. capital markets are the best, deepest, most liquid and fairest in the world, thanks in large part to credible financial reporting. There may be surface appeal to easier standards, but the marketplace shows that high-level standards pay off in the long run."

EXECUTIVE SUMMARY

■ DENNIS BERESFORD CONTINUES to see a role for a strong, independent FASB that maintains a balance between prescriptive rules and CPAs' judgment.

■ HE BELIEVES THE FASB WILL address issues raised by the AICPA special committee on financial accounting—but slowly.

■ ALTHOUGH TECHNOLOGY IS changing how financial information is used, Beresford said traditional statements will continue to be the bedrock.

■ DESPITE THE CONTROVERSIES, Beresford is pleased with the continuing good relationship with the Securities and Exchange Commission and looks forward to a profitable partnership with the AICPA accounting standards executive committee as well.

■ BERESFORD SEES INCREASING international involvement for the FASB but stresses the FASB's advantages over the IASC.

■ HE CALLS ON ALL ACCOUNTANTS, even those not involved in accounting and auditing, to support the standard-setting process.

RICHARD J. KORETO is a *Journal* news editor. Mr. Koreto is an employee of the American Institute of CPAs and his views, as expressed in this article, do not necessarily reflect the views of the AICPA. Official positions are determined through certain specific committee procedures, due process and deliberation.

JUDGMENT OR PRESCRIPTION?

Much of the accounting standards discussion, both internationally and within the U.S. business community, centers on the problem of judgment vs. prescription. How much leeway do you allow companies and how stringent should you be to protect the public? The IASC and Great Britain, in particular, he said, tend to favor GAAP that allows more room for judgment; sometimes they see the FASB as overly prescriptive. "That's not really true, however. There will always be room for judgment. We'll never try to issue a standard saying, for example, 'Here's the exact formula for a bank to calculate its loan losses.' " He said the issue of judgment vs. prescription is not always as simple as it seems. Many erroneously assume that businesses always ask for more leeway and auditors always want rigid rules. "But recently a representative from a corporation on the emerging issues task force said about a particular issue, 'Can we be very specific here? I want to know *exactly* what my company will have to do.' " Beresford looks at the whole financial accounting community as the FASB's customers, and "if the customers want a set of clearly defined rules in a certain area, we'll try to give it to them."

Beresford said with each standard the FASB issued, it wanted to present accountants with a statement of what it was trying to achieve, including some guidelines to consider. "But in the end the company and the auditor nearly always have to exercise a lot of judgment. Sometimes we've felt a need to be very prescriptive, as with capitalization of leases; such decisions are made case by case." He doesn't believe there is, or should be, an overarching approach. Beresford said most people in the financial community were well intentioned. "If we are ever overly prescriptive, it is because we don't want to offer loopholes to the few who aren't." He pointed out that it may look at times that the FASB is favoring business, while at other times it is being too restrictive. "It's really a balancing act. In fact, I would say that in the last 10 years, *balance* was my word to live by."

THE FASB AND THE PROFESSION

An increasing number of CPAs no longer are involved in financial accounting or auditing; FASB pronouncements seemingly have become inapplicable to many in the profession. Beresford voiced his opinion on the continuing relationship between the FASB and the over 300,000 U.S. CPAs. "I understand there are CPAs who say that because of the nature of their practices they don't have much interest in the FASB." Beresford doesn't have anything against consulting and diversification, but he warns CPAs not to lose touch with their roots in financial accounting and auditing. "I hope the CPA consultants realize that auditing and accounting are still the foundation; they're what being a CPA is all about. There's a professional responsibility for all CPAs to support the development of GAAP and generally accepted auditing standards. This is what distinguishes us from non-CPAs." Without this foundation, he argued, the CPA designation might melt away. "You'd be left with the American Institute of X."

At least for now he sees continued support from the entire profession. "It's been a wonderful part of the job seeing how many people give up their time to serve on task forces and write comment letters on our exposure drafts. I felt I could call nearly any CPA cold, introduce myself and get help on a key issue I was working on. The whole process depends on a lot of participation."

WORDS OF WISDOM

Beresford was reluctant to tell his successor (still unnamed) how to handle the job, but he did have some general advice that also helps explain why the FASB has been successful and how it can continue to thrive. "I've kept a positive attitude and didn't let my energy or enthusiasm flag, despite 10 years of controversy," he said, noting that even though CPAs and the business community respect the board and the process, they can still bicker over individual issues. "I've listened to all points of view—I think that's important." Recently, on separate occasions, two people who had strongly disagreed with him on certain positions told him that despite their vociferous disapproval, they respected him personally for his willingness to meet with and listen to people. "I was proud to hear that; I hope my successor realizes reaching out and listening are a key part of the job."

His only other advice is to get a dog. "After a day of debating with your colleagues, with firms, with businesses, with the SEC, it's good to come home to a dog that gives you unconditional affection."

Goodbye Connecticut, hello Georgia. Beresford is pleased with his new position: He will be executive professor of accounting at the J. M. Tull School of Accounting at the University of Georgia, Athens. And although he plans to continue to speak and write on a variety of accounting issues, he had one final message to the profession as chairman: "I want to thank the AICPA and all the CPAs who have spent so much time these past 10 years helping with the financial accounting process."

Challenges to the Current Accounting Model

Some profound and thoughtful observations for the next 100 years

By Robert J. Swieringa

We come to an age of technology, information, and global competition with a financial accounting model that was fashioned almost 100 years ago. In the early twentieth century, the balance sheet was the most important financial statement. Cost was viewed as a practical and satisfactory basis of valuation for assets held for use or sale, except that fixed assets were depreciated and inventories sometimes were written down to amounts that were below cost.

The historical cost, transaction-based model that emerged in the early 1900s generally has served us well over the years. But several areas are unclear and continue to present challenges.

Fair Value

The current accounting model is a mixed-attribute, transaction-based model. It is often described as based on historical costs; but the attributes are not limited to historical costs—current market values, net realizable values, and present values are used too.

That mixed-attribute model has worked reasonably well over the years. But some believe the mixed-attribute model should be replaced with a fair-value model. Fair value is the price that would be obtained under normal conditions between a willing buyer and a willing seller.

The Public Oversight Board of the SEC Practice Section of the AICPA urged the FASB to study comprehensively the possibility of fair value accounting. The GAO recommended the FASB consider the development of a market value rule for all financial instruments. However, a top-level government working group on financial markets that included former Treasury Secretary Lloyd Benston, Federal Reserve Chairman Alan Greenspan, and SEC Chairman Arthur Levitt, urged the FASB to go slow on market value rules for financial instruments, and the AICPA Special Reporting Committee recommended that the FASB not devote attention to value-based accounting at this time. The Association for Investment Management and Research (AIMR) has authorized a comprehensive study and report of the opinions of the entire AIMR membership on the role of market values in financial reporting.

Most recently, the GAO, in its report, *The Accounting Profession's Major Issues: Progress and Concerns,* stated its concerns about the mixed model and made a pitch for financial instruments at fair value and more forward-looking information about opportunities and risks.

The debate at the FASB has not been about changing to a different model. Rather, the debate has been about changing the mix of the attributes in the current model. The debate has not been whether to use fair values, but

In Brief

At the Crossroads

The accounting model used today is one developed during the Industrial Age. It has served us well over the years, but several areas are unclear and continue to present challenges.

■ The debate at the FASB has not been whether to use fair value, but when to use fair value.

■ Estimates for uncertainties have become increasingly complex and difficult as exemplified by the accounting for postretirement health-care benefits and for obligations for certain closure or removal costs of long-lived assets such as nuclear power plants.

■ The current accounting model will be challenged by more flexible and fluid organizational arrangements, increased investments in intangible or soft assets, more extensive use of financial instruments to manage various risks, and changes in information technology.

Former FASB member Robert Swierenga's observations clearly and thoughtfully present the challenges for the next generation of standard setting. As he states, we are indeed at the crossroads in financial reporting.

when to use fair values. The debate has focused on four questions.

Should Fair Value Be Used to Initially Measure Certain Assets? That debate has taken place in the context of contributions (FASB Statement No. 116, *Accounting for Contributions Received and Contributions Made*), mortgage servicing rights (FASB Statement No. 122, *Accounting for Mortgage Servicing Rights*), and stock-based compensation (FASB Statement No. 123, *Accounting for Stock-Based Compensation*). Contributions and stock-based compensation are required to be recognized at fair value, but mortgage servicing rights are required to be recognized at carryover basis.

Should Fair Value Be Used to Remeasure Certain Assets if Recorded Amounts Are Not Likely to Be Recovered? That debate has taken place in the context of loan impairment (FASB Statement No. 114, *Accounting by Creditors for Impairment of a Loan*) and asset impairment (FASB Statement No. 121, *Accounting for the Impairment of Long-Lived Assets and for Long-Lived Assets to Be Disposed of*). An assumption inherent in an enterprise's statement of financial position prepared in accordance with GAAP is that recorded amounts for assets will be recovered. If that condition does not hold, recorded amounts generally are adjusted. But, should those amounts be adjusted to fair value? Impaired loans may be measured at fair value, but impaired long-lived assets are required to be measured at fair value.

Should Fair Value Be Used to Account for Certain Assets that Are Readily Marketable? That debate has taken place in the context of marketable debt securities (FASB Statements No. 115, *Accounting for Certain Investments in Debt and Equity Securities,* and No. 124, *Accounting for Certain Investments Held by Not-for-Profit Organizations*). During an extended period of reduced interest rates, financial institutions reported significant amounts of realized gains while concurrently having underwater investment portfolios. That behavior was described as gains trading, cherry picking, or snacking. Statement No. 115 retains amortized cost for some held-to-maturity debt securities, but Statement No. 124 requires that not-for-profit organizations account for all debt securities at fair value.

Should Fair Value Be Used to Account for Certain Assets When Underlying Rights Are Changed or Unbundled? Loans or receivables can be pooled or packaged into homogeneous portfolios and transferred to a trust or special-purpose entity that then issues debt or equity securities. Through the securitization process, receivables are changed or unbundled into new rights and obligations. Should those rights and obligations be recorded at fair value? FASB Statement No. 125, *Accounting for Transfers and Servicing of Financial Assets and Extinguishments of Liabilities,* requires that

The Stock Illustration Source

some of those rights and obligations be recorded at fair value and that some be recorded at carryover basis.

Uncertainties

Another unclear area under the traditional model is how to deal with uncertainties. Uncertainties about valuations are largely avoided by relying on amounts established in bargained exchange transactions. Yet, the results of transactions must be classified, and assets and liabilities represent future benefits or sacrifices. Some wish to minimize uncertainty by expensing all costs when incurred, unless there is clear evidence of future benefit, by requiring a rigorous association of costs and revenues, or by minimizing the use of estimates and allocations by sticking as close to cash accounting as possible.

Accounting tends to be viewed as objective and precise and as reflecting measures of past transactions and events. Yet, those measures are based on assumptions or estimates about future events. All balance-sheet accounts reflect estimates and assumptions.

Estimates are becoming more prevalent because contractual relationships are becoming more prevalent. Accounting for contracts is easy if they are simple, discrete, and of short duration; if they reflect limited relations between the parties; if precise measures exist for objects of exchange; if no future cooperation is anticipated, and if no sharing relations exist.

Accounting for contracts is difficult if contractual relationships are complex and of long duration, if they reflect close relations between the parties, if some objects of exchange cannot be measured currently, if some future cooperation is anticipated, if sharing relations exist, if some troubles are anticipated, and if interactions are assumed.

Complex contractual relationships exist for parent and subsidiary affiliations, financial instruments, contributions, postretirement benefit arrangements, compensation plans, insurance arrangements, warranty and service arrangements, regulated enterprises, software contracts, and so forth.

Accounting for objects of exchange that cannot be measured currently makes extraordinary demands on accountants as measurers. Consider postretirement health-care benefits—arrangements that may cover up to 80 years. Those benefits are in kind and indexed rather than fixed, the contracts are not as well defined as pension contracts are, and contracts are changing as arrangements evolve.

Realization of software assets has become increasingly uncertain because of ever increasing volatility in the software marketplace, compressed product cycles, increased competition, and diverging technology platforms.

But, also consider reclamation costs that can cover up to 90 years, decommissioning costs, and the costs of significant extended warranties. All of those costs rely heavily on estimates of uncertain future events to make initial and subsequent measurements. Accountants are increasingly making interim measures of unfolding events. Estimates are difficult; changes in estimates are prevalent.

Consider the February 1996 FASB Exposure Draft—*Accounting for Certain Liabilities for Closure or Removal Costs of Long-Lived Assets.* Measuring those liabilities for long-lived assets such as nuclear power plants requires estimates of uncertain future events. The amounts and timing of expected future payments for closure or removal activities have to be projected over periods ranging from 40 to 60 years. The payments have to be discounted back to their present value at an assumed interest or discount rate to reflect the time value of money, and the discounted amounts have to be allocated between current and future accounting periods. Between now and then, laws and technologies may change. Actual payments may differ dramatically from expected amounts.

The expanded use of estimates in financial reporting is being driven by the increased reliance on contractual relationships and by the increased uncertainty associated with judgments, assumptions, and estimates.

A New World

The financial accounting model we bring to the new era was shaped by the existing corporate arrangements for large, complex, and more or less permanent business enterprises that invested heavily in tangible assets. That model will be challenged by more flexible and fluid organizational arrangements, increased investments in intangible or "soft" assets, more extensive use of financial instruments to manage various risks, and changes in information technology.

Alliances and Partnerships. There is an increased use of alliances and partnerships between telecommunications, entertainment, and information services companies; between pharmaceutical companies; between software companies; and between technology companies. The term "merger lite" has been used to describe arrangements in which talent and resources are combined, but each partner retains the right to link with others and retains its financial and other resources.

Where some alliances and partnerships reflect well-defined legal boundaries that are supported by contractual agreements, others reflect organizational arrangements that transcend legal boundaries by using the talent, resources, or governance structure of more than one entity. A "virtual entity" is formed to emphasize functional considerations. Highly specific assets are committed to the new arrangements, and those assets are integrated to develop and deliver products and services to the market, but the ownership of those assets is retained by the partner entities.

Alliances and partnerships essentially decouple decision rights from access to talent, resources, and sharing relations. Generally, the equity method is used to account for investments in alliances and partnerships, but those investments may represent only one of the many features of the arrangements.

Other companies are spinning off single-product or single-function companies. A technology company (Thermo Electron) that testified at the public hearing about the October 1995 FASB Exposure Draft, *Consolidated Financial Statements: Policy and Procedures,* has multiple public subsidiaries, each with joint ventures, licensing arrangements, and other links that form and dissolve in just months or even weeks. The company spins out certain of its businesses into separate subsidiaries that then sell a minority interest to outside investors. As a result of those sales and similar transactions, the company records gains in income that represent the company's increased net investment in its subsidiaries. Those gains have represented a substantial portion of the net income reported by the company in recent years. That company has brought the decoupling of decision rights and residual claims and the reporting of those gains to a new art form. Other companies are following the example of Thermo Electron.

Reported earnings can continue to be transaction-based and cost-based, and gains and losses from price and other changes can be recognized as a component of comprehensive income.

Intangible or "Soft" Assets. Attention is shifting away from tangible assets to intangible assets. Companies that are building soft assets are now among the fastest growing segments of our economy. Service companies are investing significant amounts in employee and other training, technology companies are making significant investments in intellectual capital and research and development, and retailers and others are investing in internally-developed brands, customer loyalty, and satisfaction levels.

The SEC held a symposium on intangible assets in April 1996. The objective of the symposium was to identify specific financial reporting problems and to explore potential improvements to the financial reporting model.

The accounting issues about intangible assets are not new. In the late 1960s and early 1970s, there was a great deal of interest in recognizing investments in research and development and in human resources. A subfield called human resource accounting emerged and flourished. However, a watershed event was the issuance of FASB Statement No. 2, *Accounting for Research and Development Costs,* in 1974. That statement required that all research and development costs as defined be charged to expense when incurred.

In issuing Statement No. 2, the Board expressed concerns about the high degree of uncertainty about future benefits of individual research and development projects at the time the costs are incurred and the lack of a direct causal relationship between expenditures and benefits. The Board concluded that although future benefits from a particular research and development project could be foreseen, they generally could not be measured with a reasonable degree of certainty and therefore failed to satisfy the suggested measurability test for accounting recognition as an asset.

In March 1996, the FASB received a letter from the Software Publishers Association that requested that the Board reconsider FASB Statement No. 86, *Accounting for the Costs of Computer Software to Be Sold, Leased, or Otherwise Marketed.* The letter noted that where Statement No. 86 was based on an inventory model approach, sales of software have become more analogous to services or subscriptions than to inventoried goods.

The letter observed that the product cycle has shortened from several years in the mid-1980s to 18-24 months in the mid-1990s to less than 12 months today. Software development is increasingly funded by periodic maintenance fees, database software often is updated on a daily basis, and some online services charge on a number-of-images-used basis. Software companies find it increasingly difficult to meet the "technological feasibility" criteria of Statement No. 86.

The Software Publishers Association believes realization of software assets has become increasingly uncertain because of ever increasing volatility in the software marketplace, compressed product cycles, increased competition, and diverging technology platforms. It further believes that capitalized costs no longer are relevant to most users of financial statements and that the cost and effort to develop the information required by Statement No. 86 do not justify the benefit from recording an asset. Given the high degree of uncertainty in the product development cycle of most software, the association believes that software development costs should be classified as research and development expenses and charged to expense when incurred.

Financial Instruments. In the past 20 to 25 years there has been an increased use of financial instruments. We have experienced a sea change in finance. Fundamental changes in global financial markets have transformed the financial activities of all entities. Increased volatility in foreign exchange and interest rates and other market prices have greatly increased market, credit, and liquidity risks. Efforts to manage those financial risks, competition, and government deregulation in financial markets and services; structural changes in the economies and taxation of different countries; and technological advances in computers and information services have stimulated financial innovation.

The Board's decision to add the project on financial instruments and off-balance-sheet financing to its technical agenda in May 1986 was, in part, a response to that sea change in finance. That project was expected to develop broad standards for resolving accounting issues raised by financial instruments as well as those raised by the inconsistent accounting guidance and practice that had developed for those instruments over the years.

Where the FASB may have been somewhat ahead of the curve in 1986, it has fallen behind in the 1990s. After 10 years of effort, the Board has yet to come to grips with financial instruments. Instead of developing broad standards, the Board has issued a patchwork of inconsistent standards for marketable securities, loan impairment, and other issues. Those standards have been contentious because they have raised questions about the continued reliance on bargained exchanges and amortized cost.

The debate about financial instruments currently is focusing on derivatives. There is limited guidance about how to account for derivatives. The authoritative literature does not specifically cover many derivatives, so accounting for them is based on analogy to existing literature or on what has been done elsewhere in similar circumstances. Often the accounting depends on the intended use of the derivative and what is said to be the economics of the transaction. Derivatives are accounted for differently depending on whether they are intended to be used as a hedging instrument. Some derivatives that receive hedge accounting treatment may actually increase the enterprise's exposure to risk.

FASB Statement No. 119, *Disclosure About Derivative Financial Instruments and Fair Value of Financial Instruments,* improved disclosures of information about the way entities use derivatives. But, improved disclosures are not likely to be sufficient. The value of some derivatives can change many times faster and many times more than that of most traditional assets and liabilities.

The FASB has been at an impasse about how to account for derivatives and hedges. The hedge accounting model currently used for derivatives is the deferral method. That method, which dates back to the early 1900s and was developed for simple hedging arrangements, links changes in the values of the derivative to a balance or transaction with exposure to market risk and defers certain unrealized and realized gains and losses in the interest of "matching." The method is complex and its effects are not readily apparent to users of financial statements. The authoritative literature has limited the use of that method to specific circumstances. A fundamental issue is whether that method should be applied more generally. The FASB Exposure Draft on *Accounting for Derivative and Similar Financial Instruments and for Hedging Activities* was issued in June 1996. While proposing that all derivatives be measured at fair value, it maintains many of the concepts of the historic hedge accounting model.

Some are concerned that smaller entities are no longer preparing and issuing general-purpose financial statements based on generally accepted accounting principles.

Crossroads

The existing mixed-attribute, transaction-based financial reporting model has exhibited incredible staying power over the years. That model made the transition from farm to factory, and survived the challenges of the inflationary 1970s and the financial-institution crisis of the 1980s. It also is important to recognize that many of the challenges are at the margin and are not central to the model.

However, I believe financial reporting faces an important crossroads. A crossroads is defined as a place where two or more roads meet, as a place where different cultures meet, or as a crucial point or place.

Two very different paths are being advocated at this crucial point. One path is to delimit financial reporting. Some believe financial reporting has strayed too far from the reporting model that emerged in the early 1900s. Some believe more reliance should be placed on price aggregates that result from bargained exchanges and on matching revenues and expenses to measure income. Concerns have been expressed about the increased use of fair values, present values, and estimates in financial reporting.

Some are concerned that smaller entities are no longer preparing and issuing general-purpose financial statements based on generally accepted accounting principles. Some also are concerned about the costs of developing those financial statements and the extensive disclosures that are included.

Concerns also have been expressed about the usefulness and cost effectiveness of existing disclosures and about the increasing volume of disclosures in financial statements. Some have called for the elimination of less useful disclosures and for elimination of redundant requirements that result in essentially the same information being repeated in various sections of a financial report.

The other path is to expand financial reporting. Some believe too much reliance continues to be placed on bargained exchanges and on matching revenues and expenses to measure income. Some believe that value added by productive activity, discovery values, and gains and losses from price changes and other changes should be recognized in financial statements.

Some believe financial reports should provide more information about plans, opportunities, risks, and uncertainties; should focus more on the factors that create longer-term value; and should better align information reported externally with the information reported internally.

I don't know which path will be taken. But the outcome of two recent initiatives may provide some indication about the future path of financial reporting.

The first initiative is the February 1996 FASB Invitation to Comment, *Recommendations of the AICPA Special Committee on Financial Reporting and the Association for Investment Management and Research,* that solicits views on the recommendations made in the December 1994 report of the AICPA Special Committee on Financial Reporting. That report recommended the development of a comprehensive model of business reporting that would include financial and nonfinancial data, management's analysis of those data, forward-looking information, information about management and shareholders, and background about the company.

The Invitation to Comment also solicits views on the recommendations expressed in the November 1993 position paper of the AIMR. That report describes financial analysis and discusses globalization of capital markets, accessibility of computing power, and the increase in economic activities that do not "fit" within the historic cost accounting model. That report discusses the qualitative characteristics of financial reporting and recommends improvements for financial reporting issues that the AIMR believes will be significant during the 1990s and beyond.

The second initiative is the June 1996 FASB Exposure Draft on *Reporting Comprehensive Income.* That proposal can be viewed as a relatively insignificant effort to tidy up the reporting of certain items that bypass the income statement and are reported directly in equity. But that view does not adequately reflect the potential of reporting comprehensive income.

Many people have strongly resisted attempts to include gains and losses from price and other changes in reported earnings. Reporting comprehensive income provides a way to recognize those gains and losses outside of earnings. Reported earnings can continue to be transaction-based and cost-based, and gains and losses from price and other changes can be recognized as a component of comprehensive income and reported in statements of income or financial performance. Reporting comprehensive income would—

■ facilitate articulation of financial statements and would make nonowner changes in equity distinct and transparent.

■ be consistent with the United Kingdom's "statement of total recognized gains and losses" that was introduced as a supplement to the "profit and loss account."

■ be consistent with the comprehensive statement of activities that is required by FASB Statement No. 117, *Financial Statements of Not-for-Profit Organizations.*

■ be consistent with a growing literature about accounting-based valuation and comprehensive income.

Discussions on these two initiatives will play an important role in determining the future path of financial reporting. All the items on the FASB's technical agenda will be completed or very near completion in a short period of time. Important decisions will be made in the months ahead.

Robert J. Swieringa, PhD, *a former member of the FASB, is now a professor in the practice of accounting at the Yale School of Management.*

The importance of computer literacy.

Keeping in Step with the Competition

BY ANITA DENNIS

How can CPAs help their companies gain a marketing advantage? One CPA uses his technology expertise to bring his employer into the age of electronic commerce, giving it a distinct edge among retailers in the highly competitive fashion industry. His experience in automating many of his business's most important functions and in decentralizing computer responsibility throughout the organization can serve as a model for other CPAs striving to derive the most value from information technology opportunities.

LISA QUIONES/BLACK STAR

Etienne Aigner CFO Michael Cangemi spearheaded a technology upgrade and the quick response program that has helped the footwear maker get a leg up on the competition.

A PRACTICE NICHE

Michael Cangemi started out in public practice, where he developed a specialty in electronic data processing auditing, the use of computer resources in the audit process. He later used this knowledge overseeing financial auditing and management information systems for a *Fortune* 500 company and then moved to the position of director of EDP auditing with a large accounting firm when the corporation relocated. One of the firm's clients, the Hartstone Group, a British company that was looking to acquire fashion businesses in the United States, called in Cangemi to review the computer systems of an acquisition prospect, the Etienne Aigner Group, during the due diligence process. Because company managers were looking for a computer-literate chief financial officer and executive vice-president, they offered Cangemi the job.

His first challenge at Aigner was to bring the business up to speed technologically. The company, which designs and distributes women's quality footwear and accessories to major department stores, had a mainframe computer and a lot of internal complaints about its computer system. Cangemi knew that some giant retailers, such as Wal-Mart, had computerized their supply chains. "I saw a huge opportunity for a fashion company to get its computer operations in shape and use them to gain a competitive advantage," Cangemi says.

QUICK RESPONSE

To that end, the company sought faster communications with its customers through electronic data interchange (EDI) to allow Aigner and its customers to swap information, such as orders, electronically. In the retail industry, this is part of the quick response process, a relative of just-in-time inventory control that uses EDI and automatic inventory replenishment programs. But introducing the

From *Journal of Accountancy,* July 1997, pp. 89-92. © 1997 by the American Institute of Certified Public Accountants, Inc. Reprinted by permission.

When Cangemi took over his position, he made users—and not management information systems staff—responsible for their own technology.

required systems can be time-consuming and complicated, which in 1993, when Cangemi started at Aigner, made the process seem daunting to all but the largest companies. To expedite the process, Cangemi created a start-up system that allowed the company to receive purchase orders (POs) from various retailers on a PC and then print them out for the customer service department. A more sophisticated version of the system would have transferred all of the information electronically, rather than sending a printout to customer service. But Cangemi knew it would take a great deal of time and money to bring his company up to the state of the art, so he installed this interim step to get it started.

While his first system was a very primitive version of quick response, it made the process much easier for Aigner's retail customers, who had no idea how their orders were handled once received. During his first year on the job, Cangemi's division brought the company's system up to speed by upgrading its internal computer operations and by building the necessary connections in its computer system to allow it to dial into the two major national EDI networks, run by GE and IBM, and to pull down orders from the major department stores that are its customers.

Once Aigner began receiving POs electronically, the company moved on to electronic disbursement of items called advance ship notices. "When a customer buys a pair of shoes," Cangemi explains, "a store such as Macy's checks its inventory level and submits an order to us electronically; we process it in our computer system. When we are ready to ship, we send the store an advance ship notice. Because the store knows the order is coming, it can set up its computer system in its distribution center to read our barcode and move the order across the retailer's distribution center in a day."

The company can receive orders via EDI for as many as 6,000 to 10,000 pairs on a big selling day; individual orders can be for as few as one pair of shoes or as many as 2,500. Fast turnaround and movement through the store's channels mean lower inventory costs for the retailer, which makes Aigner an attractive company to deal with. In an ideal situation, the system should allow the retailer to send Aigner an electronic PO on day one, perhaps a Monday after a heavy shopping weekend; Aigner can ship its product to the retailer the next day; and the product can be back on the selling floor before the next weekend.

Cangemi also took steps to ensure that his staff keeps informed, placing them on voluntary interindustry communications standards committees that determine how systems work across the entire retail industry. "We wanted to be sure we built our systems to the right standards," so the staff had to understand industrywide standards. Such cooperation to ensure consistency among those involved in the process is crucial, Cangemi explains. "You don't want Federated Department Stores' Macy's stores to design one electronic PO and the May Co.'s Lord & Taylor stores to design another, because then you spend a lot of money trying to read each one's documents."

Cangemi helped introduce quick response into a large part of the company's business. In 1996, it was used in 24% of total footwear sales and in 19% of handbag sales. It is more efficient than the old method, Cangemi says.

Company Profile

Name: Etienne Aigner Group.

Locations: New York City; Edison and Sayreville, New Jersey; Los Angeles.

Date founded: 1950.

Sales: Over $220 million.

Number of employees: Approximately 900.

Form of ownership: Parent company, Hartstone Group PLC, is publicly traded in the United Kingdom.

What we produce: Finely crafted women's footwear, handbags and accessories.

Our main customer: All major department stores plus company outlet and retail stores.

EXECUTIVE SUMMARY

■ ONE CPA's EXPERIENCE IN AUTOMATING many of his business's most important functions and in decentralizing computer responsibility throughout the organization can serve as a model for other CPAs striving to derive the most value from information technology opportunities.

■ THE COMPANY SOUGHT FASTER and more efficient communications with its customers through electronic data interchange. By taking small steps toward sophisticated operations, the company was able to achieve its goals and impress customers.

■ ANOTHER STEP WAS TO DECENTRALIZE responsibility for technology across the organization. In addition, the company replaced its mainframe with PCs and upgraded its software, all the while staying within its technology budget.

ANITA DENNIS is a *Journal* contributing editor.

The company's experience demonstrates that widespread computer capabilities, plus the right software, can vastly improve operations without costing a great deal.

"Previously, you would send out a shotgun of product periodically. You would pick shoes from sizes 5 through 12 and guess at how many of each. The selling pattern would never match exactly, so the retailer would hold on to a huge chunk of inventory and sell it until the end of the season, when the store would discount it or try to return what was left to us. With quick response, there are few returns because the store receives orders based on what it sells." An unusual selling pattern at any one store then can be reflected in inventory models.

The company also is now sending invoices electronically and hopes to receive payment through electronic funds transfer within the next couple of years. Cangemi also would like to refine the system to get a better sense electronically of what stores have actually sold, not simply what they have ordered.

The customers are pleased with the company's efforts. "The retailers compliment us on how well quick response is doing," Cangemi says. The program puts them ahead of the competition in the handbag business, he says, because so few others have anything like it. In its footwear line, where quick response is more common, it keeps the company in step with its competitors.

How else can the company make its products easier to purchase? "In retail, the future is direct sales to consumer," Cangemi says. "The world of retail will be broken down into recurring necessity purchases and spontaneous or not as regular purchases. In either case, stores will be able to reduce inventory."

To take advantage of direct sales, the company is planning to start a store on the Internet and distributing a printed catalog so its customers don't have to go to stores to buy their products. Although women's fashions don't seem like automatic recurring purchase items, Cangemi sees some opportunities. For example, one woman professional he knows has a favorite pair of Aigner pumps that she replaces about every three months. "Once you like a shoe, you'll buy it again," he predicts. Such customers can use the Internet to set up regular orders.

LESSONS LEARNED IN AUDITING

In addition to changing its communications with customers, the company also has altered internal attitudes about technology. When Cangemi took over his position, he made users—and not management information systems staff—responsible for their own technology, based on an insight he gained from his EDP auditing experience. Cangemi believes that the people who use technology should have a solid understanding of it.

"EDP auditing grew up as a separate function because many people were uncomfortable dealing with computers," he observes. But Cangemi thinks separation of expertise is a mistake. "If the auditors delegated the work to an EDP audit team, the team didn't understand the audit job they were trying to do. They understood only the technology, so there was missed potential" for a better understanding of all aspects of the engagement, he says. "You can't make the needed refinements if you're just farming out the work." The same problems occurred in industry. "Businesses also created MIS departments because staff in other areas didn't want to deal with computers, when in fact in the retail business you have a computerized cash register. Technology shouldn't belong to MIS; it should belong to the retail people."

Cangemi spearheaded an effort to rid the company of its mainframe, brought in PCs for all personnel and then turned to each department to take the next steps. "If the design department wants computer-aided design, design department staff members are going to lead the project. They are going to select the system rather than have the MIS people tell them what to do." The company offers whatever assistance users need to understand their options, including computer training and the support of the MIS department, which actually has grown in the wake of decentralization. Although different departments can make their own software choices, systems that are used corporatewide, such as general ledger, must be centralized.

Shifting responsibility from MIS to users wasn't easy, he reports. Cangemi faced a battle to get his philosophy accepted. However, once decentralization was implemented, attitudes changed. "People really understand and support it. Now they propose projects and their implementation plans, and the MIS department reviews them and helps in planning."

To implement this kind of change, Cangemi must keep himself informed about new technology. Conferences and user groups help him to understand software packages, he says, while his position as editor of the *IS Audit & Control Journal,* published by the Information Systems Audit & Control Association, alerts him to new developments in the field.

For Further Reading:

EDI Control, Management and Audit Issues, published by the American Institute of CPAs information technology membership section.

Managing the Audit Function: Corporate Audit Department Procedures Guide, 2nd ed., by Michael P. Cangemi, published by Wiley & Sons.

Quick Response, published by the American Institute of CPAs information technology membership section.

THE BOTTOM LINE

How much has this computer revolution cost the company? Cangemi says it has resulted in significant savings. When he was hired, the company was considering spending $1 million on an IBM ES9000 system to speed its operations. Cangemi insisted it was better software, not more expensive hardware, that would solve the problem. "The systems were antiquated and spending $1 million on a faster computer wouldn't have fixed them." He scrapped the mainframe in favor of an RS6000 Unix box with an open systems environment for a total cost of $150,000. The move also helped lower personnel costs when three operators running the mainframe around the clock were replaced by one part-time operator. "We spent our money replacing software," he says, such as the new Lawson Financial Systems software bought for $100,000 and the specialized footwear industry package used in distribution. The company also installed Novell network software and Windows, created the quick response program and gave laptops to all the sales people in the field. "All of that fit into the old budget," he says, "and we upgraded a great deal."

DECENTRALIZING EXPERTISE

The company's experience demonstrates that widespread computer capabilities, plus the right software, can vastly improve a business's operations without costing a great deal of money. It shows, too, that the first step toward a sophisticated system can be a small one. In order to make a viable transition, management must be committed and knowledgeable, however. If senior management is not in charge of the information system, Cangemi says, companies often hire someone to run an area in which all staff should be knowledgeable. He suggests that when top executives are replaced, companies seek people who "at a minimum can manage technology—and who can drive it, if possible." For companies and their executives, computer literacy is crucial, he believes. "You're very late if you don't have it already. The world of electronic commerce is already here."

Speeding the delivery of high-quality information.

12 Tips to Make Financial Operations More Efficient

BY BARBARA KEVLES

Corporate accounting departments often are limited by tradition. Established procedures perpetuate a pervasive mind-set of "This is the way it's always been done." But the introduction of a new accounting software package or the review of one already installed gives an accounting staff the opportunity to overhaul day-to-day financial operations for a company's benefit. At such junctures, reengineering basics such as financial processing, the general ledger, project accounting and treasury management may shave labor costs, speed monthly closings, improve cash management and help a company become more profitable.

As Jerry F. White, director of the Caruth Institute of Owner-Managed Business at Southern Methodist University's Cox School of Business in Dallas, points out, "Efficient financial reporting is essential to making management decisions on a timely basis, before a problem compounds. The faster you have high-quality information, the quicker management will be able to take corrective action."

According to Lisa Robinson Waugaman, SAP technical project director at Quaker State Corp. in Las Colinas, Texas, and formerly a senior manager of process transformation at Ernst & Young in Dallas, the best reengineering practices "consolidate routine processing, streamline time-consuming tasks of little advantage or eliminate data duplication by more fully using software capabilities." The 12 ideas presented in this article can work for *Fortune* 500 companies as well as small to midsize businesses using standard software packages. While these tips can be applied to ongoing financial programs, when a company introduces new software, Waugaman advises it's better to revise essential financial procedures before going online.

ACCOUNTS RECEIVABLE

Make use of lockbox processing. CPAs who work for companies with a high volume of customer payments should consider lockbox processing instead of manually recording customer payments in accounts receivable. Under this arrangement, customers mail payments to a post office box, usually at a local bank. This gives a company obvious tangible benefits. The more quickly a bank deposits payments in a company's account, the sooner the company earns interest. The bank can transmit a computer file of remittance information electronically to be applied automatically to the company's computerized receivables. CPAs can define software options to match incoming payments and unpaid orders by criteria such as dollar amount, invoice number or date—or any combination. If necessary, Waugaman says a company should expand the criteria it uses to match incoming data with outstanding receivables to totally eliminate manual intervention except for unidentified customers or amounts.

Improve credit management. Many companies take orders and ship goods without checking customer credit because sales people get paid for making sales, not for collecting bills. Yet delays in credit checks can cause a company to lose money by increasing its bad debts. In such cases, it's advisable for a company to switch to a software package that allows credit checks to be made during order entry. If a company's current software already permits this, CPAs should encourage greater compliance with this procedure. According to Waugaman, a good

Companies can speed T&E processing by eliminating manual approval by managers in favor of direct electronic submission for payment.

software program still allows the sales force to maintain its order volume but puts a hold on orders from customers with poor credit. The credit manager can then decide whether to release or cancel orders from these customers.

ACCOUNTS PAYABLE

Streamline processing of travel and expense reports. CPAs need to scour the repetitive expenses processed by their companies' accounts payable departments for better time management measures. A good place to start is with employee travel and expense reports (T&Es). They absorb a fair amount of staff overhead expense because of the time required for approval and the details involved in setting up payment entries.

To streamline T&E processing, employees should be asked to submit reports electronically, with precoded charges. "Precoding removes the time-consuming burden of coding," says Waugaman, who points out another electronic advantage. "Addition errors are likely to occur in manual computations, whereas electronic spreadsheets validate the totals."

Waugaman suggests another time-saving measure. Companies can speed T&E report processing by eliminating manual approval by managers in favor of direct electronic submission for payment. This avoids the trap of an expense report languishing in a manager's inbox and an unwarranted delay in the reimbursement process. Employee accountability can be monitored through computer-generated, monthly departmental reports for audit or manager review for exceptions to internal policies. Or the software can be programmed to generate reports on employees who exceed T&E limits.

TIP 4 ***Change the vouchering of purchase order items.*** When companies buy inventory, raw materials or even supplies and services, insufficient purchase order information can waste valuable time of accounts payable staff who must review invoices against purchase orders for verification. Companies can eliminate this problem by asking the employee or department making the purchase to provide key financial information such as charge code, payment terms (rapidity of payment), payment method (wire or check) and the vendor's remittance address. Waugaman suggests companies also ask the purchasing employee or department for the tax code that shows how the product will be used because it may have an impact on state and local taxes. For example, labor to maintain or repair a piece of machinery may require special tax handling. These procedures prevent time lost in verifying information or in having to return invoices to the originating department.

Discrepancies between amounts ordered and a shipment's actual invoice also can disrupt accounts payable processing. According to Waugaman, "without knowing whether the purchasers will accept shortages or surpluses, accounts payable personnel have to set these transactions aside and await further directions." To avoid this frustration, companies can set up a tolerance in the software program for deviations either by vendor or by product. Waugaman says it could be zero tolerance, necessitating a perfect match, or 10% tolerance of under or over the amount of the shipment.

In lieu of this three-way match (purchase order=goods received=invoice received), a company also has the option of a two-way match (purchase order=goods received).

EXECUTIVE SUMMARY

■ CORPORATE ACCOUNTING departments must overcome the reluctance on the part of others within their companies to make changes to established procedures. Such changes—often accompanying the installation of new accounting software—can help cut labor costs, speed monthly closings and help companies become more profitable.

■ IMPROVEMENTS CAN BE MADE IN several areas, including accounts receivable, where companies can consider making use of lockbox processing to get deposits into their bank accounts faster. Companies also can use software programs to make credit checks before goods are shipped, minimizing losses from bad debt.

■ IN THE AREA OF ACCOUNTS PAYABLE, companies can streamline travel and expense report processing, change the vouchering of purchase order items, implement the use of a corporate purchase card for small purchases and consider outsourcing freight payment processing.

■ GENERAL LEDGER IMPROVEMENTS can be made by capturing tax information when source documents are processed, adopting a standard chart of accounts for the entire company and reducing the monthly closing time by fully using software options.

■ CHANGES ALSO CAN BE MADE IN PROJECT accounting, treasury management and fixed assets to set up separate coding for specific projects, accelerate bank reconciliations and integrate fixed assets with the general ledger.

BARBARA KEVLES is a Texas-based business writer. A past contributing editor to *Working Woman* and *Global Custodian,* her articles have appeared in the *Journal of Accountancy, New York*, the *Dallas Business Journal,* the *Houston Business Journal,* the *Denver Business Journal* and the *Dallas Morning News.*

Companies can relieve accounts payable of reconciling shipments and shipping documents by outsourcing these payments to a third party.

With select major vendors, accounts payable staff can do away with invoices altogether by instituting payment terms based on the goods received. "It requires a strong vendor relationship," cautions Waugaman, "and a foolproof method for accurately capturing the amount of goods shipped." Such arrangements work well with vendors with whom a company has a high volume of transactions.

Use a corporate purchase card for small purchases and employee travel. Rather than having accounts payable deal with voluminous items under $100, a company should distribute a purchase card to an employee in each department. In that way, the accounting staff can consolidate multiple bills for small-ticket items into one check and avoid numerous checks requiring envelope stuffing, postage and maintaining multiple vendors in the software system.

Although many companies micromanage by allocating every item on a corporate card bill to a specific charge code, the cost of this activity should be weighed against the value the company receives. Waugaman has seen instances when every item on a company Visa bill is charged to a different code because management worries about capturing every cost to the penny. But she says it's not worth the time and labor for someone to check the validity of these items, assign charge codes to them and perform hundreds of entries. Typically, one charge code per card simplifies the accounting.

Companies also can cut the volume of bills received by accounts payable by issuing company cards to individual employees who travel regularly on company business. If companies do not follow this approach, accounts payable may have to dedicate one or two people to reconciling such things as airline tickets charged to the company with employees' expense accounts. Using company charge cards in employees' names abolishes these jobs by shifting the reconciliation and payment burden to employees, who have the incentive to submit expense reports quickly to make their credit card payment deadlines. Waugaman stresses that special issues, such as discounted airfares requiring early purchase months before T&E submissions, should be worked out so employees are not penalized.

Outsource processing of freight payments. Normally, an accounts payable clerk handles multiple pieces of paper to reconcile shipments and shipping documents and then manually keys in each freight bill. Companies can relieve accounts payable of this process by farming out these time-sensitive payments to a third party. For a fee, a vendor will perform the reconciliation, audit bills for accurate charges, do the remittances and provide companies with periodic information feeds for automatic entry into financial records. Outsourcing won't be cost-effective unless a company's shipping volume justifies it.

GENERAL LEDGER

Capture tax information when source documents are processed. Many companies record a purchase—for internal repairs or maintenance, for example—and review it later to determine the appropriate tax treatment. "Don't handle a transaction twice," advises Waugaman. "Record it once for both management and tax reporting purposes." She says the latest software is designed to handle tax needs with greater efficiency. If a company's package lacks this feature, another piece of software can be purchased and "bolted" onto the existing system.

Adopt a standard chart of accounts. Every division, business unit and subsidiary of a company should use the same list of accounts (receivables, payables, cash) that makes up the company's general ledger. In addition, corporate accounting should issue standard guidelines by which to code transactions. Standardized accounts and account numbers throughout the company ensure more accurate reporting in the consolidation process.

Reduce the monthly closing time. Publishing monthly financial statements in the middle of the succeeding month, as is the norm for many companies, prevents top management from reacting on a timely basis to changes in the business world. Revamping the financial system with a fully integrated software package can drastically shorten this lag. Such programs automatically feed subsystems such as accounts payable into the general ledger, thereby eliminating the time and labor needed to manually total subledgers, reconcile any imbalances with the general ledger and key entries into the ledger. This not only may reduce processing time for companies that do monthly closings but also may produce tremendous cost savings.

PROJECT ACCOUNTING

Set up separate coding for project management. To capture the costs of an ongoing capital expense item such as building an addition to a company facility, CPAs should set up separate coding for the project under accounts payable so those costs are integrated into the general ledger. This eliminates handling a transaction twice, says Waugaman, first for payment purposes and then for review by the project manager, who compares the ongoing project costs with budgeted costs. If a company's current software package lacks this feature, a standalone package may be purchased that both feeds into accounts payable and is accessible for project management.

TREASURY MANAGEMENT

Accelerate bank reconciliations. Depending on the volume of checks a company writes, CPAs may wish to download information on checks cleared from the bank daily rather than monthly. Such daily routines—more manageable than the usual volume at month's end—also can speed monthly closings. With the help of integrated software packages or special interface software written by a programmer, a company's financial software can read bank records daily, automatically match cleared outstanding checks and update the accounts payable check file.

FIXED ASSETS

Integrate fixed assets with general ledger. This system typically is overlooked during a review to modernize financial operations because it has little impact on a company's day-to-day operations. Fixed assets demand corporate accounts that track information for tax purposes, the financial statements and depreciation. Typically, when capital expenditure projects are finished, they are capitalized as fixed assets that immediately begin to generate depreciation expense. Says Waugaman, "If a software package integrates those data subsystems with accounts payable and the general ledger, then fixed asset subsystem updates automatically appear in the general ledger. This ensures that finished capital projects become fixed assets in a timely manner and won't get lost." Such integration also eliminates one more task from the monthly closings list.

STREAMLINE AND ENERGIZE

CPAs can use a multitude of ideas to streamline and energize the financial operations of the typical corporate accounting department. Although such modifications can improve financial reporting and realize savings in staff costs, a lot of companies say they are too busy or don't have the time to change. To overcome such resistance, Waugaman suggests, "Pick one or two items that can make the biggest difference in operations and make them priorities." Other ideas can be implemented later, when attitudes change. The alternative is to support the status quo, have disgruntled employees and publish outdated financial statements.

Fraud Prevention and the Managem

RICHARD A. TURPEN, CPA, AND FRANK M. MESSINA, CPA

We've implemented JIT, TQM, ABM, BPR, and SCM, but what are we doing about F-R-A-U-D?

Over the last decade management accountants have had to be quick learners, embracing a bewildering array of new concepts, all designed to transform their organizations into world-class competitors. While success stories of the latest management innovations abound, news concerning an old problem is not encouraging. Fraud is still a major threat to businesses, and statistics show that it is getting worse.

A recent KPMG Peat Marwick survey of America's largest companies found both a greater incidence of fraud overall and a higher rate of occurrence within companies as compared to the previous year.[1] We will look at a similar survey of smaller organizations, a group that represents the more typical American business. Patterned after the KPMG study, our project tried to identify areas where management accountants might be most effective in preventing and detecting fraud, as well as areas where their companies are the most vulnerable.

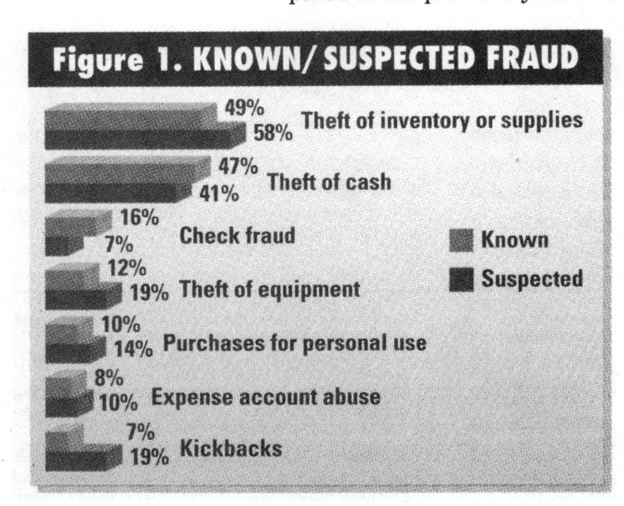

Given the numerous management initiatives of recent years, what we found was surprising. Although sophisticated frauds still occur, employee theft of cash and other assets continues to be the most reported type of fraud plaguing U.S. businesses.

WHO THE COMPANIES ARE

With support from the Cooperative Management Division of the USDA's Rural Business and Cooperative Development Service (RBCDS), KPMG Peat Marwick, and the National Society of Accountants for Cooperatives, we mailed a survey to each of the more than 4,000 U.S. agribusiness cooperatives that RBCDS tracks annually.[2] Their database includes a wide range of industries with different operating volumes. On the whole, however, most cooperatives are relatively small and thus more typical of many American businesses.

There were many reasons for choosing cooperatives. First, they represent a major sector of the American economy. More than 47,000 co-ops operate in the United States, in industries that span agriculture, food, retail, hardware, utilities, and healthcare.[3] These companies generate over $100 billion annually. Agricultural co-ops alone account for $59 billion in value and hold 13 places on the list of the Fortune 500.[4] In fact, this prominence is expected to grow. *The Wall Street Journal* reports that cooperatives are poised to dominate the small business sector in the next decade as this form of organization spreads to new fields.[5]

Second, cooperatives were chosen because they are typical of many businesses both in form and function. They are corporations, organized by the stockholders to provide economic benefits to their members. The members also enjoy a tax benefit in that cooperative earnings derived from member business are taxed once (like partnerships and S-corporations), unlike income from general business C-corporations. As for operations, co-ops purchase supplies, provide services, and engage in marketing, processing, dis-

In the rush to prepare for the new world economy, some companies are forgetting traditional fraud prevention techniques.

ent Accountant

tribution, and even research and development. About a quarter (24%) of the co-ops in our sample perform multiple functions and nearly half (46%) operate in more than one industry.

Finally, cooperatives are generally small to midsize and often have less investment in sophisticated security and control systems. Almost all the co-ops in our sample (95%) reported total annual sales/revenues of $50 million or less. Like most small businesses, they may be at greater risk of fraud and abuse, making them a useful population for study.

THE FRAUDS DISCOVERED

Of the 563 cooperatives that participated in our survey, nearly half (47%) reported known or suspected occurrences of fraud. The highlights of their survey disclosures are summarized in Figure 1.

Theft of current assets tops the list of the most common types of fraud, with nearly half of the victims reporting known thefts of inventory/supplies (49%) or cash (47%). An even greater percentage (58%) of the cooperatives suspected further instances of stolen inventories. Other areas of known or suspected vulnerability include check fraud (16% and 7%), equipment theft (12% and 19%), and kickbacks (7% and 19%).

Although sometimes inappropriately regarded as less serious offenses, improper purchases made for personal use (10% and 14%) and expense account abuse (8% and 10%) also were frequent problems for the cooperatives. As they did for inventory theft, more co-ops reported suspected than known incidences, indicating the difficulty employers often have in uncovering these types of fraud.

Other offenses also reported by the respondents include accounts receivable manipulation, false invoices or phantom vendors, credit card

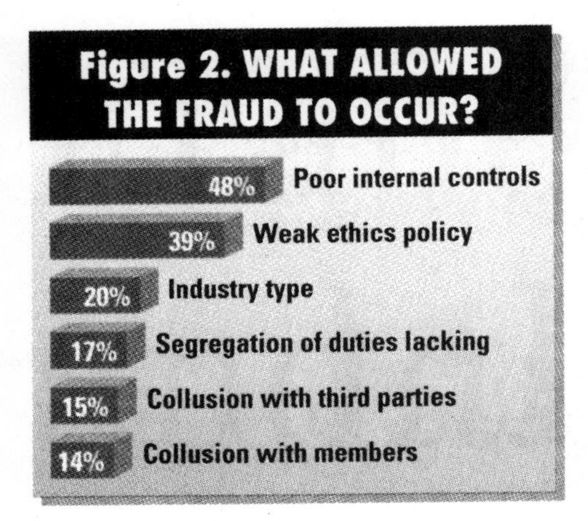

fraud, bid rigging or price cutting, conflicts of interest, payroll fraud, falsification of financial statements, diversion of sales, and product substitution. None of the reporting rates for these frauds exceeded 5%.

Loss estimates provided by the cooperatives for the most common of these frauds—current asset thefts—range from less than $100 to $350,000—substantial numbers when you consider that the largest loss disclosed by a single co-op for all fraud types combined totaled approximately $600,000. More telling perhaps are the overall loss figures represented as percentages of income. The data indicate that for 30% of the co-ops, total known fraud losses amounted to 5% or more of net earnings.

Figure 3. WHAT "RED FLAGS" WERE PRESENT?

54% Unexplained losses
22% Poor internal controls
20% Decline in employee morale
20% Change in employee lifestyle
14% Unusual expenditures
10% Internal audit findings ignored

The survey presents a profile of the perpetrators. The majority were employed as staff personnel in marketing, sales, or customer service and had been working for the co-op for three to five years. Most of the fraud took place over a period of one year or less.

Figures 2-4 summarize the cooperatives' disclosures as to what allowed these frauds to occur and how they were discovered. Not surprisingly, co-ops most often blamed poor internal control (48%, Figure 2). A sizable number (39%), however, indicated a weak ethics policy or code of conduct as having contributed to the fraud. These responses provide further evidence that developing a corporate culture that stresses honesty and scrupulous behavior is not only the right thing to do, but also it produces real savings as well.

Figure 4. HOW WAS THE FRAUD DETECTED?

40% Internal controls
35% Specific investigation
34% Employee tip
29% Internal audit procedures
18% By accident
9% Member tip

Some industries are at greater risk for fraud, the third most often mentioned factor (20%) contributing to theft. Sound control systems and strong ethics policies become all the more important in such an environment. An important control is adequate segregation of duties. Lack of attention to this feature was the fourth most cited problem in the survey (17%), followed closely by collusion (14% and 15%). As professional auditing standards state, collusion is always a possibility, even in the most strictly controlled environment. Where fraud prevention is difficult, fraud detection takes on greater importance.

In the majority of cases reported in our survey, certain "red flags" appeared prior to the fraud discovery, most often in the form of unexplained losses (54%, Figure 3). Poor internal control also was listed by about a quarter of the co-ops (22%), indicating at least an awareness of their susceptibility to fraud even if they chose to do nothing about it. This failure to act serves as a warning to companies because it suggests that many of the frauds reported here might have been prevented. Finally, a third major omen, one often ignored, was a marked behavioral difference in the employee—either a decline in morale (20%) or a change in lifestyle or behavior (20%). Severe depression, discontent, and living beyond one's means can signal fraudulent activity. Managers who ignore such signs clearly put their companies at risk.

Many of the frauds were uncovered through specific investigations, initiated in response to these early warnings (35%, Figure 4). Other good news from the survey is that for the majority of co-ops (40%), fraud most often was revealed through internal controls. Internal audit procedures also frequently were cited as an important means of detection (29%). On the other hand, a large number of discoveries were the result of information coming to management's attention outside formal channels, either through employee (34%) or member (9%) tips, or merely by accident (18%).

HOW THEY RESPONDED

Management's response to a known or suspected fraud can serve as an effective deterrent. In this respect, our survey results are not encouraging. Although the dismissal of the employee involved (44%, Figure 5), a formal investigation (21%), or the involvement of law enforcement agencies (18%) were frequent outcomes, a sizable number of cooperatives chose to keep quiet about the matter (27%) or merely to allow the employee to resign (16%). As for other steps taken (21%), the one most often mentioned was no action at all, either due to a lack of proof or the employee's departure prior to the detection of the fraud. Relatively few co-ops chose to use their discovery as an opportunity to set an example (8%, not shown). The reasons for not bringing fraud to light are varied. Some companies simply may want to avoid adverse publicity. Others may fear copycat reoccurrences of the fraud. Ironically, unless companies show a willingness to pursue wrongdoers aggressively, they may create the impression of weakness, if not outright tolerance for misconduct. Thus, they may foster the very activity they're seeking to prevent.

Some of the findings do give reason for optimism. A number of the cooperatives indicate that they now have taken or plan to take steps designed to prevent future frauds. Not surprisingly, reviewing and improving internal controls (93%, Figure 6) and segregating critical duties and functions (76%) were the measures most commonly cited, followed by performing more extensive background checks of employees (72%) and bonding those who have access to negotiable assets (64%). Focusing management's attention on fraud (64%) and developing or revising ethics policies or codes of conduct (63%) also frequently were mentioned. The latter result is significant because data from the U.S. Sentencing Commission shows that an effective ethics program can prevent an organization from being prosecuted, or it can help reduce fines in federal cases involving employee wrongdoing.[6]

THE LESSONS THEY OFFER

For management accountants concerned about the potential for fraud in their own organizations, the experiences of our survey participants provide several important lessons. The traditional types of fraud are still the most common, and they require continual management attention to basics. Companies always are vulnerable to theft of cash or other assets. Adequate background checks of employees are essential, as is an ongoing program for monitoring and evaluating internal control. Above all, red flags should never be ignored. Management must respond immediately to any warning sign.

Perhaps the most significant finding in our survey comes from those cooperatives that did *not* report fraud. The following comment was all too typical: "We are a small town business and employees are from our local area. There is no reason to suspect fraud, because our employees are trustworthy and competent." Unfortunately, many companies learn too late that certain employees are able to commit fraud chiefly because management does consider them "trustworthy."

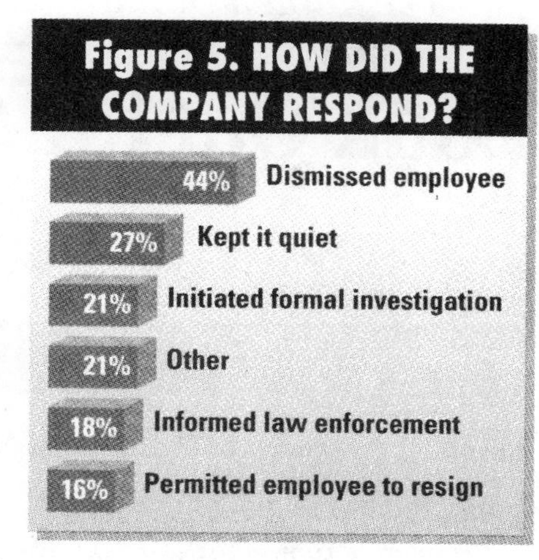

Management accountants continue to face new challenges and a business environment characterized by accelerating change. In the drive to ready their organizations for the next century, they must make sure that among the management initiatives there is a sound program of fraud prevention.

Figure 6. WHAT PREVENTATIVE ACTIONS HAVE BEEN TAKEN/ ARE PLANNED?

Taken	Planned	Action
77%	16%	Improve existing internal controls
65%	11%	Segregate critical duties
61%	11%	Investigate employees
60%	4%	Bond employees
45%	19%	Train management
44%	19%	Strengthen code of ethics

Richard A. Turpen, CPA, Ph.D., is an associate professor of accounting at the University of Alabama at Birmingham, Birmingham, Ala. He submitted this article through the South Birmingham Chapter, of which he is a member. He can be reached at (205) 934-8820.

Frank M. Messina, CPA, DBA, is an assistant professor of accounting at the University of Alabama at Birmingham, Birmingham, Ala. He is a member of the South Birmingham Chapter and can be reached at (205) 934-8820.

[1] KPMG, *1994 Fraud Survey*, 1994.

[2] In order to encourage participation in the study, it was essential for us to provide the cooperatives with assurances of confidentiality. Therefore, we purposely conducted our survey in a manner that makes identification of the respondents impossible. As a result, we have no way of knowing which specific cooperatives contained in the database returned their questionnaires.

[3] Among the many cooperatives familiar to American consumers are Land O'Lakes, Ocean Spray, Sunkist Growers, and Tree Top, Inc. Other sectors are represented by ACE Hardware Corp., ServiStar Corporation, and CARE, one of the world's largest private relief organizations.

[4] Bruce L. Anderson, Brian M. Henehan, and J. Robert Kelchner, *Putting Cooperation to Work—A Handbook for Rural Businesses, Economic Development Groups and Planning Agencies.* Cornell Cooperative Enterprise Program at Cornell University, Ithaca, N.Y., 1995.

[5] Timothy L. O'Brien, "Franchises Spearhead Renewed Popularity of Co-Ops," *The Wall Street Journal*, November 29, 1993, p. B2.

[6] Larry Ponemon, "'Effective' Ethics Programs," MANAGEMENT ACCOUNTING, December 1995, p. 22.

But I've known him for years. How could it happen?

Look Out for Cletus William

By John E. McEldowney, Thomas L. Barton, and David Ray

The internal control structure, particularly the control environment, is often weak at not-for-profit organizations. A case study of an embezzlement provides some background for CPAs regarding the conditions that often exist that increase the potential for fraud.

Charles Counter scanned the computer screen for the number. He found it in cell H87 of the spreadsheet: $61,238.16. Charles leaned back in his chair, took his glasses off, and rubbed his eyes.

He had known Cletus William for 31 years. Cletus was the man who had welcomed him to the recreation center at First Church when he was just 12-years old. Cletus was always at the church—working in the office, fixing broken kneelers, adjusting chemicals in the recreation center pool. Cletus was the resident handyman and he knew everybody.

Now Cletus William was accused of the unthinkable—stealing $61,238.16 from First Church. Charles could hardly believe it. He had never known Cletus to even utter a mild profanity, much less steal from the church that had been the center of his life.

What had gone wrong, he thought? What had happened to Cletus...? But Charles couldn't help but wonder something else. What kind of system allows this level of theft for ten years without discovery?

Providing accounting and auditing services for not-for-profit entities can create significant problems for the CPA. The environment surrounding this type of entity, the management style normally associated with these enterprises, and the diversity of problems connected with these organizations often make any engagement related to not-for-profits a challenging venture.

An example of a recent fraud that went undetected for a number of years in a religious organization illustrates the unique problems often encountered in providing services to a not-for-profit organization. While the actual case deals with a church fraud, the lessons learned from this type of engagement can be applied to any not-for-profit.

The First Church Internal-Control Structure

Charles Counter, a CPA, was hired by the church after the discovery of a $60,000 theft. Church officials asked Charles to explain how their accounting system allowed something like this to occur. Charles was also asked to suggest improvements to help prevent this type of fraud in the future.

As is the case with many small businesses, Charles found the internal-control structure of First Church was lacking in a number of areas. Those responsible for monitoring record-keeping operations of the church had limited accounting knowledge. Charles concluded a number of fraudulent acts could have easily been detected had the governance board only recognized the improper accounting treatment for certain transactions. For example, Cletus was able to siphon off funds on a number of occasions and record charges to "salary advances." These amounts were never repaid, but instead were written off to expense accounts. A basic knowledge of accounting would have helped identify this type of recording discrepancy.

Another control weakness was related to the entity's attitude and understanding of internal accounting control in general. Not only were the leaders of the church not knowledgeable of basic accounting practices, but they also lacked a sufficient understanding of key controls that should have been in place when dealing with highly liquid assets. Additionally, there appeared to be an apparent lack of concern over weaknesses present in the internal-control structure. After all, it is a church, and everyone there is assumed to be of the highest moral character. This is possibly the worst case scenario for any organization.

Church leaders were inactive and ineffective in their oversight function. For example, on numerous occasions, Cletus, the church administrator, wrote large checks out to cash, and subsequently deposited them into his own account. No one challenged this practice. Additionally, he would generate extra paychecks for himself. He would generate one payroll check and have it signed by an authorized check signer. He would then generate another check and have it signed by a different check signer. Nobody but Cletus ever reconciled the bank statements to spot the duplicate payroll payments.

The lack of involvement of church leaders was most apparent in the area of general expense payments. Cletus wrote checks for basic expenditures that greatly exceeded previous disbursements for those areas. For example, checks were written for over $500 for supposed expenses related to a special occasion breakfast. Comparison with previous years revealed this outlay to normally total about $50.

Additionally, the oversight board placed too much reliance on the expertise of the individual performing the accounting function. In this case, the accounting work was done by one person—Cletus William. Cletus was known as someone who could do just about anything, and, unfortunately, he lived up to that reputation. He was given total control and oversight responsibilities for the accounting system and basic cash expenditures. The only minimal exception to this was the area of payroll. In this case, payroll checks had to be signed by someone other than Cletus.

This presented no great obstacle though, because Cletus was responsible for all data that generated those paychecks. Additionally, no verification of the data was ever performed by various authorized payroll check signers. Cletus was able to generate greatly [inflated] payroll checks. On numerous occasions, these checks were written for five to six hundred dollars more than called for. Additionally, since he was responsible for compiling and signing all payroll tax documents for the church, he was able to manipulate tax records to show a much lower salary. In this way, he was also able to avoid significant income taxes.

Final assessment of the payroll area indicated over $9,000 of income tax withholding taxes were owed to the IRS due to Cletus' manipulations.

The church never thought about separation of duties, the very basic precept of internal control that provides an effective safeguard of highly negotiable assets. The governing body was uninformed, uninvolved, and very trusting of the one person who could best take advantage of the situation. Unfortunately, Cletus did exactly that.

Not-for-Profit Environment and Problems

The previous scenario reflects a number of issues that could relate to any not-for-profit entity. The issues and basic environment under which most not for profits operate are basically the same.

Ineffective Controls. Not-for-profit organizations by their nature often are involved in noble and idealistic activities seeking to improve society and the well being of all. The leaders are often devoted and very conscious of the ir eleemosynary objectives. They take for granted that all involved with the activity are of a similar bent and disposition and think there is no need for controls against employee dishonesty. Unfortunately, that is just not the case. Even when directly confronted by church elders about his thefts, Cletus William maintained he had not stolen anything: the money was owed him for additional work not covered by his employment contract, or was needed to offset a cut in pay the church board had enacted three years earlier.

This scenario could unfold in almost any not-for-profit. Hospice: "None of our people would steal money from those under our care." Drug treatment center: "None of our people would steal money from these poor drug-ravaged souls." Neighborhood recreation center: "None of our people would steal money from these underprivileged kids." Yet people can and do steal from these organizations and often create their own elaborate justifications for their actions.

Leaders of not-for-profit organizations have responsibility to implement practices and policies businesses use to discourage employee fraud and embezzlement. To rely on employees' consciences or sense of moral duty is to invite serious problems. And in many cases the absence of reasonable controls can provide a temptation to the employee with a financial burden or an expensive habit. However, all too often their leaders don't understand this.

Dominant Leadership. Not-for-profit enterprises are often under the leadership of dominant personality types. These personalities can work at odds with what is considered to be a proper internal-control structure. For example, in the medical field, medical doctors are often found in leadership positions. They are used to being in charge in the operating room or clinic and expect to see a carryover of this authority into the business aspects of the not-for-profit's activities. When this happens, because of a lack of understanding, suggestions for improvements and comments related to significant internal control weaknesses can be viewed as unimportant and not receive proper consideration.

Overemphasis on Enterprise Goals. Another related issue often prevalent in not-for-profits is the problem encountered when the goal of the enterprise supersedes all else. When the entity is managed by a dominant personality, this issue becomes even more pronounced. In one medical rehabilitation center, the basic premise that drove the enterprise was to provide as much service to as many individuals as was humanly possible. Unfortunately, as with many not-for-profits that receive state assistance, the funds supplied from year to year can vary greatly. Instead of looking more towards the future and anticipating changes, the unskilled manager may inappropriately cling to an objective that is untenable in the face of diverse swings in funding. Couple this with a management attitude that brooks no interference with goals of the enterprise, and disaster may be not far ahead.

Lack of Accounting Orientation and Education. Because of the focus on the purpose and objectives of the typical not for profit, there is often a significant lack of accounting education and orientation on the part of management. For example, in one enterprise, directors of the institution were extremely competent at diagnosing drug dependency problems and outlining recovery programs for patients. However, they failed to recognize the antiquated and expensive nature of their operations. As long as funding from the state was adequate, operations ran fairly smoothly. Once they experienced a significant downturn in funds however, they had to markedly curtail their treatment program because funds were no longer available. In this case, management lacked the expertise to appropriately budget and plan for the future. Their perspective was so oriented towards the accomplishment of the goals of the enterprise they lost sight of the fact the entity must stay solvent to provide those services.

Additionally, not-for-profits have historically relied heavily on volunteer assistance, and volunteers are often given accounting or management duties for which they have little qualification. Or the organizations have so little money budgeted for a key position, that highly qualified people have no interest in applying.

First Church was paying Cletus William $12,000 a year to be church administrator. At the $12,000 salary, First Church would have been fortunate to hire a first-class bookkeeper, much less a church administrator. This was obviously an unrealistic salary for the level of managerial and financial responsibilities Cletus was assigned to undertake. Something had to give. Either Cletus would perform at a substandard level, or he would be inclined to supplement his salary off-the-books to bring it to something more approximating market level. In Cletus' case, it was the latter.

Failure to Operate Entity in a Business-like Fashion. An ancillary problem normally faced by most not for profits is the failure to operate the entity in a business-like fashion. As previously discussed, the goal of the not-for-profit becomes the end aim for everything done on a daily basis. Projects are initiated, patients are admitted, or campaigns are launched without regard for common business issues. This failure to treat the enterprise as a business is probably the most prevalent and perplexing attribute of a not for profit.

It is in this area the accountant experiences the most frustration. Often, management does not know of the existence of basic system and accounting control concepts, much less recognize the need for their implementation.

CPAs often encounter people who believe not-for-profits cannot be run like businesses and are expected to lose money every year. But the simple fact remains a not-for-profit that consistently loses money can not, in the long run, survive.

It is not unusual for the CPA to hear something like this from not-for-profit personnel (in this case, a mental health counselor): "I've got people out there ready to do harm to themselves and you want me to do paperwork!" A good response would be: "If you don't do the paperwork, you can't collect your fees, and you'll go out of business. What will happen to all the people who depend on you?"

Additionally, a strong, financially healthy not-for-profit will be able to render even better services to its clients. How can not-for-profit employees do their best work when they're worried about being laid off? Financial strength can also help a not-for-profit weather funding cuts from the government or funding organizations such as United Way.

Negative Viewpoints Regarding the Accounting Function. It is not uncommon for accountants within the not-for-profit organization to be relegated primarily to bookkeeping functions. While they may possess the professional skills to be of real service to the entity, they are kept out of the decision-making process. Financial positions lack any real power or influence. The result can be job dissatisfaction and high turnover of the position.

Also, many not-for-profit managers, view accounting and finance departments as a necessary evil. Accountants and auditors are generally regarded as a regulatory or governing board requirement that inhibits the accomplishment of the organization's goals.

If the accounting and finance departments are not viewed as being important, then the policies and procedures implemented by these "bean counters" are not likely to be considered important either. These policies and procedures may not be consistently enforced or enforced at all.

Over Reliance on One Individual. When a not-for-profit organization hires a competent individual in the accounting and finance area and the agency director delegates significant authority to this person, a very different scenario is created. Under these circumstances, this individual establishes, implements, monitors, and enforces the controls within the entity. In many ways, nothing happens without the approval and signature of this person.

Heavy reliance is placed on the knowledge and actions of the one competent person. As a result, CPAs engaged to audit the entity tend to rely heavily on the controls in place in a manner similar to that found in an owner-managed, small business.

The problem with this scenario is obvious. The person is not an owner; therefore the CPA's reliance on owner controls is not only unwarranted but possible misplaced. Reliance on owner controls is based on the notion of an owner with his or her own capital at risk being actively involved in the day-to-day operations of entity. It is reasonable to assume the manager/owner would not try to steal from himself. However, the same would very rarely hold true for the key financial person in a not-for-profit enterprise; they have no vested interest in the firm.

The CPA must understand the role of the board of directors and top management for the potential absence of mitigating controls. The key question is how much reliance should be placed on any one individual, no matter how trusted or competent that person might be.

There are other aspects of the not-for-profit entity that also make the CPA's reliance on "owner controls" unrealistic. Since there is no profit motive, concentration is on the program, and not on financial performance or efficiency. The basic viewpoint in this type of environment is, "If we are getting by financially, there is little need for any attention." It is exactly this lack of attention that allows fraudulent activities to occur.

Volunteer Boards. Not-for-profit organizations are characterized by volunteer boards of directors or trustees. The volunteer nature of their oversight activities can often create a situation where little effort is generated to ensure a properly working internal-control structure exists. In one instance, after catching an executive director of a very large not-for-profit agency misappropriating assets, the manager was simply reprimanded by the board. When questioned why the director was not fired, one board member replied, "You have got to remember we are volunteers. We have our own businesses to run. We don't have time to run this one too."

Role of the CPA as Adviser

When interacting with a not-for-profit organization, the CPA often finds him- or herself in either the role of an accountant providing management services or of auditor. As an auditor, the CPA may generate management letter comments addressing the entity's internal-control structure and other areas where efficiency can be improved. In both these capacities, there are several ways a CPA can enhance his or her role as an adviser to a not-for-profit.

The CPA should seek to educate top management in their understanding of the importance of the control environment, as well as the importance of their accounting and finance staff.

One way to educate top management is to design and clearly and completely explain simple control systems. For example, almost everyone understands the need to balance his or her own checkbook, but few understand the necessity of physical control over voided checks.

Additionally, few in the not-for-profit enterprise understand the relevance of internal control to their corporate mission of helping people. The CPA must learn to communicate on the level and in the language of the manager. The CPA must also contend with a very different mind set and priorities than with a typical for-profit CEO.

Providing services to a not-for-profit can be a risk-laden venture. It is only through patient and professional communication that the CPA can hope to provide a viable service for the not-for-profit, while minimizing the existing potential risk exposure.

Thomas L. Barton, PhD, CPA, *is a professor and KPMG Peat Marwick Fellow at the University of North Florida.* ***John E. McEldowney, DBA,*** *is an Associate Professor at the University of North Florida.* ***David Ray, MBA, CPA,*** *is Assistant Director for Ambulatory Care Services, Hermann Hospital, Houston, Texas.*

Principles *Build* Profits

BY CURTIS C. VERSCHOOR

Some 35 years ago Milton Friedman made his classic contention that "a corporation's [only] social responsibility is to make a profit." While this philosophy remained relatively unquestioned for several decades, it has been criticized increasingly in recent years, particularly by stakeholders who are directly affected by corporate activities. These days, a company's impact on such stakeholders—including customers, employees and franchisees, suppliers, and the communities in which a company operates—is serving as an emerging benchmark of corporate performance. In that light, I want to examine the relationship between a corporate ethics code and a company's performance, both financially and nonfinancially. As experts in control systems and performance reporting, management accountants and financial managers should take leadership roles in this area, particularly at a time when accountability is beginning to transcend the bottom line.

Implementing and enforcing a code of ethics can help companies reap success—fiscally and socially.

THE TREND TOWARD ETHICAL BEHAVIOR

The legacy of social activism in the 1960s and 1970s is impacting corporate decisions today as special interest groups have grown increasingly vocal about environmental issues and Third World working conditions. Furthermore, more than 75% of consumers claim they would switch brands and retailers to support a worthy cause. Thus, heightening concerns for social and environmental responsibility have placed further constraints on corporations already facing new realities of financial prudence and fiduciary accountability from their institutional investors. To emphasize, one in 10 investment dollars is placed with some ethical or social criterion in mind. In fact, investment assets managed with social or ethical screens amount to nearly $200 billion. It is obvious, then, that many people want to invest for profit with principle so they can express their personal values with their financial assets.

Given this climate, politicians, social activists, scholars, employee and consumer groups, and even some legal experts are attempting to determine appropriate parameters of corporate social performance and how they should be incorporated into business operations. For example, corporate responsibility was a key political plank in the victorious Labor Party's platform in the U.K. Domestically, President Clinton sponsored the first Conference on Corporate Citizenship and convened a Summit on America's Future, stressing the significance of volunteerism. He also recently introduced the Apparel Industry Partnership Code of Conduct, which addresses external and internal monitoring of labor practices.

On the corporate front, ethical standards have become a higher priority ever since the passage of the Federal Sentencing Guidelines in 1991. In fact, a 1991 Conference Board survey showed that 84% of respondents had a corporate code of ethics. But is there a connection between ethics and corporate performance? Since Friedman issued his manifesto, researchers have attempted to assess the relationship between a corporation's financial performance and social performance with varying results. A little-researched but increasingly pertinent issue is the role of an ethical corporation's internal controls in its success, both financially and socially.

As management accountants and financial managers know, "internal control" is the most common term used to describe the processes an organization uses to achieve its objectives. It is recognized as the cornerstone of corporate governance. Management's public reporting of internal corporate controls originated in the early 1970s, pursuant to an initiative by public accountants. The movement for public reporting gained even greater momentum in the late '70s, after numerous ethical lapses led to intensified public scrutiny of corporate accountability. The resulting Foreign Corrupt Practices Act of 1977 requires all publicly held companies to maintain an adequate internal accounting control system.

A decade later, in 1987, the Treadway Commission recommended that the Securities & Exchange Commission (SEC) require all public companies to include a statement on internal controls in their annual reports that would acknowledge management's responsibilities for a broadly defined set of internal control objectives, discuss how the company was fulfilling these responsibilities, and provide management's assessment of the effectiveness of the internal controls. Although the SEC never implemented this mandate, three-quarters of large public companies decided voluntarily to publish an internal control report each year. Far fewer, however, provide an assessment of the adequacy of internal controls.

THE CURRENT STATE OF INTERNAL CONTROLS

This issue intrigued me. I wanted to find out if the effective use of codes of ethics made a difference in the financial and nonfinancial performance of companies, so I decided to analyze the annual reports of the largest 500 publicly held U.S. corporations (by sales and revenue) as listed in the 1996 *Business Week* 1,000. I divided these companies' annual reports into three categories for comparison: A—No management report; B—Report but no mention of ethics; C—Report with mention of ethics.

I found that 74.6% of the annual reports included a management statement describing the company's responsibility for financial reporting and for establishing and maintaining an effective internal control system. Furthermore, 54% of the reports commented on the adequacy of their system for achieving a variety of control objectives, including the safeguarding of assets, the authorization of transactions, and proper external financial reporting.

I found that almost all companies employed the same general means of fulfilling management's internal control responsibilities: audit committee oversight, actions of internal auditors, and work of the external audit firm. While the specific content of the reports and the depth varied considerably from company to company, there were consistent patterns in scope and language. (Previous research has shown that wording of a company's management report remains consistent over time.)

Unfortunately, despite their initiative in reporting internal controls, only 33.6% of the reporting companies (126) specifically mentioned a code of conduct or ethics system. This lapse was somewhat unexpected, as current accounting literature—especially SAS No. 78[1] and the COSO report (*Internal Control: Integrated Framework*)[2]—emphasizes the importance of an organization's integrity and ethical values on maintaining effective controls.

HOW DO COMPANIES EMPHASIZE ETHICS?

Among the companies that did apply a code of conduct or ethics standard to their internal control system, the language they used to define this code varied considerably. Some companies mentioned an ethics program almost in passing when listing such control practices as proper personnel selection and training. Others placed a much greater weight on ethics as a control factor. Still others made a point of emphasizing management's responsibility in this capacity.

Here are some examples of the wording companies are using when they incorporate ethics into their internal control system as an integral part of their corporate philosophy.

Johnson & Johnson

"It has always been the policy and practice of the Company to conduct its affairs ethically and in a socially responsible manner. This responsibility is characterized and reflected in the Company's Credo and Policy on Business Conduct, which is distributed throughout the Company. Management maintains a systematic program to ensure compliance with these policies."

Campbell Soup

"The company believes that its long-standing emphasis on the highest standards of conduct and business ethics, set forth in extensive written policy statements, serves to reinforce its system of internal accounting control."

DuPont

"The company's business ethics policy is the cornerstone of our internal control system. This policy sets forth management's commitment to conduct business worldwide with the highest ethical standards and in conformity with applicable laws. The business ethics policy also requires that the documents supporting all transactions clearly describe their true nature and that all transactions be properly reported and classified in the financial records."

Pittston

"Management has also established a formal Business Code of Ethics which is distributed throughout the Company. We acknowledge our responsibility to establish and preserve an environment in which all employees properly understand the fundamental importance of high ethical standards in the conduct of our business."

IBM

"We believe that it is essential for the company to conduct its business affairs in accordance with the highest ethical standards, as set forth in the IBM Business Conduct Guidelines. These guidelines, translated into numerous languages, are distributed to employees throughout the world, and reemphasized through internal programs to assure that they are understood and followed."

These examples illustrate more than a mere mention of a code of conduct. While most public companies have been motivated to higher ethical standards by the legal consequences of the Sentencing Guidelines, these companies and others with similar philosophies demonstrate a greater commitment to ethics by virtue of their description of actions for maintaining internal control.

COMPARING REPUTATION, PERFORMANCE, AND ETHICS

As the next part of my research project, I wanted to ascertain whether the 126 companies in Group C of the *Business Week* 500 differed from the remaining 374 companies in terms of their financial and nonfinancial or social performance. To do this assessment, I compared how the three groups were rated for reputation and financial performance based on *Fortune* magazine's 1997 survey of "America's Most Admired Companies" and *Business Week's* 1997 ranking of historical financial performance.

The Business Week analysis. The most surprising finding is that the companies with a defined corporate commitment to ethical principles also fared better financially. In 1997, *Business Week* decided to drop its reporting of the 1,000 largest publicly held companies. Instead, it prepared an analysis of the financial performance of the companies included in the S&P 500 Index. Using only historical results, *Business Week* ranked each company into quintiles for eight financial measures: total return for one and three years, sales growth for one and three years, profit growth for one and three years, net margin, and return on equity. The company quintile rankings for these eight factors were combined with "a slight weighting for sales volume" to yield an overall financial performance ranking. The 1997 *Business Week* analysis included 376 or 75.2% of the initial 500-company sample from the 1996 *Business Week* 1,000.

According to the 1997 analysis, the companies in Group C had a strong and statistically significant higher average financial performance than those in Group A or Group B. Using the Mann-Whitney U Test, the probability that the difference in performance ranking between the average of Group C and Group A companies was due to chance is .0095. The comparable probability between Group C and Group B companies is .0097. In contrast, the probability that the difference between Group A and Group B companies was due to chance is a very large .4559. Thus, the probability that Group C's higher financial performance rankings were not due to chance is more than 99%.

Fortune's "most admired." Five of *Fortune*'s eight key attributes track stakeholder concerns either directly or indirectly. These attributes are innovativeness; ability to attract, develop, and keep talented people; quality of management; quality of products or services; and community and environmental responsibility. The other three measures are entirely financial. They are value as a long-term investment, financial soundness, and use of corporate assets.[3]

To conduct its survey, each year *Fortune* asks senior executives, outside directors, and financial security analysts to assign ratings of 1 (low) to 10 (high) to each of the eight attributes for four to 10 companies in their own industry. For purposes of comparison, the 60 industry subgroups used by *Fortune* for its 1997 *Fortune* 1,000 listing were compressed into 49 categories. In general, the companies included were the largest in their industry. To afford an immediate overview, the scores from the eight criteria were averaged into a composite reputation score. Using *Fortune*'s assessment, then, the scores of 431 companies were reported in 1997, and 417 were reported in 1996. When I compared these *Fortune*-selected companies with the 500 top companies in the *Business Week* study, I obtained a match of 308 firms for 1997 and 287 for 1996.

Table 1.

	Business Week Mean Rank	**1997 *Fortune*** Mean Score	**1996 *Fortune*** Mean Score
N =	376	308	287
LOWER Value means	Better	Worse	Worse
Group A–No Management Report	258.3056	6.2832	6.3038
Group B–No Mention of Ethics	243.0729	6.3997	6.4349
Group C–Mention of Ethics	200.1518	6.8122	6.7562
Probability A vs B is chance	.4559	.3353	.3089
Probability A vs C is chance	.0095	.0001	.0016
Probability B vs C is chance	.0097	.0002	.0047
Statistical measure	Mann-Whitney U	One-way ANOVA	One-way ANOVA

Study results. Using the one-way analysis of variance technique, I found a statistically significant difference between the average 1997 *Fortune* reputation score for Group C companies (whose management mentions ethics) and the scores of Groups A (no management report) and B (no mention of ethics) companies (see Table 1). But there was no significant difference between the average scores of companies in Group A and Group B. The probability that the difference between the 1997 Group C mean reputation score of 6.8122 and the Group A mean score of 6.2832 was due to chance is only .0001. The probability that the difference in mean reputation score of 6.8122 for Group C companies and 6.3997 for Group B companies was due to chance also is low—only .0002. In other words, the probability that the higher *Fortune* scores linked to mention of a code of conduct or ethics was not caused by chance is more than 99%. For the 1996 *Fortune* scores, the comparable probabilities are .0016 for Groups C and A and .0047 for Groups C and B.

While this strong association does not prove causation, it certainly suggests it. The comments of Coca-Cola Chairman and CEO Robert Goizueta illustrate the strength of a commitment to ethics. He says in *Fortune* that "Employees with integrity are the ones who build a company's reputation. Working for the Coca-Cola Company is a calling. It is not a way to make a living. It's a religion." It is not surprising, then, that Coca-Cola was ranked at the top of the "Most Admired Companies" list in both 1996 and 1997.

Of the 10 highest-ranking companies in 1997, five are in Group C, two are in Group A, and one is in Group B. The other two companies were not in the *Business Week* 500-company sample I studied.

Of the 10 "Least Admired Companies" in 1997, only one is in Group C—Kmart. While Kmart's management report presents honorable-sounding objectives, the company's ranking in the *Business Week* study is, nonetheless, a lowly 428 out of 495. Its management report reads, "The Company has adopted a code of conduct to guide our management in the continued observance of high ethical standards of honesty, integrity, and fairness in the conduct of the business and in accordance with the law. Compliance with the guidelines and standards is periodically reviewed and is acknowledged in writing by all management associates." Evidently a stated commitment to ethical behavior is a helpful but not absolute determinant of success.

IMPORTANCE OF PROPER IMPLEMENTATION

It should be emphasized that the mere presence of an ethics program—particularly one that does not cover all stakeholders or that is not implemented properly throughout the organization—is not sufficient. Even the most comprehensive code will not ensure ethical behavior without commitment from top management and effective monitoring.

Texaco, Inc., stands as a classic example of this cautionary tale. The company has all the outward appearances of an effective ethics control system. Its management report clearly says, "It is Texaco's long-established corporate policy to maintain a control-conscious environment and an effective internal control system throughout its worldwide operations . . . [with] Corporate Conduct Guidelines which require that all employees maintain the highest level of ethical standards." Furthermore, its 1996 proxy statement describes implementation of a number of standing committees to oversee and enforce internal controls, including an Audit Committee that reviews internal controls; a Public Responsibility Committee that reviews and makes recommendations regarding the policies and procedures affecting the company's role as a responsible corporate citizen, including those related to equal employment opportunity, health, and environmental and safety matters; and a Compensation Committee that assures the company's compensation structure incorporates programs that motivate performance in "full compliance with Texaco's vision and values."

Yet, despite all these well-intentioned measures, Texaco's system permitted one of the more egregious cases of internal control failure in history. Ultimately, control weaknesses caused Texaco's continued failure to comply with antidiscrimination statutes, in spite of the many oversight functions the directors reported performing. The landmark $176.1 million discrimination suit settlement against Texaco last March involving alleged widespread prejudice and intolerance in employment, pay, and promotions of women and minorities serves as a sobering reminder that even the best-laid control measures can fail without constant vigilance.

Texaco, however, has taken dramatic measures to improve internal controls in the future. The company has agreed to appoint an independent Equality and Tolerance Task Force to bolster internal control and has committed $35 million to fund this endeavor over the next five years. Activists have stated that the settlement terms should be a model for other corporations.

Indeed, Texaco's delegation of governance functions to an external group seems without precedent in its breadth and scope. Task Force recommendations for changes in practices affecting diversity in procurement, franchising, distribution, and employment generally must be adopted by management under penalty of court sanction. Also, the unlimited access granted the Task Force to any and all activities of the corporation could result in a costly and cumbersome duplication of efforts that could have been performed much more effectively and efficiently by a properly structured internal corporate audit function in the first place.

CONTROLS DO MAKE ETHICS EFFECTIVE

There is a statistically significant link between a management attitude favoring strong controls that emphasize ethically and socially responsible behavior and favorable corporate performance, both financially and socially. Yet it is critical that a company implement and maintain the controls. Reengineering efforts make teamwork and self-motivated activities even more crucial to corporate success. As *Fortune* has written, "[A company's] good name [reputation] is to strong financial performance as chicken is to egg." But the reputation must be deserved and not simply the result of clever public relations.

Senior management should realize that corporate ethics has become a mainstream management issue, not limited to safeguarding assets, compliance, or financial reporting. Because of downsizing, greater emphasis must be placed on "soft" controls like teamwork, trust, and loyalty, which are closely related to ethics and the corporate culture.

Management accountants and financial managers have many roles to play in assuring that organizations have strong controls integrating ethics and social responsibility. Not only should the corporate mission consider the interests of all stakeholders, but the design and operation of its implementation must be effective. The corporate audit function must have breadth of scope and adequate resources. Furthermore, other monitoring activities must be effective as well. Investors are becoming increasingly wary of high-sounding mission statements that may exist in the absence of accountability. In addition, management accountants should work toward more clearly defined informative structured disclosures to stakeholders that properly portray corporate ethical, social, and environmental performance and the presence of control systems to ensure their continuance.

Curtis C. Verschoor is the Ledger and Quill Alumni Research Professor in the School of Accountancy at DePaul University in Chicago. He is a member of the Northwest Suburban Chicago Chapter, through which this article was submitted. He can be reached at (847) 381-8115, phone, or e-mail, cverscho@condor.depaul.edu.

[1] American Institute of CPAs (AICPA), Auditing Standards Board, Statement on Auditing Standards (SAS) No. 78 *Consideration of Internal Control in a Financial Statement Audit: An Amendment to Statement on Auditing Standards No. 55*, New York: AICPA, 1995.
[2] Committee of Sponsoring Organizations of the Treadway Commission (COSO), *Internal Control—Integrated Framework*, New York: AICPA, 1992.
[3] A consensus is lacking as to whether *Fortune*'s criteria are appropriate for assessing corporate performance, either socially or financially. It seems that the major demarcations of a company's reputation—reliability, credibility, trustworthiness, and responsibility—are not defined and measured adequately even though they are as important to social performance as they are to financial performance.

HIGH-TECH SALES: NOW YOU SEE THEM, NOW YOU DON'T?

In most industries, goods are shipped, the product works, and the customer pays. But in high technology, confusion abounds over when a sale is really a sale. Sometimes, the product is shipped, and a sale is recorded—but the product has bugs, and customers balk at paying. Worse, aggressive salesmen have been known to ship goods without a purchase order at the end of a quarter to make their quota.

Investment bankers, money managers, and accountants worry that more companies than ever may be booking sales before they have occurred. "With the slump in the industry, salesmen are even more aggressive because commissions are shrinking," says David Clements, managing partner of Arthur Andersen & Co.'s San Jose (Calif.) office. "I didn't think there were any tricks I didn't know," grumbles Thomas I. Unterberg of L. F. Rothschild, Unterberg, Towbin. "But in the past months, I've learned three new ones."

Investors are suing DSC Communications Corp. and its auditor, Arthur Andersen, after DSC restated reports for six quarters because sales were booked too soon. DSC's stock price then fell by half. Wall Street has since badgered other high-tech companies about their accounting policies, says Dave H. Williams, chairman of Alliance Capital Management Corp.

Many companies, such as Network Systems Corp., chalk up sales when merchandise leaves the loading dock. "We've had a long record of successfully installing some rather complex systems," says Richard A. Fisher, Network's chief financial officer. DSC's policy was to record a sale on shipment, too, but not necessarily to the customer's site. In one case, sales were booked when merchandise went to a warehouse GTE Spring Communications Inc., a major customer, had leased. When Spring's own business failed to live up to expectations, it cancelled the orders.

WARNING BELLS. Analysts now say DSC's questionable sales might have been detected as early as June when

WHERE RECEIVABLES LOOK HIGH IN HIGH TECH: A COMPUTER SCAN

Company	Average number of days to collect on a sale*	Company	Average number of days to collect on a sale*
UTL	242	Scan-Optics	144
C3	231	Seagate Technology	143
DSC Communications	217	Data Switch	143
Radiation Systems	184	Porta Systems	141
Network Systems	181	Silicon General	140
Aydin	178	Computer Entry Systems	137
Masstor Systems	163	Computervision	132
CPT	155	Ungermann-Bass	131
Microdyne	154	Intecom	131
T-Bar	144	Applied Data Research	126

INDUSTRY AVERAGE: 65

*Receivables at 6/30/85 divided by average sales per day since 7/1/84
DATA: STANDARD & POOR's COMPUSTAT SERVICES INC.

it became apparent that accounts receivable were growing faster than sales. "I had suspicions that something was going wrong," says Douglas Whitman, an analyst at San Francisco's Hambrecht & Quist. "But the company completely denied there were any problems." DSC maintains that its accounting policies conformed to industry practice. "It would not have been a problem if Spring's business had taken off on plan," says William R. Tempest, DSC's general counsel.

A search by Standard & Poor's Compustat Services Inc. (table) showed that DSC was taking 217 days to collect its bills, up 22% from a year ago. "Everybody on the Street had been pestering DSC about it," says Karen Mulvany, an analyst at L. F. Rothschild.

The pros say that investors should look carefully at the relationship between sales, as displayed on the income statement, and receivables, which appear on the balance sheet. If the time to collect on a sale is significantly higher than the industry average of about 65 days, a warning bell should sound. It may simply mean that companies are lenient in their collection practices. "We've been more patient lately with our customers," says Network Systems' Fisher. Or it could mean that a customer has agreed to pay in stages as a very large order is being manufactured—an acceptable accounting treatment. That's mainly why Radiation Systems Inc.'s receivables are high, says Robert L. Pevenstein, the company's vice-president for finance.

But a higher-than-normal collection time could signal that some sales are being recorded even though no firm agreement on the purchase has been reached. The Securities & Exchange Commission has charged a few companies with exaggerating sales, but usually long after the quarter in question. On Oct. 10 the SEC completed its review of Chronar Corp., a maker of solar energy devices. The commission charged that the company recorded a sale at the end of its fiscal 1982 year, even though negotiations to sell its product had not been completed, and the transaction ultimately fell through. In August the SEC told American/Davey Corp., a maker of hydraculic-gear pumps, to "reverse out" sales booked at the end of its fiscal 1982 period. And in a complaint against Datapoint Corp., the SEC charged it with recognizing sales before the orders were placed. All three agreed to the changes without admitting or denying guilt.

Although the commission only catches a few cases, it hopes that those it does highlight will serve as an object lesson. But ultimately investors and analysts must depend on management integrity and the company's independent auditors. When the demand for high-tech products was growing at 30% annual rates, booking sales for one quarter when they should have gone into an even loftier next quarter mattered little. Now it can be a major distortion. "We did not meet our sales targets for the third quarter," admits Radiation's Pevenstein. "But the credibility that you lose when you report a sale that isn't one is far worse than missing a projection."

By Stuart Weiss in New York

INVESTIGATIONS

NUMBERS GAME AT BAUSCH & LOMB?

It may have used dubious methods to inflate yearend sales

Late last year, Bausch & Lomb Inc. hastily summoned its 32 independent contact lens distributors to a meeting at the company's Rochester (N.Y.) headquarters. As the distributors filed into the Dec. 13 meeting, they figured something big was up.

They weren't disappointed. Harold O. Johnson, the longtime head of B&L's contact lens unit, announced a change in sales strategy. B&L wanted to cut its direct shipments to eye doctors and funnel more business through the distributors. To ensure they could meet rising demand, Johnson told distributors they'd have to boost inventories.

Then came the bombshell. B&L's sales representatives gave each distributor a list of lenses to buy. The amounts were staggering: up to two years' of inventory. Moreover, prices were at least 50% more than B&L charged just three months earlier—and the lenses had to be bought by Dec. 24, when B&L closed its 1993 books. Johnson says he made it clear that anyone refusing to take their quota would lose their distributorship. "When your No. 1 vendor says you'd better take it or else, what're you going to do?" says James K. Butner, president of Doctor's Optical Supply Inc. in Vinita, Okla. In the end, all but two agreed—and by January, B&L dropped the two holdouts.

Hard-nosed tactics? You bet. The distributors swallowed close to $25 million worth of goods in the waning days of 1993, boosting B&L's U.S. contact lens sales 20%, to $145 million, and providing about half the division's $15 million in earnings for the year. Now the transaction has come back to haunt B&L. In June, it announced that "high distributor inventories" in its contact lens and sunglass businesses would severely hurt 1994 results. Third-quarter profits plunged 86%, to just $7.7 million. Analysts expect profits for the year to fall 37%, to $121 million, while sales are expected to fall slightly to $1.8 billion. Since late May, B&L's stock has slid from 50 to the low 30s.

"ASSURANCES." But an investigation by BUSINESS WEEK has revealed that the late December transaction was accompanied by questionable accounting practices. In interviews with more than a dozen of B&L's distributors, most tell a remarkably similar tale: Company executives promised that the distributors wouldn't have to pay for the lenses until they were sold and said that a final payment would be renegotiated if the program flopped. "Payment terms were scheduled, but I had verbal assurances that they wouldn't force through payment. If sales weren't sufficient, they said they would reevaluate with an eye toward extending the terms," says David T. Rusch, president of Firestone Optics Inc. in Kansas City, Mo. Ten months after the sale, B&L had collected less than 15% of the money—and some distributors never paid a dime for lenses worth hundreds of thousands of dollars.

If the distributors' tales are accurate, several accounting experts agree that Bausch & Lomb appears to have violated accounting principles for revenue recognition. If payment was contingent on the distributors' own sales, that would be a consignment sale. "If the distributors were told they didn't have to pay for inventory until they sold it, the company is supposed to hold off booking the revenues," says Robert S. Kay, professor of accounting at New York University's Stern School of Business. "[It] has no sale to record. It merely has inventory."

Furthermore, Howard Schilit, a professor at American University and expert on accounting irregularities, says "revenue should be recognized only when the risk has passed from seller to buyer." Based on the facts supplied by BUSINESS WEEK, he says, "by shipping out huge amounts of inventory, the company seems to have artificially created revenues on products not ordered by its customers. It's outright wrong."

Bausch & Lomb CEO Daniel E. Gill declined BUSINESS WEEK's requests for an interview. But other Bausch & Lomb executives strongly deny charges of accounting irregularities. They portray the sale as a failed marketing program. They concede that distributors were told they could pay only for what they sold during the first six months but insist that final payment for the lenses was due in June. "It has always been our policy with distributors that what they buy, they own," says Johnson. "I said two things specifically at that [December] meeting: The payment must be paid when it comes due, and 'you own this inventory.' I don't know how anybody could misread that." Stephen C. McCluski, B&L's controller, says the company's financial staff and its outside auditors, Price Waterhouse, twice reviewed the contact lens transactions. "Our accounting treatment was appropriate," he says. Price Waterhouse declined to comment.

Although B&L also suffered from excess inventory in its sunglasses business, the company says that problems in U.S. contact lenses account for roughly half its third-quarter earnings drop. In October, B&L agreed to take back roughly three-quarters of the December inventory and discount the rest, resulting in a $20 million sales reserve in the third quarter. The 60-year-old Johnson stepped down from his post at midyear but remains on the payroll until next March, when he will retire. B&L says he had planned to retire early. Yet B&L's troubles may just be beginning. A shareholder class action filed in June accuses the company of misleading investors by falsely inflating sales and earnings. B&L says the suit is "without merit."

SECOND PLACE. Led first by its contact lens unit and later by explosive growth in sales of its Ray Ban sunglasses, B&L had been a stellar performer: Through 1993, it posted 12 straight years of double-digit growth in earnings before nonrecurring charges. But growth has been tougher in recent years. The contact lens business, which accounts for 17% of sales, has been hammered. B&L stuck too long with traditional lenses, while the market shifted to frequent-replacement models and to disposable lenses pioneered by Johnson & Johnson. In 1992, J&J elbowed perennial leader B&L into second place in the U.S.

Johnson says B&L tried to perform a tricky balancing act: ramping up sales of the newer lenses while maintaining a strong piece of the shrinking but far more profitable market for traditional lenses. But with resources short, he decided to let distributors take a larger share of the traditional lens business.

Johnson describes the December sale as a great deal for the distributors. If they bought more traditional lens inventory, B&L would allow them to sell to large accounts. Johnson says the distributors needed the inventory to serve such accounts. Moreover, the shift was accompanied by promotional programs. "We said to our distributors, 'You become our agent,'" says Johnson. "'We'll move our warehouse into your warehouse.'" Distributors' reactions, Johnson adds, were "excellent."

But if distributors welcomed the idea many say they were very unhappy about the inventory. They say they already had 4 to 12 months' worth of supplies after an earlier promotion in September. They add that B&L refused to let them simply order more inventory as needed later on—and they wondered why the orders had to be made in the 11 days before B&L's fiscal year ended. "It was just a blatant attempt to make their numbers," says Michael W. Elton, contact lens marketing manager at Omega Group in Dallas. Johnson denies that the quickly organized promotion was tied to the yearend. Instead, he says B&L believed that distributors would be more motivated to sell its products if they had stock on hand that they were committed to paying for.

But distributors say they weren't committed to pay. After the Dec. 13 meeting, B&L asked each to sign a purchase agreement and a promissory note. Distributors would make five small monthly payments, with a final balloon payment of around 60% due in June. B&L charged no interest on the inventory in the meantime. Even B&L's McCluski says the

A Marketing Push— Or An Accounting Gimmick?

SEPTEMBER, 1993

Independent contact lens distributors say B&L asks them to buy four to six months' worth of inventory. B&L says buildup supported new marketing program, but distributors say uneven results leave them with 4 to 12 months' inventory in early December.

first payments were not firm. "[For] the first six months, the payment terms were based on the distributors' sell-through of that inventory," he says, adding that payment "didn't have to be a specific amount a month."

Yet many distributors say B&L's sales reps promised orally that the balloon payment would be extended if they didn't sell the lenses. B&L says that while Johnson told distributors he would "reevaluate the program" if it didn't work, there was no specific talk of extending payment. But two distributors say they protected themselves in writing. "I had an addendum [to the note], so to speak, that we had no obligation to pay," says Butner. "If push came to shove, all they could do was to take it back." Rusch of Firestone Optics added a clause reserving the right to return the lenses for full credit in lieu of payment.

B&L says it can't find Butner's note and says that the add-on clauses were not legally binding. But accounting expert Schilit says such written agreements "underscore why this shouldn't be recorded as revenue," since they indicated questions over whether the distributors had assumed the risks for the inventory.

Several distributors simply refused to sign the promissory note. "I never signed anything to pay in intervals," says Everett West, vice-president in charge of contact lenses at Omega Group. "I told them, if you want to put inventory in my house, fine. But we weren't responsible for payment until we sold it."

Once the lenses reached the distributors, the merchandise sat around for months, often unopened. "I had boxes piled seven feet high in my employee break room for a year," says Butner of Doctor's Optical. While the plan to shift sales to distributors did improve business for many, the uptick was small. One problem: B&L continued to sell lenses directly to high-volume eye doctors and chains. An executive at one small optical chain says it could buy Optima FW lenses directly for $9 early this year, well below the $11.90 B&L charged distributors for the same lenses.

By June, when the final balloon payment fell due, many distributors say they hadn't sold a single lens from the December inventory. McCluski concedes that few of the 30 made the balloon payment. B&L's accounting staff tried to collect the money during the summer but met fierce resistance. "I told 'em, your company is a bunch of liars," claims one. "They told us when they shipped it, it was on a pay-as-you-use-it basis. We didn't use it, so we weren't obligated to pay for it." Although B&L stopped shipping new orders to some distributors, it did little to force collection—which accounting experts say hints at the consignment nature of the sale. "It's a tough call, but the facts suggest that there was clearly an understanding by the distributors" that they wouldn't have to pay until they sold the product, says NYU's Kay. "The proof of the pudding is that [B&L] didn't enforce" the payment terms.

"THEY'VE BEEN FAIR." After Johnson stepped down as head of the contact lens division last summer, new head Carl E. Sassano agreed to take back most of the lenses. Some distributors sent back nearly the entire purchase. Others shipped back about two-thirds and were given two months to pay for the rest at a big discount. The move has quieted much discontent. "They've cleaned up our warehouse," says Michael Abbruzzese, president of Target Industries in Cohasset, Mass. "They've been fair. They saw they made a mistake and tried to rectify it."

But cleaning up the inventory problem has done little to address B&L's real competitive troubles. Moreover, B&L's proxy lists Johnson as earning a 64% performance-related bonus on top of his $275,000 salary for 1993, thanks to performance "substantially in excess" of company goals. B&L wouldn't address Johnson's bonus but says the yearend sale accounted for only "a small fraction" of bonuses paid to contact lens executives. But it also noted that "the company has altered its executive compensation systems to assure that equal attention is focused on the balance sheet as well as the income statement." It may be none too soon. With the shareholder suit charging that CEO Gill and other top executives may have also received unduly large bonuses stemming from overstated 1993 sales, B&L's accounting and legal problems could be just beginning.

By Mark Maremont in Rochester, N.Y.

DEC. 13, 1993

B&L calls a meeting and tells distributors to take additional inventories ranging from one to two years' worth or face cutoff. B&L says the buildup was needed for programs aimed at getting high-volume accounts to buy from distributors rather than the company.

DEC. 24, 1993

Insisting lenses be ordered by Dec. 24, B&L rushes out shipments. That adds sales of $25 million, but distributors say B&L gave verbal assurances they'd only pay for lenses when sold. B&L says small payments were set through June, when balance was due.

JUNE 15, 1994

With the new promotions flagging, less than 10% of the inventory is sold—or paid for. When the final payment falls due, most distributors refuse to pay. Meanwhile, B&L continues to sell directly to some high-volume accounts at prices below what distributors paid.

OCTOBER, 1994

With the majority of the inventory unsold, B&L takes most back. Distributors pay sharply discounted prices for the rest. B&L's third-quarter revenues drop 10%, to $449 million, and earnings plummet 86%, to $7.7 million, due to inventory reduction efforts and price cuts.

First In, First Out

Paying FIFO Taxes: Your Favorite Charity?

Gary C. Biddle

University of Washington

In one of the most puzzling rituals of American business behavior, thousands of U.S. companies are once again preparing their annual reports using FIFO rather than LIFO inventory accounting. By so doing, they will pay as extra taxes funds which could be used for expansion, capital replacement or dividends.

Under FIFO, or the first-in, first-out assumption, inventory costs flow through the firm as if on a conveyor belt. Costs are assigned to units sold in the same order the costs entered inventory. As a result, during periods of rising prices, older and thus *lower* costs are subtracted from revenues when determining reported (and taxable) earnings.

In contrast, under LIFO, or the last-in, first-out assumption, inventory costs are accumulated as if on a coal pile, with the newest costs being removed from the top and assigned to units sold. Unless a cost layer is liquidated by depleting inventories, it can remain in the base of the pile indefinitely. Thus, during periods of rising prices older and lower costs can remain in the balance sheet inventory accounts while the newer and *higher* costs are used to calculate earnings. Compared to FIFO, reported earnings in most cases drop. But so do taxable earnings. The company can keep more cash for itself and for shareholders.

According to their latest annual reports, three long-time LIFO users—Amoco, General Electric and U.S. Steel—have together saved more than $3 billion in taxes compared to what they would have paid using FIFO.

LIFO was deemed acceptable for tax purposes in 1939, and it's been used widely in selected industries, notably steel and petroleum, since the late 1940s. A large number of firms switched to LIFO in 1974, a year of high inflation. And for 1980, American Hospital Supply, Eli Lilly, Clorox and Williams Cos., among others, have announced they're making the switch.

Yet the vast majority of companies continue to use FIFO. Some managers are perhaps reluctant to incur additional LIFO bookkeeping costs. Some have perhaps dismissed LIFO's tax advantages in light of variable year-end inventory levels or less than galloping prices. Others may believe that since LIFO would result in lower reported earnings, stockholders are content to pay the extra FIFO taxes.

How much extra are stockholders willing to pay? In a forthcoming study in the "Supplement to the Journal of Accounting Research, 1990," I compare the inventory levels and accounts of 106 New York Stock Exchange firms which used FIFO, with those of 106 competitors that adopted LIFO between 1973 and 1975. From 1974 to 1978, by my estimates, the 106 FIFO firms paid an average of nearly $26 million each in additional federal income taxes, thanks to their policy of sticking with FIFO. For 1974 alone, these additional taxes averaged nearly $12 million per firm—more than 1½ percent of their sales.

Indeed there are good reasons to suspect that the additional taxes paid by FIFO firms put them at a competitive disadvantage. The accompanying table compares estimates of the additional taxes

*FIFO firms LIFO competitors	1974–1978 Additional FIFO taxes	LIFO tax savings
	(in millions of dollars)	
* Federal Paper Board	$8	
Mead Corp		$46
* J.P. Stevens	29	
Burlington Inds		44
Cone Mill		28
* Jewel Companies	36	
American Stores		18
* Masco Corp.	15	
Wallace-Murray		13
* Minn. Mining & Mfg	118	
Eastman Kodak		204
* Smith International	32	
Dresser Inds.		125
Hughes Tool Co.		22

paid by six FIFO firms, with the amounts saved by direct competitors that adopted LIFO or extended its use in 1974.

FIFO firms, of course, do not typically disclose the additional taxes they have paid. I have estimated these amounts, however, using industry specific price indexes and assumptions about procurement to come up with the differences between FIFO and LIFO based earnings. The additional FIFO taxes shown in the table equal these differences multiplied by the corporate income tax rate (then 48%).

The estimates of additional FIFO taxes assume that LIFO is applicable to all of a FIFO firm's inventories. As a result, these amounts may be overstated for firms like Smith International which hold significant portions of their inventories in other countries where LIFO is not permitted. However, the amounts that have been saved by LIFO competitors may understate the potential savings in cases like American Stores where LIFO has been adopted for only a portion of domestic inventories.

The amounts presented suggest that a number of firms have paid millions of dollars each in additional taxes by using FIFO rather than LIFO for domestic inventories. It is unlikely that bookkeeping costs could account for such sums. And fears of negative stockholder reaction appear unfounded in light of the efficient markets research documenting investor preferences for cash flows. While there are some unusual circumstances (like falling prices or inventory levels) in which LIFO could yield smaller cash flows, it is puzzling why so many firms in so many industries have continued to use FIFO.

Perhaps companies sticking to FIFO are showing their support for some worthy federal program. But wouldn't it make more sense to contribute some LIFO tax savings to a favorite tax-deductible charity? Or perhaps I have ignored an important LIFO cost or FIFO benefit. If so, please let me know.

For Some Companies, FIFO Accounting Makes Sense

Michael H. Granof

University of Texas at Austin

Daniel G. Short

Kansas State University

The use of FIFO, or the first-in first-out inventory accounting method, may not be so puzzling after all.

It is frequently argued that LIFO, the last-in first-out method, provides companies with substantial tax savings by permitting them to determine their cost of goods sold as if the items purchased last—at presumably higher prices—were in fact the ones sold. Financial analysts and business school professors often wonder why companies using FIFO, or another method called the weighted average, are paying millions of dollars in extra taxes—funds that would otherwise be available for expansion, capital replacement and dividends. The conventional explanation is that companies use FIFO in order to boost their reported earnings, even at the expense of their after-tax cash flow. But we have just concluded a survey that makes clear this interpretation is usually wrong.

We asked the controllers of 380 corporations that have not adopted LIFO why they haven't. We received 213 answers. Our survey convinces us that many companies have legitimate reasons for not climbing aboard the LIFO bandwagon.

For one thing, we found that most non-LIFO companies are *not* incurring a tax penalty. On the contrary, in a number of circumstances, the FIFO or weighted-average method can reduce tax payments.

Over 16 percent of our respondents indicated that the prices of their goods held in inventory have been declining. This was especially true of firms in high technology industries, but was also reported by firms in less glamorous industries such as steel and meat packing. In periods of declining prices, LIFO serves to accelerate recognition of taxable gains and, therefore, results in higher tax payments.

Many controllers—17%—told us that their firms as a whole or various of their subsidiaries are using tax loss or tax credit carryforwards. These carryforwards make it advantageous for the firm to accept the currently higher earnings that go with FIFO in order to have correspondingly lower earnings in the future, when the firm will again be in a tax-paying position.

Some managers explained that adoption of LIFO would prevent them from taking advantage of the "lower of cost or market" rule. This feature of the tax code (which is not available to firms that use LIFO) enables firms that have incurred losses on selected inventory items to give them immediate tax recognition. When LIFO is adopted, inventory must be stated at original cost. Previously recorded losses must be recovered and taxes must be paid on that amount.

Many managers have already taken advantage of a recent relaxation of the LIFO conformity rule. Normally a firm that uses LIFO for tax purposes must do so for financial reporting purposes. As a result of a ruling last year by the Second Circuit Court of Appeals in a case involving Insilco Corp., a parent company may now report the results of a subsidiary in its financial statements based on a method other than LIFO even though its subsidiaries calculate their taxable earnings using LIFO.

In addition, many controllers focused on various drawbacks of LIFO that could outweigh possible tax benefits. If a company's inventory balances fluctuate from year to year, LIFO increases the difficulties of cash planning. This is because LIFO subjects the company to the risk of dipping into its LIFO base—valuing for tax purposes its goods sold at the artificially low prices of past years. The company might then report artificially high profits and have to repay in a single year the accumulated tax savings of several previous years. Other controllers emphasized that the record-keeping requirements of LIFO are burdensome and costly.

While our study uncovered a number of legitimate reasons for not using LIFO, several responses seemed to lack economic support. One company said it did not use LIFO because it is "trying to maintain a record of year-to-year growth in profits, and though the impact of the change would not be material in relation

Further Thoughts on FIFO Accounting

In his Jan. 19 editorial page article, Prof. Biddle questions why so many industries have continued to use FIFO inventory accounting.

One reason may be that the managements of industries using FIFO are reluctant to reduce reported earnings. Although their reasons may appear myopic, they are nevertheless real. A recent survey by the Conference Board showed that more than 80% of medium-sized and large manufacturers had annual bonus plans for executives. The survey indicated that all plans linked bonuses to corporate performance. It appears likely that corporate performance is often measured by the amount of and by the increase in reported earnings. To reduce reported earnings even in the short-term would mean reduced compensation for these executives. This alone may account for some of the FIFO inventory companies. Until corporate managers lengthen their time horizons for determining improved corporate performance there will be reluctance to change anything that has an immediate negative impact on reported earnings.

When contemplating a change to the LIFO inventory costing method management should also be told that LIFO could cause erratic if not poor production habits in the future. This occurs when management continues to produce, to make certain that old lower costs remain in inventory and are not assigned to the cost of goods sold, while sales fall short of expectations. The result, at the very least, is a temporary involuntary buildup of inventory. This in turn often leads to the furloughing of production employees while sales catch up with past production. Once the catchup takes place the furloughed employees need to be recalled. The problem is that sometimes they have found other jobs and are not available. This is especially painful in industries where the learning curve is important.

LIFO inventory accounting does provide a company with a number of benefits, including tax benefits and improved cash flow. However, the benefits may not offset some of the problems it creates and that perhaps explains why so many New York Stock Exchange companies continue to use FIFO.

John Cerepak
Professor, Department of Accounting
Fairleigh Dickinson University
Teaneck, N.J.

I, too, have long been puzzled why so many firms continue to use FIFO. While FIFO does permit the firm to report higher "earnings" per share, it is unlikely that the stock market is fooled. Given the impressive scientific evidence supporting market efficiency, it seems more likely that share prices are geared primarily to real magnitudes, especially the ability to pay dividends, rather than to reported earnings. Surely the general decline in real stock prices witnessed during the past twelve years can be explained, in part, by widespread use of FIFO working in conjunction with ongoing inflation.

FIFO accounting harms the public in two important ways. First, the public is led to believe that profits are greater than they really are. This not only arouses public antagonism, it also fosters intervention. For example, some of the commotion during the "obscene oil profits" episode of the 1973–74 owed its origin to FIFO accounting. By overstating their profits, the oil companies seemingly almost invited the price controls and other waste-creating regulations which ensued. Second, since FIFO enriches the Treasury at the expense of stockholders, it induces a shift in scarce economic resources from the private to the public sector. This overpayment of taxes, which is unlegislated and represents a magnitude in the billions of dollars, fosters a transfer system which, because of bracket creep, already overtaxes the private sector during inflation.

Geoffrey E. Nunn
Professor of Economics
San Jose State University

---

to total profits in the first year, it would be significant in terms of year-to-year profit improvement." Another did not use LIFO because it thought that "such a switch would depress the market price of our stock. Such a switch would reduce the book value of our stock and would depress reported earnings . . . these considerations are more significant to our stock price than cash flow."

These explanations are somewhat surprising in light of the persuasive evidence that the capital markets are able to understand and compensate for differences in earning attributable solely to choices between accounting principles. But only 9 percent of the controllers gave such explanations.

Our study has convinced us that when it comes to paying taxes, most managers know what they are doing. But managers who have justification for not adopting LIFO need to be careful to explain these reasons to investors. We found that often the justification is not apparent from an analysis of financial statements. Companies that do not use LIFO for sound economic reasons should avoid being confused with companies that do not adopt LIFO for merely cosmetic reasons.

Convenient Fiction

Inventory Chicanery Tempts More Firms, Fools More Auditors

A Quick Way to Pad Profits, It Is Often Revealed Only When Concern Collapses

A Barrel Full of Sweepings

LEE BERTON

Staff Reporter of THE WALL STREET JOURNAL

Why do so many accountants fail to warn the public that the companies they audit are on the verge of collapse?

Increasingly, experts are blaming inventory fraud.

"When companies are desperate to stay afloat, inventory fraud is the easiest way to produce instant profits and dress up the balance sheet," says Felix Pomerantz, director of Florida International University's Center for Accounting, Auditing and Tax Studies in Miami.

Even auditors at the top accounting firms are often fooled because they usually still count inventory the old-fashioned way, that is, by taking a very small sample of the goods and raw materials in stock and comparing the count with management's tallies. In addition, Mr. Pomerantz says, outside auditors can fail to catch inventory scams because they "either trust management too much or fear they will lose clients by being tougher."

Growing Problem

The problem is growing fast. On Friday, Comptronix Corp., for example, disclosed that inventory manipulations played a significant role in the scandal at the once-highflying Alabama electronics company.

In November, William Hebding, its chairman and chief executive, told the Comptronix board that he and two other top officers had simply, though improperly, inflated profits by putting on the books as capital assets some expenses, such as salaries and start-up costs, related to the company's expansion. But on Friday, the company said the "fraudulent" accounting practices were started by making false entries to increase its inventory and decrease its cost of sales. Comptronix also said Mr. Hebding has been dismissed and its auditor, KPMG Peat Marwick, has resigned.

Nationwide, tough economic times have sparked a fourfold increase in inventory fraud from five years ago, says Douglas Carmichael, a professor of accounting at City University of New York's Baruch College. Paul R. Brown, an accounting professor at New York University's graduate school of business, adds: "The recent rise in inventory fraud is one of the biggest single reasons for the proliferation of accounting scandals."

Accounts Accused

Indeed, lawsuits charging accounting firms with fraud and malpractice have escalated to the point where the six biggest firms last year spent nearly $500 million—9% of their U.S. audit revenue—to defend themselves. Although auditors' failure to spot bad loans at financial institutions gets headlines, accounting experts term inventory fraud far more pervasive.

How an audit can misfire is illustrated by the way Deloitte & Touche, the auditors of Laribee Wire Manufacturing Co., failed to realize that the New York copper-wire maker was buoying a sinking ship by creating fictitious inventories.

Laribee was plagued by huge debt—almost seven times its equity—generated by a major acquisition in 1988. Meanwhile, its sales to the troubled construction industry, its major customer for copper wire, were declining. In 1990, Laribee borrowed $130 million from six banks. The banks say they relied on the clean opinion that Deloitte & Touche gave Laribee's financial statement for 1989, when the company reported $3 million in net income. A major portion of the loan collateral consisted of Laribee's inventories of the copper rod used to draw wire at its six U.S. factories.

Between Warehouses

But after Laribee filed for bankruptcy-court protection in early 1991, a court-ordered investigation by other accountants, attorneys and bankruptcy specialists showed that much of Laribee's inventory didn't

Reprinted with permission from *Wall Street Journal*, December 14, 1992, pp. A1, A5.

exist. Some was on the books at bloated values. Certain wire-product stocks carried at $2.20 a pound were selling at only $1.70 to $1.75 a pound.

Shipments between plants were recorded as stocks located at both plants. Some shipments never left the first plant, and documentation supposedly showing they were being transferred to the second plant "appeared to be largely fictitious," the report to the court found. And 4.5 million pounds of copper rod, supposedly worth more than $5 million, that Laribee said it was keeping in two warehouses in upstate New York would have required three times the capacity of the buildings, the report said.

"It was one of the biggest inventory overstatements I've ever seen," says John Turbidy, the court-appointed trustee. He estimates that inventory fraud contributed $5.5 million before taxes to Laribee's 1989 results. Absent this fraud and other accounting shenanigans, Laribee would have reported a $6.5 million loss instead of the profit, he adds. Laribee's previous top management declines to comment.

Creating phantom inventory instantly benefits a company's bottom line. Subtracting the current inventory of parts and raw materials from year-earlier figures shows the supply costs of producing items for sale. This cost, plus labor, is deducted from sales to help calculate profit. By inflating current inventories with phantom items, a company reduces stated production costs and creates phony profits.

Banks and other creditors sued Deloitte in state courts in Texas, Illinois, North Carolina and New York earlier this year for unspecified damages, charging it with malpractice and gross negligence in failing to spot the accounting manipulations at Laribee. A suit filed by Asarco Inc., a copper producer and Laribee creditor, accuses Mel Dobrichovsky, the Deloitte partner who oversaw Laribee's audit, of fraud in missing the inventory scam and other improper audit practices.

"The auditor was either taken in or missed the obvious," Mr. Turbidy says. "Giving the auditors the benefit of the doubt, I assume that it was inexperience on their part because some who showed up at Laribee's plants were fresh out of college. Otherwise, how could they have overlooked such blatant inventory manipulations?"

James T. Simmons, Laribee's former vice president for operations, says a firm later merged into Deloitte sent "three to five auditors with three years or less experience to the [Camden, N.Y., and Jordan, N.Y.] plants to check inventory." He recalls: "The faces kept changing and there was little continuity." According to several Laribee employees, a standing joke at the plants was that the next outside auditor "would be fresh out of high school." Mr. Simmons adds that Mr. Dobrichovsky "never showed up at the plants" during annual inventory counts.

Mr. Dobrichovsky, who left Deloitte at the end of 1990, declines to comment. Deloitte denies any wrongdoing and says the audits "were done in accordance with professional standards."

Common Problems

In any event, the Laribee case isn't unusual. Experts say many companies overvalue obsolete goods and supplies. Others create phantom items in the warehouse to augment the assets needed as loan collateral. Still others count inventory that they pretend they have ordered but that will never arrive.

In recent years, lawsuits have been filed against a lot of companies, including L.A. Gear Inc. and Digital Equipment Corp. Three class-action suits charge in federal district court in Los Angeles that L.A. Gear pumped up its inventories with "phantom sneakers," and one against Digital in federal court in San Jose, Calif., accuses it of failing to set aside reserves for obsolete inventory. L.A. Gear declines to comment, and Digital denies the allegations.

As critics see it, unscrupulous managers can get auditors to swallow all kinds of ruses. In one case, auditors permitted company officials to follow the auditors and record where they were making test counts of inventory, Prof. Carmichael says. "Then the managers simply falsified counts for inventory that wasn't being tested by the auditors.

In another case, the auditor spotted a barrel whose contents management had valued at thousands of dollars. Actually, the barrel was filled with floor sweepings. The auditor forced the company to subtract the false amount from inventory, Prof. Carmichael says, "but it never occurred to the auditor that this was an egregious example of intentional and pervasive fraud. To be that blind suggests incompetence or worse."

Many Staffs Inadequate

Prof. Carmichael adds that spotting inventory fraud requires bigger staffs than some accounting firms now have or are willing to send out to do inventory sampling. In the slow economy, the firms, facing reduced revenue growth and client demands for audit-fee concessions, have been pushing out partners and lower-level staff to cut costs. "With their jobs in peril, remaining auditors are less likely to make waves for fear of losing a client and possibly their jobs," says Howard Schilit, an associate professor of accounting at American University in Washington, D.C.

According to professional standards, outside auditors are supposed to watch carefully how company personnel count inventory and make counts themselves for a representative sample. The sample usually ranges from 5% to 10%, experts say. But current auditing standards don't spell out the sample's size, which depends on the auditor's judgment, nor how the inventory should be counted, says the American Institute of Certified Public Accountants, which sets the standards.

Alan Winters, the institute's director of auditing research, says it is difficult if not impossible for an outside auditor to spot inventory fraud "if top management is directing it."

But Mr. Pomerantz of the Florida center disagrees. "If auditors were more skeptical of management claims, particularly in bad times, they would look at a far greater portion of the inventory in certain instances and do more surprise audits, which under the leeway of current standards nowadays are unusual," he says.

Fights over how auditors should handle inventory have figured prominently in the woes of Phar-Mor Inc., the troubled deep-discount drugstore chain based in Youngstown, Ohio. It recently took a $350 million accounting charge to cover losses resulting from an alleged swindle by some former managers, who were dismissed last August. The company's surviving management and Coopers & Lybrand, its former outside auditor, have each filed lawsuits charging the other with negligently failing to detect inventory fraud and other financial manipulations at Phar-Mor.

The suit by Coopers, filed in a state court in Pittsburgh, contends that previous management kept items in inventory ledgers that had already been sold, maintained a secret inventory ledger and created phantom inventory at many of the chain's stores. But a suit filed against Coopers in federal district court in Cleveland in October by Corporate Partners L.P. contends that Coopers is at fault for failing to catch the scams. Corporate Partners, which has a 17% stake in Phar-Mor, is an investment fund affiliated with Lazard Freres & Co., the investment bank.

While recent charges concerning Phar-Mor have cited the inventory-rigging problem, the Corporate Partners' suit has far more detailed allegations.

Corporate Partners contends that Coopers, in a "gross departure from generally accepted auditing standards, observed the taking of inventory at no more than five stores" and "advised Phar-Mor, in advance, of the specific stores at which Coopers would observe" the inventory counting.

Corporate Partners maintains that Phar-Mor then "refrained from making fraudulent adjustments at the five stores where it knew that the inventories would be observed . . . by Coopers. Instead, it [Phar-Mor] made its fraudulent adjustments to the inventory records of the vast majority of other stores that it knew in advance that Coopers would not review."

On June 30, 1990, the fiscal year end, Phar-Mor's balance sheet "falsified (and overstated) inventory by more than $50 million," the suit alleges, adding, "Coopers closed its eyes to the evidence that would have revealed the false and inflated inventory adjustments."

Coopers's Response

Eugene M. Freedman, Coopers's current chairman, contends that the suit lacks merit because the fund's own accountants studied Phar-Mor in 1991. He adds that the fund's accountants spent little time discussing Phar-Mor with Coopers's auditors. "They're trying to shift the blame for their inadequate due diligence and judgment" to Coopers, he contends.

Phar-Mor said last August that it was the victim of a more than $400 million fraud-and-embezzlement scheme by Michael Monus, a co-founder of the company and former president, and three other executives; all were discharged soon afterward. Phar-Mor and Mr. Monus recently filed for bankruptcy-court protection. In its suit, Corporate Partners said it would have also sued the company and Mr. Monus if they hadn't filed in bankruptcy court. Mr. Monus has declined comment.

David McLean, Coopers's associate general counsel, says the firm had to tell Phar-Mor managers where it was sampling inventories "because those stores had to be closed to do the count. You can't check a huge retail operation's inventories while the store is open."

Sometimes, however, auditors fall for the most obvious ruses.

Paul Regan, a forensic accountant in San Francisco often involved in court cases, recalls a Texas company being acquired by a California computer concern. He says the auditor test-counted two types of computer chips, finding 500 of one and 300 of the second at the acquired company. The next day, the acquired company's controller called the auditor and told him that "an hour after you left, 1,500 more chips of the first variety and 1,000 of the second arrived in a shipment," he says. But the auditor "never checked back to see if the new chips were for real. It was a complete scam and helped the acquired company double its reported profits." Mr. Regan says.

—Martha Brannigan in Atlanta contributed to this article.

Cash Flows, Ratio Analysis and the W. T. Grant Company Bankruptcy

Although they surfaced as a gusher rather than a trickle, the problems that brought the W. T. Grant Company into bankruptcy and, ultimately, liquidation, did not develop overnight. Whereas traditional ratio analysis of Grant's financial statements would not have revealed the existence of many of the company's problems until 1970 or 1971, careful analysis of the company's cash flows would have revealed impending doom as much as a decade before the collapse.

Grant's profitability, turnover and liquidity ratios had trended downward over the 10 years preceding bankruptcy. But the most striking characteristic of the company during that decade was that it generated no cash internally. Although working capital provided by operations remained fairly stable through 1973, this figure (which constitutes net income plus depreciation and is frequently referred to in the financial press as "cash flow") can be a very poor indicator of a company's ability to generate cash. Through 1973, the W. T. Grant Company's operations were a net user, rather than provider, of cash.

Grant's continuing inability to generate cash from operations should have provided investors with an early signal of problems. Yet, as recently as 1973, Grant stock was selling at nearly 20 times earnings. Investors placed a much higher value on Grant's prospects than an analysis of the company's cash flow from operations would have warranted.

James A. Largay, III and Clyde P. Stickney

The W. T. Grant Company was the nation's largest retailer when it filed for protection of the Court under chapter XI of the National Bankruptcy Act on October 2, 1975. Only four months later, the creditors' committee voted for liquidation, and Grant ceased to exist. The collapse of Grant is a business policy professor's dream—ambiguous marketing strategy, personnel compensation based on questionable incentive schemes, financially and administratively unsound credit operations, centralization versus decentralization issues and poorly conceived and poorly executed long-range plans. Problems of this magnitude do not develop overnight, although they often surface as a gusher rather than a trickle.

As we will show, a traditional ratio analysis of Grant's financial statements would not have suggested the existence of many of these problems until approximately 1970 or 1971. As recently as 1973, Grant stock was selling at nearly 20 times earnings. Perhaps investors believed that Grant would continue to prosper despite many years of consistent but lackluster performance; after all, the company had been in existence since the turn of the century, paying dividends regularly from 1906 until August 27, 1974. But Grant's demise should not have come as a surprise to anyone following its fortunes closely; a careful analysis of the company's cash flows would have revealed the impending problems as much as a decade before the collapse.

Stock Prices and Ratio Analysis

Prior to 1971, Grant's stock had tended to perform like other variety store chain stocks. Beginning in June or July of 1971,

James Largay is Professor of Accounting at the College of Business and Economics, Lehigh University. This article was written while he was Coopers & Lybrand Visiting Associate Professor of Accounting at The Amos Tuck School of Business Administration, Dartmouth College. Clyde Stickney is Associate Professor of Accounting at The Amos Tuck School of Business Administration, Dartmouth College.

The Authors thank the Tuck Associates Program for its financial support.

Exhibit I W.T. Grant Company Stock Prices and Selected Ratios For the Fiscal Years Ending January 31, 1966 to 1975

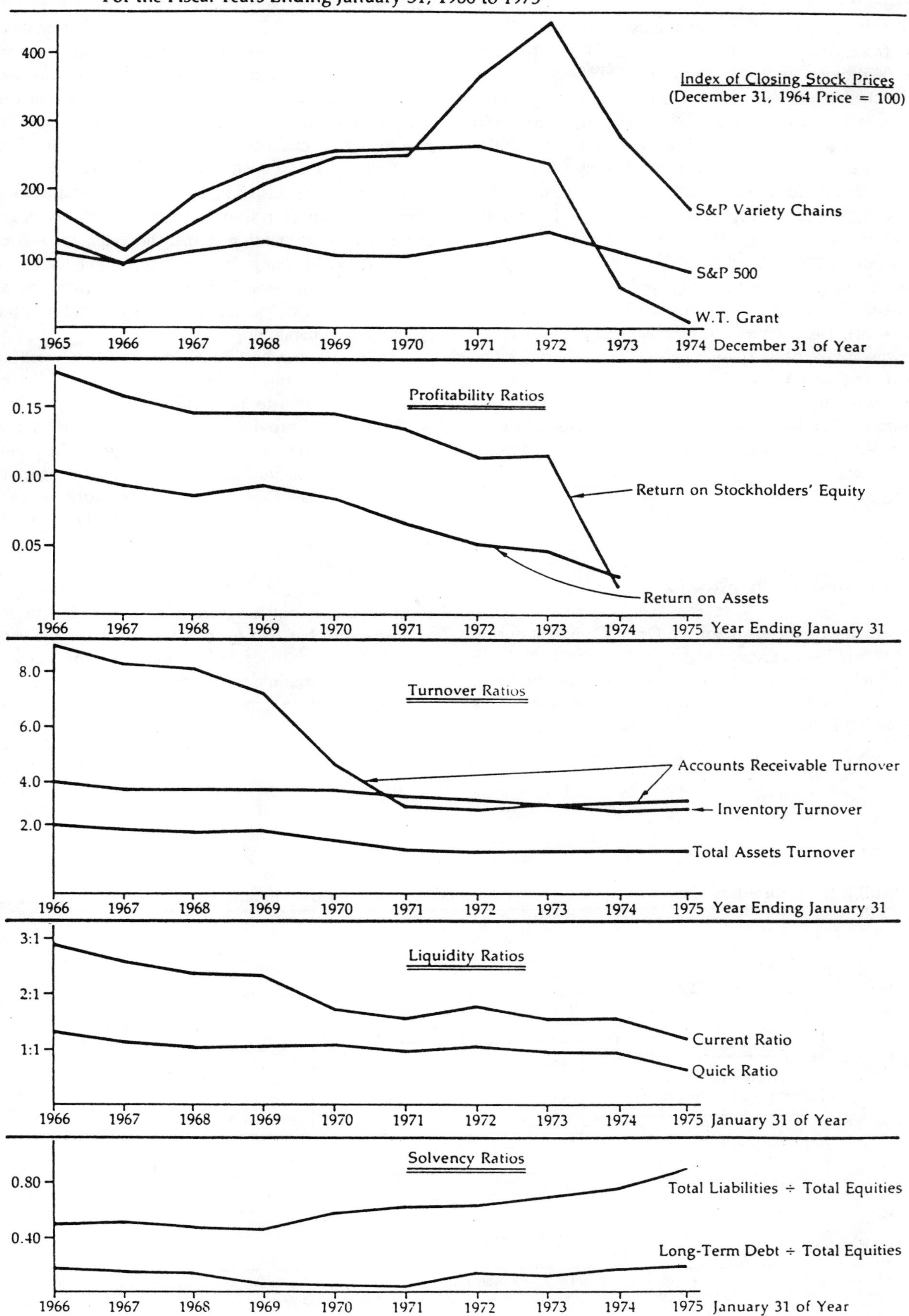

however, the stock price performance of Grant and the other variety chains parted ways.

Exhibit I presents data on monthly closing prices and various ratios from Grant's financial statements for the 10 years preceding bankruptcy in 1975. The top panel shows the December 31 closing price for Grant's stock for each year expressed as a ratio of the closing price on December 31, 1964 (i.e., the December 31, 1964 closing price equals 100). It also shows the values of the Standard & Poor's Variety Chain Stock Price Index and the Standard & Poor's 500 Composite Stock Price Index at the end of each year, each expressed as a ratio of its value on December 31, 1964.

The bottom four panels in Exhibit I shows the trends in Grant's profitability, turnover, liquidity and solvency ratios over the fiscal periods between 1966 and 1975 (ending January 31 of each year). The profitability, turnover and liquidity ratios tended downward over this 10-year period. The solvency ratios reflect increasing proportions of liabilities in the capital structure. The most significant deterioration in these ratios, however, occurred during the 1970 and 1971 fiscal periods, leading the stock market's recognition of Grant's problems by approximately one year.

Net Income and Cash Flows

The most striking characteristic of the Grant Company during the decade before its bankruptcy was that it generated virtually no cash internally. The company simply lost its ability to derive cash from operations. After exhausting the possibilities of its liquid resources, it had to tap external markets for funds. As the failure to generate cash internally continued, the need for external financing snowballed.

Most textbooks in corporate finance, investments and financial statements analysis devote little attention to computing or using cash flow from operations. Yet the calculations are straightforward enough. One starts with working capital provided by operations from the statement of changes in financial position, adds changes in current asset accounts (other than cash) that decreased and current liability accounts that increased and subtracts changes in current asset accounts (other than cash) that increased and current liability accounts that decreased. In accounting terms, the calculation is equivalent to adding credit changes in working capital accounts and subtracting debit changes. Exhibit II summarizes the process of converting working capital provided by operations to cash flow provided by operations.

Exhibit III graphs Grant's net income, working capital provided by operations and cash flow provided by operations for the 1966 to 1975 fiscal periods. Note how poorly working capital provided by operations correlates with cash flow from operations. The financial press frequently refers to "cash flow," defined as net income plus depreciation. This measure of cash flow approximates working capital provided by operations, which (as Exhibit III shows) may prove a very poor surrogate for the cash flow actually generated by operations.

While Grant's net income was relatively steady through the 1973 period, operations were a net user rather than provider, of cash in all but two years (1968 and 1969). Even in these two years, operations provided only insignificant amounts of cash. Grant's continuing inability to generate cash from operations should have provided investors with an early signal of problems.

Exhibit II Computing Cash Flow Provided by Operations from Published Financial Statements

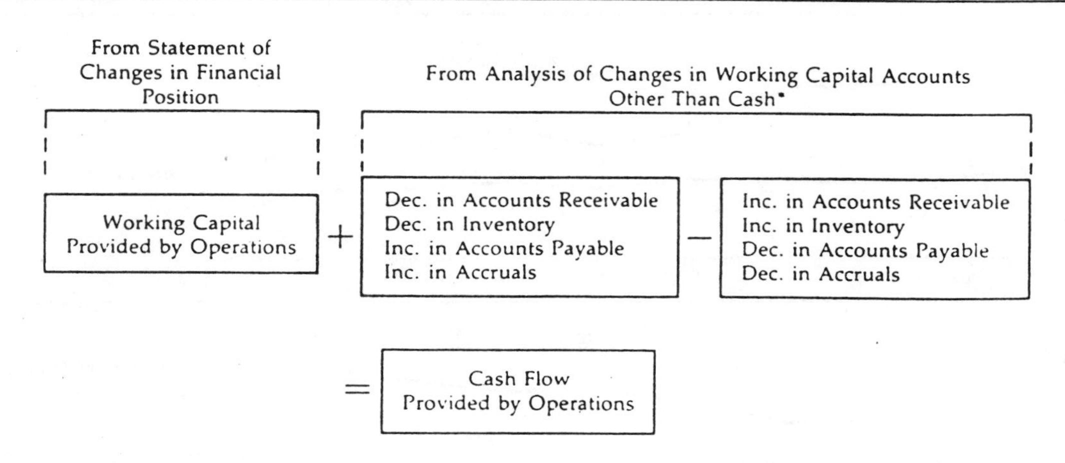

*Accounts such as "Bank Loans" and "Current Portion of Long-Term Debt" must be excluded from the analysis. Even though treated as current liabilities, they represent neither cash provided nor cash used by operations.

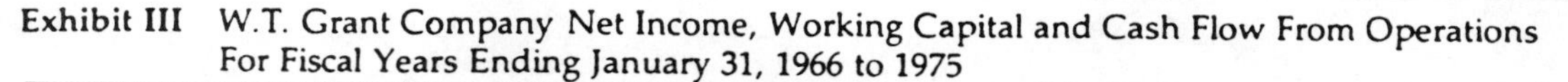
Exhibit III W.T. Grant Company Net Income, Working Capital and Cash Flow From Operations For Fiscal Years Ending January 31, 1966 to 1975

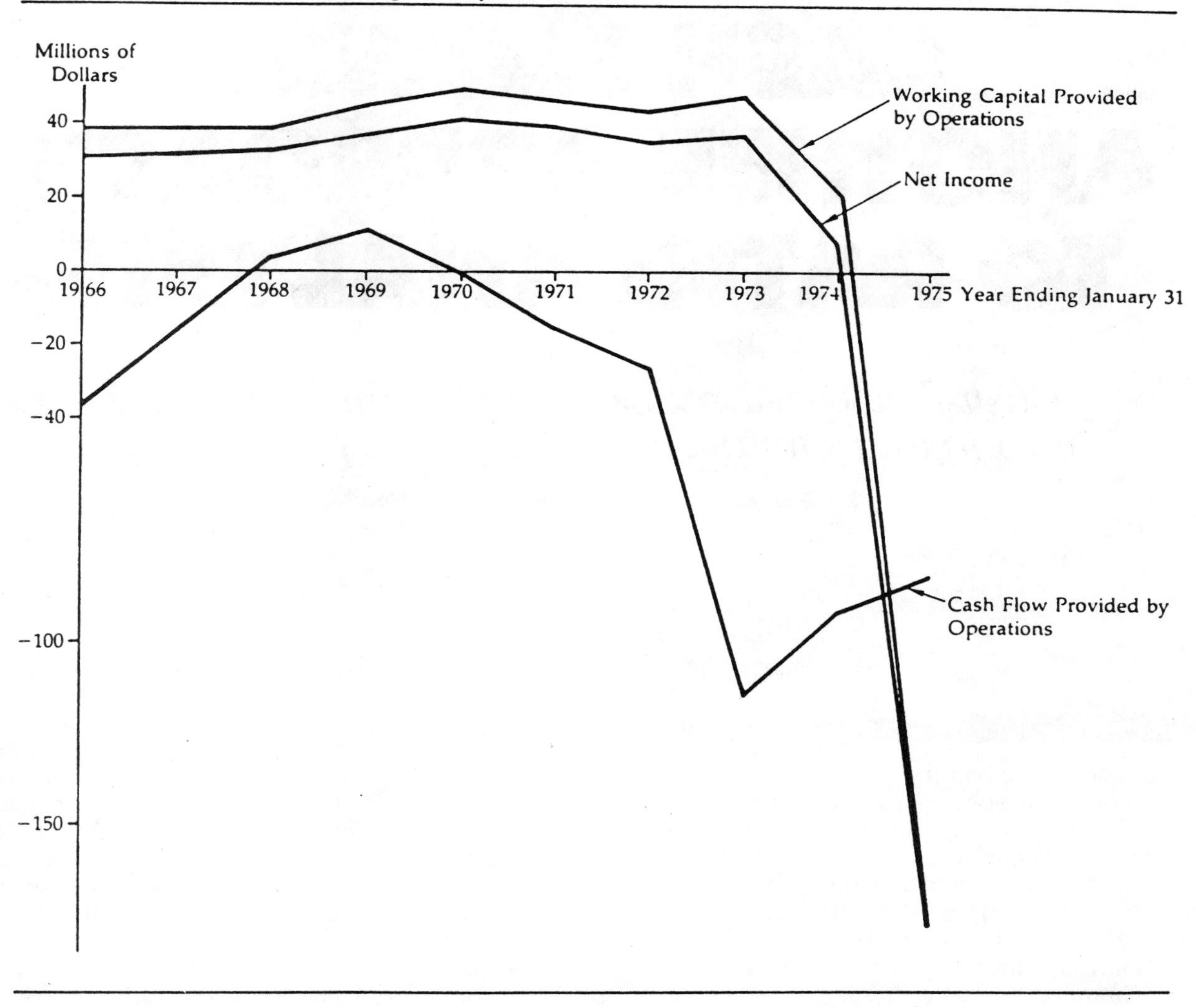

Was the Market for Grant Stock Efficient?

In an efficient market, stock prices continually reflect all publicly available information about a company's past performance and future prospects. The evidence presented here, however, seems to suggest that W. T. Grant Company was a counterexample to market efficiency.

Operations were a net user of cash in eight of Grant's last 10 years. Between January 31, 1966 and January 31, 1973, Grant's sales nearly doubled, but its earnings and earnings per share remained virtually unchanged. Despite its failure to translate vastly increased sales into additional profits, Grant's price-earnings ratio on January 31, 1973 was about twice what it had been on January 31, 1966.

We compared Grant's price-earnings ratios with those of similar variety chains (Kresge, McCrory, Murphy and Woolworth) over the 1965–75 period. Until 1973, Grant's price-earnings multiple tended to exceed the multiples of the other variety chains, with the exception of Kresge. Traders in Grant stock during the company's last decade placed a much higher value on Grant's prospects than an analysis of the company's cash flow from operations would have warranted.

CASH FLOWS: ANOTHER APPROACH TO RATIO ANALYSIS

Cash-flow-based ratios are useful in evaluating a company's financial strength and profitability.

by Don E. Giacomino and David E. Mielke

One product of accounting evolution in the United States is the use of ratios for analyzing financial statements. Originally developed as short-term credit analysis devices, ratios can be traced as far back as the late 19th century. Since then, analysts have developed many financial ratios that are widely used by practitioners and academicians.

A relatively recent development has been the Financial Accounting Standards Board requirement to prepare a statement of cash flows. To date, little has been done to suggest a comprehensive set of cash flow ratios with the potential to evaluate financial performance. Scattered empirical evidence in published studies does not identify a complete set of useful ratios.

Relative performance evaluation is one important use of cash flow ratios, which can be viewed in terms of sufficiency and efficiency. *Sufficiency* describes the adequacy of cash flows for meeting a company's needs; *efficiency* describes how well a company generates cash flows relative both to other years and to other companies.

This article proposes some cash-flow-based ratios that can be used for relative performance evaluation. We conducted an empirical study of cash flow statements to provide some industry averages and to determine if the potential exists to develop benchmarks for the ratios by industry. These benchmarks can play an important part in evaluating the relative sufficiency and efficiency of a company's cash flows.

DON E. GIACOMINO, CPA, DBA, is associate professor and chairman, Department of Accounting, Marquette University, Milwaukee, Wisconsin. He is a member of the Wisconsin Society of CPAs and the American Accounting Association. DAVID E. MIELKE, PhD, is associate professor of accounting, Marquette University. He is a member of the AAA.

The authors gratefully acknowledge support from Arthur Andersen Alumni research grants in 1989 and 1991.

USE OF RATIOS

Analysts use ratios to predict financial variables and to evaluate relative performance. They group ratios into liquidity and profitability categories to predict bankruptcy, the probability of loan defaults and stock prices. Relative performance evaluation assumes comparing a company's performance to that of a chosen industry or benchmark ratio filters out the performance effects of common uncertainties, leaving only company-specific performance. In such evaluations, other companies' performance provides information about a specific company's performance.

Although recent studies yielded apparently contradictory results, most cash flow studies show the value of cash flow data. This is especially true in predicting bankruptcy and financial distress. Little has been done with respect to using cash flow ratios for relative performance evaluation.

CASH FLOW RATIOS

Our study provides a starting point for developing some benchmarks (norms or standards) for cash flow ratios. The cash flows from the operating activities classification on the statement of cash flows generally summarize the cash effects of transactions and other events involved in determining net income. Operating activities involve an enterprise's primary activities—the production and delivery of goods and services. They are the enterprise's primary focus and the primary variable of interest in this study. Cash from operations is a component of each of the ratios shown in exhibit 1, which have been classified as sufficiency or efficiency to describe their potential use in relative performance evaluation.

Sufficiency ratios. The cash flow adequacy ratio directly measures a company's ability to generate cash sufficient to pay its debts, reinvest in its operations and make distributions (dividends) to owners. A value of 1 over a period of several years shows satisfactory ability to cover these primary cash requirements. The long-term debt payment, dividend payout and reinvestment ratios provide further insight for investors and creditors into the individual importance of these three components. When expressed as percentages and added together, these three ratios show the percentage of cash from operations available for discretionary uses.

Although a company could use cash generated from financing and investing activities to retire debt, cash from operations represents the main source of long-term funds. The debt coverage ratio can be viewed as a payback period; that is, it estimates how many years, at the current level of cash from operations, it will take to retire all debt.

The depreciation–amortization impact ratio shows the percentage of cash from operations resulting from add-backs of depreciation and amortization. Comparing this ratio to the reinvestment ratio provides insight into the sufficiency of a company's reinvestment and the maintenance of its asset base.

Over several years, the reinvestment ratio should exceed the depreciation–amortization impact ratio to ensure sufficient replacement of assets at higher current costs. This ratio also can be used as an efficiency evaluation. A company would be considered more efficient if depreciation and amortization have a relatively low impact on cash from operations.

Efficiency ratios. Investors, creditors and others concerned with a company's cash flows are especially interested in the income statement and earnings measures. The cash flow to sales ratio shows the percentage of each sales dollar realized as cash from operations. Over time, this ratio should approximate the company's return on sales. The operations index compares cash from operations to income from continuing operations. It measures the cash-generating productivity of continuing operations. Cash flow return on assets is a measure of the return on assets used to compare companies on the basis of cash generation (as opposed to income generation) from assets.

Sufficiency and efficiency ratios are examples of information available to financial statement users from the cash flow statement. It's important to remember that, as in all ratio analysis, isolated ratios provide limited information about a single period. The ratios become more useful when computed for a period of years to determine averages and trends and when compared to industry averages.

STUDY RESULTS

Because they have the largest number of companies among the *Fortune* 500, we selected the electronics, food and chemical industries for our study. In 1988, these industries respectively ranked third, fourth and fifth in sales and third, fourth and sixth in assets among the *Fortune* 500. All companies in each industry were asked to provide their 1988 annual reports. Exhibit 2 shows an industry breakdown of the 99 companies that responded.

Each respondent included a statement of cash flows complying with FASB Statement no. 95, *Statement of Cash Flows.* Cash flow ratios were computed for 1986 through 1988 using the data from the annual reports. Exhibit 3 shows the three-year averages for each ratio by industry.

DATA ANALYSIS

The cash flow adequacy ratio depicts the extent a company's cash from operations covers payments on long-term debt, purchases of assets and dividend payments. A value of 1 might be considered a reasonable target. Based on mean values, none of the industries generated sufficient cash from operations to cover its primary cash requirements. The percentages of companies that had the cash to meet the target were electronics, 45%; food, 28%; and chemicals, 31%.

EXECUTIVE SUMMARY

- CASH FLOW RATIOS CAN help evaluate a company's financial performance in terms of both strength and profitability.
- SUFFICIENCY RATIOS evaluate the adequacy of cash flows for meeting a company's needs. Efficiency ratios evaluate how well the company generates cash flows relative to other years and other companies.
- CASH FLOW DATA CAN be particularly helpful in predicting bankruptcy and financial distress. Ratios are most useful when computed over a period of years to determine averages and trends.
- DEVELOPING BENCHMARKS for cash flow ratios in a particular industry may make the ratios more meaningful, enabling a company to compare its performance to that of similar companies.
- A STUDY OF COMPANIES in the electronics, food and chemical industries has yielded some useful ratios for evaluating cash flow adequacy, long-term debt payment, dividend payout, reinvestment, debt coverage and the impact of depreciation–amortization. Information on the ratio of cash flow to sales, the operations index and the cash flow return on assets also can be helpful.

EXHIBIT 1
Cash flow ratios

Sufficiency ratios

Cash flow adequacy	Cash from operations / Long-term debt paid + purchases of assets + dividends paid
Long-term debt payment	Long-term debt payments / Cash from operations
Dividend payout	Dividends / Cash from operations
Reinvestment	Purchase of assets / Cash from operations
Debt coverage	Total debt / Cash from operations
Depreciation–amortization impact	Depreciation + amortization / Cash from operations

Efficiency ratios

Cash flow to sales	Cash from operations / Sales
Operations index	Cash from operations / Income from continuing operations
Cash flow return on assets	Cash from operations / Total assets

From 1986 through 1988, cash flow adequacy declined in the electronics and chemical industries but increased in the food industry. Electronics showed a large decrease (.91 to .80) in 1988 and food showed a large increase (.82 to .95), while chemicals showed a decline of 2 percentage points per year.

For the three-year period, less than half the companies had sufficient cash flow from operations to cover primary cash requirements. Three-year averages varied from .85 (food) to .89 (electronics); no significant differences between industries were found for the cash flow adequacy ratio.

Since each represents a major component of the denominator in the cash flow adequacy ratio, the long-term debt payment, dividend payout and reinvestment ratios are discussed by industry. For the electronics industry, the data showed increased reinvestment in assets and dividends paid relative to cash from operations and a decrease in debt retirement from 1986 to 1988. For 1988, asset reinvestment exceeded cash from operations.

From 1986 through 1988, food companies showed increases for long-term debt payments, dividends and reinvestment in assets. Relative to electronics, food and chemical companies spent a greater portion of cash from operations on long-term debt retirement. All three industries showed a tendency toward increased asset reinvestment during the period. Two industries (electronics and chemicals) showed decreases in the portion of cash from operations devoted to debt retirement.

Dividend payout showed consistency between years and between industries, approximating 20% of cash from operations over the three-year period for all three industries combined and showed stability from year to year. Debt coverage indicates the number of years required for cash from operations to repay all debt. Electronics companies showed a large increase in debt coverage (from 4.07 to 10.18) in 1988, due to declining payments on long-term debt and increased debt. Food and chemicals companies reflected more stable debt coverage, with three-year averages of 6.06 and 5.62, respectively.

For the depreciation–amortization impact ratio, the three industries showed different patterns over the period. The electronics and chemicals industries had relatively stable ratios, while food companies showed a large increase in 1988.

Reinvestment ratios suggested companies were reinvesting at a rate greater than they were depreciating assets. If companies are to maintain or increase their assets, over a several-year period reinvestment should exceed the depreciation–amortization impact ratio. Except for the food industry, reinvestments were, on average,

EXHIBIT 2
Breakdown of study respondents

Industry	Companies in industry	Companies in study	Percentage of companies covered by study
Electronics	45	37	82%
Food	48	22	46
Chemicals	51	40	78
Totals	144	99	69% (average)

sufficient to cover depreciation and amortization.

Cash flow to sales is a cash-flow-based measure of return on sales. Chemical companies showed the highest three-year average cash flow return, 12%, while electronics and foods showed 9% and 6%, respectively. These differences are significant between food and chemicals for all three years, between food and electronics in 1987 and between chemicals and electronics in 1988. Since food companies earn lower accounting returns on sales than do chemicals and electronics, these results are not surprising.

When compared to accrual income from continuing operations, the cash flow from operations ratio also is useful. It reflects the extent noncash transactions are involved in the operating income computation. Over several years, cash flow from continuing operations might be expected to approximate income from continuing operations. The operations index makes this comparison. For each industry, cash from operations exceeded income from continuing operations.

Cash flow return on assets compares cash from operations to total assets. For electronics companies, the return decreased by three points from 1986 to 1988. In part, this may be explained by the large increase in the reinvestment ratio. For food and chemical companies, the cash flow returns were stable. Comparing this ratio and the annuity return on assets may provide useful information.

EXHIBIT 3

Three-year averages by industry

	Three-year value (1986–88)		
	Electronics	**Food**	**Chemicals**
Sufficiency ratios			
Cash flow adequacy	.89	.85	.88
Long-term debt payment	.28	.63	.66
Dividend payout	.22	.18	.20
Reinvestment	.85	.73	.63
Debt coverage	6.50	6.06	5.62
Depreciation–amortization impact	.63	.63	.47
Efficiency ratios			
Cash flow to sales	.09	.06	.12
Operations index	1.41	1.92	1.96
Cash flow return on assets	.10	.11	.12

USEFUL RATIOS

This article proposes nine cash-flow-based ratios for relative performance evaluation. These sufficiency and efficiency ratios provide additional information (over traditional financial ratios) about the relationship between cash flow from operations and other important operating variables. Averages for those ratios for companies in the three largest industrial groups in the *Fortune* 500 were computed for 1986 to 1988.

Only the cash flow to sales ratio showed significant differences between industries for all three years. The only other difference between industries occurred in 1988 for the operations index and the cash flow return on assets. In those instances benchmarks or cutoff values may be advisable by industry. For all other ratios, the results suggest common interindustry averages might be appropriate. While this study has provided new information about the potential value of cash-flow-based ratios, there is unlimited potential for additional research.

The Dangers of Creative Accounting

DAVID SCHIFF

David Schiff is the editor of Emerson, Reid's "Insurance Observer," a quarterly newsletter that analyzes the insurance industry.

THERE'S AN OLD STORY ABOUT A PUBLIC COMPANY LOOKING to hire a new accounting firm. Candidates for the job were asked, "what does two plus two equal?" Auditor after auditor replied, "Four," and was turned away. Finally, the last candidate arrived and was asked the same question. After thinking a moment, he answered, "What number did you have in mind?"

He got the job.

This joke has more truth to it than many realize. Although investors usually focus on corporate earnings when evaluating common stocks, earnings aren't precise figures. They are approximations arrived at using generally accepted accounting principles, and they can vary greatly depending on the accounting methods chosen. Most investors, though, take a company's financial statements at face value, which can be a recipe for disaster.

Investors often go wrong by paying too much attention to one number, earnings per share, ignoring the way it was calculated and whether it was boosted by the stroke of an accountant's pen. Companies can paper over disappointingresults for a little while, but not forever; the bad news tends to come out in the end, and, when it does, it can cost investors plenty of money.

"Audited financial statements don't guarantee a company is healthy," says Loren Kellogg, a CPA whose "Financial Statement Alert" scrutinizes public companies' questionable accounting practices. "It's up to investors to determine what's really going on."

Kellogg, who works far from Wall Street in Friday Harbor, Washington, spotted troubles early at many companies, including **Cineplex Odeon, First Executive, Prime Motor Inns,** and **L.A. Gear.** He advises investors to examine carefully shareholder letters and management's discussions and analysis of financials, and to try to read between the lines.

To do that, Kellogg looks at four basic areas. First, he determines how much of a company's earnings are from operations, as opposed to onetime occurrences, such as gains from the sale of assets, securities transactions, or accounting changes, which shouldn't factor into future or current stock values based on earnings.

Next, he looks for any warning signs in the balance sheet, income statement, or cash flow statement. For example, are profit margins shrinking? Are inventories and receivables growing too fast? Is the company generating cash?

There are many ways that companies can goose their earnings—investors need to read between the lines.

Then he makes sure the company hasn't changed to more favorable accounting methods, or he checks whether it used methods different from the ones its competitors use. Although all companies use GAAP (generally accepted accounting principles), they still have considerable leeway when preparing their financials, and changes in accounting methods can provide a onetime boost to earnings. Finally, Kellogg looks for assets or liabilities on (or off) the balance sheet that might affect future earnings.

The presence of these warning signs doesn't necessarily mean a company is a bad investment, any more than the presence of a crack in a ship's hull means it's going to sink. However, investors should be aware of potential problems, just as a sailor would want to be aware of that crack. And, if there were several cracks. . . .

There are many ways companies can goose their earnings, but warning signs often appear in their financial statements. Here are some common ones.

HIDDEN PENSION LIABILITIES In the first quarter of 1990, **General Motors** boosted earnings by 10%, not by selling more cars, but by projecting that its pension fund would achieve an 11% annual return rather than a 10% annual return, and by assuming retirees' lifespans would be two

From *Worth*, March 1993, pp. 92-94. © 1993 by Capital Publishing Company. Reprinted by permission.

years shorter. These nonrecurring, "low quality" earnings are not the sort of thing on which one wants to put a multiple, but unless an investor had paid attention, he wouldn't have even been aware of them. As it turned out, these earnings were illusory. A year and a half later General Motors announced a charge of up to $1.9 billion because pension liabilities were likely to exceed the earlier, overly optimistic projections.

CAPITALIZING EXPENSES INSTEAD OF WRITING THEM OFF Considered by many to be the country's best-run airline, **Southwest Airlines** did this when it changed its accounting for airframe overhauls, the periodic maintenance and upgradings performed on planes. Southwest had previously subtracted the costs from earnings when the overhauls were performed, which is what other large airlines do. Beginning in 1992, perhaps because it was faced with rapidly increasing expenditures, Southwest amortized these costs over ten years, even though the money had been spent. This increased earnings by 13¢ per share—about 20%—in 1992. Going forward, it's impossible to compare the company's earnings with those of other airlines on an apples-to-apples basis—unless an analyst adjusts Southwest's figures, as Jack T. Ciesielski, publisher of Baltimore-based "The Analyst's Accounting Observer," has done.

Sierra On-Line, which makes computer software, switched to more liberal accounting standards in its fiscal year ending March 1991 and now capitalizes most of its software development rather than expensing it. Had Sierra continued using its former standards, its 1992 pretax operating earnings would have been a mere $524,000 rather than $5.375 mIllion. This is especially significant because at a recent stock price of $16¾, Sierra is sporting a $120 million market capitalization and selling for more than 25 times last year's earnings. Considering that sales and earnings are down this year, those capitalized software development costs will have to lead to a big increase in sales and earnings in the future just to support the current stock price at that multiple.

Sierra isn't necessarily breaking any rules, although it might be stretching them. An investor, however, can't simply look at the bottom line to get the answer. The question that must be asked is whether the accounting treatment chosen is truly reflective of economic reality.

WHEN RECEIVABLES OR INVENTORIES GROW FASTER THAN SALES Receivables rising faster than sales often presages an earnings problem. When business slows, management will sometimes load the pipeline (their distributors, for example) with products (shipped on credit) that can't easily be resold. This can be kept up for a while, but not indefinitely. In the meantime, receivables surge, which is a tip-off there might be a problem. Ultimately, the fact that demand is weak will be apparent, either by a decline in sales, a write-off of receivables, or both.

That's similar to what happened to **Community Psychiatric Centers,** a high-flying growth company with a long history of rising earnings. Receivables kept growing until they amounted to 123 days of sales, versus an industry average of about 70 days. This signaled a collection problem: Perhaps the company was delivering services to customers who couldn't pay. "Overpriced Stock Service" picked up on this and recommended a short sale at $28⅞ in July 1991. Community Psychiatric ultimately took a $37 million charge for uncollectible receivables. The stock is now at $9½.

NEGATIVE CASH FLOW To many analysts, cash flow is more important than earnings. After all, cash is what a company must use to pay its bills. Many companies repeatedly report "earnings" but don't generate any cash. Investors have to be wary of these situations.

McDonnell Douglas, the largest U.S. defense contractor, is a prime example of a company whose reported earnings are so misleading as to be meaningless, according to a shrewd analyst who's shorting the stock and prefers anonymity. Although McDonnell reported total net earnings of $33.87 per share between 1988 and 1991, cash flow was *negative* $2 billion. An outflow of funds of this magnitude is, in and of itself, sufficient to make

BIG BLUE

You Could Have Seen It Coming

In the mid '80s, IBM looked like the preeminent growth stock. Earnings rose from $9.04 a share in 1983 to an all-time high of $10.77 in 1984, a solid 19% gain. And the stock traded up in the stratosphere, as high as $175⅞.

Yet, the warning signs of Big Blue's flagging growth were visible way back then, and you didn't have to know a minicomputer from a mainframe to spot them; you had only to peruse the annual financials.

According to Thornton O'Glove, author of "Quality of Earnings," IBM's 1984 earnings were boosted by $1.23 per share by a lower tax rate, a oneshot increase in 1983 expenses, more aggressive pension plan assumptions, and a more liberal method of depreciating equipment. The "adjusted" earnings growth was a meager 5.5%—not the stuff growth stocks are made of. Too many investors, however, persisted in viewing IBM as it once was—even though the numbers indicated otherwise. This was a costly mistake. IBM stock recently hit a low, at $46½.

one suspicious, even if everything else appears to be okay, which in McDonnell's case, it doesn't.

The analyst also questions the company's credibility, noting that McDonnell failed to remove four MD-11s from its order books in the first quarter of 1992 even though Guiness Peat Aviation stated in its own IPO prospectus that it had cancelled these orders.

He also cites McDonnell's aggressive accounting compared with that of other defense companies. Although McDonnell and General Dynamics have the same potential liabilities on the A-12 program, General Dynamics has taken charges more than twice those of McDonnell. And McDonnell uses a 9% discount rate on its pension liabilities, compared with General Dynamics' 7½%. A higher discount rate means lower charges and higher reported earnings. (McDonnell's earnings also increased by $221 million of pension income between 1989 and 1991.)

On December 31, 1991, just in time to improve the appearance of its year-end balance sheet, McDonnell sold an MD-11 flight simulator and leased it back. Who bought the simulator? McDonnell Douglas Finance Corp., a wholly owned subsidiary. This transaction, and an $80 million loan from the finance company, had the effect of increasing McDonnell's cash on hand by $110 million. The offsetting liability showed up on the consolidated balance sheet as debt of the finance company.

McDonnell's stock has been volatile. After touching $26½ at the beginning of 1991, it rebounded to more than $80 by the end of the year, went back to $34, and is now in the $50s. This analyst thinks that taking into consideration the items previously mentioned, as well as the debt and poor prospects for the businesses, McDonnell stock is worthless.

WHOSE EARNINGS? Henley Group, a 1980s conglomerate run—not very successfully—by overcompensated asset-shuffler Mike Dingman, used a simple technique that gave the appearance of greater shareholder's equity and earnings than actually existed. By consolidating its 52%-owned subsidiary, **Henley Manufacturing,** on its September 30, 1988, interim financial statement, Henley Group recorded $22 million in additional income and added $113 million of extra net worth to its balance sheet. But Henley Group would never receive any of these reported earnings or equity because it had granted Henley Manufacturing an option to purchase its 52% stake for $115 million—a price far below market value, and $113 million less than its carrying value—and because it was a virtual certainty that Henley Manufacturing would exercise that option. Since the ultimate ownership of Henley Manufacturing was beyond Henley Group's control, it was misleading to take credit for assets and earnings that would never accrue value to Henley Group.

Although this number in question was relatively small given Henley Group's size, it was indicative of Henley's treatment of its shareholders.

CONSERVATIVE ISN'T NECESSARILY RIGHT Even seemingly conservative accounting practices can give the wrong impression. LIFO (last-in, first-out) is generally regarded as the preferred method of accounting for inventory in the income statement, but it can produce misleading results. For example, if layers of lower priced LIFO-costed inventory are "invaded" and sold at current prices, current earnings power is overstated. An example is **Culbro,** which produces White Owl cigars. It reported earnings per share of 72¢ in 1990 and $1.15 in 1991. But, as Jack Ciesielski points out, these earnings were due to the liquidation of lower-cost LIFO inventory. Without these liquidations, Culbro would have lost 3¢ and $1.30 in those years.

Although too-clever accounting doesn't necessarily mean that a company is a bad investment, it is something that should influence an investment decision. Remember, the numbers in a company's financials are often judgment calls. And just because a company's financials conform to GAAP, it doesn't mean the numbers are right. In his book *More Debits Than Credits,* accounting professor Abraham Briloff suggested that GAAP was something of a misnomer, and that a more appropriate acronym for accounting might be derived from Cleverly Rigged Accounting Ploys.

Maybe he was on to something.

New Accounting Standards and the SMALL BUSINESS

The focus is different for a small business.

By Daniel M. Ivancevich, Susan H. Ivancevich, Anthony Cocco, and Roger H. Hermanson

When the FASB issues accounting standards, very often the affected companies have some choices regarding implementation. SFAS No. 123, *Accounting for Stock-Based Compensation,* allows adopters to choose between financial statement recognition and footnote disclosure of a new method of accounting for the cost of employee stock options. SFAS No. 118, *Accounting by Creditors for Impairment of a Loan—Income Recognition and Disclosures,* was issued as an addendum to a prior standard for the express purpose of allowing creditors to select among adoption alternatives pertaining to the method of interest income recognition. SFAS No. 106, *Employers' Accounting for Postretirement Benefits Other than Pensions,* permitted firms to choose between two methods of recognizing the previously unreported accrued cost for benefits earned by employees up to the adoption date.

In Brief

What's More Important?

What's more important for the small business, the balance sheet or the income statement? Some FASB pronouncements permit alternative accounting choices that impact the balance sheet and income statement differently.

In exploring the answer to this question, the authors survey how lending officers assess the credit worthiness of two sets of companies. At issue is the adoption of SFAS No. 106 and whether the companies took the full one-time catch up charge or accrued for it ratably over some future period. The first group of financials that lending officers were asked to assess were those of companies that chose to record the one-time full provision and liability. The second group was of financial statements of companies that chose to defer and spread the liability.

The lending officers reported different conclusions depending on the approach the companies chose. And yet there is no real difference between the two groups of financials.

The objectives of financial reporting may differ for small versus large businesses, especially large public companies. Accordingly, when confronted with alternatives for adopting new accounting standards, the financial reporting strategy considerations may be different for smaller businesses.

Consideration Differences of Small and Large Businesses

For a larger public company faced with adoption choices regarding a new accounting standard, attention is normally directed toward the effects the standard will have on the income statement. The alternative selected often is the one with the most favorable or least unfavorable effect on earnings and earnings per share (EPS). Public companies attract investment capital from investors who often use earnings and EPS as a basis for their investment decisions.

For nonpublic companies, attracting fresh investment capital is often not an important consideration. A sole proprietor, partners in a partnership, or owners of a closely-held corporation have already committed capital to the enterprise, and the impact on earnings of various adoption choices is not likely to change their commitment. To obtain additional funds, attracting creditor capital is usually of primary importance for these smaller nonpublic companies. A sufficiently large line of credit is the lifeblood of many small businesses. Creditors often require periodic submissions of audited financial statements prepared in accordance with generally accepted accounting principles (GAAP). This demand by creditors for audits is the primary reason that new GAAP accounting standards must be adopted by small businesses.

When evaluating a company that has applied for a business loan or line of credit, a creditor will typically focus on the company's ability to meet its debt obligations. Much of the key information used by creditors to evaluate a company's ability to meet its debt obligations, such as leverage and liquidity ratios, are based on balance sheet accounts. Accordingly, it could be argued that the potential balance sheet impact of the standard alternatives should be more heavily considered by small businesses than the potential income statement impact.

Do the choices made by small businesses regarding the accounting standard alternatives selected have economic consequences for the decisions of creditors and potential creditors? Specifically, if one alternative has a more favorable income statement impact, and a second alternative

Reprinted with permission from *The CPA Journal,* July 1997, pp. 22-25.

TABLE 1
MEAN RISK AND LOAN AMOUNTS BY GROUP

Treatment Group	Number of Observations	Mean Risk	Mean Loan Amount* (In Thousands)
One-time charge (Group IR)	24	2.6538	168.214
Amortization (Group DEFER)	31	2.5371	286.109

* Significant difference between treatments at the 0.05 level

TABLE 2
NUMBERS OF RESPONDENTS USING BALANCE SHEET RATIOS AND EARNINGS

Elements	Group IR*	Group DEFER*
Debt-to-equity	14 (58.33%**)	21 (67.74%**)
Current ratio	16 (66.67%)	19 (61.29%)
Earnings	4 (16.67%)	4 (12.90%)
Number of observations	24	31

* Numbers in this column represent the number of respondents that cited the element.

** Percentage of respondents citing the element (number of respondents citing the element/number of observations).

has a more favorable balance sheet impact, will a small business be better served by selecting the first or second alternative if its main goal is to obtain credit capital? To explore this question, we examined the effect that adoption alternatives of a particular accounting standard had on the decisions of loan officers. SFAS No. 106, *Employers' Accounting for Postretirement Benefits Other than Pensions,* was used as the basis for this inquiry.

The Adoption Alternatives Available Under SFAS No. 106

SFAS No. 106 requires companies to use accrual accounting and expense the cost of these benefits as they are earned by employees. SFAS No. 106 granted firms a choice of adoption alternatives regarding how to account for the previously unreported accrued cost for benefits earned by employees up to the adoption date. This one-time accrual was referred to as the transition obligation. Companies were required to choose between two adoption alternatives:

One-time charge: Recognize the entire amount of the liability on the balance sheet in the adoption year, with an offsetting charge to net income as a cumulative effect of a change in accounting principle.

Deferred recognition: Amortize the transition obligation to compensation expense over future periods, and record a portion of the liability each year over the same time period.

The new recognition of this liability results in a decrease in equity and increase in debt.

Financial Statement Considerations For Adopting SFAS No. 106

Many large public companies elected to take the one-time charge against net income and book the entire liability in the year of adoption. For instance, General Motors recorded a $20.72 billion expense of this item in 1992. As a result, its net worth declined by nearly 80%. The motivating factor for this financial reporting decision was to temper the income statement effect. Although the one-time charge dramatically lowered EPS, the classification of this decrease as a cumulative effect of a change in accounting principle was appealing to many companies. First, operating income was not affected. Further, this classification made the charge "standout" as a one-time-only event. The negative impact on EPS was mitigated by the disclosure of the different components of the EPS in the financial statements and because investment analysts tend to discount such one-time charges in projecting future income and determining firm value.

Large public companies realized that deferred recognition would result in a drag against earnings well into the future. Even worse, this earnings decrease would be buried in compensation expense. Thus, not only net income, but the important subtotal, operating income, would be lowered each year by the amortization expense. The advantages provided by the one-time charge—coupled with the disadvantages of deferring the charge—spurred many large, public companies to select immediate recognition.

What about small, nonpublic companies? There appears to be little data available regarding the percentage of small companies that selected the one-time charge versus those that chose to defer recognition. Is it possible that small, nonpublic companies may have been better off by selecting deferred recognition? Certainly, that question is impossible to answer without knowing all of the facts and circumstances unique to each company. It is possible, however, to make some general observations. As discussed previously, the balance sheet impact of a new accounting standard, in all likelihood, is more important than the income statement impact for smaller companies seeking to obtain creditor capital.

To test this theory, we conducted a survey to explore the differential impact of the two adoption alternatives available under SFAS No. 106 on the decisions of creditors. The description and the results of the survey are discussed in the next section.

Description of the Survey

We sent questionnaire packets to two groups of loan officers. Loan officers were selected randomly from the *Thompson Bank Directory* (Thompson Financial Services, Skokie, IL, 1993). Each packet contained a set of financial statements for a small, fictitious plastics manufacturer and a two-page questionnaire. The financial statements consisted of comparative balance sheets, income statements, and notes to the financial statements.

The financial statements mailed to each group were identical, except for the manner in which the transition obligation was handled. One group of loan officers received financial statements that reflected immediate recognition (Group IR); the other group received financial statements that reflected amortization over 20 years (Group DEFER). The financial statements contained footnote disclosures on: 1) inventories; 2) property, plant, and equipment; 3) accrued and other current liabilities; and 4) noncurrent liabilities. The footnotes were identical for both groups, except for noncurrent liabilities. The only distinction in this footnote pertained to the account titled "deferred compensation," which differed in the way the transition obligation was handled.

Each questionnaire asked the respondent to examine the company's financial statements, and to assess the riskiness of the company and to determine the loan amount that he or she would be willing to lend the company. The exact questions asked were as follows:

Question 1 (Q-Risk): Based on your review of the information provided, what is your assessment of the riskiness of XYZ company. Please rate your response on a scale of one to five, where one represents very low lending risk and five represents very high lending risk.

Question 2 (Q-Loan): Assume XYZ company has unpledged assets to meet your collateral needs and there are no restrictions on the amount you may loan or the availability of bank funds to loan, what amount would you loan XYZ company?

No special attention was given to the handling of the transition obligation, and neither group was aware of the existence of the other group. We did not want to bias the respondents by making them aware of the purposes of the survey.

Results of Survey

We received 27 responses, of which 24 were usable for Group IR, and 35 responses, of which 31 were usable for Group DEFER. The mean responses to the questions Q-Risk and Q-Loan are presented in *Table 1.* The results of Table 1 show that Group IR, which received financial statements based on immediate recognition, perceived the company to be a higher lending risk (although not significantly higher) than Group DEFER. Further, they would make the Group IR company eligible to borrow a significantly lesser amount than the Group DEFER company.

Was it primarily the difference in the balance sheets (debt-to-equity) analyzed by loan officers for Group IR and Group DEFER, or was it the difference in the income statements (EPS) presented for the two groups that propelled these results? The answer to this question is critical, because it may provide small businesses with some insight as to how they should focus their financial reporting strategies to obtain credit capital when adopting new accounting standards.

We also collected data pertaining to which components of the financial statements were employed by loan officers in making their loan decisions. The loan officers were requested to list any components of the financial statements, ratios, and other information used to answer Q-Risk and Q-Loan. These results are presented in *Table 2.*

Although various elements were noted by the respondents, we were primarily interested in what percentage of loan officers used the basic balance sheet ratios that measure leverage and liquidity and how many respondents focused on income statement elements/ratios such as earnings and EPS. As displayed in Table 2, many more respondents in both categories listed debt-to-equity (leverage) and the current ratio (liquidity), as opposed to earnings, as elements that were used in the decision making process regarding Q-Risk and Q-Loan.

It is interesting that these differences were discovered at all, since SFAS No. 106 merely recognized a previously unrecorded existing liability and did not establish a new liability. The failure to detect the content of SFAS No. 106's disclosures causes negative economic consequences for small companies choosing the one-time charge.

Look to Balance Sheet Effect

When alternatives are available regarding the adoption of a new accounting standard, it is of the utmost importance that a financial reporting strategy be adopted for the small business that best suits the needs of the business. For many small businesses, the relevant financial statement users are creditors and potential creditors, and these "users" tend to focus more heavily on a company's ability to meet its debt obligations than on earnings because of the short-term nature of money loans. This information may be found on the balance sheet and the results of this study support this assertion. Thus, when assessing the implementation alternatives of new accounting standards available, small business financial reporting strategy may need to assign more importance to the balance sheet impact of the various alternatives.

Daniel M. Ivancevich, PhD, *and* ***Anthony Cocco, PhD, CPA,*** *are assistant professors of accounting, and* ***Susan H. Ivancevich, PhD, CPA,*** *an assistant professor of hospitality finance and accounting, all at the Universityof Nevada, Las Vegas.* ***Roger H. Hermanson, PhD, CPA,*** *is regents professor of accounting and Ernst & Young JW Holloway Memorial Professor, Georgia State University, Atlanta.*

Sales are booming—so why are profits sagging?

Surviving Explosive Growth

BY CHRIS MALBURG

The company president looks up wearily from his cluttered desk and says to the chief financial officer (CFO), "I don't get it. Sales are booming. Each year we see gains of 25% to 35%. We're three years old and already we're the darling of our industry. So—how come we're not making more profit?"

Such a conversation, or one very much like it, is not that unusual at fast-growth companies. Most entrepreneurs know that success is elusive in the early years, but few realize the danger when revenues soar suddenly. This article examines the symptoms of dangerous corporate growth and offers remedies that accountants can prescribe to their clients or employers.

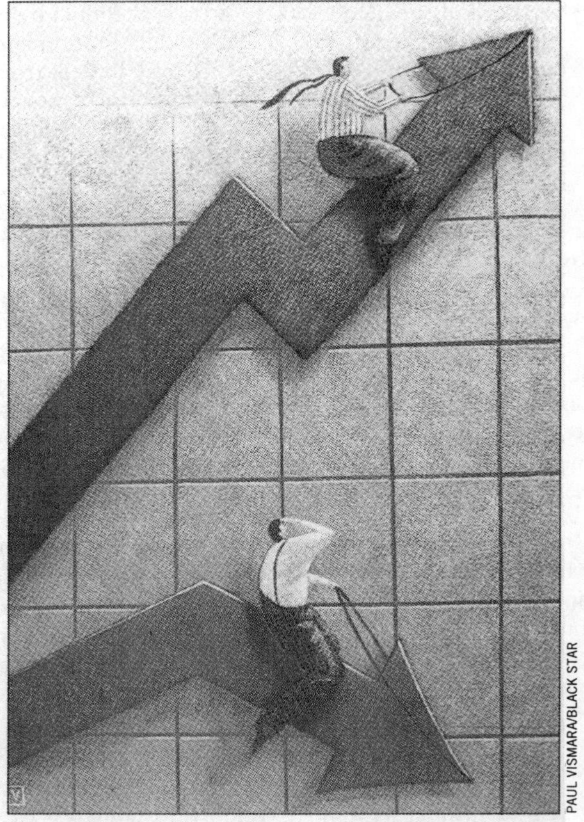

PAUL VISMARA/BLACK STAR

ORGANIZATION STRUCTURE

Companies undergoing explosive growth often have flat organizational structures. For example, it's not uncommon for the company president to have direct control over 10 or even 20 employees. Everyone reports directly to the company head—sales, marketing, purchasing, finance and accounting, warehouse, manufacturing, shipping, receiving, human resources. As a result, the president becomes a major decision bottleneck.

Procedures that worked well when annual sales were $10 million break down when sales suddenly explode tenfold. Crucial decisions stagnate in endless bottlenecks waiting for one overloaded manager with authority to focus and act.

A case in point: The CFO of one fast-growing company allowed accumulated compensating bank balances to balloon to $3 million more than the agreed minimum. It wasn't because the CFO was incompetent or neglectful; he simply was overloaded and had failed to delegate this responsibility.

The first step to take to remedy the problem is to reorganize management into a conventional pyramid—one in which management responsibilities are delegated to second- and possibly third-tier managers. That single step gives the president time to think, plan, oversee and advise—which is what the top manager should be doing. On paper, the solution looks simple, but getting people to buy into it can be difficult.

If it's so good for the business, why do so many people resist such a change? The first obstacle is the boss. He built the company from scratch. The management structure during that successful period was simple: everyone reported to him. The question now is: Can he get his ego out of the way and recognize that, although he may have been the reason for the business's initial success, now he's overcommitted and has become the cause of chaos? If he can't, such a company—even if sales continue to soar—may collapse into bankruptcy.

If a company can get past that initial obstacle, it's ready to tackle the second one: resistance from middle management. In a fast-growth company with one line of reporting, that may include nearly everyone in the company.

From *Journal of Accountancy*, December 1997, pp. 67-72.

When the sales staff is overworked and undermotivated, the evidence can be found in the customer complaint file—if anyone has the time to compile one.

Most managers will resist suddenly reporting to a second- or third-level manager, viewing withdrawal of their once free access to the president as a demotion. Overcoming their objections will take time and patience. Top management must understand that their stated objections may camouflage their real concern—which is loss of direct access to the boss.

STAFF QUALIFICATIONS

People don't always grow at the same pace or in the same direction that a business grows. Too often loyal managers who started with the company are given duties beyond their skills and experience in the hope that they will grow into their new jobs. But if they are overworked, they may not have the time or energy to learn new skills. To close this gap, management must more rigorously evaluate key players, assessing their professional credentials and experience. If employees are found to lack the skills needed to function in new jobs, management must either offer training programs to bring them up to speed or move them out.

In addition, it's important that every critical job has a backup person. Management should use these questions to determine the effectiveness of a backup program:

- How often do the backup people fill in to keep in practice and on top of changes in the job procedures?
- To what extent are they cross-trained?
- Who does the fill-in's job when the backup person is called to duty?

FINANCE AND ACCOUNTING

One sign a company is heading for trouble: When the finance department provides management with loads of raw data rather than information that's been interpreted so it's useful to top management. Without that, busy managers are forced to invest precious time figuring out what the raw data mean.

A case in point: The finance department issues a daily profit margin report to manufacturing and sales executives listing all 50 company products. Few, if any, of the managers have the time to translate the data into useful information.

An example of a better report—one that truly delivers useful information and probably takes no longer to provide—is an exception report that cites only those items (if any) that have fallen below established profit margin minimums.

Here are some tip-offs that the finance department is not properly doing its duty:

- Management letters from the auditors are ignored.
- Financial statements and management reports are inaccurate, not timely or not done at all.
- Bank accounts are not reconciled in a timely way.
- Product profit margins are estimates.

One way to help manage explosive growth is to install a balanced performance measurement system. (For more on this subject, see "A Smarter Way to Run a Business," JofA, Jan.97, page 48.) This is simply a scorecard that employs three steps:

1. Identify the key measurements needed to monitor the enterprise's overall business (production output, sales, inventory turnover, raw material costs).

2. Develop a process for routinely comparing key process measures (such as production output) and results measures (such as return on investment) against the previously established benchmarks.

3. Set up a routine decision-making process for acting on information produced by the performance measurement system to make any necessary midcourse corrections of strategy.

EXECUTIVE SUMMARY

- MOST ENTREPRENEURS KNOW that success is elusive in the early years, but few realize how dangerous it is when success comes suddenly and explosively.
- THE UNDERLYING PROBLEM for such companies is its organizational structures: Everybody reports to the boss. The solution: Create a competent middle management level.
- ONE SIGN OF TROUBLE is a finance department that provides management with loads of raw data rather than useful information. An example of a better solution: an exception report showing only the items (if any) falling below established profit margin minimums.
- FAST-GROWING COMPANIES are aggressive by nature. But often they forget excessively low bad debt can be as troublesome as bad debt that's too high. Unnecessarily restrictive credit policies leave money on the table that could enhance overall profit even after allowance for a slightly increased bad-debt expense.
- FEW THINGS EAT UP PRECIOUS working capital faster than slow-moving inventory. Determining whether inventory turns over sufficiently to maximize the investment in working capital can be done. Do this by relating inventory turns to the turnover of accounts payable and accounts receivable.

CHRIS MALBURG, CPA, of Palos Verdes Estates, California, consults for organizations undergoing explosive growth. His e-mail address is Crmalburg@aol.com.

Often companies forget that bad-debt totals that are too low can be as troublesome as too much bad debt.

Such a scorecard system places the accounting and management reporting departments where they belong—smack in the middle of the information flow needed to guide the company.

SALES SYMPTOMS TO MONITOR

When the sales staff is overworked and undermotivated, the evidence can be found in the customer complaint file—if anyone has the time to compile one.

The basic problems: Do salespeople share their company's good fortunes—that is, is their compensation linked to their results? Equally important, does the sales staff get guidance on which products and services are more profitable to the company than others? In many fast-growing businesses, the answer to both questions is no. One solution: Management should set higher commission rates for more profitable products to reflect the strategy for meeting profit margin targets.

Customer credit is another area that explosive growth companies tend to ignore. Such businesses, by their nature, are aggressive. But often companies forget that bad-debt totals that are too low can be as troublesome as too much bad debt. Unnecessarily restrictive credit policies in effect leave money on the table that could enhance overall profit even after allowance for a slightly increased bad-debt expense.

Next, management must determine who makes credit decisions. Sometimes the same people who once made $2,500 credit decisions now make $250,000 decisions—and often they use the same criteria and methods. Questions to ask:

- Is there a credit policy and a formal credit review committee?
- Is there a written credit authority hierarchy to establish clearly defined credit-granting authority limits for specific individuals?
- Does the company make credit decisions on the fly? Such informal decisions often circumvent established policy because there is simply no time.
- Are the wrong people (such as commissioned sales staff) a part of the credit-granting decision? The head of sales should be a nonvoting member of the credit policy committee. While the committee needs this person's market savvy, recognize that sales people have a bias for giving high credit as an inducement to sales.

When Everyone Reports to One Boss, These Problems Surface

Problems that typically occur when a company has a flat organizational reporting structure:

➤ Unrelated duties are delegated to inappropriate departments or individuals. This often occurs when one person or a department fails at the job so the task is transferred to someone who can do it—regardless of appropriateness.

➤ Because everyone is so rushed keeping up with the expansion, internal controls are compromised—leading to errors and inviting fraud.

➤ With the staff juggling too much, workloads gets unbalanced, often resulting in excessive, and expensive, overtime or worse: more errors and lapses in judgment.

INVENTORY CONTROL

Few things eat up precious working capital faster than slow-moving inventory. Management must determine the number of inventory turns; are the cycles sufficient to maximize investment in working capital? This should be handled by relating inventory turns to the turnover of accounts payable and accounts receivable. Many explosive growth companies are cash poor so they must turn their receivables faster than their payables. A well-managed fast-growth company first sells inventory and then collects from customers before actually paying suppliers.

Returned merchandise is another opportunity to grow without financial pain. Returned merchandise requires quick shipment back to the manufacturer for debit to accounts payable.

Does a real-time computer link exist between the perpetual inventory system and the order-entry system? Often fast-growing businesses fail to establish this link. If the inventory and the sales order listings are not equal (and the difference is not due to late-entered sales), there's a problem. Without this vital link, the sales staff cannot know what is available to sell.

Management also needs to assess the adequacy of the inventory back-order system. Fast-growth companies usually experience an increase in back-ordered merchandise. An effective automated order system ensures that inventory is truly out of stock. This prevents needless waste of working capital by ordering items already on hand or in transit from suppliers.

Characteristics to look for when assessing the adequacy of the back-order system:

- Automatically notifies buyers of the need to reorder specific items. Some systems even cut purchase orders automatically.
- Accurately tracks order status and arrival times.
- Allocates inventory to the proper customer orders.
- Interfaces with inventory and sales-order-entry systems. This is necessary to track back-order status and tell which sales orders were indeed back-ordered.

WAREHOUSE OPERATIONS

Managers should walk through the warehouse. The stresses and strains of explosive growth usually are obvious: racks groaning under the weight of overstocked merchandise;

Organizations undergoing explosive growth may have already outgrown their present banks' capabilities—and that may actually hinder operations.

stockpiles of similar items scattered throughout the warehouse; lack of a specific location for processing returned merchandise.

Often the warehouse is so busy that the personnel simply don't have time for such housekeeping. However, those are the things that allow a warehouse to contribute to overall profit.

The high-tech systems for modern warehouses sometimes get ignored as managers who started with the enterprise when it was small now lack the time to keep up with innovations. Some modern enhancements that might help include

- Automated inventory-tracking systems that control cycle counts and tell workers where specific items are stored.
- Barcode scanners with remote radio frequency computer uplinks for use on the warehouse floor that tell stock pickers the location of specific items.
- Picking and put-away scheduling systems that optimize warehouse travel routing and improve productivity.

Reviewing the labor expense for the warehouse, including overtime costs, is a must. Explosive growth companies tend to automatically throw more people at problems because they think they can afford it. Determining whether the warehouse runs the proper number of shifts, identifying peak staff demand and comparing that with the number of people actually on the warehouse floor at that time are key steps. Often simply changing the timing of a shift or overlapping shifts during periods of peak demand offers a more cost-effective solution than additional overtime.

Sometimes companies are just too busy to look at shipping details. Freight discount is often one area that suffers in this way. Many fast-growth companies fail to realize that, with their sudden clout, they can negotiate deeply discounted freight rates. Often they blindly pass on the entire discount to their customers. That's a mistake for two reasons:

- Customers may not understand or appreciate this gesture, so there is no marketing advantage in passing along the discount.
- The company is squeezing its own profit margin.

Keeping Your Company Vision at 20/20

During periods of rapid growth, overworked executives often overlook the company's long-term vision. Instead, they merely react to daily crises. It's critical that management review specific performance statistics at least monthly. Such a review should include

- Complete financial statements.
- Cash and working capital sufficiency.
- Actual results compared with budget.
- Profit margins by product.
- Sales statistics compared with targets.
- Personnel and staffing needs.
- Credit limits.
- Purchase trends.
- Product availability.

What to Ask the Bank

Ask a bank these questions to find out whether it really serves the needs of a fast-growing business. Does the bank

- Have sufficient capital to accommodate suddenly increased financing requirements?
- Offer automated treasury workstations that reduce the workload of the cash manager?
- Have automated cash transfers, electronic data interface and electronic funds transfer services?
- Provide a choice of receiving an invoice and paying directly for services or does it insist on payment through earned credit on compensating balances through account analysis?
- Have lock boxes with appropriate and frequent pick-up times?

PURCHASING KNOW-HOW

Companies caught up in extremely competitive markets often make their profits on the purchasing side. But during periods of rapid expansion, management's attention sometimes focuses exclusively on doing the deal and getting the best price. Maintaining profit margins takes a back seat. Top managers should see if this is not the case by looking at the overall inventory purchasing discipline to find out whether

- Someone studies demand cycles to make sure sufficient (but not excessive) inventories are in stock at the right time.
- The purchasing discipline includes a computation to determine the most economic order quantities.

Explosive growth companies are afraid of running out of stock and not making that next sale. Some take extraordinary measures to ensure that does not happen. Consequently, safety stock balloons.

More evidence of purchasing problems is panic buying—buying that circumvents normal purchasing procedures or requires extraordinary measures to complete. Panic buying usually indicates that purchasing systems may not have caught up with suddenly exploding product demand. The result is frenzied buying that

- Fails to take advantage of quantity discounts.

■ Increases freight delivery costs when buyers too often say, "We must have it—get it here whatever way is fastest."

It's dangerous for a company to have just one vendor for critical supplies: If something happens to that vendor, the company could be in deep trouble. But it also takes time to develop backup vendors. Since purchasing agents at fast-growth companies are under extreme pressure to negotiate deals, track purchase orders and manage the back-order system, they rarely have the time to qualify new vendors. Nevertheless, this is a very important task.

WORKING CAPITAL MANAGEMENT

The most obvious symptom of corporate treasury problems is an excessive number of bank accounts. Dormant accounts may contain significant balances the business could use elsewhere. Further, they require precious time to reconcile each month, so it makes sense to consolidate the accounts.

When looking at the yields on short-term investment of excess cash, it's not uncommon to find funds invested at below-market rates or large balances constantly stuck in overnight instruments (such as repurchase agreements). Such funds can be applied more profitably—for example, by repaying part of the outstanding line of credit.

Also, management should take a close look at the bank the company uses. Organizations undergoing explosive growth may have already outgrown their present banks' capabilities—and that may actually hinder operations. For the questions to ask the bank to see whether it meets company needs, see the side bar, "What to Ask the Bank."

Internal cash controls take precious time to maintain. When there is already too much to do, busy staffers sometimes ignore control procedures. Management must watch for compliance with cash control policies such as

■ Reviewing and signing off on bank account reconciliations.

■ Independent approval of short-term investments.

■ Independent reconciliation of brokerage statements.

■ Sending brokerage confirmations of investments directly to an independent person within the company.

Watch for the surprise arrival of large cash receipts or disbursement demands. Do this by comparing the cash flow forecast (every growing company should have one) against actual cash inflow and disbursements for several time periods. Sooner or later a cash flow surprise will force the company to take out an emergency loan at inflated rates. Or it can put a company in a position where cash received is underemployed. The result is the yield on liquid assets is not maximized. All are costly and wasteful.

COMPUTER RESOURCES

One sure sign that a company's needs have outstripped its computer resources is the proliferation of standalone systems—those running independently of the corporate network. Explosive growth companies tend to stretch their computer resources, and system degradation or outright crashes are common.

What to do?

Begin by assessing the adequacy of routine data backup and recovery procedures. Although most companies back up data, during time crunches they may neglect testing those routines by staging an actual recovery using the backed-up data to see whether the procedure really works.

The software versions the company uses—which must be examined—should be recent, if not the latest, versions. Fast-growth companies sometimes are too busy to stay current with new updates. Instead, some try patching customized solutions into canned packages as a short-term fix. However, such fixes often create problems because the more extensive this customization, the more difficult it is to convert to the next generation of software.

MANAGEMENT DECISIONS

Explosive-growth companies can be so single-minded about growth that they frequently take on additional business simply because it's there—failing to consider the impact on profit margins, working capital and cash requirements. Growth simply for its own sake—rather than profit—becomes obsessive.

Another clue that swift growth has overburdened management is uncharacteristic hesitation to make decisions—often referred to as *analysis paralysis.* The philosophy may seem to be *better the devil we know than one we don't.* While foot-dragging is never good even under normal circumstances, during explosive growth, it can be fatal.

Recognizing the symptoms associated with rapid growth and knowing what to do about them make accounting professionals all the more valuable to their clients and employers. Managers not overwhelmed by one urgent crisis after another can effectively help calm the rocky course of expansion.

The FASB introduces new rules for comprehensive income.

How Companies Report Income

BY RANDALL W. LUECKE AND DAVID T. MEETING

The pendulum of income reporting is again changing direction. At different times over the years, businesses have used two major income reporting concepts. Under the *current operating performance concept,* extraordinary and nonrecurring gains and losses are excluded from income; because those gains and losses are taken directly to equity and bypass the income statement, this is sometimes called the "dirty surplus" method. Under the *all-inclusive (comprehensive) concept,* all items, including extraordinary and nonrecurring gains and losses, go to the income statement; the result is a "clean surplus," since all gains and losses are reported in the income statement.

The AICPA Accounting Principles Board moved toward the all-inclusive income concept in 1966 when it issued Opinion no. 9, *Reporting the Results of Operations,* and later reaffirmed this concept in Opinions nos. 20, *Accounting Changes, and 30, Reporting the Results of Operations—Reporting the Effects of Disposal of a Segment of a Business, and Extraordinary, Unusual and Infrequently Occurring Events and Transactions.* The FASB followed the all-inclusive concept, except when changes in certain assets and liabilities were not reported in the income statement but, rather, were included as a separate component of equity. Pronounce-

EXECUTIVE SUMMARY

■ WITH ITS ISSUANCE OF STATEMENT NO. 130, Reporting Comprehensive Income, the FASB is moving closer to the all-inclusive method of income determination. The statement is effective for fiscal years beginning after December 15, 1997.

■ AN ENTERPRISE REPORTS comprehensive income—nonowner changes in equity—to reflect all of the changes in its equity resulting from recognized transactions and other economic events in a period. Statement no. 130 requires companies to report in a financial statement for the period in which they are recognized all items meeting the definition of components of comprehensive income.

■ STATEMENT NO. 130 DIVIDES comprehensive income into net income and other comprehensive income, which includes foreign currency items, unrealized holding gains and losses on marketable securities defined as available-for-sale and additional minimum pension liability adjustments. The statement does not address the recognition or measurement of comprehensive income but, rather, establishes a framework that can be refined later.

■ COMPANIES HAVE THREE WAYS TO display comprehensive income, including the one- and two-statement approaches and displaying it in the statement of changes in equity. The FASB discourages use of the third method because it hides comprehensive income in the middle of the financial statement.

■ AS THEY UNDERTAKE IMPLEMENTATION of Statement no. 130, companies must decide what format they will use in reporting comprehensive income. They also must decide whether to show components of comprehensive income net of reclassification adjustments and whether to show the components on a before- or aftertax basis.

RANDALL W. LUECKE, CPA, CMA is vice-president–administration and treasurer of International Approval Services, Cleveland. IAS is a division of the Canadian Standards Association. DAVID T. MEETING, CPA, DBA, is associate professor of accounting at Cleveland State University.

With the issuance of *Reporting Comprehensive Income,* the FASB has moved closer to the all-inclusive income determination method.

ments with such exceptions are FASB Statements nos. 52, *Foreign Currency Translations,* 80, *Accounting for Futures Contracts,* 87, *Employers' Accounting for Pensions,* and 115, *Accounting for Certain Investments in Debt and Equity Securities.*

Starting with Statement no. 12, *Accounting for Certain Marketable Securities,* in 1975, the FASB used a hybrid of the operating performance and the all-inclusive concepts. More recently, in Statement no. 130, *Reporting Comprehensive Income,* it moved closer to the all-inclusive income determination method. This article explains this and other important aspects of Statement no. 130 and offers implementation guidance companies can use as they begin to comply with the statement.

WHAT IS COMPREHENSIVE INCOME?

In Concepts Statement no. 5, *Recognition and Measurement in Financial Statements of Business Enterprises,* the FASB said a full set of financial statements for a period should show

1. Financial position at the end of the period.
2. Earnings (net income).
3. Comprehensive income (total nonowner changes in equity).
4. Cash flows during the period.
5. Investments by and distributions to owners during the period.

FASB Concepts Statement no. 6, *Elements of Financial Statements,* went on to define comprehensive income as the change during a period in an enterprise's equity from transactions and other events and circumstances from nonowner sources, including all changes in equity except those resulting from investments by owners and distributions to owners. Although the FASB generally has followed the all-inclusive income concept, it occasionally has made specific exceptions by requiring that companies not report certain changes in assets and liabilities in a statement reporting results of operations but, instead, include them in balances within a separate component of equity in a statement of financial position. These exceptions are summarized in exhibit 1.

...AND WHY REPORT IT?

A business reports comprehensive income to reflect all changes in its equity that result from recognized transactions and other economic events of the period—other than transactions with owners in their capacity as owners. Historically, companies displayed some of these changes in a statement that reported the results of operations, while other changes were included directly in balances within a separate component of equity in a statement of financial position.

Exhibit 1: Items Included in Other Comprehensive Income

Here is a listing of accounting standards that—prior to Statement no. 130—required certain items to bypass a statement of income and to be reported in a balance within a separate component of equity in a statement of financial position.

Item	Citation
Foreign currency translation adjustments.	Statement no. 52, paragraph 13.
Gains and losses on foreign currency transactions that are designated as, and are effective as, economic hedges of a net investment in a foreign entity, commencing as of the designation date.	Statement no. 52, paragraph 20(a).
Gains and losses on intercompany foreign currency transactions that are of a long-term investment nature when entities to the transactions are consolidated, combined or accounted for by the equity method in the reporting enterprise's financial statements.	Statement no. 52, paragraph 20(b).
A change in the market value of a futures contract that qualifies as a hedge of an asset reported at fair value under Statement no. 115.	Statement no. 80, paragraph 5.
A net loss recognized pursuant to Statement no. 87 as an additional pension liability not yet recognized as net periodic pension cost.	Statement no. 87, paragraph 37.
Unrealized holding gains and losses on available-for-sale securities.	Statement no. 115, paragraph 13.
Unrealized holding gains and losses that result from a debt security being transferred into the available-for-sale category from the held-to-maturity category.	Statement no. 115, paragraph 15(c).
Subsequent decreases or increases in the fair value of available-for-sale securities previously written down as impaired.	Statement no. 115, paragraph 16.

Statement no. 130 does not address the recognition or measurement of comprehensive income. These will be addressed in future pronouncements.

Exhibit 2: ABC Co.–Available-for-Sale Securities

Available-for-Sale Portfolio	1/1/9X	3/31/9X	6/30/9X	9/30/9X	12/31/9X
Stock A 100 @ $10	$1,000	$1,080	$1,300	$1,400	
Other portfolio stocks	$15,000	$15,500	$16,300	$16,700	$17,400
Total portfolio	$16,000	$16,580	$17,600	$18,100	$17,400
Gain per quarter (included in comprehensive income):					
Stock A		$ 80	$ 220	$100	
Other stocks		500	800	400	$700
Total unrealized gain		$580	$1,020	$500	$700
Cumulative unrealized gain		$580	$1,600	$2,100	$2,800
Reclassification to realized gain (included in net income)					$(400)
Net unrealized gains for the year, after reclassification adjustments, before tax					$2,400

Sale of Stock A		
	Sale price @ 10/1/9X	$1,400
	Cost/basis	1,000
	Realized gain	400
	Tax @ 25%	100
	Aftertax gain	$ 300

Statement no. 130 requires that all items meeting the definition of components of comprehensive income be reported in a financial statement for the period in which they are recognized. Thus, Statement no. 130 amends the accounting standards listed in exhibit 1 to require that changes in the balances of items that—under those statements—had been reported directly in a separate component of equity in a statement of financial position now be reported in a financial statement and displayed as prominently as other financial statements. Items that are required by accounting standards to be reported as direct adjustments to paid-in capital, retained earnings or other nonincome equity accounts are not to be included as components of comprehensive income.

THE VIEW FROM FASB 130

As defined in Statement no. 130, comprehensive income is the same as that in Concepts Statement no. 6 except Statement no. 130 divides it into net income and other comprehensive income, where net income is calculated the same as in the past and other comprehensive income includes (1) foreign currency items, (2) unrealized holding gains and losses on marketable securities defined as available-for-sale in Statement no. 115 and (3) additional minimum pension liability adjustments under Statement no. 87. In the past, companies did not include these other comprehensive income items in the income statement. Instead, the items were taken directly to a separate component of equity. Statement no. 130 does not affect the *measurement* of the three items included in other comprehensive income; it affects only *where* the information is presented.

Statement no. 130 does not address the *recognition* or *measurement* of comprehensive income; future pronouncements will address these issues. Rather, the FASB took several initial steps toward implementing a framework that establishes the first elements of comprehensive income, leaving further refinements for later.

Every business that provides a full set of financial statements reporting financial position, results of operations and cash flows must follow Statement no. 130. However, it does not apply to a company that has no items of other comprehensive income, nor does it apply to not-for-profit organizations. Statement no. 130 is effective for fiscal years beginning after December 15, 1997. Since total comprehensive income must be reported on interim financial statements, calendar-year corporations had to start reporting comprehensive income in the first-quarter statements of 1998. Statement no. 130 does not require companies to disclose comprehensive income in a specific place in the interim financial statements, nor does it require that they report the separate components of other comprehensive income.

WHAT TO INCLUDE AND WHERE

Items included in net income are displayed in various classifications, including income from continuing operations, discontinued operations, extraordinary items and cumulative effects of changes in accounting principle. Statement no. 130 does not alter those classifications or other requirements for reporting results from operations.

Since net income is a component of comprehensive income, items included in both must be adjusted to avoid double counting. For example, companies would have to adjust gains on investment securities classified as available-for-sale that were realized and included in net income for the period that also were included in other comprehensive income as unrealized holding gains in earlier periods or the present period. Statement no. 130 refers to these as reclassifcation adjustments.

Consider, for example, ABC Co. In the year it adopted Statement no. 130, it had activities relating to marketable securities defined as available-for-sale under Statement no. 115. Information on the company's portfolio—stock A in particular—is summarized in exhibit 2. At January 1, 199X, the company's portfolio consisted of 100 shares of stock A, which had a cost and market price of $10 per share and a portfolio of other stocks with a market price of $15,000. At March 31, 199X, the market price of stock A was $1,080 and that of the other stocks was $15,500. The market price for all the stock was $16,580—$580 more than the cost. ABC recognized an unrealized gain of $580 as other comprehensive income in its first-quarter financial statements. In the second and third quarters, it recognized and reported an additional $1,020 and $500, respectively, in other comprehensive income.

For the first three quarters, the total unrealized gain on stock A was $400; this amount was reflected in other comprehensive income. The company sold stock A on October 1, 199X, for $1,400, resulting in a realized gain that ABC included in its net income computation. If the company makes no adjustment to comprehensive income, the $400 gain is double counted. In exhibit 3, however, ABC includes in its statement of income and comprehensive income the $400 gain in income from operations of $25,000. In other comprehensive income, a ($400) reclassification adjustment—or ($300) aftertax—is included for ABC's sale of stock A.

A company must determine reclassification adjustments for each classification of other comprehensive

Exhibit 3: One-Statement Approach to Reporting Comprehensive Income

ABC Co.
Statement of Income and Comprehensive Income
Year Ended December 31, 199X

Revenues		$ 28,000
Expenses		(5,000)
Other gains and losses		1,600
Gain on sale of securities		400
Income from operations before tax		25,000
Income tax expense		(6,250)
Income before extraordinary item and cumulative effect of accounting change		18,750
Extraordinary item, net of tax		(5,600)
Income before cumulative effect of accounting change		13,150
Cumulative effect of accounting change, net of tax		(500)
Net income		12,650
Other comprehensive income, net of tax:		
Foreign currency translation adjustments		2,400
Unrealized gains on securities:		
Unrealized holding gains arising during period	$ 2,100	
Less: Reclassification adjustment for gains included in net income	(300)	1,800
Minimum pension liability adjustment		(600)
Other comprehensive income		3,600
Comprehensive income		$16,250

ABC Co.
Notes to the Financial Statements
Year Ended December 31, 199X

Note X

During the year, the ABC Co. adopted FASB Statement no. 130, *Reporting Comprehensive Income.* Statement no. 130 requires the reporting of comprehensive income in addition to net income from operations. Comprehensive income is a more inclusive financial reporting methodology that includes disclosure of certain financial information that historically has not been recognized in the calculation of net income.

During the year, ABC Co. engaged in numerous transactions involving foreign currency, resulting in unrealized gains of $3,200 before tax. In addition, the company at yearend held securities classified as available-for-sale, which have unrealized gains of $2,400 before tax. Finally, in compliance with Statement no. 130, the company as part of comprehensive income recognizes a beforetax increase in minimum pension liability of $800. The beforetax and aftertax amount for each of these categories, as well as the tax (expense)/benefit of each, is summarized below.

	Before Tax	Tax (Expense)/ Benefit	After Tax
Foreign currency translation	$3,200	$(800)	$2,400
Unrealized holding gains	2,800	(700)	2,100
Reclassification adjustment for gains included in net income	(400)	100	(300)
Minimum pension liability	(800)	200	(600)
	$4,800	($1,200)	$3,600

Note: This statement has been formatted in accordance with format A, one-statement approach, on page 42 of Statement no. 130.

income, except for minimum pension liability adjustments. The adjustment for foreign currency translation is to be limited to translation gains and losses realized on the sale or substantially complete liquidation of an investment in a foreign entity. A company may display reclassification adjustments on the face of the financial statement or in the notes to the financial statements.

DISPLAYING COMPREHENSIVE INCOME

Statement no. 130 provides three different approaches to displaying comprehensive income. Exhibits 3 and 4 illustrate the one-statement and two-statement approaches, respectively, to reporting comprehensive income. Exhibit 5, illustrates how a company can display comprehensive income in the statement of changes in equity.

In exhibit 3, net income is in the middle of the statement. This burying of net income with comprehensive income as the bottom line may not appeal to investors and accountants who are used to seeing net income as the bottom line. Components of other comprehensive income are shown before reclassification adjustments, and therefore no note disclosure is required for the reclassification adjustments of the available-for-sale securities that have unrealized gains of $400 before tax. Since the other comprehensive income is shown after tax, the notes to the financial statements must show the beforetax amounts, the tax expense/benefit and the aftertax amounts of each component of other comprehensive income.

Exhibit 4 illustrates the two-statement approach. The income statement is typical of one calculated in the past. The statement of comprehensive income begins with net income from the income statement, and other comprehensive income is added to calculate comprehensive income. Because other comprehensive income is presented after tax, a note is needed for the income before tax, the tax expense/benefit and the aftertax amounts of each component of other comprehensive income. This approach leaves the income statement unchanged from past income statements and adds an addi-

Exhibit 4: Two-Statement Approach to Reporting Comprehensive Income

ABC Co.
Statement of Income
Year Ended December 31, 199X

Revenues	$ 28,000
Expenses	(5,000)
Other gains and losses	1,600
Gain on sale of securities	400
Income from operations before tax	25,000
Income tax expense	(6,250)
Income before extraordinary item and cumulative effect of accounting change	18,750
Extraordinary item, net of tax	(5,600)
Income before cumulative effect of accounting change	13,150
Cumulative effect of accounting change, net of tax	(500)
Net income	$12,650

ABC Co.
Statement of Comprehensive Income
Year Ended December 31, 199X

Net income		$12,650
Other comprehensive income, net of tax:		
Foreign currency translation adjustments		2,400
Unrealized gains on securities:		
Unrealized holding gains arising during period	$ 2,100	
Less: reclassification adjustment for gains included in net income	(300)	1,800
Minimum pension liability adjustment		(600)
Other comprehensive income		3,600
Comprehensive income		$16,250

ABC Co.
Notes to the Financial Statements
Year Ended December 31, 199X

Note X

During the year, the ABC Co. adopted FASB Statement no. 130, *Reporting Comprehensive Income.* Statement no. 130 requires the reporting of comprehensive income in addition to net income from operations. Comprehensive income is a more inclusive financial reporting methodology that includes disclosure of certain financial information that historically has not been recognized in the calculation of net income.

During the year, ABC Co. engaged in numerous transactions involving foreign currency, resulting in unrealized gains of $3,200 before tax. In addition, the company at yearend held securities classified as available-for-sale, which have unrealized gains of $2,400 before tax. Finally, in compliance with Statement no. 130, the company as part of comprehensive income recognizes a beforetax increase in minimum pension liability of $800. The beforetax and aftertax amount for each of these categories, as well as the tax (expense)/benefit of each, is summarized below.

	Before Tax	Tax (Expense)/ Benefit	After Tax
Foreign currency translation	$3,200	$ (800)	$2,400
Unrealized holding gains	2,800	(700)	2,100
Reclassification adjustment for gains included in net income	(400)	100	(300)
Minimum pension liability	(800)	200	(600)
	$4,800	($1,200)	$3,600

Note: This statement has been formatted in accordance with format B, two-statement approach, on page 43 of Statement no. 130.

A company generally must determine reclassification adjustments for each classification of other comprehensive income.

tional statement of comprehensive income. An alternative would be for a company to present the data before tax, subtract the total tax and in the notes disclose the amount of tax applicable to each component of other comprehensive income.

Exhibit 5 uses a statement of changes in equity approach, where net income, other comprehensive income and comprehensive income are displayed. This method involves the fewest changes from current reporting. The FASB discourages companies from using this method because it tends to hide comprehensive income in the middle of the statement.

An entity should transfer the total of other comprehensive income for a period to a component of equity that is displayed separately from retained earnings and additional paid-in capital in a statement of financial position at the end of an accounting period. That component of equity should have a descriptive title such as "accumulated other comprehensive income." A company's disclosure on the face of the statement, in the statement of changes in equity or in notes to the financial statement of accumulated balances of each component of accumulated other comprehensive income should correspond to the classifications used in other financial statements for components of comprehensive income.

IMPLEMENTATION GUIDELINES

Companies must display net income, comprehensive income and other comprehensive income in one of the three recommended formats. The first decision a company should make is the format it will use in reporting comprehensive income. The second decision is whether to show the components of other comprehensive income net of reclassification adjustments. If it shows the components in this way, then the notes must display the unadjusted information.

Another decision companies face is whether to show the components of other comprehensive income on a beforetax or aftertax basis. If the components are shown before tax, then the company must display the aftertax amount applicable to each component of other comprehensive income in the notes to the financial statements. If the components of other comprehensive income are shown after

Exhibit 5: Statement of Changes in Equity Approach to Reporting Comprehensive Income

ABC Co.
Statement of Changes in Equity
Year Ended December 31, 199X

	Total	Comprehensive Income	Retained Earnings	Accumulated Other Comprehensive Income	Common Stock	Paid-in Capital
Beginning balance	$107,700		$17,700		$30,000	$60,000
Comprehensive income						
Net income	12,650	$12,650	$12,650			
Other comprehensive income, net of tax						
Unrealized gains on securities, net of reclassification adjustment (see disclosure)	1,800	1,800				
Foreign currency translation adjustments	2,400	2,400				
Minimum pension liability adjustment	(600)	(600)				
Other comprehensive income		3,600		3,600		
Comprehensive income		16,250				
Common stock issued	30,000				10,000	20,000
Dividends declared on common stock	(2,000)		(2,000)			
Ending balance	151,950		$28,350	$3,600	$40,000	$80,000

Disclosure of reclassification amount:

Unrealized holding gains arising during period	$2,100
Less: reclassification adjustment for gains included in net income`	(300)
Net unrealized gains on securities	$1,800

NOTE: This statement has been formatted in accordance with format C, statement of changes in equity approach (alternative 1), on page 44 of Statement no. 130.

Statement no. 130 should be viewed as the FASB's first step in developing a framework for reporting comprehensive income.

tax, as they are in exhibits 3 and 4, the company must display the beforetax amount and the tax implications relative to each component in the notes to the financial statements. Finally, the company has options in how to display the individual components of accumulated other comprehensive income—either in the financial statements or in the notes to the financial statements.

To make these decisions, a company should immediately develop the data from prior periods so it can simulate past results under today's rules. A company should prepare post-forma financial statements for prior years to see how the company's statements *would have looked* had Statement no. 130 been in effect during that time. Although publicly reporting companies tend to try to "manage" their net income, it is much more difficult to manage comprehensive income than it is to manage net income. Companies should analyze the post-forma statements to gain insights about how future statements will apear to investors.

Finally, a company should also keep in mind that, in the future, standard setters may include additional items in comprehensive income. Potential candidates for inclusion are additional accounting for pensions and gains and losses on transactions in derivative instruments. With an eye to the future, companies should begin to position themselves for the eventual inclusion of these components.

THE FIRST STEP

Companies should view Statement no. 130 as the FASB's first step on a considerable journey. Having established with this statement the framework for reporting comprehensive income, the FASB will go on over the next several years to refine accounting standards to add more elements to this framework, rendering comprehensive income more and more inclusive. If the objectives of reporting comprehensive income are met, financial statement readers should gain additional insights into a company's activities, which should enable them to better anticipate its future cash flows.

Understanding Global Standards

When your company goes global, examine the differences between the international standards and GAAP.

BY ANNE J. RICH, CMA

In the past, U.S. businesses did not have to pay attention to International Accounting Standards (IAS). But as the business world shrinks and the number of international transactions grows, most U.S. businesses recognize they must adapt to a global environment. Within this context, understanding the increasingly rigorous IAS is becoming a necessary skill for management accountants.

SUPPORT FOR USING IAS

Why should American accountants begin to change their perception about International Accounting Standards?

- Many countries already use IAS, and management accountants should be aware of their impact on U.S. standards.
- International transactions are increasing at an amazing rate, and U.S. companies will have to evaluate foreign companies in order to extend credit and vice versa.
- With the growth of American subsidiaries abroad, companies are required to report in the subsidiary's host country as well as consolidating using U.S. generally accepted accounting principles (GAAP). Preparing financial statements using two or more accounting standards is very costly—using the International Accounting Standards would lower this cost. (For a look at some of the differences between U.S. accounting standards and IAS, see sidebar on next page and Table 1.)
- Finally, the number of joint ventures with foreign corporations has increased. As U.S. companies and foreign companies become partners, the exchange of information would be facilitated by a common format. China, for example, uses the IAS for the regulation of its joint ventures.

Here are some additional reasons for supporting International Accounting Standards.

Capital markets—Ignoring the International Accounting Standards could place U.S. companies at a competitive disadvantage. Many international corporations are looking to U.S. capital markets for financing. European companies have indicated that all they need is U.S. acceptance of the International Accounting Standards Committee (IASC) principles and they will be eager to list on the New York Stock Exchange (NYSE)—as they do on the London and Hong Kong stock exchanges. Daimler Benz recently listed on the NYSE, but it is the only German company to do so. American investors do not have easy access to investing in foreign companies. We can expect in the near future that many U.S. corporations will seek financing from international capital markets.

IOSCO—One of the more significant drivers of international standards for accounting is the International Organization of Securities Commissions (IOSCO). This organization has been working with the IASC to reach agreement on mutually acceptable international standards of accounting and disclosure for international securities offerings and other foreign lists. For example, several IOSCO members require foreign issuers to present financial statements in conformity with IAS. If IASC is able to meet all of IOSCO's requirements, IOSCO will accept international standards for accounting in cross-border public offerings.

The World Bank—Another supporter of IAS is the World Bank. It prefers, to the extent possible, that project accounts be maintained in accordance with generally accepted international standards. Many developing countries use the Standards.

Multinational companies—International Accounting Standards are receiving increased recognition from multinational companies. This situation exists particularly in countries where the Standards are accepted as either the preferred accounting principle or as allowed alternatives. For example, Ciba-Geigy Limited Group, Switzerland, changed its accounting system on January 1, 1993, in order to comply with the IAS and with the European Community's directives. Shanghai Petrochemical in the People's Republic of China uses IAS as its principal accounting policies. The 1994 Annual Report for Anglo American Corporation, South Africa, states the accounting policies substantially comply with the International Accounting Standards.

SEC—The Securities & Exchange Commission (SEC) is working with IOSCO and the IASC. The SEC now will accept cash flow statements from foreign issuers that conform with IAS 7. The SEC also has accepted as equivalent information value to GAAP the international standard for amortization of goodwill, the distinction between acquisition (purchase) and unitings of interests (poolings) in business combinations, and foreign subsidiaries

DIFFERENCES BETWEEN IAS AND GAAP

Are there any major differences between U.S. accounting standards and the IAS? See Table 1 for a quick overview. Here are some more in-depth differences:

- Disclosure of Accounting Policies (IAS1)—IAS allows more than one method.
- Inventories (IAS2)—This Standard values inventories at lower of historical cost or net realizable value. Net realizable value has a more specific meaning than the GAAP definition of market value. As mentioned earlier, LIFO inventories are reconciled to FIFO, which is a requirement similar to that of the SEC. Most large companies, therefore, will have no difficulty meeting the IAS requirement.
- Depreciation (IAS4)—This Standard requires depreciable assets to be disclosed according to a major class grouping, such as property, plant, and equipment. The rates used to compute the depreciation also are disclosed.
- Cash Flow (IAS7)—The revised Standard, effective January 1, 1995, complies with U.S. GAAP except for certain exemptions for some organizations, the treatment of bank overdrafts, the treatment for operating cash flows associated with the purchase and sale of dealing or trading securities and loans, the cash flows associated with extraordinary items, and the detailed disclosure by major category of other assets and liabilities acquired or disposed of in subsidiaries. There could be controversial differences for some industries.
- Research and Development (IAS9)—This Standard is less stringent than GAAP after the Statement of Financial Accounting Standards (SFAS) 2. IAS9 allows development expense to be deferred if it meets certain criteria.
- Retirement Benefit Costs (IAS19)—The Standard does not address the additional minimum liability.
- Business Combination (IAS22)—The IAS is a departure from GAAP in that it requires the amortization period for expensing goodwill to not exceed five years unless there is justification for a longer period—not to exceed 20 years. Also, where the aggregate fair value of net identifiable acquired assets exceeds the cost of acquisition, the excess (negative goodwill) should be treated as deferred income and recognized as income on a systematic basis or allocated over individual depreciable nonmonetary assets acquired in proportion to their fair values. It is a significant area of contention. Additionally, pooling may be applied to a broader group of transactions, and the IASC's concept of control is different from GAAP.
- Related Party Disclosures (IAS24)—The Standard requires additional disclosures than required under GAAP. GAAP does not require disclosure of items in the ordinary course of business, such as compensation.
- Accounting for Investments in Associates (IAS28)—The differences occur when using financial statements with a different reporting date.
- Financial Reporting of Interests in Joint Ventures (IAS31)—While the proportionate consolidation method is the benchmark treatment for reporting interests in joint ventures, the equity method is an allowed alternative.

operating in the currency of a highly inflationary economy.

FASB—The Financial Accounting Standards Board (FASB) is watching the International Accounting Standards carefully. A major project of the FASB is consolidations—the United States is out of step with the IASC on that issue. In 1993, the FASB stated that its project on earnings per share (EPS) had two objectives: to simplify procedures for the computation of EPS by U.S. companies and to make U.S. standards on EPS compatible with international standards. The FASB is coordinating its project with the IASC's work on EPS. In September 1994, the FASB and the IASC Steering Committee met to discuss a number of issues for which the two organizations have reached different conclusions.

INTERNATIONAL ACCOUNTING STANDARDS COMMITTEE

The organization that has had the most significant impact on developing international standards for accounting is the International Accounting Standards Committee. The IASC was formed in 1973 in order to improve and harmonize financial reporting and focuses primarily on developing and publishing International Accounting Standards. The Committee is located in London, England, and includes more than 100 organizations representing more than 80 member countries.

The objectives of the IASC are:

- to formulate and publish in the public interest accounting standards to be observed in the presentation of financial statements and to promote their worldwide acceptance and observance;
- to work generally for the improvement and harmoni[z]ation of regulations, accounting standards and procedures relating to the presentation of financial statements.[1]

The IASC Board comprises representatives of accounting organizations from 13 countries and representatives from a maximum of four organizations other than accounting but with an interest in financial reporting. The Board includes representatives from Australia, Canada, France, Germany, India, Italy, Japan, Jordan, The Netherlands, the Nordic Federation of Public Accountants, South Africa, United Kingdom, and the United States. In addition, there are representatives of the International Coordinating Committee of Financial Analysts' Associations. The U.S. representative is the AICPA.

The Board also meets with the IASC Consultative Group, an international group that comprises representatives of users and preparers of financial statements and standards-setting bodies, as well as observers from intergovernmental organizations. The FASB, for example, is a member of the Group. The IASC is funded by professional accountancy bodies and other organizations on its Board, the International Federation of Accountants (IFAC), and by contributions from multinational companies, financial institutions, accounting firms, and other organizations.

Similar to the FASB, the IASC adds topics to its work program, sets up

TABLE 1 / STATUS OF INTERNATIONAL ACCOUNTING STANDARDS (IAS) AS OF NOVEMBER 1994

IAS No.	Title	Effective January 1	Conforms to U.S. GAAP?
1*	Disclosure of Accounting Policies	1975	Yes
2*	Inventories	1995	Yes, additional disclosures required if company uses LIFO
3	Superseded		
4*	Depreciation Accounting	1977	Yes
5	Information to be Disclosed in Financial Statements	1977	Yes
6	Superseded		
7*	Cash Flows Statement	1994	Yes, minor differences
8	Net Profit or Loss for the Period, Fundamental Errors and Changes in Accounting Policies	1995	Yes
9*	Research and Development Costs	1995	Some differences
10	Contingencies and Events Occurring After the Balance Sheet Date	1980	Yes
11	Construction Contracts	1995	Yes
12	Accounting for Taxes on Income	1981 under revision	
13	Presentation of Current Assets and Current Liabilities	1981	Yes
14	Reporting Financial Information by Segment	1983 under revision	
15	Information Reflecting the Effects of Changing Prices	1983	Yes
16	Property, Plant and Equipment	1995	Yes
17	Accounting for Leases	1984	Yes
18	Revenue	1995	Yes
19*	Retirement Benefit Costs	1995	Some differences
20	Accounting for Government Grants and Disclosure of Government Assistance	1984	Yes
21	The Effects of Changes in Foreign Exchange Rates	1995	Yes
22*	Business Combinations	1995	Yes, except for goodwill treatment
23	Borrowing Costs	1995	Yes
24*	Related Party Disclosures	1986	Yes, minor differences
25	Accounting for Investments	1987	Yes
26	Accounting and Reporting by Retirement Benefit Plans	1988	Yes
27	Consolidated Financial Statements and Accounting for Investments in Subsidiaries	1990	Yes
28*	Accounting for Investments in Associates	1990	Some differences
29	Financial Reporting in Hyperinflationary Economies	1990	Yes
30	Disclosure in the Financial Statements of Banks and Similar Financial Institutions	1991	Yes, minor differences
31*	Financial Reporting of Interests in Joint Ventures	1992	Yes, minor differences

*For more detail, see sidebar, "Differences between IAS and GAAP."

steering committees to develop Statements of Principles, prepares Exposure Drafts, and, ultimately, presents International Accounting Standards.

To date, the IASC has issued 31 International Accounting Standards and two major Exposure Drafts: financial instruments and income taxes. The Board also has issued a guideline titled "Framework for the Preparation and Presentation of Financial Statements."

In 1987, the IASC decided there were too many acceptable alternative accounting treatments in its Standards and began a project to look into this matter. In January 1989, E32, "Comparability of Financial Statements," was published, which represented the culmination of the first stage of the project. It dealt with 29 issues concerning existing Standards that allowed too many choices of accounting treatments. A second document, "Statement of Intent on the Comparability of Financial Statements," was issued in June 1990 as a result of feedback to the Board.

The "Statement of Intent" identified three issues—research and development, inventories, and capitalization of borrowing costs—on which the Board decided to make substantive changes. The IASC also identified 21 issues it considered noncontroversial and on which Standards would be published without any changes from the E32 proposals.

The IASC has identified a broader base of users of financial statements than the FASB. The IASC includes as users: present and potential investors, employees, lenders, suppliers and other trade creditors, customers, governments and their agencies, and the public. Financial statements must provide information about the financial position, performance, and changes in financial position that is useful to a wide range of users in making economic decisions.

International Accounting Standards recognize accrual accounting and the going-concern concept. Many of the qualitative characteristics found in the FASB's Conceptual Framework also are found in the International Accounting Standards Committee's Framework. The definitions of assets, liabilities, and equity also are very similar. Finally, the recognition principle is similar to that used in the United States.

Recently, the IASC decided to reduce the number of accounting alternatives and began its Comparability Project. As a result, in 1993, many alternative treatments were eliminated with the issuance of 10 revised International Accounting Standards. Some issues were resolved by identifying a benchmark treatment—the preferred method—and an allowed alternative.

The most controversial problem the IASC settled is the treatment of inventories. In earlier drafts, LIFO accounting for inventories was to be eliminated. Effective January 1, 1995, however, FIFO is the benchmark treatment, and LIFO is the allowed alternative treatment. If LIFO is selected, then the company must provide disclosures that reconcile differences between income using LIFO and income following the benchmark treatment, FIFO. Reconciliation is achieved by disclosing the difference between the amount of the inventories as shown in the balance sheet and either (a) the lower of the amount arrived at in accordance with the historic cost using FIFO or the weighted average cost and the net realizable value or (b) the lower of current cost at the balance sheet date and the net realizable value.

IASC PROJECTS

What are the current and future projects of the IASC? The outstanding issues in "Statement of Intent on Comparability of Financial Statements" relate to IAS 25, "Accounting for Investments." The IASC will consider this Statement as part of its larger project on financial instruments. It has taken a lead role in the development of accounting standards related to this subject. Now IASC is reviewing IAS 17, "Accounting for Leases." Here the issue is recognition of finance income on a finance lease.

In 1988, the IASC began its review of IAS 12, "Accounting for Taxes on Income." In 1989, it published E33. As a result of strong negative comments, it has just issued another Exposure Draft before approving a revised Standard along with a Background Issues document. The document indicates there are two approaches to the liability method: the balance sheet liability method and the income statement liability method. Previously, the IASC recommended the income statement method. The new Standard, E49, adopts the balance sheet liability method that was developed by the FASB. While the international standard now has the same theoretical approach to accounting for income taxes as GAAP, there still is one area of difference. The IASC decided that it would not permit the recognition of the deferred tax liability in certain cases where the consideration paid for an asset implicitly takes into account its nondeductibility for tax purposes. Long-term assets with a tax base less than cost and nondeductible goodwill amortization are exceptions to deferred tax liabilities. Negative goodwill and government grants are exceptions to deferred tax assets.

In September 1994, IASC published a draft Statement of Principles titled "Reporting Financial Information by Segment." In this document, the IASC recognized there are two popular approaches to defining segments, namely, the business segment approach and the management approach. The former is proposed by the IASC's Steering Committee, while the latter is the approach being developed jointly by the FASB and the Canadian Institute of Chartered Accountants. The IASC has requested input from accountants before it issues a final report.

The IASC also is developing Standards on intangible assets, earnings per share, agriculture and presentation of financial statements, and post-retirement benefits.

THE FASB AND THE IASC: WORKING TOGETHER

Until recently, the AICPA played a more formal role than the FASB with the IASC. In an effort to communicate more effectively, the FASB formed an informal "working group." Beginning in 1991, the working group conducted meetings to enhance communication among standards-setting bodies and to explore conceptual and technical issues about which they have common concerns. They initially focused on one problem that confronts standards setters worldwide—the role of future events for recognition and measurement.

In August 1994, the FASB published a special report, "Future Events: A Conceptual Study of Their Significance for Recognition and Measurement." The principal author is L. Todd Johnson of the FASB. The study represents the combined thoughts of the Australian Accounting Standards Board, the Canadian Accounting Standards Board, the IASC, the United Kingdom Accounting Standards Board, and the FASB. This project also was published by the IASC.

When the FASB proposes changes to GAAP, U.S. accounting professionals respond passionately. It is time for a broader perspective. Management accountants should monitor and participate in the global standards-setting process to ensure their voice is heard.

Anne J. Rich, CMA, CPA, Ph.D., is professor of accounting at Quinnipiac College, Hamden, Conn. She is a member of the New Haven Chapter, through which this article was submitted, and can be reached at (203) 281-8787.

[1]International Accounting Standards Committee, *International Accounting Standards*, IASC, London, England, July 1992, p. 4.

THE IAS EXPRESS GAINS STEAM

Once considered as likely as Esperanto, international accounting standards could become acceptable by the year 2000.

BY LOUISE NAMETH

After years of being stuck on what seemed a permanent siding, the idea of a uniform global accounting code may finally be on track to acceptance.

Momentum built sharply last year after an improved set of international accounting standards, or IAS, took effect in January—albeit with the United States, Japan, and Canada as holdouts—clearing the way for hundreds of companies around the world to begin embracing a single set of procedures. The model created by the International Accounting Standards Committee (IASC) was approved by national standard-setters in London, Switzerland, Hong Kong, and elsewhere for use in cross-border listing requirements. Indeed, on a recent visit to Shanghai, Fidelity Investments fund manager John Hickling found that more than half the 20 companies he called on are complying with IAS.

"Standards are converging throughout the world," says Hickling, who manages Fidelity's $4 billion overseas group of funds. And there is little feeling these days, he adds, that the United States has "a monopoly on all that is best or correct in accounting."

Were new international standards to win full acceptability—and usher in an alternate set of procedures differing somewhat from U.S. generally accepted accounting principles (GAAP) in such areas as business consolidations, tax accounting, and treatment of derivatives—it would have significant implications for American financial executives and their corporations. "Major multinational companies domiciled in other countries [would be] adopting these standards in order to list and raise capital in the U.S.," says Pat McConnell, managing director at Bear Stearns & Co. and an analyst delegate on the IASC board. "Therefore, U.S. corporations will be competing for capital with these companies."

And because "the ultimate goal is for these companies to be reporting under IASC standards with no U.S. GAAP reconciliation," she says, U.S. multinationals must "be aware of the way that their competitors are reporting their results." The Institute of Management Accounting is one U.S. organization represented on the IASC board, and numerous other entities are watching the IAS developments closely.

"As U.S. firms become more global, it will make more sense, from an internal management point of view, to have one set of internationally accepted accounting standards," says Trevor Harris, a Columbia Business School professor and author of a study comparing IAS and U.S. GAAP.

While IAS gathered steam last year, a blueprint was drawn up in July for a schedule to refine core procedures that could satisfy the regulatory authorities of more than 113 countries—including the United States—by as early as mid-1999.

SOME SKEPTICS

The "IAS Express" could still be derailed during its three-year run, of course. Despite the growing acceptance, some skeptics within major multinationals question whether universal acceptance can ever really be achieved. Reto F. Domeniconi, executive vice president/finance, control, and administration at giant Swiss confectioner Nestlé, for example, says it is "a pipe dream" that the world can adopt uniform standards any time soon. And, he adds, "it is unthinkable that all of the 70 major plus 50 minor countries in which we operate would ever have a uniform set of standards." While Nestlé's internal standards are in full accordance with IAS, the executive suggests that it might be more practical globally for stock-exchange listings to be based on "a mutual recognition among the world's leading accounting standards, which all have their strong and weak points without any one of them appearing to be overall superior to others."

And were the United States and other key countries to continue to balk, IAS likely would go the way of Esperanto—that oft-thwarted attempt at an internationally accepted language. One concern among U.S. finance executives is that more flexible standards could open the floodgates to an array of foreign offerings on the domestic U.S. exchanges, thus raising the cost of capital.

THE SEC STANCE

But in anticipation of 1999, the U.S. Financial Accounting Standards

RICHARD DOWNS

From *CFO,* March 1996, pp. 68-71. © 1996 by CFO Publishing Corporation. Reprinted by permission of *CFO,* The Magazine for Senior Financial Executives.

Board has been preparing a study comparing U.S. GAAP and IAS. And significantly, the Securities and Exchange Commission now hints that it might soon withdraw its opposition to IAS, long based on an assumption that any international standards would be more lax than U.S. GAAP. If international planners can protect investors and solve certain sticky accounting problems, such as how to deal with standards governing the fast-changing area of financial instruments, the United States could well jump on board, says Richard Reinhard, the SEC's associate chief accountant.

"If the IASC comes up with reasonable answers, around the year 2000 international standards will become acceptable," says Reinhard, who has been involved with the global negotiations since 1988. And in a world hungry for access to U.S. capital markets, that would be a giant step for international standards.

The SEC official, whose agency is often seen as the world's top accounting cop because of its exacting array of standards, notes that even U.S. GAAP could be strengthened in some areas—such as financial instruments and procedures for valuing property, plant, and equipment, where there's actually more information provided under IAS.

CONTROVERSY IN EUROPE

Some of the biggest proponents of IAS are European multinationals that for cultural reasons don't want to accept the U.S. version of GAAP, even to help them tap this country's prime capital markets.

Swiss-based Roche Holding Ltd. (known as Hoffman–La Roche in the United States) embraces the idea of uniform standards. From his office down a sparkling white hall lined with contemporary art—making the huge drug company's headquarters resemble one of Basel's many art galleries—Dr. Henri Meier, the CFO, notes that keeping up with local statutory and fiscal accounts in approximately 100 countries is expensive. He favors converting to a

SUMMARY OF ADJUSTMENTS BY ACCOUNTING PRACTICE/THE BAYER GROUP

Accounting Policy	As Reported to Revised IAS	From Revised IAS to U.S. GAAP
A Acquisitions, business combinations, and consolidations	Capitalize and amortize goodwill. Additional disclosures.	Adjust for retroactive write-off of goodwill.
B Foreign currency translations	Use current rate for all assets and average rate for income statements. Use current rate for all transaction balances.	
C Shareholders' equity	Adjust for tax-related items. Reclassify minority interest. Additional disclosures.	
D Property, plant, and equipment	Capitalize certain leases. Additional disclosures. Possibly capitalize development costs.	Capitalize borrowing costs.
E Investments	Additional disclosures.	Additional disclosures. Adjust to portfolio basis of calculation of lower of cost and market value.
F Discontinued operations and changes in accounting policies	Potential reclassification and disclosure.	Potential reclassification and disclosure.
G Taxation	Additional disclosures.	Additional disclosures. Possible deferred tax asset from net operating loss carryforwards.
H Postemployment benefits	Consider future salaries and alternate interest rates. Additional disclosures.	Additional disclosures.
I Revenue recognition	Use percentage of completion (potential only).	
J Segment reporting	Disclosure of identified assets.	Additional disclosure of depreciation.
K Related party transactions		
L Statement of cash flows	Reclassify.	
M Other items	Treat bond discount as contraliability.	Management discussion and analysis. Additional disclosure of earnings per share.

IMPACT OF ADJUSTMENTS ON SHAREHOLDERS' EQUITY/THE BAYER GROUP (12/31/93)

Area Covered	As Reported to Revised IAS (millions)	Revised IAS to U.S. GAAP* (millions)	Comments
Acquisitions, business combinations, and consolidations	DM 0.0	DM 1,116.7	Retroactive adjustments for previous write-offs of goodwill.
Foreign currency translation:			Recognition of unrealized foreign currency gains.
Unrealized gains	12.0	0.0	Use of current rate method.
Translation	(429.0)	0.0	
Shareholders' equity:			
Dividends	.0	0.0	
Minority interest	479.0	0.0	Minority interest presented separately from shareholders' equity.
Other	78.0	0.0	Reversal of the "special item with an equity component" (net of applicable deferred taxes) and reversal of tax write-downs.
Property, plant, and equipment:			
Interest capitalization	0.0	0.0	
Revaluation	0.0	0.0	
Development costs	0.0	0.0	
Investments	0.0	0.0	
Discontinued operations and changes in accounting policies	0.0	0.0	
Taxation (1)	0.0	NQ	Possible deferred tax asset from operating loss carryforwards.
Postemployment benefits	(16.)	0.0	Additional accrual allocated over the remaining service life.
Other	21.0	0.0	Reversal of future maintenance costs.
Net adjustment to shareholders' equity	DM (813.0)	DM 1,116.7	
Shareholders' equity as reported at 12/31/93	DM 18,160.0	DM 18,160.0	

DM 1 = 0.579 US$ at 12/31/93. *U.S. generally accepted accounting principles as required for foreign private issuers filing Form 20-F.
NQ Potential difference has not been quantified. (1) The tax effects of all other adjustments are reflected in the other adjustment amounts.

Source: Trevor Harris, Columbia University (1995 study)

"It took us three or four years and some management changes before almost universal acceptance," says Jim Cronin, GEC Alsthom's managing director.

single set of accounts—at a Sfr 50 million reduction in Roche Holding's costs.

"Once people know what the definition is," says Meier, "it doesn't matter which system you use."

At the sprawling facilities of German chemical and pharmaceuticals giant Bayer AG, executives aimed both to cut costs and to improve their fiscal understanding of Bayer units when they adopted IAS. "We wanted a cost-efficient way of developing a better basis for internal decision making," says Bernd Joachim Menn, head of Bayer's corporate accounting and reporting. "In the past, we had lengthy internal guidelines whereby we translated data from 350 subsidiaries. Now, it's easier for both our auditors and our managers to understand. The result is a better, more mature body of information from our subsidiaries.

Bayer continues to keep a separate set of accounts for tax purposes covering the legal corporate entity, as defined by German law. There's some criticism of this approach, but Menn says that reflects "an irrational fear that if you allow for alternative accounting measures it will destabilize the system, and the entire tax structure will change." To allow for the difference in tax treatment between IAS and German GAAP, Menn merely uses two fixed-asset schedules. Rather than adding to cost, he says, he's just going public with a set of accounts normally used for internal purposes.

"If you calculate internally for a product, you need a period-by-period depreciation schedule, as the first year of the product is not profitable," he notes. Accelerated depreciation "might go up to as high as 33 percent for tax purposes and then start to decline," Menn notes, describing what German tax law requires. But for Bayer's own internal accounting purposes the firm already uses the straight-line depreciation method. Since that's the same straight-line approach IAS now calls for, there isn't any real additional work involved for Bayer in complying in that area.

GEC ALSTHOM TRIES IAS

The ornate facade of GEC Alsthom NV's classical-style Paris office building hides a no-nonsense, engineer-friendly interior at the power and transportation company, the result of a 1989 merger between part of the U.K.'s General Electric PLC, and France's Alcatel NV and Alcatel Alsthom. Here, IAS is helping resolve internal differences that the public never learned about.

It hasn't always been easy, though. GEC Alsthom was born in accounting confusion—with the British and French systems differing dramatically, with consolidated accounts having to be produced quarterly to satisfy two separate fiscal-year schedules, and with separate information having to be provided to meet U.S. GAAP requirements for New York Stock Exchange–listed Alcatel Alsthom.

When GEC Alsthom made a progressive attempt to report according to IAS—instituting reporting methods at the lowest levels of management—it met fierce resistance from some of the staff. Already reeling from the merger between two cultures with historically frosty relations, employees viewed the introduction of monthly management accounts as a tool of cost-cutting that could be destructive to the work force.

SOME PROBLEM AREAS

Among the more controversial areas for international standard-setters are those that relate to internally developed intangibles, a category that includes everything from mailing lists to a publisher's masthead to a drug in development. "In the U.S. you capitalize research, but you don't capitalize development," says Bayer's Bernd Joachim Menn. "In the evolution of a drug, when does research become development? Once you start development, if you don't get drug approval, you're not sure how that will affect your future cash flows."

One other particularly controversial area in the bid for global acceptance of IAS involves valuing financial instruments—a task that is a moving target because market changes often make it difficult to draft regulations adequate to the new financial products being offered. Indeed, this sticky area is the only one that has so far managed to evade scheduling by IASC working committees.

The valuing of financial instruments is a particularly controversial area in the bid for global acceptance of IAS.

The financial-instruments debate rages on two levels, according to Menn, who is a member of a new IASC steering committee. "For fixed assets and current assets, normally what is done in the U.S. is to use acquisition value for fixed and market value for current." But, he points out, "under the strictest interpretation of German accounting, for example, you should use acquisition or below, but never a value above acquisition." The European prudence principle, in its simplest form, dictates that asset values be reflected at acquisition levels until the asset is sold. That entrenched tradition conflicts with Americans' preference for valuing current assets at market, and thus could be a tough barrier for international regulators.

Menn says the regulators concerned about the financial-instruments area are also struggling to set up special treatment of banks and insurance companies, as opposed to nonfinancial corporations. Banks and insurers often hold financial instruments, or even gold and silver, for trading purposes. "The problem," he says, "is that if you go this way, what happens to the rest of the [nonfinancial firms], which use these instruments for a variety of [nontrading] purposes"—such as hedging, for example? In much of Europe, nonfinancial companies would likely reflect financial instruments at acquisition value.—L.N.

THE ROAD TO U.S. ACCEPTANCE OF IAS

On January 1, 1995, a single set of international procedures is adopted by the 45-delegate International Accounting Standards Committee (IASC), representing 14 countries. The United States, Japan, and Canada are among holdouts to accepting IAS as an alternative to their local codes. The committee, develops a work plan through July 1999 to propose revisions for the standards on the way to final, global IAS.

■ The United States, while reaffirming U.S. GAAP as the only acceptable standard, continues monitoring the progress of IAS through the Securities and Exchange Commission. The Financial Accounting Standards Board reviews the differences between U.S. GAAP and IAS. Among the American organizations following the process through their own delegates to the IASC are the following: the Institute of Management Accountants; the Association for Investment, Management, and Research; and the American Institute of Certified Public Accountants.

■ At the end of the IASC work plan—which provides timetables for discussion of IAS revisions involving tax-related matters, intangibles, and accounting procedures for R&D and financials instruments, for example—17 working committees are to present their draft proposals to the whole IASC board. The board must approve the entire set of standards unanimously for IAS to be retained globally.

■ With such unanimous approval, the International Organization of Securities Organizations would recommend to its 113 members that they accept IAS as an alternative to their own accounting principles.

■ The SEC would consider accepting IAS as an alternative to U.S. GAAP for foreign registrants. Prior to the drafting of IASC's 1995 work plan, the SEC presented the committee with a series of "reservations" covering treatment of issues ranging from leveraged buyouts to certain types of financial instruments. ■

"That feeling ran quite deeply, not only in France, but also in other units which were not used to comprehensive monthly accounting," says Jim Cronin, GEC Alsthom's managing director. "It took us three or four years and some management changes before almost universal acceptance.

"People acted very quickly to produce the information," says Cronin. "It took them somewhat longer to understand what they were producing."

Indeed, say company executives, once the perception of a threat to their jobs vanished, employees discovered that the monthly IAS approach helped them get a better handle in such areas as cash management.

The company's cash on hand has doubled since the joint venture was formed—tangible proof that accounting measures can influence operations at the lowest levels.

Generally, though, the greatest pressure for IAS simply reflects the rapid internationalization of investing. In the United States, more institutions and individuals are looking for investment opportunities. Corporate fund managers sent 4 percent of their investment dollars abroad in 1986, a percentage expected to triple in 1998, according to research firm Greenwich Associates.

Regulators and issuers of securities must pay attention to global competition for capital, insists Professor Harris of Columbia University. "The SEC can protect investors more by adopting IAS, because they can invoke oversight," he says. "Our investors are investing in these countries regardless of whether they're there or not."

Louise Nameth is a New York–based writer.

Unit 2

Unit Selections

Key Points to Consider

- Competition has helped change how businesses operate. One key change is in the area of managerial accounting. What do you think the role of the management accountant will be in the twenty-first century? Do you think traditional management accountants will be able to make the transition necessary to succeed in the future? Explain.
- Is activity-based costing a fad or a costing system that will become a permanent method in the majority of companies? Defend your answer.
- Many improvements to budgeting have been suggested. How many companies do you think focus on the numbers instead of the overall goals? Why is it hard to change the way budgeting is done in a firm?
- Quality is a much-discussed topic in business. The articles in this unit implied that quality and cost savings go hand in hand. Why then do many firms produce products and offer services of low quality? Do you think the trend in U.S. firms will be to produce higher quality products and services in the upcoming century? Why or why not?
- Computer technology has changed the role of the accountant. What technological changes do you think will be developed in the future? How will these changes impact accounting and the role of accountants? How serious do you think the Year 2000 problem is? What will be the long-term impacts of this problem?

Links

www.dushkin.com/online/

19. **American Bar Association (ABA)**
 http://www.abanet.org/
20. **American Institute of CPAs (AICPA)**
 http://www.aicpa.org/
21. **Activity-Based Costing (ABC)**
 http://www.pitt.edu/~narst8/Welcome.html
22. **Break-Even Analysis**
 http://web.miep.org/bus_plan/break.html
23. **Information Technology Association of America (ITAA)**
 http://www.itaa.org/
24. **International Federation of Accountants (IFAC)**
 http://ifac.org/StandardsAndGuidance/InformationTechnology.html
25. **MFR Assurance Services**
 http://www.mfrgroup.com/fraud.htm
26. **TAPNet**
 http://www.tapnet.com/nav.htm
27. **World Wide Web University**
 http://www.csun.edu/~vcact00g/acct.html

These sites are annotated on pages 4 and 5.

Managerial Accounting

It seems that financial accounting has always overshadowed the importance of management accounting; however, the rapidly changing and competitive business environment may at last allow management accountants to share center stage with financial accountants.

The changing role of management accountants is discussed in two articles in the first subsection of this unit. In "Finance's Future: Challenge or Threat?" Stanley Zarowin notes that the "frantic pace of management accountants will continue" and the future business role of CPAs will be significantly different. Zarowin predicts that only half of all CPAs will be able to make the transition to the new roles. The new roles required of management accountants focus on financial management, business strategy, and the management of information and technology, as opposed to number crunching and data collection. The third subsection article proposes a philosophical base for management accountants equivalent to financial accountants generally accepted accounting principles.

The other articles in this unit are divided into categories most often discussed in managerial accounting courses. Some selections offer applications of topics discussed in textbooks, while others offer new and innovative strategies to traditional topics.

Cost accounting systems are addressed in the next three selections. The history of cost accounting from the Industrial Revolution to the present is documented in the article "Cost/Management Accounting: The 21st Century Paradigm." Standard cost systems, once viewed as a great improvement in accounting systems, are now being questioned as to their value. In "Updating Standard Cost Systems," Carole Cheatham illustrates how companies can improve their standard costing systems to better serve their needs in an ever-changing and highly competitive manufacturing environment. Next, the true story of Claudia Post, entrepreneur, offers an interesting and easy-to-understand situation common to many small businesses. Claudia is one of the few that realized before it was too late that her future success depended on developing, implementing, and understanding a cost accounting system.

As companies have tried to improve their cost accounting systems, one method that has gained acceptance is activity-based costing. Activity-based costing is generally described in accounting courses in the context of manufacturing concerns; however, this method works in service type firms as well. "Using ABC to Determine the Cost of Servicing Customers" provides a case study of a service business and how they used activity-based costing to reduce costs. While activity-based costing has proved beneficial to many firms, not all companies have found this method useful. In Kip Krumweide's article, the reasons for success or the lack thereof are presented. Even the U.S. Post Office has used activity-based costing in order to be more competitive and innovative. The article "How ABC Changed the Post Office" examines a case study of the Post Office experiences.

Applications of cost-volume-profit analysis are discussed in the subsection. In the article "Multidimensional Break-Even Analysis," the traditional textbook model of break-even analysis is expanded to allow comparison of a firm to its competitors. Kevin Thompson explains in the article "Planning for Profit" how break-even analysis can be a simple tool for small businesses wanting to streamline expenses and increase profits.

Budgeting is a much talked-about area, yet change has been slow. The traditional approach to budgeting in most companies and textbooks is a number-crunching approach. While the numbers are important, firms should not lose sight of the overall goals of the firm. An innovative approach to budgeting is suggested in the article "Is It Time to Replace Traditional Budgeting?" The process and challenges of setting up a budgeting and planning system are discussed in a second subsection selection.

A new realization in accounting is that measuring nonfinancial items such as customer expectations and levels of quality is equally important to measuring the financial information. Quality of raw materials does not necessarily mean higher costs, as is illustrated by Kathleen Rust in the article "Measuring the Costs of Quality." Rapid and constant change is causing management to question the value of traditional financial reporting. The next two selections address the need for better information to be reported and the need to measure both financial and nonfinancial performance. Companies are also just beginning to realize that cost control is largely determined during product design, an area where management accountants have not been prominent players.

The final selections in this unit address the ever-important area of information technology. "Arrivederci, Pacioli? A New Accounting System Is Emerging" discusses the weaknesses of the traditional double-entry bookkeeping system. This revolutionary article explains how debits and credits could disappear from accounting systems. Then, two selections explain the Year 2000 software compliance problem and the many implications for accountants.

The new role faced by management accountants.

Finance's Future: Challenge or Threat?

BY STANLEY ZAROWIN

As the Bob Dylan song of the 1960s warned, "The times they are a-changin'." Management accountants certainly can attest to the sagacity of those lyrics. But how exactly will the changing times affect CPAs in the years ahead?

Change is not new to management accountants. After all, they are expected to be jacks-of-all-trades and to leap nimbly from one priority to another—handling accounts receivable one day, payables the next, human resources a week later, closing the books at the start of each month and—most demanding of all—dropping whatever they are doing to provide instant information and analysis on everything from inventory to cash flow.

But as Yogi Berra put it, "The future ain't what it used to be." While it's clear that the frantic pace of management accountants will continue, and it's equally clear that the business role these CPAs will play in the years ahead will be significantly different, what is less clear is how many of today's accountants will be willing—or able—to adjust to what many in the profession are now calling the New Accounting.

What is the New Accounting?

An anecdote will help with the definition. Some years ago, when a *Fortune* 500 company was seeking a new chief financial officer—a search that went on for more than half a year—the president kept rejecting candidates even though they showed ample skills and experience with traditional financial tasks: digging into balance sheets, trimming costs and managing money with sophistication. He even rejected candidates who qualified as so-called business partners—those who understood how the business ran, including marketing and production, and could provide shrewd business advice to top management. "Sure, I want a business partner," the president said, "but I also want someone who can be more than that. I want someone who can help me accelerate change in this organization. I want a change agent."

Exhibit 1: Shrinking Finance Costs

Because of reengineering, finance department costs, as a percent of total revenue, on average have dropped 37% since 1988.

Cost as a percentage of revenue

1988 Baseline	1995	1996
2.2%	1.5%	1.4%

Source: The Hackett Group

HISTORICAL PERSPECTIVE

The new accountants are change agents and more—much more. It's the *more* that creates problems for many management accountants. But before defining what the *more* is, some historical perspective.

The most significant shift in the role of management accountants began in the 1980s, triggered largely by the introduction of the personal computer (PC). Top management recognized that the PC could do more than just warehouse data: It could be an analysis tool, generating what-if scenarios ("What if we lowered the price of widget X but boosted the price of widget Y?"), data searches ("How did widget X sell in St. Louis in February?") and real-time reporting ("How many widget Xs do we have in the warehouse today?")

So, in addition to all the traditional tasks of the finance department, the PC—the tool that was supposed to make a CPA's life easier—suddenly added new burdens. From

"There is nothing less useful than to do a little better that which should not be done at all," says Peter Drucker, the modern-day management sage.

then on, accounting was launched on a new journey, but it was a journey into unchartered waters by professionals without a compass and trained to steer a quite different course. What *was* very clear was that the columnar pad was dead—long live the computerized spreadsheet! And now accountants were being asked to do more than record historical financial records; they were invited—sometimes ordered—to get out from behind their data, become analytical and proactive, look into the future and join with management in making and taking responsibility for all those tough decisions. Further, top management expected the accounting department, in addition to its demanding role processing transactions, to serve as

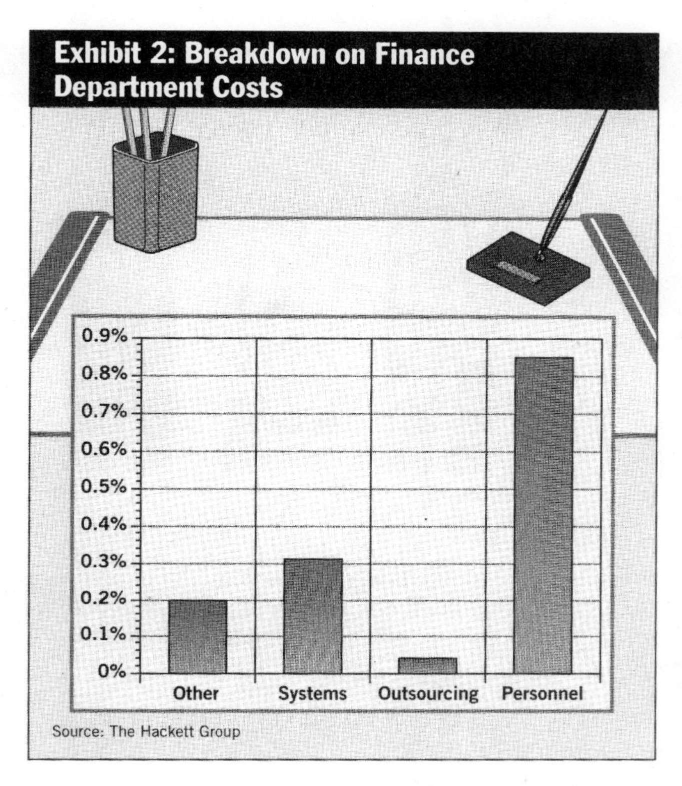

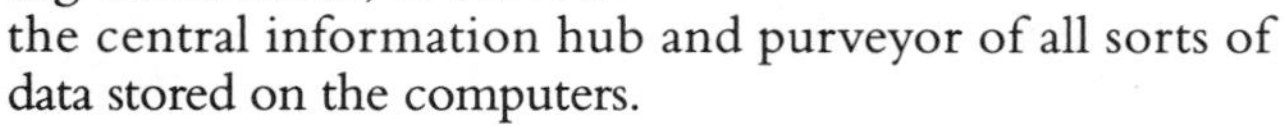
the central information hub and purveyor of all sorts of data stored on the computers.

KEENER COMPETITION

While all this was going on, the culture of American business was undergoing a sea change, too: Competition among business enterprises was becoming keener—thanks in large part to the efficiency and data-analyzing power of the computer. To stay competitive, top management generally realized that just selling more goods and services was not enough. So it added two new priorities: Improve the quality of products and services and increase productivity. As a result, American business went on a forced march in search of inefficiencies. The idea was to find them and fix them.

But management sage Peter Drucker and others said that was not enough: "There is nothing less useful," lectured Drucker, "than to do a little better that which should not be done at all." Business heard the prescription, and soon a new buzzword—*reengineering*—crept into the management litany and quickly redefined American business. The idea behind reengineering is to go beyond seeking efficiencies and to ask, *Is this business process (report, study, procedure) really necessary? And, if it is, how can it be designed to better serve the business?*

One of the natural fallouts of reengineering is downsizing: If a task is unnecessary, so, too, are the people who perform that task. Downsizing whipped through nearly every business, producing a mixed bag of results—in some cases creating bottlenecks because of manpower shortages, while in others effectively eliminating deadwood in organizations, lowering costs and jump-starting sagging profits. As a result, today's business profits are generally at or near record highs and product and service quality has risen appreciably. But anxiety over job security—especially among middle managers, the job function of most management accountants—has become what can best be described as a national malaise. It's only because business is so good today—effectively resulting in 0% unemployment for finance professionals—that this anxiety among CPAs has abated somewhat. But any dip in the business cycle will surely reignite the job security issue.

One of the first departments to face reengineering was finance—it was both a natural and easy target because much of its work lends itself to what the reengineering consultants call *metrics*—quantifying the cost and impact of business processes. Once a metric is determined, it can be compared with metrics taken some time earlier and later to determine its true value to the business. But before many top managers let the reengineering consultants loose to redesign the organization, they wisely undertook benchmarking studies to measure how bad—or how good—the metrics of their current processes were. In most cases, they were not good at all.

There's no question that reengineering works. In the decade or so since reengineering was first employed among mostly large and medium-size organizations, the average cost of running a finance department in those businesses has plummeted some 37%—to 1.4% of an organization's total revenue from 2.2%. (See exhibits 1 and 2.) These numbers come from Gregory Hackett, president of The Hackett Group, a Hudson, Ohio, consulting firm that has benchmarked nearly 1,000 companies (see "How Does Your Finance Department Measure Up," JofA, Jan. 97, page 50). To be sure, not all of those savings came directly from reengineering business processes; some resulted from trimming payroll. With payroll representing about half of a typical finance department's cost, it's not hard to extrapolate

In the years to come, we should expect another one-third reduction in the number of people in finance. Those cuts will have a sizable impact on accountants.

how those process improvements swelled the unemployment lines.

HEADS ROLL

Has American business cut, improved and reengineered as much it can? Hackett thinks not. Of the companies that have undertaken reengineering—and these mostly are among the *Fortune* 1000—he sees the potential for further improvements of as much as 50% in the next few years. That would bring down the average cost of running a finance department to as low as 0.7% of total revenue from the current level of 1.4%. How will such a reduction affect head counts? According to Hackett, we should expect another one-third reduction in the number of people in finance. Those cuts may include some clerical staff, but they also will have a sizable impact on accountants.

Is that as low as it can get? Hackett speculates that, based on the many reengineering studies his company has conducted, the theoretical bottom is about 0.3% of revenue—which implies another 50% cost reduction, and that, too, means the head count will be trimmed even more.

Okay, you may argue, but all this is somewhat speculative and theoretical and, anyway, we're talking about averages and trends—not specific jobs.

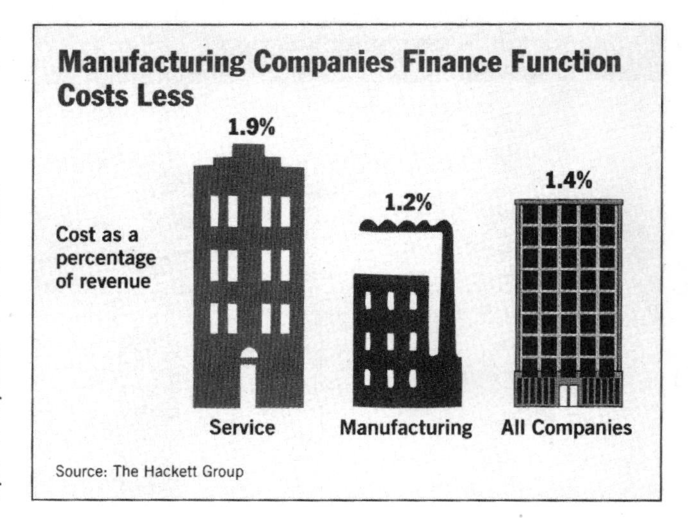

Let's talk specifics. While hard projections are impossible to come by, some anecdotal evidence that will affect the future may be useful. Phillip Ameen, CPA, controller and vice-president of General Electric, says that, generally speaking, for the last several years GE has not hired accountants for entry-level positions in the finance department and "we have no current plans to change that policy." GE is certainly not discriminating against accountants; it also avoids hiring MBAs and business majors for those jobs. Instead, he explains, the company searches for bright people who are adaptable—not those who are stuck in yesterday's business paradigm.

Once hired, the new employees are put through GE's rigorous financial training management program so they can do what the company considers to be the highest priority work of the finance department: analysis of data to support decision making by GE's top management. At the same time, the finance department has become the hub for business data—distributing information as needed throughout the enterprise.

This represents a shift from the traditional role of finance, where most, if not all, of accountants' resources were focused on transaction processing—so-called back of-

EXECUTIVE SUMMARY

■ THE ROLE OF MANAGEMENT accountants is changing, but it's unlikely they all will be able, or willing, to make the adjustment to those changes.

■ TWO ROLES THEY will be expected to play are those of business partner and change agent.

■ TO UNDERTAKE THESE new tasks, they must be prepared to become knowledge workers, setting up a computer infrastructure so they can become the hub for data—distributing information as needed throughout the enterprise.

■ ONE VIEW IS THAT ONLY ABOUT HALF of all CPAs will be able to make the transition from reporters of historical data to business partners and change agents. The other ones, if they are retained in their jobs at all, likely will become high-level clerks.

■ HERE ARE SOME WAYS ACCOUNTANTS can prepare for tomorrow: (1) Develop facilitation skills so you can excel as a change agent. (2) Think of yourself not so much as an accountant—one who balances the books—but as a knowledge professional. (3) Get used to not just looking back at historical data. (4) Recognize that it takes great courage to give up what works well now for something you know will replace it in the future.

STANLEY ZAROWIN is a senior editor on the *Journal*. Mr. Zarowin is an employee of the American Institute of CPAs and his views, as expressed in this article, do not necessarily reflect the views of the AICPA. Official positions are determined through certain specific committee procedures, due process and deliberation.

For many companies, transaction processing represents nearly 70% of their finance departments' costs, which leaves precious little time for analysis and thinking.

fice work. For many companies, transaction processing represents nearly 70% of their finance departments' costs, which leaves precious little time for analysis and what in the New Accounting has become the most important of all jobs—*putting your feet up on the desk and thinking.*

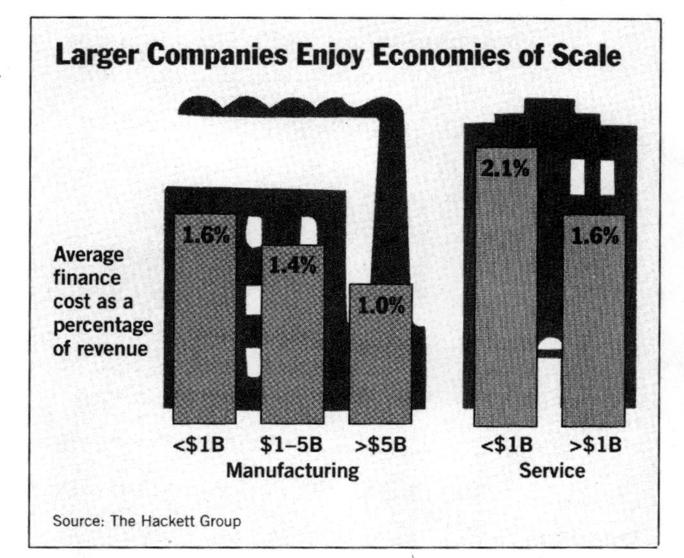

KNOWLEDGE SKILLS

Information—very current and useful information—is the lifeblood of today's business, and if tomorrow's accountants expect to be included in management's decision making, they will have to be the key personnel involved in developing, configuring and dispensing information throughout the organization. Peter Senge, head of the Centre for Organizational Learning at the Massachusetts Institute of Technology, says that today's companies owe their competitive edge to their ability to learn and to keep on learning.

"Learning," adds Shoshana Zuboff, a professor at Harvard Business School, "is the new form of labor and the heart of productive activity." And one of the primary sources of this learning? The professionals who control the information.

Management accountants' first priority, then, is to construct executive information systems so eventually line managers and others can tap into the data warehouse and easily and speedily extract the information they need to keep the business competitive.

The new accountant, then, must be ready for all of the above roles, and that includes

- Developing an in-depth understanding of all aspects of a business.
- Becoming a data hub for the business' information warehouse
- Applying analytical skills so new trends can be spotted and forecasts provided.
- Taking on the role of a business partner—providing insightful advice to top management.
- Recognizing what needs changing and then taking up the cause with effective presentation skills—in short, becoming a change agent.

To cordon off enough time for the prerequisite thinking and analyzing necessary for accountants to be effective business partners and change agents, the drudge work must be taken off their plates and shunted to computer systems that excel at handling transaction processing.

To make this transition, CPAs will have to shift their thinking and work habits. Hackett, for his part, is not optimistic that all the CPAs who work in business and industry are willing, or even able, to make that transition. To a large extent, their formal training—both in school and in subsequent jobs—rarely prepared them for many of these new tasks. For one thing, accountants are expected to be exacting, which is why monthly closings often consume many days as they conduct searches for last-minute transactions—even if those last-minute transactions are effectively small change and will have little impact on closings' results.

But are such exacting closings even necessary in the first place? Since top management generally puts little faith in the numbers that are generated by the monthly closing—and don't find much practical use for the numbers anyway—one wonders why so much time and energy is spent on the activity. Some companies, like Motorola, are beginning to wonder whether a virtual closing—a process in which computer systems handle many of the details and less attention is given to extracting a number that's correct right down to the pennies—is close enough. It certainly saves time and manpower and money.

As the controller of an automaker recently proclaimed at a business seminar, "When it comes to some reporting and forecasting, close enough is good enough." When he spoke those words, however, some of the accountants in the audience groaned. It's those groaners who probably won't be able to make the transition.

Since Hackett's firm conducts reengineering consultations for many *Fortune* 1000 businesses and thus examines his clients both before and after, he's well qualified to answer the question, How many CPAs will be capable of making the transition?

His assessment: "We find that only about half of them make it. The other ones, if they are retained in their jobs at all, become, in effect, high-level clerks." Given the salary disparity between clerks and professionals, it isn't hard to forecast the future of those CPAs who can't make the transition.

It takes great courage to give up what works well now for something that you know will replace it in the future.

The irony, Hackett adds, is that our society long ago adapted to change. While many may not like it, change today is deeply imbedded in the business culture, and we believe that if we're not changing, something's wrong. The old adage, "*If it ain't broke, don't fix it*", has changed to, "*If it's old, fix it—whether it's broken or not.*"

He adds that CPAs as a group are not in tune emotionally with change. They feel most comfortable with well-defined procedures, they dread uncertainty and they want the books to balance. But while "*close enough is good enough*" may be perfect for forecasting and seeking trend lines, it will not balance the books with the degree of accuracy that's traditionally been expected of and by accountants. However, in today's business environment, that job is best left to the computer systems, which can be programmed to handle it efficiently and economically.

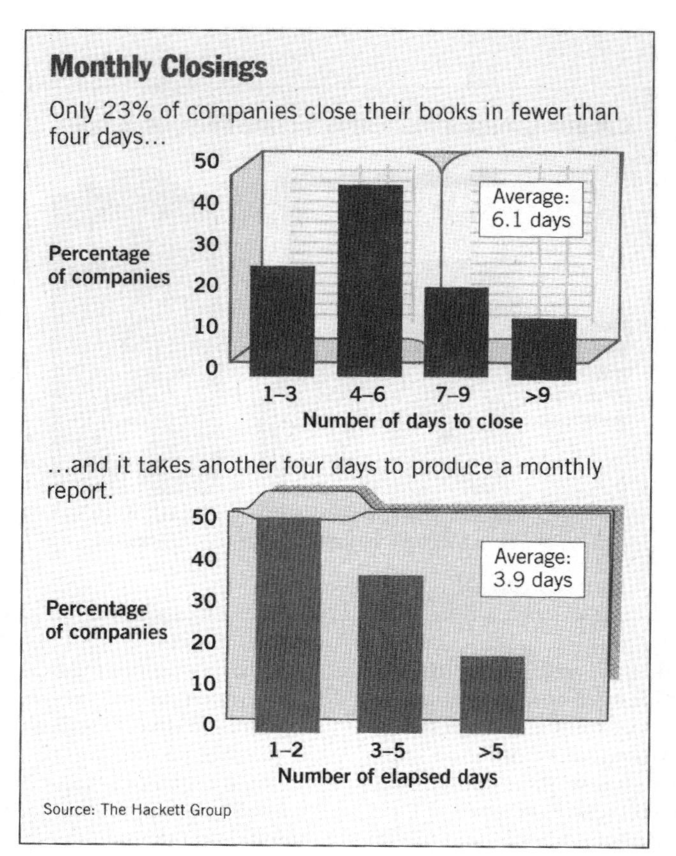

What should an accountant do to prepare for tomorrow? Here are some suggestions:

Facilitation: To be an effective change agent requires persuasion and facilitation skills—the ability to create and deliver formal presentations that use information as a tool to convince others that change is not only good but also necessary. For some, facilitation skills are an inborn gift; not so for most accountants, who tend not to be people-oriented. That's not to say they can't learn the skills. But it takes time and practice.

Knowledge: CPAs should think of themselves not so much as accountants—those who balance the books and post billings—but as knowledge professionals. Discover where the information is and how to mine it as a resource. Learn who needs the data and in what form, and build a computer infrastructure so it's readily available to the organization. Recognize that while knowledge has always been power, in today's fast-paced, highly competitive business world speedily delivered knowledge often means survival.

Discover the other departments in your organization that need what you can supply. Think of yourself as a partner to these departments. Financing's job is to knit together the basic elements of decision making: forecasting, budgeting, strategic planning, reporting, benchmarking. In other words, by integrating these functions, finance becomes a chief driver of the decision- making process (see "Becoming a Business Partner," JofA, Mar.97, page 72).

Foresight: Get away from just looking back, putting the accounting magnifying lens only on historical data. Start to look ahead—using a telescope. Use yesterday's data as a guide for tomorrow, but remember the old adage—"*History surely repeats itself, but not always in quite the same way.*"

Risk: Accountancy training stresses risk reduction—or at least risk identification of what's known. But change requires a willingness to examine the unknown, which, in turn, implies risk taking. It takes great courage to give up what works well now for something that you know will replace it in the future. Or, viewed from the other side of the coin, *if you always do what you've always done, you'll always get what you always got.*

Outsourcing: Don't be rigid in thinking about outsourcing. Many finance departments raise a knee-jerk objection to it because they fear it will erode their power. The day may come when it's economical to outsource even the entire finance department. But, remember, if you're prepared to assume the new role as knowledge guru, such a move will not be traumatic for you.

Analysis: Recognize that the only way to really know whether change is called for is to measure what you're doing. In your new role as a facilitator and change agent, get to know the metrics and be involved in benchmarking so you'll know when it ain't worth fixing. Be open to such innovations as the virtual close, rather than investing a week in a mechanical operation that fewer and fewer top managers find especially useful.

As a CFO at a *Fortune* 500 firm put it in trying to convince his accounting staff to think out of the box, "Thanks very much, but the beans have already been counted. Time to rethink your jobs."

It's Not Your Father's Management Accounting!

BY C. S. "BUD" KULESZA, CMA, CFM, AND GARY SIEGEL, CPA

Numbers crunching and data collection alone are a thing of the past. Now our profession has entered the realm of financial management, business strategy, information technology, and information management. What else lies ahead?

What knowledge, skills, and abilities do we need as management accountants to keep pace with the changes in our profession? That question is difficult to answer. Try as we will, we only have a picture of what is being practiced at one point in time. If we look at a series of these point-in-time pictures, particularly of leading-edge companies, we soon gain insight into the direction management accounting is moving. Most important, it becomes all too obvious that direction is all we ever will have, as we are a profession that will continue to add value only as we remake ourselves to meet the ever changing needs of our environment.

Much of our metamorphosis has been evolutionary rather than revolutionary—until the last five to 10 years, that is. Few professions can say they have experienced the degree and speed of change that management accounting has experienced.

WHAT ARE THE CHANGES?

Not since 1492 with the invention of double entry accounting by Fr. Luca Pacioli has anything impacted accounting as much as the silicon chip. Information technology—both hardware and software—has become remarkably available and affordable. Over the past few years, automation has increased dramatically, system capability has expanded enormously, and integrated information systems have been developed. Many traditional accounting functions have been computerized and centralized and have been shifted from management accounting to clerical staff. Electronic mail and electronic data interchange (EDI) are used extensively.

These changes have made information more accessible than ever. Closing the books at year-end used to take weeks. Now many companies close in a few days or are near virtual close. Consequently, the finance staff can get results to management in a fraction of the previous time.

Also, the days of entering data and producing basic reports are over. Management accountants must interpret and analyze data and do financial planning and financial modeling. Many people we interviewed as part of IMA's Practice Analysis[1] said it isn't as important to know what the numbers are as to know what the numbers mean. These comments are consistent with businesses wanting more involvement from management accountants throughout the entire business process. A Hewlett-Packard finance manager summed up the change: "We are not accountants; we are analysts and business partners."

And here are more changes: Routine/mechanical transactions are being automated and centralized; companies are being reengineered; processes are changing; the idea of continuous improvement is not just a slogan—it's for real; the focus is on the customer; and there is a mandate to use costs in a forward-looking way. As a result, management accountants no longer are performing many of the traditional functions connected to "accounting" in its data collection and statement preparation aspects. Instead, management accountants are taking on a new role, one with much more financial emphasis than traditional accounting.

At all professional levels in the finance function in the companies we visited (see sidebar), data collection, data entry, and straightforward reporting of data are being replaced by explanation, interpretation, and analysis of data. In their new role, management accountants are business partners, members of cross-functional teams, change agents, and organizational educators. They refer to themselves not as "accountants" but as members of the "finance function" because finance has a broader connotation than accounting. Accounting is perceived as a system that reports on what happened in the past, while finance focuses on the future. In fact, in two companies we visited, management accountants shun the word finance and call themselves decision-support specialists. They reason it is a much better description of what they do.

But regardless of how they refer to themselves, management accountants see their role as distilling diverse information, putting it into a useful format, and facilitating management decision making. Clearly, they are spending less time on transactions and more time working with other functions or enterprise business opportunities.

What other changes are coming? In the words of the accounting executives we interviewed as part of the Practice Analysis project:

In our organization, we are trying to fashion ourselves into a provider of distilled information that the senior managers can act on very quickly versus providing a bunch of data and letting them sort through it. (US West)

Fourteen years ago the job was to get the numbers in the right columns, get the books closed at month-end. What we are asking people to do is not only close the books but help people manage the business so we can be more effective and more profitable and more operationally effective. (Hewlett-Packard)

(The role of finance) will progress toward less data gathering and more data analysis and consultation kind of work so that it will take a more skilled person to help teams and get them focused on understanding their costs. We are getting to a point now where everybody has a PC. I think it's important that we move to a mode where we've got things so integrated that a manager can point and click and see information and then ask questions. Then we should be sitting with them to help them understand and to answer some of their questions and to help them analyze. (Caterpillar)

...Change is accelerating as we go. The change in the last five years is much more dramatic than, say, the previous five or 10...Now the accountants are not only the interpreters, but they help drive management toward the proper response to what the numbers are telling us and toward helping tie together the financial results with the business strategies. We're going from a number-crunching-type mode to a business partnership, more strategic approach. (ITT Automotive)

Run-of-the-mill finance departments are spending all their time building the reports and throwing them over the fence. Leading-edge finance departments have got the reports just coming through, and they're spending their time analyzing the data and telling the management team what they need to know. (Boeing)

It is critical that both financial and nonfinancial people understand the total context in which their company operates. Not only do finance staff need to understand the whole business to be most useful, but engineers and manufacturing staff need to understand costs and how important they are. This transference of such management accounting skills as strategic cost management gives leading companies a better-quality solution to enterprise business problems. It is not unlike transferring quality knowledge to production workers so they can build quality into the product rather than inspect it out.

TEAMWORK

The trend toward business partnering and working on cross-functional teams has fostered an increase in interaction. Most accounting/finance staff report spending a substantial proportion of their time working with other departments. That means good communication skills are of paramount importance. These "soft skills," once considered "nice" to have, now are "necessary" for successful employment.

The new roles require finance staff to be more accessible, to stop policing, and to become full partners on a team. In many organizations the transition from control and compliance to trust and respect may be difficult because of past practices or because some managers may not believe we management accountants can quickly adapt to new ways of doing business. Therefore, as a profession, we have to build good working relationships with people in other departments. This is especially important given the trend in many companies to locate management accountants in the departments they service rather than in accounting departments that are physically isolated from the people they have to work with. Some of the companies we interviewed described the interactions of their finance staffs with other departments in the following manner:

We are involved on teams where [products are being developed]. The service we provide is financial analysis. We try to bring certain analytical skills [to the table] to evaluate and identify alternatives and then to model that from a cost and benefit perspective. There are many different tools we bring in terms of statistical or financial type analyses. (Ohmeda)

Our accountants have a seat in accounting, but we ask them to be out of their seat more often than they are in it because what they ought to be doing is working as a business partner with the production managers. They need to help the managers understand ways to do things better in the manufacturing process. Instead of just an MOH (manufacturing overhead) number that is applied for cost accounting reasons, we want to provide production managers with data that say, "Here is what is driving your overhead structure; here is what you can fundamentally do different to drive your costs down." (Hewlett-Packard)

Note: Being part of a team helps people learn more about their company:

I try to make sure that as many people as I can are involved in various teams because what that does is give them a sense of what other functions are working on—it gives them a sense of contributing to the organization. (Ohmeda)

BECOMING BUSINESS PARTNERS

Suddenly management accountants are in demand in all aspects of business. The management accountant's broad knowledge of the organization, coupled with his/her strong analytical skills and familiarity with available information, makes him/her a valuable business partner. How do companies describe this trend toward business partnering?

...we have gotten away from just being a policeman or bookkeeper to being more an advocate of management and working hand in hand with management on influencing or molding the decisions that are made by the various organizations within the company so that finance has a true input. Now you are more a partner. You can advise others that if they do one thing, the impact on the financial results will be that. (Abbott Labs)

I see the role as consultant rather than cop. I think by analyzing a department's function we should be able to come up with recommendations that will increase efficiencies. (Gates)

In this organization there has been a lot of effort to build bridges and to partner as opposed to being the watchdogs of the organization. That is what auditors end up being, and that is what traditionally accountants got pigeonholed into. I think that has changed. I think there are a lot of people here that are very receptive to that change. We hear from people that we are helpful. (Ohmeda)

SEEING THE BIG PICTURE

Executives want data to be presented in a context that is meaningful to them. To be successful, accountants need to broaden their perspective so they can understand and explain things in business rather than financial accounting terms. To accomplish this goal, management accountants need to increase their general understanding of the business environment inside their company as well as their company's industry. Focusing on the important assumptions underlying a strategy or problem or doing things faster (timeliness) is more important than the preciseness of the calculation.

GETTING THERE

In the past, management accountants weren't noted for their interactive skills or interest in other areas of the business. As a result, organizations haven't been proactive in involving the finance staff in the business decision-making process. Financial professionals who are interested in changing the way they interface with the rest of the organization must take the first step to show they are high-level contributors who can add value to the process. Once they prove to their organization that they are supportive, willing to expand their overall business knowledge, and share their financial acumen, the demands for their services will soar.

Managers at Boeing report that members of their company's finance staff are working hard to get other departments to include them in the decision-making process:

It's been a long, hard road. The finance people used to be very adversarial. They would just automatically say no. They were paid to do that. Today it's not so much saying, no, it's how you say no or how you work with others so they come to that conclusion themselves. In years past the work statement would be developed, finance folks would go off into their world somewhere else, come up with some numbers, and say, "Here's what the numbers say, and you guys can't do this." The biggest thing is we had to get out of the control mode. We had to move from control to enable. The finance function of this company had been in a control mode for a long time, so the change isn't overnight. You have to earn others' trust.

DEFINING THE EXPECTATIONS

Companies expect management accountants to have solid technical skills and strong interpersonal skills coupled with solid business acumen. Sound like a lot to expect? It is, but it's the price management accountants pay for having one of the most involved, broad-based, and interesting jobs.

Taken together, the technical and job function changes have led to higher expectations about the performance of management accountants:

You notice none of my people are called clerical this or that. They are all analysts. That is deliberate. I expect them to think, to know what the end point is, what our expectations are. Once they have done that, as long as they've got the capability, I give them the resources and let them do their job. That is a huge change. (Takata)

Good oral and written communication skills are essential because finance staff need to be able to distill information and then communicate it clearly:

We are speaking to senior managers who don't have a lot of time. You have to be crystal clear, very crisp, very good at articulating, particularly if you are trying to persuade in five minutes. (U S West)

You obviously have to have the tools to do the job, but to communicate your answers and your conclusions to somebody else so that they understand it—that's the key. (ITT Automotive)

Accountants must do multi-faceted decision support, decisions at an operating level, at a divisional level, at a corporate level. People must float across division and functional lines in providing support and almost integrating into the operations. (Abbott Labs)

The world we're describing isn't specialized like we were trained to be. It needs more generalists. A generalist has to be able to take the detail data, which will be managed by a computer system, supposedly with some smarts to it, and interpret it for use by the management team. That means financial professionals are going to take the financial data, the human resources data, and the scheduling data and the other metrics that the business manager needs and report out to the guy. They're going to have much more general knowledge of how the business works.

Also, they need a strong capability of using software enabling technology, the ability to use a suite of software or processing database, spreadsheets, graphic tools, the ability to access data out of many legacy systems. It's a required piece of the toolkit which wasn't the case five years ago. Five years ago, you could rely on some systems person to go and write an extract report gathered out of a mainframe or something like that. That is not our world today. (Boeing)

WHAT'S AHEAD?

Everyone we interviewed expects the trend we have described to continue. Management accountants, frequently called finance staff, will do less accounting and more financial analysis and business partnering. While there is agreement on the direction, there are differences by company in predictions about how fast and how far change will go. These differences probably are rooted in where the company is now, the speed at which its practices are changing, and the organization's attitude toward change. One company's present practice is another company's future practice.

As a profession, few can compare to management accounting and its ability to remake itself as the needs of business change. The transition from transactional activities and control to more financial management, analysis, and decision support is directly in concert with the business demands of today. The emphasis on using accounting to move the business forward rather than look historically at the past is evident everywhere we look. Professional organizations and universities alike have recognized this change in the business environment by focusing their programs to help individuals meet these new demands. As individuals we need to be aware of the changing business needs so that we can determine the best way to meet those needs and then implement those changes actively

COMPANIES INTERVIEWED

As part of the Practice Analysis of Management Accounting, in-depth, in-person interviews were conducted at nine leading-edge companies to understand what management accountants are doing today and where the profession is headed:

Abbott Laboratories	Abbott Park, Ill.
Boeing Company	Renton, Wash.
Caterpillar	Aurora, Ill.
Gates Rubber Co.	Denver, Colo.
Hewlett-Packard	Fort Collins, Colo.
ITT Automotive	Auburn Hills, Mich.
Ohmeda	Louisville, Colo.
TAKATA Inc.	Auburn Hills, Mich.
U S West	Englewood, Colo.

The interviews, conducted from June through August 1995, focused on how the profession is changing and the skills that are needed to make the transition.

The Practice Analysis information presents a clear picture of where management accounting was, where it is now, and where it is heading in the future. You can use the information to prepare yourself, your staff, and your companies for new accounting . The Practice Analysis is available on the IMA home page on the Internet at www.imanet.org under the category IMA Materials.

within our organizations. We must make certain that we have the knowledge, skills, and abilities to change ourselves and our organizations. If we don't, we and our organizations will be left behind as progress passes us by. As the adage goes, change is the only constant.

C.S. "Bud" Kulesza, CMA, CFM, is senior vice president and controller of ITT Automotive and a member of IMA's Board of Directors where he is a national vice president.

Gary Siegel, CPA, Ph.D., is an associate professor in the School of Accountancy at DePaul University and president of the Gary Siegel Organization, an independent opinion research and behavioral accounting firm.

1Gary Siegel, CPA, and C.S. "Bud" Kulesza, CMA, CFM, "The Practice Analysis of Management Accounting," MANAGEMENT ACCOUNTING, April 1996, pp. 20-28. The original research can be found in Gary Siegel, *The Practice Analysis of Management Accounting*, Institute of Management Accountants, Montvale, N.J., 1996.

Managerial Accounting Needs a Philosophical Base

BY RICHARD VANGERMEERSCH, CMA

There is a considerable void in the literature of management accounting. Management accounting seems to be a free-standing phenomenon without a deep philosophical base. There have been some extremely well-thought-out works in accounting such as Mautz and Sharif's *The Philosophy of Auditing*, Littleton's *Structure of Accounting Theory*, and Scott's *Cultural Significance of Accounts*, which form a philosophical basis for generally accepted accounting principles (GAAP).[1]

There are no complementary works in the field of management accounting although McFarland's *Concepts for Management Accounting* and Marple's *Toward a Basic Accounting Philosophy* seem to be searching for managerial accepted accounting principles (MAAP) but don't seem to get any further than managerial accepted accounting practices.[2]

If management accounting were solidly grounded in a basic philosophy, it would facilitate the teaching of cost/management accounting as well as the practice of management accounting. I prepared a list of 50 proposed managerial accepted accounting principles, and I presented them to my students in cost/management accounting. Many improvements were suggested.[3] The MAAP list presented here is not intended to be inclusive, and I realize MAAP will vary from organization to organization. It would be wise for each organization to develop its own list for distribution to its management accountants. I would like to collect as many of these lists as possible so that ideas can be exchanged. What follows is an edited list of proposals in four general categories.

TIMELY AND ACCURATE INFORMATION

- Communication must be clear, direct, and appropriate. Management accountants must become communicators.
- Managerial accounting must seek the truth. And two qualities of the truth should be especially valued: that it can be pragmatic and that it can be specific to particular situations.
- Management accountants must have the freedom to create. Without this freedom, they cannot adapt to different companies, to different timing horizons, and to different managements.
- Management accountants need to delineate best practices in MAAP. A

Reprinted with permission from *Management Accounting,* June 1997, pp. 45-47.

source for best practices could be an open-ended survey of top corporate finance officials. As best practices are defined, they should be published in the introductory comments in companies' accounting manuals.

- Managerial accounting must be allowed flexibility in responding to time periods.

  There must be rigorous training in the four time periods of economic theory: very short run, short run, intermediate run, and the long run. Managerial accounting needs to be aware of the many concepts of cost and how these concepts relate to the four economic time frames. These concepts are too numerous to list here. While it may be logical to operate in an incremental revenue minus incremental cost in the short run, this logic fails in the intermediate run and is not a relevant approach for the long run. There are numerous examples of American businesses and entire industries going bankrupt because of pricing behavior. The length of time in each of the four economic time frames must be determined continuously by each organization. There must be a managerial team set up to handle this issue.
- Managerial accounting is number- as well as dollar-oriented. Resources with number implications include such items as employees, materials, the plant, land, and machinery.

DIRECTION AND MOTIVATION

- Management accounting is a profession. The Certified Management Accountant exam and status must become better known. Management accounting pertains to organizations in all types of settings: profit, not-for-profit, and governmental. The general public should be made aware that good management is found not only in the profit sector.
- Management accounting needs to go beyond the pragmatic. The development of the intellectual growth of the management accountant will contribute to his or her success.
- Management accountants should operate within the context of the code of ethics that has been developed and published.
- Management accountants must assume that their tasks are important. How else can they convince others of the importance of the field?
- Management accountants must be able to relate their work to the managerial functions of planning, control, and evaluation. Management accountants must strive for the same level of performance in administration, marketing, and MIS as they do in manufacturing.
- Managerial accounting must generate a higher net income to the organization through better managerial decisions. Ultimately, managerial accounting comes down to a net income figure. If it does not, users will not relate very well to management accounting.
- Participative management is a positive philosophy. Management accounting systems and management accountants must be in the forefront of any "be the best you can be" movement.
- Management accounting should focus on incentive systems at all levels of the organization. Variances are just the beginning of the analytical process and not the end of it. Variances are just the start of the "sleuthing process" for management accountants. If the organization does not provide a training program, and/or fund an MBA degree, the management accountant must design and fund his own training program or graduate education. Too many management accountants reach their plateau too soon.
- Management accountants must be just as concerned with measuring and controlling liquidity as they are with measuring and controlling income. Unless equal weight is given to liquidity, there never will be an improvement in bankruptcy statistics. In order to achieve liquidity, the management accountant always must conclude his analysis of a decision with its effect on the cash budget.

ADVANTAGES OF MAAP OVER GENERALLY ACCEPTED ACCOUNTING PRINCIPLES (GAAP) AND TAX ACCEPTED ACCOUNTING PRINCIPLES

- Financial accounting and managerial accounting should be complementary in nature, not competitive. Every cost/management accountant should be well versed in the philosophy, principles, and practices of financial accounting.
- Managerial accounting always must be aware of GAAP and tax accounting practices. They won't go away. They must be dealt with by the organization and must be constantly on the minds of management accountants.
- Management accounting must weigh information overload against the simplicity of just following GAAP and tax accounting. There is a need for a sound training program in accounting for nonaccountants. Managerial accounting can break away internally from GAAP by different internal reporting of such items as research and development costs, computer software costs, major marketing efforts, direct costing, life cycle, and value-chain accounting. Again, middle and top management must be involved, and a training program must be established to explain the internal reporting system. If managerial accounting breaks away from GAAP, managerial accounting must be sure to reconcile to GAAP and tax accounting. Without integration and understanding, managerial accounting will become trivialized.

MORE SPECIFIC TOPICS

- Management accountants must be able to demystify the cost allocation process. They should not be the only ones in the organization to understand this process.
- Management accountants need to recreate the one strong tie between industrial engineers and management accountants. A standard cost card is based on the invaluable engineering concept of standardization.
- Management accountants must be well read in the literature of management as well as in the practices of budgeting. Too many accountants view management as "touchy-feely" in nature and not deserving of study.
- Management accountants must become as knowledgeable about

estimation of sales figures as marketing executives.

- Management accountants must not be locked in by budgets and standards and must be able to make changes because of subsequent information. One year is too long to wait for corrections.
- Management accounting must have policies governing inventory, and these policies must be built into the accounting system. The recent emphasis on just-in-time (JIT) is indicative of this need.
- Management accounting should incorporate capacity as an important concept. Not only are there different ways of measuring capacity (ideal, practical, normal, budget), but there are different numbers of capacity for each of these time periods (short, intermediate, and long runs).
- The concept of opportunity costs must become a key analytical tool of the management accountant and be explained carefully to all users.
- Management accountants can use the job-order procedure in many more instances than just accounting for units produced—for instance, R&D, major marketing programs, human resource costs, and major maintenance projects. Long-term effects must not be drowned by short-term net-income considerations. A job-order-based, "off the ledger" system must be developed for key items like those mentioned above to combat short-run thinking. The job-order approach can be used for many purposes other than that of a specific manufacturing job.
- Managerial accounting must be able to project ranges of revenues as well as ranges of costs and expenses. This projection must be done at all levels and at all points in the organization. Costs displayed without accompanying revenues present an incomplete picture. Management accountants must display the same level of interest in revenues as they do production costs.
- Management accountants must have a sound knowledge of the literature and practice of the pricing function. As there is not a good accounting text on this issue, management accountants need special guidance on this issue. While pricing may not be a function of the management accountants, they should be on the pricing team. If there is no pricing team, an organization should consider creating one.
- Management accountants should abhor waste. For too long, waste has been rationalized in too many organizations. Waste should be controlled by numbers as well as dollars. This is one issue about which management accountants can do a great deal for society. Management accountants should lead efforts to move treated waste to waste; move wastes to scrap; move scrap to by-products; and move by-products to joint products. Again, a proactive role must be assumed.

There are two corollaries to the proposed MAAP principles that were not included in these groupings. One is that the field of management accounting needs to develop MAAP. Before one can have managerial accepted accounting practices, one must develop managerial accepted accounting principles. These practices must be tied to guides for actions, but these guides for actions need to be framed within a coherent philosophy. The other is that it will take years to develop into a cohesive and coherent package.

The concepts I have presented represent a start in the development of managerial accepted accounting principles. Not only will there be many more concepts added to MAAP, but there will be a deepening of each as well. This deepening will occur when the many classic books on cost/management accounting are analyzed for their contributions to MAAP. Let's give our field a more explicit philosophical base.

Richard Vangermeersch, CMA, is a professor of accounting at the University of Rhode Island at Kingston, R.I. He is a member of the Providence Chapter of the IMA, through which this article was submitted. Professor Vangermeersch can be reached at (401) 874-4338.

[1] R.K. Mautz and Hussein Sharif, *The Philosophy of Auditing*, Monograph No. 6, American Accounting Association, 1961. A.C. Littleton, *Structure of Accounting Theory*, Monograph No. 5, American Accounting, 1953. L.C. Scott, *Cultural Significance of Accounts*, Scholars reprint.

[2] Walter B. McFarland, *Concepts for Management Accounting*, New York, National Association of Accountants (now IMA), 1966. Raymond P. Marple, *Toward a Basic Accounting Philosophy*, New York, National Association of Accountants (now IMA), 1964.

[3] A graduate student, Matthew White, suggested a grouping system, which is followed in this article.

COST/MANAGEMENT ACCOUNTING

The 21st Century Paradigm

The old individually focused control concepts inherent in standard costing and responsibility accounting may be counterproductive in today's world.

WILLIAM L. FERRARA, CPA

Certificate of Merit, 1994-95

What will the field of management accounting look like in the 21st century? To find out, let's consider four paradigms that cover its recent history. These paradigms provide us with an intriguing review of the current scene from a historical perspective (see Table 1) and an opportunity to focus on unresolved issues. Ultimately, we can consider adjusting and even combining paradigms in anticipation of a new one for the 21st century.

For continuity and simplicity, we'll consider each paradigm in the context of both product costing and the determination of selling price. This context is useful especially because the current vogue of activity-based cost analysis emphasizes improved product costing in order to arrive at better pricing decisions.

Paradigm A: Turn of the century until the 1940s—the era of the Industrial Revolution plus. Paradigm A conjures up the image of an early-day industrial engineering type such as Frederick Taylor who was interested in what costs should be, that is, standard costs. These engineering-driven standards were typically a function of product specifications, time and motion studies, and the like. The costs involved were direct materials, direct labor, manufacturing overhead, and even marketing and administrative costs, all of which were tied together in a total cost per unit of output.

Added to the total cost per unit was a desired profit or markup, and the sum of total cost and desired profit yielded a target selling price per unit. In many instances, the total cost per unit excluded marketing and/or administrative costs, which were included as a factor in the desired profit. The ultimate result was still the target selling price per unit—the price that would yield desired profitability if projected costs per unit could be achieved.

Two issues of contention surface immediately with Paradigm A:

1. What volume of activity should be used to determine unit costs?
2. How should desired profit be determined?

The variety of answers typically offered is amazing even if both questions are put to an audience of practitioners representing various departments of the same company, as I have done over many years.

Table 2 shows possible answers for the "volume of activity" question, which must be addressed to determine total unit costs for Paradigms A, B, and C. Answers usually lean in the direction of expected volume or something referred to as standard or normal volume. A rather difficult aspect of the expected volume answer is its implicit circular reasoning—expected volume assumes a selling price while it is being used to determine unit costs and ultimately a "target" selling price.

The answers for the "desired profit" question typically used to be very subjective or rule-of-thumb oriented. In recent years, however, up-to-date return on investment and cost of capital concepts have been considered in the most prevalent answers.

As we move on to subsequent paradigms, these two questions or issues of contention remain, and others emerge.

Paradigm B: The 1940s until the 1980s—the era of cost-volume-profit analysis and direct costing. Paradigm B introduces the distinction between fixed and variable costs, which ultimately leads to cost-volume-profit

Reprinted with permission from *Management Accounting*, December 1995, pp. 30-34, 36.

analysis and direct costing. The fixed/variable cost dichotomy and its implications encompass the most dynamic developments in management accounting from the 1940s to the 1980s.

On the surface, not much seems to change between Paradigms A and B other than the distinction between fixed and variable costs as part of a total unit cost and a target selling price. However, even a cursory consideration of Tables 1 and 2 reveals a refinement of one of our issues of contention, that is:

1. Variable costs per unit are determined by engineering standards and analytic techniques, which means that the volume of activity issue relates essentially to fixed costs.
2. Furthermore, many variable costs have become more fixed over time. Union contracts and labor legislation have affected labor costs in just this fashion.

The issue of how to determine desired profit remains an issue of contention as we move to Paradigms C and D.

Variable costs per unit for direct materials and direct labor are determined easily by the engineering specifications for materials and labor requirements. Similarly, the per-unit amounts of other variable costs can be calculated. Techniques that typically are variations of regression analysis isolate the variable cost per unit as the "b" coefficient in flexible budget formulations.

Deriving variable costs per unit via engineering standards and analytic techniques leaves us with only the fixed costs to consider when determining the volume of activity to divide by in deriving per-unit costs. None of the other issues related to the volume-of-activity question changes from our earlier discussion, except that many variable costs have become more fixed over time. In essence, the issue of volume of activity to divide by has become a larger issue as the relative amount of variable costs has diminished and the relative amount of fixed costs has increased.

Paradigm C: The late 1980s and the early 1990s—the era of activity-based costing. Much of the recent, exciting revival of interest in cost/management accounting relates to Paradigm C, which embodies activity-based costing (ABC). On the surface, Paradigm C considers only two additional variable costs in the development of a total cost per unit. Recognition of these additional variable costs is designed to improve the accuracy of a total unit cost, which then should improve the determination of selling prices and product mix decisions.

The new or additional variable costs of ABC relate to product complexity and product diversity. As shown in Tables 1 and 2, there are three elements of variable manufacturing cost under ABC:[1]

1. Costs that vary with units of product.
2. Costs that vary with product complexity, such as number of batches.
3. Costs that vary with product diversity, such as number of products.

The implications of the new categories of variable costs initially suggest a decreased number of fixed costs, but *further consideration of ABC leads me to suspect that the supposed additional variable costs are really fixed costs.*

This additional issue of contention could revive the controversy over "direct costing versus absorption costing," a paramount issue of the late 1950s and 1960s. Look at the ABC literature. It doesn't take much to see the possibility that ABC is nothing more than an updated, revised, and most likely, more accurate version of absorption costing.

It's unfortunate that the advocates of ABC virtually have ignored the significance of Paradigm B's direct costing implications that were put forth so eloquently by J. S. Earley in 1955. According to Earley, the new management accounting "implied basing decisions on their estimated effects on marginal balances and contribution margins rather than upon 'full cost' calculations. It involves consistent references to variable costs and 'specific' fixed costs where these are relevant—and neglect of those costs unaffected by decisions."[2]

Another interesting facet of cost/management accounting virtually ignored by the advocates of ABC is the emergence of Paradigm D. This paradigm, which appears to have had its origins in Japan (Hiromoto), has the potential to revolu-

SUPERSTOCK

Old manufacturing systems, like the cash register production line above, have given way to the new production line systems, but some elements remain the same.

tionize cost/management accounting as it implicitly asks ABC enthusiasts, "What do costs have to do with the determination of selling prices? With the exception of cost-based pricing contracts, the market determines the price, and the role of cost is to help determine whether or not it is wise to enter the market or stay in the market."[3]

Paradigm D: The 1990s and beyond—the era of market-driven standard (allowable or target) costs as opposed to engineering-driven standard costs. Under Paradigm D we no longer look to the development of a total unit cost in order to help determine a selling price. Instead we use the selling price we believe the market will allow to help us determine the cost that the market will allow. Peter Drucker has referred to this concept as price-led costing as opposed to cost-led pricing.

The allowable or target cost per unit is a market-driven standard cost that has to be met if desired profits are to be achieved. Paradigm D questions the validity of any paradigm based on engineering-driven standard costs. Perhaps after some 90 years, the engineering-driven standard costs of Frederick Taylor and his contemporaries have been partially or wholly displaced by market-driven standard costs.

We still have the issue of how to determine desired profit with Paradigm D. However, Paradigm D creates a whole series of provocative new issues such as:

1. All that counts is that total cost per unit ultimately must not exceed the allowable or target cost if the desired profit is to be attained. This idea may mean that now the distinction between fixed and variable costs is either irrelevant or considerably less relevant.
2. If we truly believe in continuous improvement, then the allowable or target cost per unit must be reduced over time.
3. The way we work may have to change in order for us to reduce costs. Ultimately, this change can lead to the empowerment of our own workforce for, as we all know, often it is those closest to the action who can lead us on the path of continuous improvement.

This issue of continuous improvement via empowerment involves all people in the workforce—those in the factory, in procurement, in marketing and distribution, and in administrative offices.[4] Continuous improvement even creates the possibility of more positive relationships

Table 1. A HISTORICAL REVIEW OF COSTING/PRICING ISSUES VIA FOUR PARADIGMS

Costing/Pricing—Paradigm A Turn of the Century Until the 1940s: The Era of the Industrial Revolution Plus	
Direct materials	XX
Direct labor	XX
Manufacturing overhead	XX
Marketing and administrative	XX
Total cost per unit	XX
Desired profit (markup)	XX
Target selling price per unit	XX

Costing/Pricing—Paradigm B The 1940s Until the 1980s The Era of Cost-Volume-Profit Analysis and Direct Costing	
Variable costs	XX
Direct materials	XX
Direct labor	XX
Variable manufacturing overhead	XX
Variable marketing and administrative	XX
Total variable cost per unit	XX
Fixed costs	
Fixed manufacturing overhead	XX
Fixed marketing and administrative	XX
Total fixed cost per unit	XX
Grand total cost per unit	XX
Desired profit (markup)	XX
Target selling price per unit	XX

Costing/Pricing—Paradigm C The Late 1980s and Early 1990s: The Era of Activity-Based Costing	
Variable costs	
Direct materials	XX
Direct labor	XX
Variable manufacturing overhead	
Variable with number of units	XX
Variable with product complexity (number of batches)	XX
Variable with product diversity (number of products)	XX
Variable marketing and administrative	XX
Total variable cost per unit	XX
Fixed costs	
Fixed manufacturing overhead	XX
Fixed marketing and administrative	XX
Total fixed cost per unit	XX
Grand total cost per unit	XX
Desired profit (markup)	XX
Target selling price per unit	XX

Costing/Pricing—Paradigm D The 1990s and Beyond: The Era of Market-Driven Standard (Allowable) Costs	
Selling price (given competitive setting)	XX
Less desired profit	XX
Allowable or target cost per unit	XX

with suppliers and customers, again to reduce costs and increase quality and performance.[5] Tom Johnson, one of the early enthusiasts of ABC, stated the case for continuous improvement as follows: "Do activity costing if you must. But don't fool yourself into thinking that ABC will help you become a global competitor. For that, get busy with the improvement process!"[6]

REFINING AND FOCUSING ISSUES OF CONTENTION

Look at Paradigm D again. The two questions or issues of contention for Paradigm A concerning desired profit and level of volume remain, but they are easier to deal with in the era of Paradigm D. Given our current knowledge of cost of capital concepts, we can deal effectively with desired profit in terms of the level of profit needed to keep the suppliers of capital (debt and equity) satisfied given a particular profit planning horizon.

In terms of the volume of activity issue, Paradigm D can yield an answer that would have been considered only tentatively under earlier paradigms because of its implicit circular reasoning. For example, given the selling price being considered, one could argue for using the expected volume of activity at that selling price for the time period being considered—whether a month, or a quarter, or a year. The resultant expected cost per unit then could be compared to the allowable or target cost per unit of Paradigm D. An unfavorable comparison should produce a questioning attitude concerning what can be done about costs (fixed, variable, or other) or expected activity via alterations in pricing and promotion strategies that would improve the situation. The answers to such questions could provide the continuous improvements of which Johnson spoke.

When viewing volume of activity after the fact, one should shift to calculating actual costs per unit using the actual volume of activity. The result would be a comparison of allowable (target) costs, expected costs, and actual costs per unit. Especially useful would be the comparison of expected and actual costs per unit in terms of what caused the difference, if any, that is, inability to achieve anticipated continuous cost improvements and/or inability to achieve expected volume for the product promotion and pricing strategies chosen.

Table 2. THREE HISTORICAL PARADIGMS RELATIVE TO CALCULATING AND USING UNIT PRODUCT COSTS*

Paradigm A
Calculating and Using Unit Product Costs
Ignoring the Distinction Between Fixed and Variable Costs

Manufacturing costs	
Direct materials	$ 200,000
Direct labor	250,000
Manufacturing overhead	450,000
Marketing and administrative costs	500,000
Total	$1,400,000

Paradigm B
Calculating and Using Unit Product Costs
Using the Distinction Between Fixed and Variable Costs

Variable costs		
Direct materials	$	1.00 per unit
Direct labor		1.25 per unit
Manufacturing overhead		.50 per unit
Marketing and administrative		.25 per unit
Total	$	3.00 per unit
Fixed costs		
Manufacturing overhead	350,000	
Marketing and administrative	450,000	
Total	$ 800,000	

Paradigm C
Calculating and Using Unit Product Costs
The New Ideology of Activity-Based Costing

Variable costs		
Direct materials	$	1.00 per unit
Direct labor		1.25 per unit
Variable manufacturing overhead		
Variable with number of units		.50 per unit
Variable with product complexity (number of batches)		.40 per unit
Variable with product diversity (number of products)		.35 per unit
Variable marketing and administrative		.25 per unit
Total	$	3.75 per unit
Fixed costs		
Manufacturing overhead	$ 175,000	
Marketing and administrative	450,000	
Total	$ 625,000	

Note: Volume levels to be considered for determining unit costs: actual volume–last period; average actual volume–e.g., past five years; expected volume–next period; average expected volume–e.g., next five years; capacity; other possibilities–standard or normal volume, given that these volume levels can be precisely defined.

*The numbers in the above illustrations are intended only to be illustrative in the broadest sense. They have no other intended purpose.

THE CURRENT SCENE

Table 3 is designed to point out some remaining issues of contention. The first, concerning the volume of activity to use under Paradigm D, was the one just discussed. The remainder follow.

Diminishing product life cycles. As life cycles for many new products decrease, the reasons for using Paradigm D increase.[7] Some products don't last long enough for engineering-driven standards to be established and utilized. Such products literally must achieve the allowable or target cost of Paradigm D in their design stage if a desired profit is to be realized.

Somewhat related to shorter product life cycles is the notion of idle capacity, which no longer may be as important a costing concept as it used to be. The suggested use of expected and actual volume of activity under Paradigm D surely enhances this thought.

Strategies concerning various product lines. If a company produces both commodity-type products and specialty-type products, it might be able to use both engineering- and market-driven standard costs. Market-driven standards probably would apply more to specialty products with their shorter life cycles. Engineering-driven standards could be more appropriate for the longer life cycles of commodity products. Nevertheless, market-driven standard costs must be determined for any intensely competitive product.

Standard cost variances/responsibility accounting. When we are looking toward a total cost per unit that must meet or better the allowable or target cost, cost variances by individual cost, activity, or department seem to be less relevant. Worker empowerment within a company requires a cooperative spirit rather than a focus on the individual department and cost center. Group or total success is the key today.

The old individual cost and cost center focused control concepts inherent in standard costing and responsibility accounting may be counterproductive in today's world. The need for continuous improvement and forcing a continuous learning curve focused on total cost surely challenges one's training and earlier views.

The theory of constraints. Eli Goldratt, the Israeli physicist turned management consultant, has had an impact in recent years. His concentration on throughput, operating expense, and inventories has intrigued many management accountants. Interestingly, his theory of constraints (TOC) appears to be a refinement of direct costing coupled with linear programming.

TOC concentrates on only three variables: throughput, inventory, and operating expenses. Throughput relates to actual sales minus materials costs. Inventory consists only of purchased items at their purchased cost, and operating expenses are expenses other than materials. The objective is to focus on increasing throughput by eliminating constraints and decreasing both inventory and operating expenses.

In essence, the theory of constraints treats operating expenses as fixed and does not add any value to inventory whether it's in process or a finished state. All operating expenses plus the cost of inventory (materials) used to produce the actual throughput are considered in determining the true profitability of a period's throughput.

There is a direct costing flavor in the theory of constraints. The apparent success of TOC simultaneous with the development of ABC (a form of absorption costing) is worth examining. A detailed comparison of a number of users of both techniques certainly would be useful.

Assigning costs to product lines and within product lines. Ultimately, any cost accounting system has to deal with the twin issues of assigning costs between and within product lines. Activity-based costing may make a real contribution toward resolving both these issues.

ABC's concentration on three categories of variable costs may be especially useful. These three categories relate to the traditional notion of variability with units and the two new ideas of variability with product complexity (such as number of batches) and variability with product diversity (such as number of products). At this point in time, those of us concerned with these product-line issues must be open to alternative points of view.

LOOKING AHEAD—THE 21ST CENTURY PARADIGM

The best hope I see for a new paradigm for the 21st century would be a combination of Paradigms C and D. An alternative variation could combine Paradigms C and D with elements from Paradigm B.

Regarding the first suggestion, in our intensely competitive world marketplace it is difficult to deny the efficacy of Paradigm D. The allowable or target standard cost permitted by our competitors in the marketplace cannot be ignored. Neither can we ignore the necessity for continuous improvement.

Paradigm D, however, is not sufficient. It must be combined with a before-the-fact determination of expected actual cost and an after-the-fact actual cost. The actual costs should be determined using the

Table 3. OTHER ISSUES OF POSSIBLE CONTENTION

- Under Paradigm D, what volume of activity should be used when determining actual total cost per unit to compare with allowable or target cost per unit?
- Does the diminishing time frame for the product life cycle have an impact on the movement toward Paradigm D, especially the movement toward market-driven standard (allowable) costs as opposed to engineering-driven standard costs?
- Does a firm's strategic posture by product line allow for the possibility of different paradigms for different product lines?
- Is the old emphasis on cost variances by individual cost categories and departments less or no longer relevant in an era when the total cost from suppliers through to customers is emphasized?
- Where does the "theory of constraints" fit in? It looks like a refinement of the direct costing ideology.
- What method should be used for assigning costs to product lines and individual products within each product line?

more precise ABC method, that is, Paradigm C.

The ongoing comparison of a cost per unit allowed by the marketplace (subject to continuous improvement) with the actual and expected actual cost per unit is vital. Such a system of comparison should seek answers to the following questions:

1. What adjustments to product promotion and pricing strategies most likely will yield expected and actual volumes capable of achieving allowable costs?
2. What adjustments to our current cost structure and work procedures will enhance our ability to achieve allowable costs?
3. What adjustments to our current cost structure and the way we cooperate with suppliers and customers will enhance our ability to achieve allowable costs?

What better use could be made of cost/management accounting data than to elicit answers to these questions? The combination of Paradigms C and D provides a meaningful environment in which to use ABC in the determination of product promotion and pricing strategies. Similarly, the combination gives real meaning to ABC's role in forcing consideration of alternative cost structures.

What happens when we add a touch of Paradigm B? Charles Horngren provides the idea for combining B with C and D to develop a new paradigm for the 21st century.[8] On numerous occasions he has cautioned us about using per-unit dollar amounts rather than total dollar amounts, especially in the context of fixed costs. By using per-unit amounts, we run the risk of treating fixed costs as variable costs and potentially concentrating too much on parts of the picture rather than the total picture.

Consider a product-line income statement, which has columns for individual products as well as a total column for the sum of individual products. The total column for the product line forces us to keep an eye on "total system" results while simultaneously looking at individual products or pieces of the system.

Shifting from the per-unit concentration of Paradigms C and D can be accomplished easily by multiplying the expected actual and actual volumes for each product by the per-unit amounts at each respective volume level for each product. Then the resulting total dollar amounts can be arranged in the format of a product line income statement as described above.

If we draw the distinction between fixed and variable costs, our product line income statement can include elements from Paradigm B with C and D. For example, if the only variable costs are materials, as assumed in the theory of constraints, we easily can develop contribution margins in the context of our product line income statements. The contribution margin as well as the net income by product and product line yields an opportunity to consider both short- and long-run aspects of profitability simultaneously as individual product and total system profitability are examined.

An intriguing result of combining Paradigm B with C and D is the ability to include, in our analysis of product line income statements, aspects of product life cycles and products that are expected to be cash users vs. cash generators during different stages of their life cycles. The product line income statement in this context looks at individual products and the sum total of a product line over a time frame that encompasses the life cycle of individual products or, at minimum, a three- to five-year period.

LOOKING BACKWARD TO SEE AHEAD

Often it is useful to reconsider where we have been during various stages of our development. Especially helpful would be case studies that could lead to the fine-tuning of a cost/management accounting paradigm for the 21st century. Of interest would be:

- A detailed comparison of a number of users of the theory of constraints and ABC.
- Historical analyses of early, prominent, and successful users of Paradigm B and their current status with regard to moving toward Paradigms C and D or combinations thereof.[9]
- Historical analyses of successful companies (defined in some reasonable manner) and their current status in regard to moving toward Paradigms C and D or combinations thereof, with or without elements from Paradigm B.

The suggestions in this article relative to a paradigm for the 21st century seem especially useful. There definitely seems to be a place in management accounting for the more refined and exacting calculations of ABC. But that place seems better suited in combination with Paradigm D and perhaps Paradigm B as well, especially as we proceed to the 21st century.

William L. Ferrara, CPA, Ph.D., is the David M. Beights professor of accountancy at Stetson University, DeLand, Fla. He is a member of the Daytona Beach Area Chapter, through which this article was submitted, and can be reached at (904) 822-7421.

[1] Depending on the product or service offered, one could have the same three elements of variable costs for marketing and administrative activities as well as manufacturing activities.

[2] J.S.Earley, "Recent Developments in Cost Accounting and the 'Marginal Analysis'," *Journal of Political Economy*, June 1955, p. 237. The primary source for Earley's comments are the research studies of the Institute of Management Accountants, especially reports 16, 17, and 18 published during 1949 and 1950 on *The Analysis of Cost-Volume-Profit Relationships*.

[3] For a discussion of how Paradigm B responds to this comment, see "Profit Planning and Pricing Strategies," Chapter 15 in *Managerial Cost Accounting: Planning and Control* by W.L. Ferrara, et.al., Dame Publications, Inc., 1991.

[4] See Thomas A. Stewart, "GE Keeps Those Ideas Coming," *Fortune*, August 12, 1991, for one company's approach to continuous improvement and empowerment.

[5] See Dave Woodruff and Stephen Phillips, "Ford Has a Better Idea: Let Someone Else Have the Idea," *Business Week*, April 30, 1990.

[6] H.T. Johnson, "Let's Set the Record Straight on ABC," *Measurement Systems*, Association for Manufacturing Excellence, March-April 1992.

[7] See R. Cooper and P.B.B.Turney, *Hewlett-Packard: Roseville Networks Division*, Harvard Business School Case Study 189-117, 1989, for an illustration of diminishing product life cycles and a resultant increase in new products as well as product modifications.

[8] C.T. Horngren and G.L. Sundem, *Introduction to Management Accounting*, ninth edition, Prentice Hall, 1993, p. 201.

[9] See *Current Applications of Direct Costing*, Institute of Management Accountants, Research Report 37, 1961, for a list of companies from which to choose.

UPDATING STANDARD COST SYSTEMS

Making them better tools for today's manufacturing environment.

by Carole Cheatham

In recent years standard cost systems have been criticized by many theorists. Many of these systems measure variables no longer considered important. They need to be updated to measure variables that are currently significant in manufacturing.

Traditional standard cost systems came out of the production-driven past, when favorable price and efficiency variances were achieved through large volumes of material and intensive labor. Just-in-time systems now have led manufacturers to recognize the dangers of overproduction and poor quality. Concentrating only on input can lead to poor decisions about output—and to increased costs. Updated systems should focus on quality and production as well as price and efficiency.

STANDARD COST SYSTEMS VS. INPUT/OUTPUT ANALYSIS

A traditional standard cost analysis appears in exhibit 1. In this example, two cost variances—price and efficiency—are computed. (Variances for fixed costs are not covered in this article.) The price variance is computed on the basis of pounds purchased. In this case 2,700 pounds were purchased at a price that was $.10 above the standard, resulting in a $270 unfavorable variance.

Also, the computed efficiency variance indicates that 2,400 pounds should have been used to produce 1,200 good units but that 2,600 pounds actually were used. The extra 200 pounds at $1 per pound results in a $200 unfavorable efficiency variance.

The problem with this analysis is that it gives information only on inputs (the components of the product, such as materials and labor). Focusing exclusively on inputs is inconsistent with sales-driven concepts. In a sales-driven company, managers produce to meet specific sales orders rather than to accumulate masses of inventory. When input information is incomplete and misleading, erroneous decisions can be made. For instance, managers trying to avoid unfavorable price and efficiency variances may produce large amounts of unneeded inventories and minimize quality concerns, costing the company money.

In a production-driven environment, managers tended to avoid unfavorable price and efficiency variances by buying materials in quantity and keeping workers busy. The idea of shutting down the assembly line for any reason was abhorrent to most production managers. The result was un-

CAROLE CHEATHAM, CPA, PhD, is a professor of accounting at Northeast Louisiana University, Monroe. A member of the American Institute of CPAs, the National Association of Accountants and the American Accounting Association, she is the author of Cost Management for Profit Centers *(Institute for Business Planning, 1981).*

needed inventories that cost companies interest on the investment, storage, insurance and obsolescence.

In contrast, the just-in-time concept of production recognizes that costs associated with excess inventories need to be minimized and that efficiency and flexibility in production can better be achieved by producing smaller batches.

In the past, managers' philosophy was that costs should be minimized while quality merely had to be acceptable. This lack of attention to quality hurt the reputations of many companies and the need to rework defective units or sell them as seconds increased their costs.

Detecting and measuring quality deficiencies are as important as determining price and efficiency variances. Unfortunately, most standard cost systems being used in manufacturing ignore both production and quality concerns.

A better analysis is presented in exhibit 2. In this illustration, price and efficiency variances are isolated as are the output variances of quality and production. In this case, there were 50 defective units at a cost of $2 each, resulting in a $100 unfavorable quality variance.

There also were 200 units produced in excess of current needs. At an investment of $2 each, the extra units resulted in $400 in excess inventory, also an unfavorable production variance.

Why is the system in exhibit 2 superior to the traditional analysis in exhibit 1? Its primary advantage lies in its attention to both output and input. Price and efficiency variances also are revised to suit a just-in-time system better.

QUALITY VARIANCES

Quality variances focus attention on resources invested in units that must be reworked, scrapped or sold as seconds. In exhibit 2, 50 finished units did not meet quality standards, which resulted in a $100 unfavorable quality variance.

Under the traditional standard costing in exhibit 1, the cost of these defective units is buried in the efficiency variance. Without additional analysis, there is no way to tell how many inputs were invested in defective units or misused in other ways.

It is recognized now that a lack of quality results in higher production costs. Measurable warranty costs and the intangible costs of customer ill will also might increase if defects are not detected before the product is sold. Quality is a completely different concern from efficiency and it should be recognized and measured separately.

In exhibit 2, it is assumed that all units were 100% complete. Equivalent production calculations should be used if the units are partially complete. For example, if the 50 defective units were only one-fourth complete, then the equivalent unit figure would be 12.5 units and the unfavorable quality variance would be only $25 unfavorable (12.5 units times $2) instead of $100. Thus, unfavorable quality variances can be reduced by detecting defects earlier in the manufacturing process. Computing the

EXECUTIVE SUMMARY

■ STANDARD COST SYSTEMS need revisions to make them more useful in the new manufacturing environment. Traditional production-driven systems focus exclusively on inputs, which can lead to bad decisions, such as producing large amounts of unneeded inventories. A revised system should focus on both inputs and outputs and encourage managers to use the just-in-time concept of production, which results in small batches. This is accomplished by calculating four variances.

1. Quality variances indicate the production costs of defective units. They focus attention on the resources invested in units that must be reworked, scrapped or sold as seconds.

2. Production variances indicate excess investment in inventories. Tracking them follows the just-in-time philosophy of minimizing inventories at all stages.

3. Price variances are based on materials used in production rather than materials purchased. Calculating them results in a better evaluation of the trade-offs between price and efficiency or quality. For example, buying high-priced materials may result in unfavorable price variances but in favorable efficiency and quality variances.

4. Efficiency variances detect waste that occurs during the production process. Costs expended on units that eventually are rejected are moved to the quality variance.

EXHIBIT 1
Traditional standard cost system

Inputs (pounds):

Actual pounds purchased	2,700
Actual pounds used	2,600
Standard pounds per finished unit	2
Standard price per pound	$1.00
Actual price per pound	$1.10

Outputs (finished units):

Good units produced	1,200

Standard cost per unit:

2 pounds @ $1 = $2

Standard cost variances:

Price variance		
Actual pounds purchased at actual price	2,700 @ $1.10	$2,970
Actual pounds purchased at standard price	2,700 @ $1	2,700
Price variance (unfavorable)	2,700 @ $ .10	$270
Efficiency variance		
Actual pounds used at standard price	2,600 @ $1	$2,600
Standard pounds allowed for good production at standard price	(1,200 x 2) @ $1	2,400
Efficiency variance (unfavorable)	200 @ $1	$200

variance in this fashion motivates managers to take early corrective action rather than allowing defective units to accumulate costs until they are found on final inspection.

PRODUCTION VARIANCES

Production variances show deviations from scheduled production numbers. In exhibit 2, the production variance is $400 unfavorable because 200 excess units were produced. Viewing excess production as unfavorable follows the just-in-time philosophy of minimizing inventories at all production stages. Some authorities go so far as to view the excess as a liability, rather than an asset, for internal use. (For external use, the traditional treatment for assets under generally accepted accounting principles is necessary.)

As discussed in the article "Reporting the Effects of Excess Inventories" (JofA, Nov.89 page 131), the production variance can be used to calculate the cost of capital on excess inventories to determine the real cost of overproducing. Some companies that use a production variance view any deviation from the scheduled amount, whether over or under, as unfavorable. Underproduction is unfavorable because the company cannot meet sales demands. However, there is a greater likelihood that managers will ignore the costs of overproduction—which is why this variance also is labeled unfavorable. Actually, labeling a production variance as either over or under the scheduled amount is equally satisfactory, assuming management considers both kinds of unfavorable variances.

PRICE VARIANCES

In the new manufacturing literature, price variances have been criticized for motivating managers to ignore quality and buy low-priced materials and parts. However, the real problem is that price variances have been separated from production-related variances. Price is certainly a valid concern but it cannot be viewed in isolation or ignored. It makes more sense to evaluate price variances in terms of trade-offs.

In other words, a decision to buy high-quality materials for a particular production run may result in an unfavorable price variance but in favorable efficiency and quality variances. Or a decision to employ highly skilled workers may result in an unfavorable price variance for labor but in favorable efficiency and quality variances.

In exhibit 2, the price variance for materials is computed on the basis of materials used in production. Under the traditional standard costing in exhibit 1, the price variance is based on materials purchased because this approach isolates the variance earlier so that corrective action can be taken.

Computing the price variance on the basis of materials used in production is recommended because the trade-offs between price and efficiency or quality are more apparent if the same batch of materials is used for all variances. Suppose a company purchased a large amount of low-quality materials this week because it got a very good price. Using the traditional system, it would recognize a large favorable price variance for the week. But the potential unfavorable efficiency and quality variances would not be isolated until the materials were put into production, perhaps several weeks later. There is a much better match of the trade-offs if materials put into production are used for all comparisons.

EFFICIENCY VARIANCES

Historically, efficiency variances have been computed by multiplying excess inputs by the standard price (see exhibit 1). In recent years, this approach has been criticized for motivating managers to ignore quality concerns to avoid unfavorable efficiency variances. In other words, there is an incentive to produce a low-quality product by minimizing the amount of material used or the time spent in production.

The approach in exhibit 2 separates the efficiency variance from the quality variance. Inputs consisting of conversion time or material used in defective units are captured in the quality variance.

EXHIBIT 2

Updated standard cost system

Inputs (pounds):		
Actual pounds purchased		2,700
Actual pounds used		2,600
Standard pounds per finished unit		2
Standard price per pound		$1.00
Actual price per pound		$1.10
Outputs (finished units):		
Scheduled production		1,000
Total production		1,250
Good units produced		1,200
Defective units		50
Standard cost per unit:		
2 pounds @ $1 = $2		
Standard cost variances:		
Input analysis:		
Price variance		
Actual pounds used at actual price	2,600 @ $1.10	$2,860
Actual pounds used at standard price	2,600 @ $1	2,600
Price variance (unfavorable)	2,600 @ $ .10	$260
Efficiency variance		
Actual pounds used at standard price	2,600 @ $1	$2,600
Standard pounds allowed for total production at standard price	(1,250 x 2) @ $1	2,500
Efficiency variance (unfavorable)	100 @ $1	$100
Output analysis:		
Quality variance		
Total production @ standard cost per unit	1,250 @ $2	$2,500
Good units @ standard cost per unit	1,200 @ $2	2,400
Quality variance (unfavorable)	50 @ $2	$100
Production variance		
Good units @ standard cost per unit	1,200 @ $2	$2,400
Scheduled production @ standard cost per unit	1,000 @ $2	2,000
Production variance (unfavorable)	200 @ $2	$400

Separating the two variances allows production decision makers to evaluate the trade-offs between efficiency and quality. They can minimize production time to gain a favorable efficiency variance but this probably will increase the number of defective units and result in an unfavorable quality variance. Likewise, trying to minimize the number of defective units may result in investing more time and more material and therefore having an unfavorable efficiency variance.

In the case of hidden defects in materials, an unexpected number of units may be rejected on final inspection. Ordinarily, this would affect the efficiency variance. However, if the quality variance is separate from the efficiency variance, the quality variance would reflect the rejects but the efficiency variance would be unchanged. In other words, the efficiency variance computed in this fashion shows *true efficiency*. The production department would not be penalized by an unfavorable efficiency variance for working on units that appeared to be good. In effect, the efficiency variance becomes a tool for detecting waste that disappeared during the production process, while the quality variance detects waste that remains in the form of finished or semi-finished goods.

In production processes in which there is normal shrinkage due to evaporation or similar processes, the shrinkage would be part of the efficiency rather than the quality variance because the standard inputs allowed for total production would be adjusted. A separate yield variance could be broken out from the efficiency variance to show the effect of shrinkage.

A BETTER TOOL

The new manufacturing environment does not require dismantling standard cost systems, which have helped companies achieve their production goals for many years. However, when these goals change, the old systems need to be updated. In this case, updating consists of incorporating new variance measures into the standard cost system and focusing on key issues—inventory and quality control—that are important in the production process. Revision also narrows the scope of the traditional price and efficiency variances, making them more useful tools because their causes are easier to identify.

Are We Making Money Yet?

By learning the costs in each of her messenger service's transactions, Claudia Post transformed herself from sales addict to CEO—and not a moment too soon

SUSAN GRECO

IN DECEMBER 1994 CLAUDIA POST, the founder of Diamond Courier Service, did something that offended every cell in her salesperson's body: she began shedding business she had already sold. While her messengers delivered gift baskets of fruit and candy, Post was delivering sour news to some of Diamond's customers: "After some careful analysis, I'm forced to make a difficult decision—I have to relinquish part of my business with you." The chief executive and her sales manager had drawn up a list of clients to visit. Arthur Anderson, the Big Six accounting firm and one of Diamond's earliest customers, was on it. So was Montgomery McCracken, a prominent Philadelphia law firm—Post's own law firm, in fact. She relished making those calls about as much as she enjoyed selling her personal investments, which she also did in order to save her company.

"I can't tell you how painful it was," Post recalls. "I mean, these customers depended on me."

The timing of these *un*sales calls was particularly ironic in that just a few months earlier, the Philadelphia office of the Small Business Administration had handed Post her first business award—for civic involvement, job generation, and fast growth. She deserved the award. She had started Diamond Courier in August 1990, determined to outperform the downtown courier company that had just fired her from a sales position. Post plotted Diamond's sales growth on a straight trajectory, and it took her only 17 months to achieve her first objective, $1 million in sales. She nearly doubled that volume during the next year. "What she did was incredible," says the admiring owner of a Florida-based courier company.

In 1993, its third full year, Post's company had $3.1 million in sales. By then Diamond employed some 40 bike messengers and 25 back-office staffers and provided steady work for 50 independent drivers. There was never any ambiguity about Post's own role in the business: master networker and fearless cold caller—the sales whiz every struggling young company needs. Post put the "star" in start-up, and she was happy. "I was busy having a great time selling. Cash flow? Profit before taxes? I didn't know how to figure out any of that stuff," she says. She was a selling machine. And to be sure that she could keep on selling, Post recruited a former colleague, Tony Briscella, to step into the sales manager's role at Diamond.

It was early that year, however, that symptoms of underlying problems in the business first became apparent. The usual start-up crash crunches grew more serious and arrived more often until eventually they became chronic. By the latter part of the year, Post was helping her staff shuffle the accounts payable and decide whom to pay and when. Briscella, her new sales manager, who'd previously worked for Federal Express, had begun to complain that he couldn't get accurate operating results. "I'd hear things like 'We either broke even or made $6,000.' That," he says, "drove me crazy." Despite Diamond's continued growth, it wasn't much longer before Post had to resort to selling her jewelry and liquidating long-held stocks from her Merrill Lynch account to generate the cash she needed to pay her employees. Of course, the more her cash problems mounted, the more Post, the consummate salesperson, wanted to get out and sell. Yet she increasingly felt chained to her desk by the by-then nearly daily crises. One day an anxiety attack, which she mistook for a heart attack, sent her to the hospital. As she left, one of the office employees called after her, "Don't you die on us!"

Post didn't die, but Diamond Courier nearly did. By the spring of 1994 the company was undeniably sick, and Post remembers thinking, "Here I am with a company that's doing $3 million plus, and I have no money. I'm working a gazillion hours a week. There's something terribly wrong here."

But what? Desperate and scared, Post asked a friend in the industry to examine her books. "Claudia," he said after a cursory look, "you're headed for the rocks."

What had happened to this growth company and its founder?

> **Diamond Courier founder Post asked a friend to examine the company's books. After a cursory look, he said, 'You're headed for the rocks.'**

Reprinted with permission from *Inc.* magazine, July 1996, pp. 52-54, 56, 58, 61.

THERE WAS NOTHING WRONG WITH the service that Diamond provided to its expanding client list—at least nothing beyond the usual sorts of snafus experienced by fast-growing companies. Customers loved Post and her company. But in four years Diamond Courier had grown in so many directions that it was no longer the one business that Post had started; it was more like six. As she had pursued the simple idea of running a downtown bicycle-courier business Post had seen and gone after other opportunities. Now, besides bike-messenger services, the company was into driver deliveries, truck deliveries, airfreight services, a parts-distribution service—and even a legal service that served subpoenas and prepared court filings. Although all the businesses shared some common resources, each had its own line workers, manager, and administrative-support person, as well as its own steady customers and unique pricing and billing practices. In that respect, Diamond wasn't so different from a manufacturer that jumps into a dozen different product lines or a retailer that branches into several market niches in quick succession. The question was never, What do we do best? but always, What else can we sell?

It wasn't that diversification per se that had brought Post's business to the brink of failure. Any of the businesses Diamond now found itself in could conceivably have been profitable. The problem was that Post simply didn't know which, if any, of them were. She didn't know because she was operating on a set of reasonable but unexamined assumptions. She assumed, for instance, that if she kept selling and priced her services at market rates, she would build a profitable business. She assumed that growing volume would generate economies of scale. She assumed that if she took good care of customers, the business would take care of itself. She relied upon those and other assumptions because, as she admits now, she never took the time to question or test them. But even if she had taken the time, she didn't have the means. Consequently, Post continued to believe that sales would be Diamond's salvation when, in fact, nearly every sale she made pushed the company a little further into the red and a little closer to failure.

"Most entrepreneurs have no idea what it really costs them to produce a product or service," asserts Al Sloman. He's the veteran industry consultant recommended to Post by the friend who had examined her books and sounded the alarm. When he was hired to help her, Sloman made it his mission to get Post to understand more than the operational side of the courier business. She knew all about that. His goal was to teach her the business side of the business—to get her to understand and acknowledge that in addition to dollars in (sales), she also had to deal with dollars out (costs). If Post was going to be the chief executive of Diamond Courier, not just its chief salesperson, Sloman believed, she would need the management-accounting tools that would let her test her assumptions. Over several months in the fall of 1994, Sloman helped Post learn to use several of those tools. But just as important, he also gave her a clearer understanding of what her job as owner and manager of a fast-growing company had to be.

Chief among the tools that Sloman showed Post how to use was profit-center analysis, which amounted to showing her how to build an income statement for every business line Diamond was in. A profit-center analysis can reveal which activities—or, for that matter, which sales territories or branch operations—

BIKE DELIVERY: PROFIT AND LOSS

Post's imagined per-job P&L...

Revenue	$4.69
Messenger's pay*	$2.35
Overhead and profit*	$2.34

...and the actual P&L she uncovered

Revenue	$4.69
Messenger's pay	$4.23
Overhead (direct and allocated)	$5.01
Profit (loss)	($4.55)

*Approximate

One-year financial results for the bike-messenger profit center

Revenues (on 71,658 jobs at $4.69/job)	$336,000
Direct labor (messengers)	
Wages and commissions	$277,000
Payroll taxes	$26,000
Gross profit	$33,000
Direct overhead[1]	
Dispatching	$39,000
Customer service	$40,700
Workers' comp insurance	$6,800
Miscellaneous office expenses	$5,000
Telephone	$10,000
Allocated overhead[2]	$257,655
Total overhead	$359,155
Profit (loss)	($326,155)

[1]Includes all costs directly attributable to bike deliveries. [2]Costs not directly linked to bike deliveries but apportioned according to level of activity—number of bike jobs, for example.

are making money and which are not. For Post the analysis proved to be eye-opening.

The key to building a profit-center statement is knowing how to identify all the costs associated with a particular business activity. Sloman helped Post extract sales and cost data for each of the businesses Diamond was in by poring over work records and computer files. Line by line, they compiled the labor costs, the operating costs, and the administrative costs directly linked to each of the six business lines. They could have stopped there, but the profit picture would have been incomplete. Because Post's back office had grown so rapidly and come to generate such a large portion of total costs (sales, general, and administrative costs made up about 30%), they also had to allocate those indirect costs among the various businesses. *How* the overhead costs were allocated was crucial, because the allocation rationale would, in part, determine which businesses showed a profit and which did not. Sloman urged Post to use an allocation system known as activity-based costing. (See "Resources.") Essentially, activity-based costing assigns overhead costs to the various businesses not in proportion to their revenue shares (which is the conventional technique) but in proportion to their respective use of the company's resources. "If employees and managers could say how they used their time, we used that," says Sloman. "If not, we looked at the level of activity, say, the number of jobs per profit center" as the basis for allocating overhead.

As they proceeded through that exercise over a period of weeks, the scales began to fall from Post's eyes, and the errors induced by her earlier assumptions became painfully apparent. Nowhere had they been more misleading than in Diamond's original business—downtown bicycle-courier services.

For instance, Post had assumed that if competitors could make a living with prices lower than hers, then she had to be making money, too. She had assumed that the revenues generated by her bike-messenger business contributed handsomely to total company revenues and profit, since the bike customers were among her oldest and largest accounts. (Besides, to Post's thinking, Diamond's downtown image *was* the colorfully shirted Diamond Courier cyclist.) Because the back office was always busy, Post assumed that her bike messengers

At the center of Diamond Courier's operations today is the vehicle courier service, supported by dispatchers and augmented by downtown walkers.

were busy, too, which meant that they were working on commission, not for the minimum hourly wage she guaranteed them. And since the commission was roughly a 50–50 split, Post assumed that 50% was her gross margin.

How wrong she found that she was. The bicycle division, which she thought of as Diamond's core business, generated just 20% of total revenues and barely covered its own direct-labor and insurance costs. (See "Bike Delivery: Profit and Loss.") Worse, the division created more logistical and customer-service nightmares than any other single business, thereby generating a disproportionate share of overhead costs. Diamond wasn't making money on bicycle deliveries. It was charging customers $4.69 per job, but with fully allocated costs of $9.24 per job, the company was losing $4.55 every time a cyclist picked up a package.

Post's assumptions about her bike couriers' productivity had been completely wrong. Instead of the three deliveries an hour she assumed they made, the real figure was less than half that. So, instead of the 50% gross margins she assumed she collected on each $4.69 bike job, the real margin worked out to only 10%—not even enough to cover her overhead, never mind providing a profit.

Sloman showed Post how to perform the same kind of analysis on Diamond's other operations. She was shocked to see that four of the six—all except driver and truck deliveries—were generating losses.

One Monday morning two months after Sloman's arrival, Post made an announcement. "I've made up my mind," she said to Sloman and her managers. "I know what I have to do."

ON JANUARY 3, 1995, POST SHUT down the bicycle-messenger business, which was killing the rest of the company. She saw plainly that it was pointless to compete with operators charging $3 per delivery when she had to charge $10 just to cover her costs. (After all, the $3 operators were smaller companies focused on bikes.) And it made no sense to try to run the bike work simultaneously with the suburban and regional vehicle work, which was profitable, each job generating an average of $27.60 in revenues to cover $21.23 in costs. "We didn't need the bike service to have the vehicle service," says Post. "I knew I couldn't delay the decision, because every second was costing us money."

Was there a way to jettison the bicycle-courier business gently without losing the profitable driver jobs that come from the same customers? Post and Briscella nervously rehearsed what they'd say in face-to-face visits. A few customers wouldn't stand for it, and Post wasn't surprised when 4 of her top 30 accounts took *all* their business elsewhere. But she took her lumps up front. "I wanted to be clear and direct with my client base, and I think I gained credibility that way," she says. In the end Post kept all the large accounts that used her drivers more than her bikers.

Hard as the decision to close the bicycle operation had been for Post to make, it liberated her. No part of the business was untouchable anymore, and no part of the business was unknowable.

Within a few months, Post closed two more of Diamond's *un*profit centers—airfreight and parts distribution. Using the profit-center analysis, Sloman had prepared a pro forma income statement that showed Post she could actually increase profits by reducing sales. He showed her that by cutting $521,000 in unprofitable sales, she could eliminate $640,000 in costs. Sloman wanted Diamond to eliminate all services and customers that didn't generate a profit, but Post couldn't do that and didn't think she should.

She decided, for instance, that some services she couldn't afford to operate herself, such as airfreight, were worth brokering on occasion in order to retain clients that generated profits for her elsewhere. And she replaced a few of the bikers with walkers, who now service select customers at a premium price. Still, in 1995 she forfeited sales of about $400,000—most of them willfully.

Post also raised prices for some of the work Diamond did. Now that she knew how to wield a calculator and could compute her average cost per job, she realized that she'd priced too many jobs at or below breakeven.

Perhaps the biggest change for Post herself was that for an entire year, she stopped selling. Instead, she threw herself into the task at hand—visiting dozens of customers and writing to hundreds more affected by the changes she was making. And when that was done, she realized how much more work she still had to do—work that continues. She hasn't stopped looking for ways to trim overhead. (Her operations manager doubles as a dispatcher, for example.) And now that she understands her cost of sales—and her company's sales cycle—she is prepared for cash crunches. In other words, Post no longer views her company through the narrow prism of sales; she now has the broader view of a CEO.

Today Diamond Courier is not the greyhound start-up it once was. The office is a lot quieter now. The rock-and-roll environment is gone; Diamond's baby-boomer managers have grown up. The company is healthier. There's cash in the bank—which called recently to congratulate Post on her progress.

Post is healthier, too. She works out every day, and she's laughing again. She hasn't had to hock any stocks or jewelry in a long while; she recently rented a nice house for herself and her two sons. "I still don't balance my own checkbook, but I know now if my company is making money," she says. "Boy, do I know."

Thanks to a strong fall—a good chunk of the $400,000 in lost revenues was made up with more profitable business—Diamond managed to finish 1995 in the black, and the profits continued to accrue through last winter's snowstorms. Overall, revenue per job has more than doubled, from an average of $13 in 1993 to about $28 in 1995. Post and her managers think about sales differently, too. They're as likely to argue about which customers to drop as which prospects to pursue.

Now Post counts her blessings, along with her cash, every night. "I mean, I could have just spun out," she says. She knows so much more now. "I know what I need to break even every day," she says. "I monitor my payables. I know what my cash flow is and what's going into the bank every day. We created a budget, and I understand what it means to live budget-to-actual." A software program provides her with a daily report of revenue per job. "Look, I'm never going to be a serious financial person," she concedes, "but you own a business, it's your responsibility. I can't slough it off on somebody else. I have to know."

Articles editor Susan Greco can be reached at susan.greco@inc.com

RESOURCES

The information contained in the resources below can help entrepreneurs think smarter about costing, pricing, and business-unit profitability

ARTICLES

A free three-page executive brief on activity-based costing, a useful tool for companies whose overhead is growing as fast as their direct costs, is available from ABC Technologies, in Beaverton, Oreg. (800-882-3141). A 16-page manufacturing case study, "Why You Should Consider Activity-Based Costing," can be obtained free from *Small Business Forum* (800-419-5018). To see how the practice works in service companies, order a reprint of "Tracking Costs in a Service Organization," published by *Management Accounting* (800-638-4427, extension 280) in February 1993, which explains how Fireman's Fund uses activity-based accounting.

BOOKS

Accounting and Financial Fundamentals for Nonfinancial Executives, by Valarie Neiman and Eileen J. Glick (AMACOM, 800-262-9699, 1996, $18.95), covers the basics of cost accounting, the contribution concept, and other management tools. Two recent works demystify pricing and are well suited to service companies: *Priced to Sell,* by Herman Holtz (Upstart Publishing, 800-829-7934, 1996, $27.95); and *No Apologies Pricing* (Home Based Business Association of Arizona, 602-464-0778, 1995, $9.95), a 52-page booklet worth its price because of its wonderful simplicity.

SOFTWARE

Tracking costs is made easier with the "job costing" modules available with major accounting-software packages. See "Ledgerdemain" in the June issue of *Inc. Technology.*

EXECUTIVE ED

In a course in strategic planning offered by the respected Council of Smaller Enterprises (COSE), 30 company owners convene on Saturday mornings to analyze how they're making money (or not). Students team up with past graduates of the course, who serve as their mentors. The price: $2,695. Courses, which are held in Cleveland, Dayton, and Louisville, start in September and October. Call COSE at 216-621-3300 for more information. The 1,400-page course book can be had for $250; send a request to j.sussbauer@csuohio.edu by E-mail.

ON-LINE

A primer on how to do a business-unit "contribution-margin analysis" is available on America Online (go to key word "Inc.") under "Inc. Extra" and at *Inc.*'s Web site (http://www.inc.com).

Using ABC to Determine the Cost of Servicing Customers

Problems—and cost saving opportunities—surfaced when this small welding company conducted an ABC analysis.

Author Michael Krupnicki discusses deliveries with the city truck driver of Mahany Welding Supply.

BY MICHAEL KRUPNICKI, CMA,
AND THOMAS TYSON, CMA

Although most case studies of ABC applications have been in manufacturing, ABC can be used in a small service business to isolate costs for decision making. We conducted an ABC cost study in a small, family-run welding supply business. The purposes of the study were to determine the cost of servicing customers and to identify feasible cost reduction opportunities.

The domestic welding supply industry used to be composed of primarily local, mom-and-pop type operations. Since the 1980s, several national franchises have expanded on a regional basis by buying out these family-owned businesses. The economies of scale and deep pockets of regional chains create new competitive challenges and a need for the surviving small companies to reevaluate how they do business.

Mahany Welding Supply is a distributor of welding supplies and compressed gases in the greater Rochester, N.Y., area. It has a diverse base of customers in fields that include construction, metal fabrication, collision shops, restaurants, dentists and veterinarians, tool & die shops, gravel pits, highway departments, schools, and home hobbyists. Business is conducted out of a part store, part warehouse located near downtown Rochester. The company distributes products in four ways: walk-in trade and customer will-calls; a delivery truck that services customers within the city; a delivery truck that services a 40-mile radius of Rochester and visits one of five different geographic areas each day; and, to a small extent, UPS and common carrier shipments.

The company employs seven people. Employee 1 handles purchasing, collections, sales, auditing, accounting, and general administration; Employee 2 divides time among equipment repairs, warehousing, and sales; Employee 3 runs the city truck route; Employee 4 runs the country truck route; Employee 5, the owner and president, splits duties between outside sales and repairs; Employee 6 specializes in accounts receivable billing; Employee 7 handles accounts payable and general ledger and communicates with the firm's CPA. There is definitely no "dead wood" and very little idle time.

Under current ownership since 1959, Mahany Welding Supply has enjoyed three decades of steady growth. The owner, who operates the business in a very conservative management style, like many small, family-run business owners has financial goals limited to just staying in the black from year to year. Nonetheless, there is a growing concern that certain parts of the company have been subsidizing other parts and that profits from some customers are subsidizing losses from others.

Applying ABC principles to historical data (fiscal 1994 financials) was used to address these concerns so that the business owner actually could see the problems and evaluate ideas on how to correct them. Whether or not an ongoing ABC system meets the cost/benefit relationship necessary to implement as part of Mahany's computerized accounting system is another matter. In effect, historical data could be entered into spreadsheet templates on a regular basis to evaluate how improvements are doing.

ANALYZING THE DATA

Initially, some informal time studies were conducted, a task that was made difficult because everyone's position is cross functional and encompasses more than one job. Also, because of the chaotic nature of a small business, there is no set time to do a particular function such as 9:00 a.m.-10:00 a.m., purchasing; 10:00 a.m.-11:00 a.m., collections; and so on. It just doesn't work that way at Mahany Welding Supply, or at most small businesses, so the time studies in Table 1 are best estimates within the scope of this project.

The next step was to identify possible causal relationships between the occurrence of costs and activities as well as the underlying drivers of the activities. Company functions were broken down into 15 activities, as discussed next.

Selling. As shown by the time study, a large percentage of the employees' time is spent selling. In the case of the truck drivers, selling means time spent delivering. Mahany's drivers are driver/sales representatives, and a great deal of the company's success depends on the driver's charisma, professionalism, product knowledge, and salesmanship. It would be possible to break their time down further by splitting it into time on the road and time at customers' facilities, but not much would be gained given the scope of the project.

Typically, the cost driver for selling is either gross sales, orders received, or number of sales calls.[1] Notwithstanding, the time spent in selling was used for the allocation in this project. The company's labor expense is fixed, and salespeople spend their time on tasks they deem most important. There is no added salary expense for overtime, and there are no commissions. Using time spent as the cost driver helps to identify the nonselling activities that are performed by everyone. In addition, using time spent seemed to make the most sense for the purpose of pricing different customers.

Purchasing. Purchasing typically uses a cost driver such as the number of purchase orders (POs) issued or the number of vendors. In this project and in regard to costing customers, the number of POs issued did not seem to have a causal relationship with individual groups of customers. Instead, the number of sales invoices was used on the theory that the more invoices a salesperson writes, the more products are being sold regardless of their dollar value, and thus more of the purchasing resource is being consumed.

Collections. Historically, Mahany Welding Supply's level of collection activity has followed sales volume rather than the number of customer invoices. Because past-due receivables grow at the same rate as new receivables, sales dollars were chosen as the cost driver for collections.

Auditing. All invoices are checked for accuracy of product part numbers before being posted to the accounts receivable/billing program. Invoices are made out by hand and then entered into the computer. The time spent auditing is directly proportional to the number of invoices processed. Thus, the number of invoices processed is the cost driver for auditing.

Administration. The time spent on general administration doesn't seem to have a causal relationship with any cost driver; therefore, because of the relatively small dollar amount, administration costs were divided evenly across the five selling employees.

Table 1. ACTIVITIES, BASES, AND RATES

Activity	Base	Calculation
1. Sales	Time	See Table 2, Time Study
2. Purchasing	Number of invoices	Time spent/Total number of invoices ($6,150/13,780) = $.4463 per invoice
3. Collections	Sales dollars	Time spent/Total sales = ($6,150/$1,400,000) = $.0044 per sales dollar
4. Auditing	Number of invoices	Time spent/Total number of invoices ($6,150/13,780) = $.4463 per invoice
5. Administration	Even distribution	Time spent/Sales employees ($3,075/5) = $615 per sales employee
6. Warehousing	Sales dollars	Time spent/Total sales = ($24,650/$1,400,000) = $.0176 per sales dollar
7. Order pulling	Time	See Table 2, Time Study
8. Billing	Number of invoices	Time spent/Total number of invoices ($24,115/13,780) = $1.75 per invoice
9. AP/GL	Number of invoices	Time spent/Total number of invoices ($18,000/13,780) = $1.306 per invoice
10. Advertising	Sales dollars	Total cost/Total sales = ($3,780/$1,400,000) = $.0027 per sales dollar
11. Telephone	Sales dollars	Total cost/Total sales = ($4,620/$1,400,000) = $.0033 per sales dollar
12. Legal and accounting	Even distribution	Time spent/Sales employees ($2,500/5) = $500 per sales employee
13. Miscellaneous	Sales dollars	Total cost/Total sales = ($1,540/$1,400,000) = $.0011 per sales dollar
14. Insurance	Sales dollars	Total cost/Total sales = ($19,320/$1,400,000) = $.0138 per sales dollar
15. Rent and utilities	Sales dollars	Total cost/Total sales = ($18,200/$1,400,000) = $.013 per sales dollar

Warehousing. Although warehousing and distribution costs are not always a part of ABC studies, managing warehousing costs is critical to the profitability of industrial distributors. There is no substitute for an accurate determination and practical allocation of these costs. The particular method of cost allocation depends on the company and its products, but proper costing by specific activity and allocation to products based on their unique storage and handling requirements are critical for effective warehouse management.

At Mahany Welding Supply, warehousing essentially involves the activity of unloading freight trucks and putting away inventory. Employee 2 does nearly all of that, so the time study was fairly simple. Common cost drivers for warehousing include the number of incoming shipments, the number of line items on incoming shipments, forklift time, and storage space used. Again, because the extent of the project is on costing customers, sales dollars were chosen as the cost driver. This base is justified because nearly all types of customers use the same mix of products. There would be little if any benefit, and significantly more information collection cost, in allocating costs by space used, pounds received, or other volume-related measures.

Table 2. EMPLOYEE TIME STUDY

Activity	% Time Spent	Salary and Benefits	Dollar Allocation
Employee 1			
Purchasing	10%	$61,500	$6,150
Collections	10	61,500	6,150
Selling	55	61,500	33,825
Order pulling	10	61,500	6,150
Auditing	10	61,500	6,150
Administration	5%	$61,500	3,075
Total	100%	$61,500	$61,500
Employee 2			
Selling	20%	$61,500	$12,300
Repairing	40	61,500	24,600
Warehousing	40%	$61,500	$24,600
Total	100%	$61,500	$61,500
Employee 3			
Selling (delivering)	80%	$30,000	$24,000
Order pulling	20%	$30,000	$6,000
Total	100%	$30,000	$30,000
Employee 4			
Selling (delivering)	80%	$61,500	$49,200
Order pulling	20%	$61,500	$12,300
Total	100%	$61,500	$61,500
Employee 5			
Selling	70%	$85,000	$59,500
Repairing	30%	$85,000	$25,500
Total	100%	$85,000	$85,000
Employee 6			
Accounts receivable	100%	$18,000	$18,000
Employee 7			
AP/GL	100%	$18,000	$18,000

Note: Figures have been changed for confidentiality.

Order pulling. Order pulling often is combined with warehousing. It was treated separately and scrutinized carefully in this project because it is an area where resources were being wasted. As in the case of sales, selling time was chosen as the cost driver. In a larger and more specialized environment, the number of customer orders or line items, or even sales dollars, would be more appropriate. At this company these drivers didn't appear to have a causal relationship. The two truck drivers spend practically the same amount of time pulling their orders regardless of how many customers they are scheduled to visit.

Billing. Employee 6 is a part-time employee. She specializes in accounts receivable/billing and is the sole person who posts customer transactions. Her labor expense, as well as postage and envelopes, are caused directly by the number of sales invoices she processes. Some invoices may have more line items than others, but to break down billing costs according to the line items would not pass the cost/benefit test. Although second or third notices often are sent out, only one billing per invoice was used in the calculation.

Accounts payable/general ledger. Employee 7 is on a fixed salary. She pays bills, handles the general ledger, calls in the payroll, and corresponds with the CPA. Her activities could be broken down into fixed and variable costs. Bill paying is a variable cost and is based on the number of vendor invoices or the number of POs. The general ledger and all other functions are fixed general administration. The number of customer invoices was used for the cost driver under the assumption that the level of customer activity is related most clearly to Employee 7's workload. This base is somewhat arbitrary for lack of a causal factor.

Advertising. Advertising consists primarily of advertising specialties such as pens, calendars, shirts, hats, and other small items with the company logo on them. The advertising budget is based loosely on last year's gross sales. These tokens are given out randomly to customers regardless of the size of their account. As sales increase so does the advertising specialty activity for the following year. Sales dollars are the best driver for advertising.

Telephone. The telephone bill primarily is the cost of yellow pages advertising. Long distance calls are rare because most of Mahany's suppliers have 1-800 numbers. Telephone usage is allocated the same way as advertising—by sales dollars.

Legal and accounting. No causal relationship can be determined for this expenditure category. Thus, these costs arbitrarily are allocated evenly across the five selling employees.

Miscellaneous. Miscellaneous expenses seem to have a causal relationship with the level of sales volume. Sales dollars are used as the driver.

Insurance. Insurance premiums are based, in part, on sales volume. Sales dollars are used as the driver.

Table 3. CONTRIBUTION MARGIN INCOME STATEMENT – COMPANY PROFITABILITY BY EMPLOYEE

	Allocation Base	Total	Employee 1	Employee 2	Employee 3	Employee 4	Employee 5
Number of Invoices		13,780	5,200	1,300	3,640	2,860	780
Sales		$1,400,000	$618,000	$220,000	$268,000	$178,000	$116,000
Less: COGS		931,050	462,550	129,400	185,200	87,400	66,500
Gross margin		$ 468,950	$155,450	$90,600	$ 82,800	$ 90,600	$49,500
Less: Expenses							
Labor:							
Sales	Time	$ 175,750	$ 30,750	$ 12,300	$ 24,000	$ 49,200	$ 59,500
Repair	Time	50,100	0	24,600	0	0	25,500
Truck expense		25,400	0	0	8,600	16,800	0
Purchasing	Number of invoices	6,150	2,321	580	1,625	1,276	348
Collections	Sales dollars	6,160	2,719	968	1,179	783	510
Auditing	Number of invoices	6,150	2,321	580	1,625	1,276	348
Administration	Even	3,075	615	615	615	615	615
Warehousing	Sales dollars	24,640	10,877	3,872	4,717	3,133	2,042
Order pulling	Time	21,375	3,075	0	6,000	12,300	0
Billing	Number of invoices	24,115	9,100	2,275	6,370	5,005	1,365
AP/GL	Number of invoices	17,997	6,791	1,698	4,754	3,735	1,019
Advertising	Sales dollars	3,780	1,669	594	724	481	313
Telephone	Sales dollars	4,620	2,039	726	884	587	383
Legal and accounting	Even	2,500	500	500	500	500	500
Miscellaneous	Sales dollars	1,540	680	242	295	196	128
Insurance	Sales dollars	19,320	8,528	3,036	3,698	2,456	1,601
Rent/utilities	Sales dollars	18,200	8,034	2,860	3,484	2,314	1,508
Total Expenses		$ 410,871	$ 90,019	$ 55,446	$ 69,069	$100,657	$ 95,680
Net Income		$ 58,079	$ 65,431	$ 35,154	$ 13,731	($ 10,057)	($ 46,180)

Note: Figures have been changed for confidentiality.

Rent and utilities. Rent and utilities can be allocated in a number of ways, including square footage used. Because of the homogeneous nature of Mahany Welding Supply's product mix and the layout of the facility, it wouldn't be practical to allocate on square footage. Sales dollars were chosen as the driver on the rationale that the more goods sold, the more strain they placed upon the facility. Although rent and utilities are not a variable cost, and a rise in sales will not affect the rent or the utilities, sales dollars merely are a convenient way to allocate these costs.

DETERMINING THE RATES

Once the activities and cost drivers are determined, charging rates can be computed. One activity not discussed was truck expense. Because of the emphasis on the cost of a customer, truck expense is allocated directly to each truck driver. The activities, bases, and computed rates are shown in Table 2.

Now for the moment of truth. How much does it cost to service a customer? To start, the ABC cost allocation data were placed into a quasi-contribution margin income statement shown in Table 3. The statement reflects 1994 profit on sales based on individual salespeople, but it doesn't yet answer the four questions the project addressed initially. That is, how much does it cost to service Mahany's four types of customers?

Information derived in Table 3 can be used to determine the cost to service walk-in customers, which are handled by Employee 1 and Employee 2:

Employee 1's total expenses=$90,019; Number of invoices=5,200
Employee 2's total expenses=55,446; Number of invoices=1,300
Total=$145,465 Total=6,500
$145,465/6,500=$22.38 per walk-in customer invoice

The cost for Employee 3 to service city truck customers and for Employee 4 to service country truck customers are computed in a similar fashion:

Employee 3's total expenses=$69,069; Number of invoices=3,640
$69,069/3,640=$18.98 per city truck invoice

Employee 4's total expenses=$100,658; Number of invoices=2,860
$100,658/2,860=$35.20 per country truck invoice

The cost to service an equipment repair customer creates a problem. The company's computer system has not been set up to separate and track invoices for repairs, so repair invoices (parts and labor) made out by Employee 2 and Employee 5 are buried in the general sales figures. Obviously, the data would be more informative if management separated out these costs. In the future the company will start tracking repairs separately so that the analysis will be more accurate. The walk-in customer calculation also will be more accurate when repair invoices are separated. The problem is a minimal one for this analysis given its purpose is to determine the cost of servicing a repair customer, i.e., calculating a labor rate. The amount of Employee 2's and Employee 5's total expenses divided by the amount of time they each spend on repairs determines their hourly rates.

The hourly cost for Employee 2 to service a repair customer:
Employee 2's total expenses for repairs: $55,446 x 40%= $22,178
Number of hours paid for a year: 40 x 52=2,080 hours
Number of hours spent on repairs: 2,080 x 40%=832 hours
Repair expenses/repair hours ($22,178/832)=$26.66 per hour

The hourly cost for Employee 5 to service a repair customer:
Employee 5's total expenses for repairs: $95,679 x 30%= $28,704
Number of hours paid per year: 40 x 52=2,080 hours
Number of hours spent on repairs: 2,080 x 30%=624 hours
Repair expenses/repair hours ($28,704/624)=$46.00 per hour

Welder

MANAGERS, NOT ABC, MAKE DECISIONS

What do we do with the information now that we have it? First we must consider all the limitations that are a part of the calculations. In order for accounting data to be useful they must be reasonably accurate. Although the analysis is not exact, it is accurate enough so we can make some general conclusions.

For one thing, it is eye-opening to see that company-wide net income of $58,079 included two employees' aggregate net loss of $56,237! As with most complicated business issues, it is best not to jump to conclusions. At first glance, Employee 5's numbers appear to be of great concern. But, Employee 5 is the owner of Mahany Welding Supply, enjoys working, and is easing into retirement. Instead of simply drawing a salary and playing golf, Employee 5 contributes substantially to the business. It is difficult to quantify the value of a company figurehead who has nearly 50 years of industry experience.

Of more concern is the net loss for the country truck. Should we drop the country route? The calculations would suggest so, assuming they are accurate. But there are better solutions. The country route has been operated since 1946, and it seems foolish to abandon it without first trying to make it profitable. One factor to consider is that a fair amount of walk-in trade also is country route customers who might quit the company altogether if the route is dropped. Can we reshuffle the route so that it is more economical to run? Should we hire a salesperson to call on route customers? Should we impose a delivery charge, demand a minimum sales charge, or both?

There are many ways that the country route could be made more profitable, or at least only a marginal loser. Before the route is dropped, a keep or drop analysis should be undertaken, taking into account the revenue and overhead that would be lost with the route's elimination. Perhaps the 80%/20% rule would penalize profitable route customers if we dropped it completely. Only through careful consideration and discussion by company staff can this decision be made. Now that we know how much it costs the company per hour for repairs, a desired level of profit can be added, and an hourly rate can be set with confidence.

Actually sitting down and laying out an activity-based costing system for a real company is much more difficult than a typical textbook ABC problem. Determining what causes a cost to occur is much more difficult than it originally might seem. This project proved how important management support and adequate resources are to implement an ABC system properly. Some of the practical difficulties that we encountered include:

- Because all but one employee are salaried, labor costs are fixed in the relevant range. Regardless of sales activity, total labor expense stays the same. Thus, it is difficult to say that anything actually "drives" sales labor expense.
- Mahany's employees do several jobs each, making it difficult to nail down how much time is actually spent on a particular task.
- There is a lack of accounting data. Mahany's system needs several improvements, such as segregating repair data.
- The company is quite small and somewhat disorganized, making cost analysis difficult.
- Regression analysis, which often is used to justify allocation bases, was beyond the scope of this project.
- Effective ABC analysis requires input from different staff members. This project was performed without their assistance.

The ABC analysis indicated that 15 different activities caused costs to occur in the company. After identifying the activities, performing time studies, finding a causal link between activities and costs, computing allocation rates, and putting the data into a contribution margin format, the desired cost numbers were obtained. Even if this analysis were not refined and tried again, it still identified the costs of servicing different customers, which is the main reason the project was implemented.

Krupnicki (r.) discusses the features of a welder with a customer.

There is an old adage that says that 80% of your business comes from 20% of your customers. If this is true, it could mean that 80% of your resources are used to service 20% of your business. Is that 20% profitable? Probably not, and it could be dragging down the company. Is ABC only for companies that are under extreme competitive pressures or experiencing financial difficulties? Definitely not, for these companies obviously already are trying to come up with ideas and solutions. Companies that are doing well and think the good times will last forever are the ones that could get blindsided.

This ABC study provided information that will help Mahany's managers make better decisions. The mechanics of an ABC system are straightforward, but a company intending to conduct an ABC study must be prepared to devote sufficient resources to it. People involved in the project must spend a great deal of time looking at what really drives costs in their business by observing activities, interviewing employees, and performing quantitative methods such as regression analysis. A company that doesn't commit the necessary resources is bound to be disappointed with the results.

Michael Krupnicki, CMA, who is now president, was operations manager for Mahany Welding Supply, Rochester, N.Y., at the time the study was conducted. He also is an adjunct professor at Rochester Institute of Technology. He can be reached at (716) 271-0870.

Thomas Tyson, Ph.D, CMA, is professor of accounting at St. John Fisher College, Rochester, N.Y. He can be reached at (716) 385-8431 or e-mail: tyson@sjfc.edu. Both authors are members of IMA's Rochester Chapter, through which this article was submitted.

[1] Ronald J. Lewis, "Activity-Based Costing for Marketing," MANAGEMENT ACCOUNTING, November 1991, p. 34.

How ABC Changed the Post Office

PHOTOS COURTESY UNITED STATES POSTAL SERVICE

To meet its competition, the U.S. Postal Service ha

credit/debit card service.

BY TERRELL L. CARTER;
ALI M. SEDAGHAT, CMA; AND
THOMAS D. WILLIAMS

The U.S. Postal Service is a unique federal entity in several respects. First, the USPS, in essence, operates in a manner similar to many private sector companies. The USPS provides a variety of services, generates revenue from these services, and incurs costs and expenses as a result of its operations. Second, the USPS is unique in that it is open to private sector competition. Competition includes companies such as Federal Express, United Parcel Service, Mail Boxes Etc., and a host of other similar companies. Few other government agencies or departments operate in a similar business environment.

Retailers as well as USPS competitors have long accepted credit cards as payment options for goods and services. Moreover, new technologies are beginning to lead to a "cashless" world. Customers are seeking convenience and value, while businesses are striving for increased sales and guaranteed payment. Given the competitive forces facing the USPS and the rapid pace at which new technologies are becoming available, USPS management realized that it had to use innovative business methods to maintain and increase its market share against its competition and provide increased value to its customers while ensuring cost effectiveness.

Based on this evaluation of its position in the marketplace, the USPS engaged Coopers & Lybrand (C&L) to conduct activity-based cost studies of its key revenue collection processes and market strategy study for a national credit card and debit card program. To obtain an understanding of the cash, check, and credit/debit card activities, C&L reviewed USPS data and procedure manuals, interviewed USPS headquarters staff, and conducted telephone surveys of front window supervisors and district office personnel. Using an activity-based cost modeling approach, C&L defined the cash and check

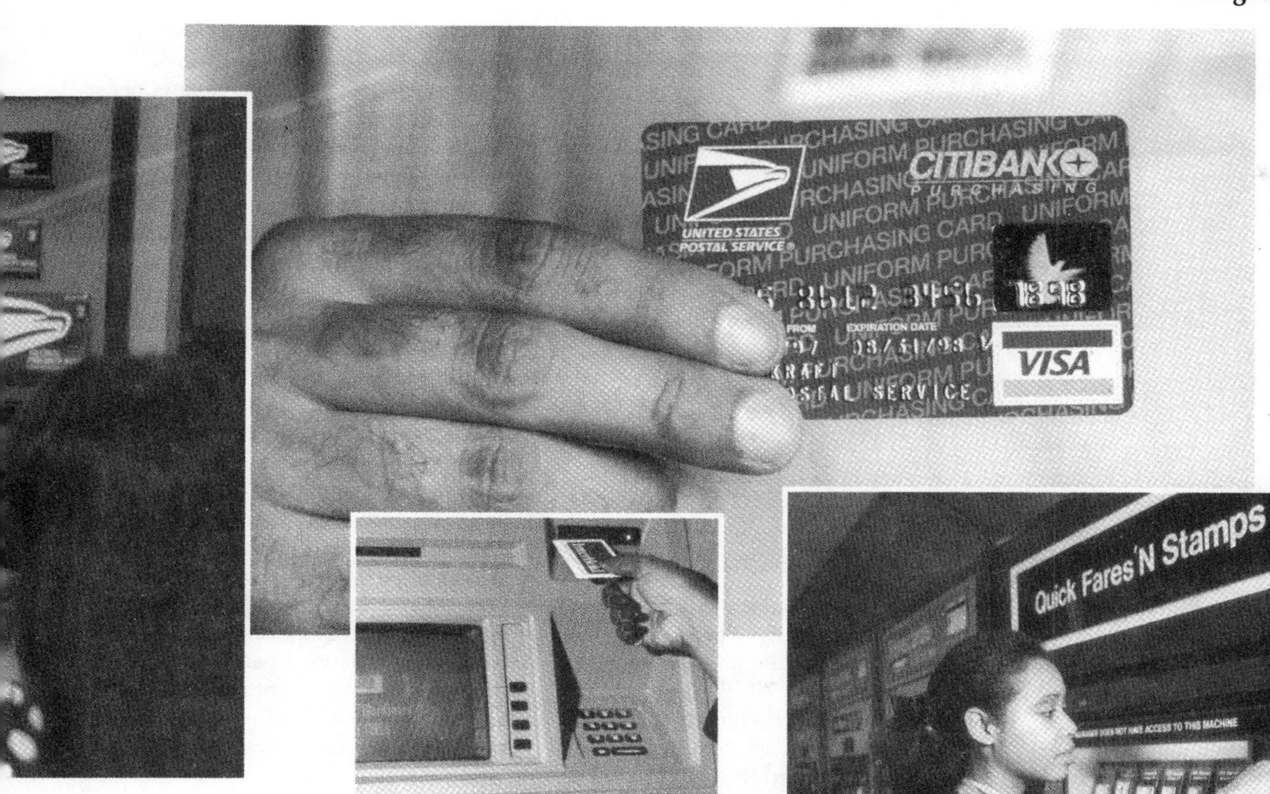

change and offer customers

process in terms of the activities that link together to make the processes. C&L also identified unit, batch, and product sustaining activities; resources for each of the activities; and the transaction volumes for each activity. Unit activity was the acceptance and processing of a payment by item. Batch activities involved close-out at the end of the day, consolidation, and supervisory review. Product activities included maintenance charges for bank accounts and deposit reconciliation (cash and checks) and terminal maintenance and training (credit and debit cards).

After building the cash and check cost models, C&L defined activity-based costs for the credit and debit card activities similarly. The components of the cash, check, and credit/debit card activities are shown in Table 1. The activity cost models for the cash and check activities are shown in Table 2. The activity-based cost models for the credit card and debit card activities are shown in Table 3.

C&L also conducted product pricing and profitability analyses of the credit/debit card test program.

In analyzing data from Phase I of the USPS credit card and debit card test market plan and the organizational costs associated with serving USPS customers through its 28,728 post offices, 9,059 stations and branches, and 1,605 community postal units, C&L identified the following issues affecting costs, product pricing, competitiveness, and customer value.[1]

1. USPS provides a limited assortment of payment options relative to the competition:

- Cash and check payments are predominant USPS payment options,
- Competitors provide credit card payment options, and
- Most USPS transactions must occur at a post office.

2. USPS generates a large volume of low-value cash transactions:

- The majority of transactions are $20 or less, and
- Transactions on a per-dollar basis are expensive to process.

3. USPS' check receipts processing is costly:

- Extra steps are required,
- Additional bank charges are incurred, and
- $3-$4 million is lost to bad checks.

4. Policies and procedures are not consistent.

5. Based on independent surveys, cash, check, and credit/debit card processes are not uniform.

Table 1. ANALYSIS OF ACTIVITIES

Cash Process Activities	Credit/Debit Card Activities	Check Process Activities
1. Receive cash	1. Process card transactions	1. Receive checks
2. Deposit cash	2. Close out point-of-sale (POS) terminal	2. Deposit checks
3. Maintain bank accounts (including cash concentration and funds mobilization)	3. Reconcile credit and debit card receipts	3. Maintain bank accounts (including cash concentration and funds mobilization)
4. Reconcile bank accounts	4. Process chargebacks	4. Reconcile bank accounts
	5. Maintain POS and telecommunications equipment	

Note: Cash is handled by USPS employees four times: 1. By the clerk when accepting payment from a customer. 2. By the clerk when counting the cash in the drawer daily. 3. By a supervisor when counting the cash before the bank deposit. 4. By another supervisor when counting the cash to verify before the deposit.

PROJECTED COST MODEL FOR USPS

The ABC study also revealed hidden and indirect costs for each of the payment activities. Combining all of the costs resulted in the breakdown shown in Table 4. C&L pointed out that "total incremental costs for a national credit/debit card program are immaterial in relation to total USPS payment processing costs that exceed $1 billion per year, based on the activity-based cost study data collected through the February/March 1994 time frame."[2] The cost data showed that the net benefit of accepting credit and debit cards would be negative through 1997. Projections showed that from 1998 through 2000, the net benefits of card acceptance would be $5.2 million, $15.6 million, and $28.8 million, respectively (see Table 5).

In summarizing these findings, C&L reported that, "Credit and debit card processing costs are relatively high at the moment due to the normal impact of process start-up, low initial volume and high initial implementation costs. However, as volumes continue to grow, projected credit and debit card costs can become competitive with current cash and check processing costs."[3] C&L also reported that "credit and debit card processing costs for retail window transactions becomes cost effective once total card revenue exceeds 3%-4% of total revenues from retail transactions. As card volume continues to displace cash and check

Table 2a. ACTIVITY-BASED COST MODEL FOR CASH PROCESSES

Unit Activities	Driver	Cost per Driver	Driver Quantities	Annual Cost
Accept cash	Number of cash transactions	$0.49	921,881,239	$451,173,288
Processing of cash by bank	Number of cash transactions	0.02	921,881,239	19,974,271
Batch Activities				
Close-out and supervisor review of clerk	Number of close-outs	5.79	28,029,443	162,255,662
Consolidation and deposit of unit's receipts	Number of deposits	16.16	9,902,381	160,016,636
Review and transfer funds-time	Number of accounts	1,884.47	7,490	14,114,698
Product Activities				
Maintenance charges for bank accounts	Number of accounts	114.32	7,490	856,286
Reconciling bank accounts	Number of accounts	1,935.94	7,490	14,500,182
	TOTAL COST			**$822,891,023**

Table 2b. ACTIVITY-BASED COST MODEL FOR CHECK PROCESSES

Unit Activities	Driver	Cost per Driver	Driver Quantities	Annual Cost
Accept checks	Number of checks	$0.98	120,173,780	$117,627,298
Processing of checks by bank	Number of checks	0.06	120,173,780	7,335,089
Processing of returned checks	Number of bad checks	25.16	143,436	3,608,400
Batch Activities				
Close-out and supervisor review of clerk	Number of close-outs	2.67	28,029,443	74,887,229
Consolidation and deposit of unit's receipts	Number of deposits	2.07	9,902,381	20,505,861
Review and transfer funds-time	Number of accounts	250.20	7,490	1,873,980
Product Activities				
Maintenance charges for bank accounts	Number of accounts	14.91	7,490	111,641
Reconciling bank accounts	Number of accounts	251.80	7,490	1,185,971
	TOTAL COST			**$227,135,469**

transactions, card costs become even more advantageous."[4]

COOPERS & LYBRAND'S RECOMMENDATION

Based on its analysis of the market test, a Gallup survey (see p.34), and market trends, C&L recommended that the USPS use a three-phase strategy to implement a national policy of accepting both credit and debit cards: Phase I—Market Test (which was already completed); Phase II—Mobilize and Market; Phase III—Modify.

PHOTOS COURTESY UNITED STATES POSTAL SERVICE

Mobilize and market. This two-step phase began with an aggressive mobilization effort to implement nationwide acceptance of credit and debit cards for selected USPS products and services at retail windows beginning with larger offices. The potential benefits were identified as increased customer satisfaction, increased sales, and improved processing efficiency. The second step was an aggressive targeted marketing campaign designed to increase credit card usage at USPS retail windows. "Studies indicate that a targeted marketing campaign can have significant impact on consumer use of debit and credit cards. A recent study concluded that the value of increased sales more than covered the additional expense of advertising."[5] The potential benefits identified were increased credit/debit card volume, increased total sales, and

Table 3a. ACTIVITY-BASED COST MODEL FOR CREDIT CARD PROCESSES

Unit Activities	Driver	Cost per Driver	Driver Quantities	Annual Cost
Process credit card	Number of credit transactions	$0.80	357,796	$287,217
Payment of credit card fee	$ size of transactions	0.01	18,512,365	252,474
Processing chargebacks	Number of chargebacks	23.87	120	2,865
Batch Activities				
Close-out terminal	Number of close-outs	1.30	160,596	208,581
Reconciling daily receipts—district	Number of stations	65.84	1,500	98,767
Process form 1908	Number of 1908s	9.04	2,884	26,072
Product Activities				
Maintain equipment	Number of terminals	275.60	1,875	516,754
Training	Number of districts	22,311.84	5	111,559
	TOTAL COST			**$1,504,289**

Table 3b. ACTIVITY-BASED COST MODEL FOR DEBIT CARD PROCESSES

Unit Activities	Driver	Cost per Driver	Driver Quantities	Annual Cost
Process debit card	Number of debit transactions	$0.86	35,262	$30,260
Batch Activities				
Close-out terminal	Number of close-outs	0.12	160,596	19,746
Reconciling daily receipts—district	Number of stations	6.24	1,500	9,359
Process form 1908	Number of 1908s	0.86	2,884	2,470
Product Activities				
Maintain equipment	Number of terminals	26.11	1,875	48,965
Training	Number of districts	2,114.16	5	10,571
	TOTAL COST			**$121,371**

Table 4. PROCESSING COSTS

Activity Processing of	Average Transaction Size	Cost Per Dollar Processed	
		Phase I Market Test	Phase II 1995-1999
Cash	$20	$.045	$.048
Checks	$51	$.038	$.040
Credit Cards	$52	$.081	$.027
Debit Cards	$49	$.071	$.015

reduced transaction costs.

Modify. This phase entailed implementing improved credit/debit card processing technology and procedures to increase the benefits and continue to reduce the costs of the national card program. C&L recommended installing online point-of-sale terminals and consolidating all card authorization and transaction processing. The national implementation would use standalone card verification terminals, and this phase would replace them with integrated equipment. The potential benefits identified would be improved processing efficiency, reduced processing costs, reduced transaction errors and rejects, and improved management information.

THE BOARD APPROVES CARDS

Senior postal management decided on the basis of the C&L analysis and a decision analysis report (DAR) prepared by USPS Finance to propose to the USPS Board of Governors ("Board") that credit and debit cards be accepted nationally at USPS retail windows. Management recommended an aggressive two-year implementation. By the end of the second year, 33,000 post offices would be equipped with 50,000 card terminals and trained USPS personnel.[6] The DAR provided the following breakdown:

Expense investment (50,000 card terminals)	$25,893,000
Installation expense	3,825,000
Total investment (fiscal years 1995 and 1996)	$29,718,000
Operating costs in first full year (FY 97)	$30,327,000

Customer service initiative with no claimed ROI

Potential cost savings and revenue enhancements not included.

It is important to note the last two points. The program, while virtually ensuring an ROI and cost savings, was not being proposed for the financial benefits. Instead, as USPS CFO Michael J. Riley said in his presentation to the Board, "It is important to note that this is a customer service initiative which does not attempt to claim a return on investment. This is in spite of the fact that many retailers report savings from processing less currency and checks, as well as increased revenue from offering this growing retail

Table 5. PROJECTED COST MODEL

Base Line	1994	1995	1996	1997	1998	1999	2000
Cash	822,856,044	879,004,435	938,710,365	1,003,001,968	1,071,923,013	1,145,819,941	1,225,066,230
Check	227,789,177	242,987,911	259,731,645	277,371,596	296,274,358	316,534,152	338,252,449
Total Cost	1,050,645,221	1,121,992,346	1,198,442,010	1,280,373,564	1,368,197,371	1,462,354,093	1,563,318,679
Card Program							
Cash	822,856,044	867,786,033	899,084,296	933,386,322	967,692,345	1,001,794,407	1,035,444,902
Check	227,789,177	238,356,354	250,021,816	259,526,699	269,039,899	278,505,217	287,864,197
Credit	1,511,405	18,948,017	46,924,315	69,641,084	96,614,272	127,254,140	161,339,635
Debit	125,709	3,112,999	13,839,778	21,074,881	29,567,163	39,187,991	49,833,387
Total Cost	1,052,282,335	1,128,203,403	1,209,870,205	1,283,628,986	1,362,913,679	1,446,741,755	1,534,482,121
Net Benefit (Cost)	(1,637,114)	(6,211,057)	(11,428,195)	(3,255,422)	5,283,692	15,612,338	28,836,558

COST PER DOLLAR

Base Line	1994	1995	1996	1997	1998	1999	2000
Cash	0.045	0.042	0.044	0.043	0.042	0.042	0.042
Check	0.037	0.035	0.036	0.036	0.036	0.035	0.035
Card Program							
Cash	0.045	0.042	0.045	0.045	0.045	0.046	0.047
Check	0.037	0.036	0.037	0.038	0.038	0.039	0.039
Credit	0.082	0.035	0.033	0.029	0.028	0.027	0.027
Debit	0.073	0.023	0.021	0.017	0.016	0.015	0.015

Note: The 1994 Model Totals were higher than actual Phase I Cost Models due to the incremental start-up costs of the national program. C&L stressed that data for this model would be subject to change as new data and information became available, and for the model to continue to be useful it would have to be updated on a periodic basis to reflect ongoing program management modification.

payment option. We base our DAR on increased customer satisfaction."[7] In October 1994, the Board unanimously approved the proposal without any modifications.

Through March 1997	Total Number of Transactions	Total Dollar Transactions	Average Ticket	Total Chargebacks*
Credit Cards	26,494,680	$1,276,263,936	$48	$61,723
Debit Cards	2,251,720	$ 118,529,332	$53	n/a

Table 6

*Chargebacks are charges that customers dispute, which, after investigating, the card companies reverse. This becomes an expense to the merchant.

THE ROLL-OUT

The next step after Board approval was to get a contract in place for a credit card processor and a vendor to supply the 50,000 card terminals. A contract was competitively awarded the following spring to NationsBank with NaBanco, a national card processor, as its subcontractor.[8] NaBanco also would supply the terminals under a contract it had with a manufacturer in Atlanta, Microbilt, Inc. In April 1995, the roll-out began.

Since April 1995, the program has broadened in scope to include phone and mail orders for stamps including philately and vending machines. Because of demand, the contract recently was modified to increase the number of card terminals shipped to more than 67,000. From a customer service perspective, credit and debit card acceptance has been a runaway success, and even with such an aggressive implementation schedule it has been difficult to satisfy demand.

This project has been a very successful customer-driven initiative. Since the roll-out began, there have been more than 300 positive news articles covering this program. Not only do customers enjoy the convenience and flexibility of not having to carry as much cash, but USPS retail window clerks, who feel safer because there is less cash in their drawers, benefit as well. USPS clerks also like card acceptance because card transactions are more accurate than counting cash, so their liability is minimized.[9]

The USPS benefits because it gets funds the next day from card transactions at a very competitive discount rate. The payment infrastructure created by card acceptance has helped the USPS launch new products and market tests more quickly. Starting credit card acceptance later benefited the Postal Service because it could add debit card acceptance at the same time with one roll-out rather than two. The USPS is now the nation's largest debit card acceptor. The program has been highly successful in all of its aims, as these important statistics show (see Table 6). See Figure 1 for the growth trends in transaction and dollar volume.

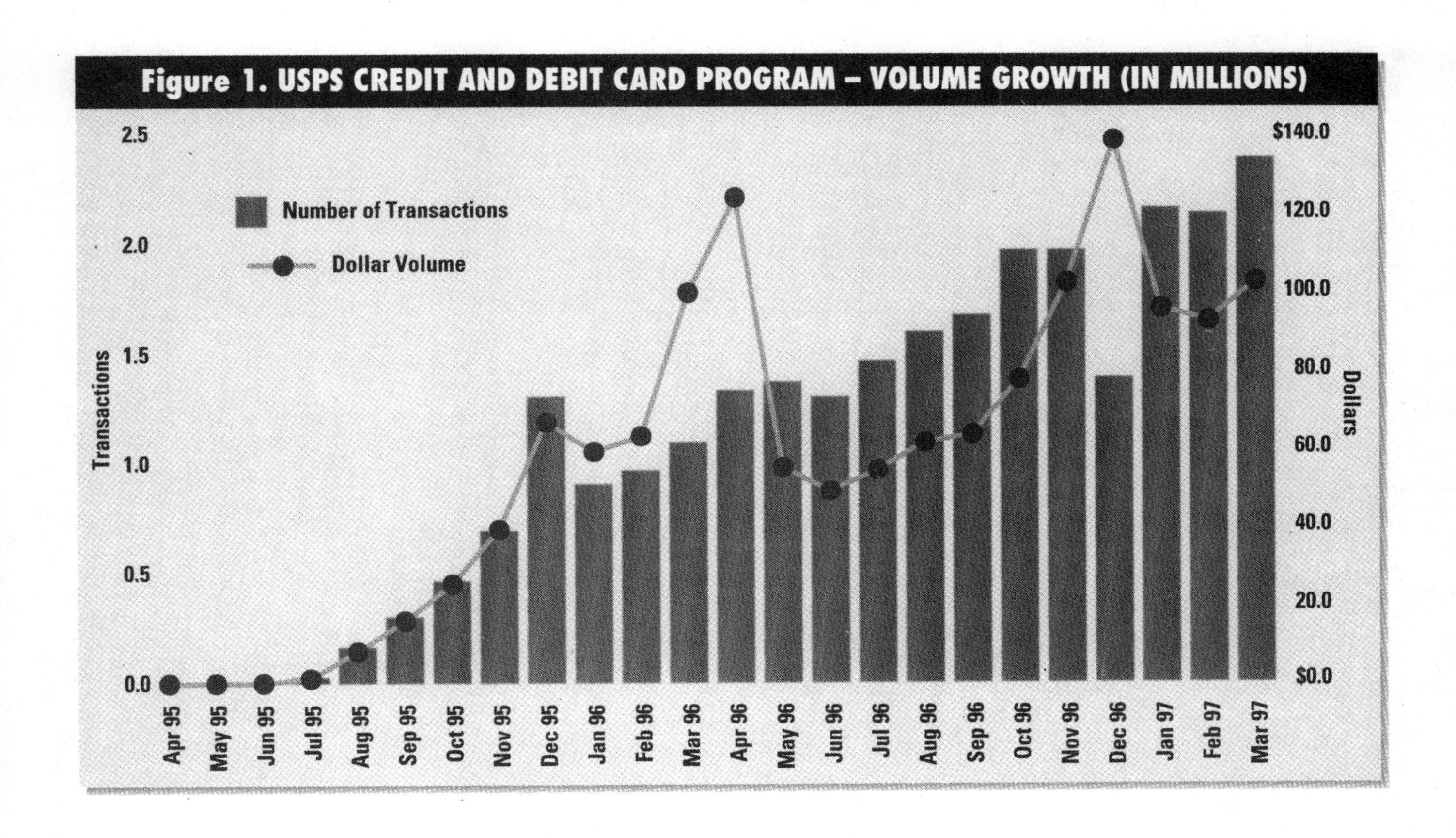

Figure 1. USPS CREDIT AND DEBIT CARD PROGRAM – VOLUME GROWTH (IN MILLIONS)

AS EASY AS ABC: MAXIMIZING VALUE

The popularity of activity-based costing and activity-based management is growing. In the private sector, hundreds of companies have adopted activity-based costing and management approaches to cost finding and cost accounting. These range from manufacturers such as John Deere to service firms such as American Express. Many have gone a step further and adopted activity-based management approaches.

Now, local and national public sector organizations are beginning to apply activity-based costing and activity-based management to the task of reinventing government. These organizations range from the road maintenance department in Indianapolis to enormous federal agencies such as the USPS as described here.

Earlier attempts at improving government operations have been largely unsuccessful. Activity-based costing and activity-based management approaches are allowing these government organizations to discover and take advantage of four elements missing from earlier performance improvement attempts. They include:

- Financial and performance information systems that enable and encourage managers to make strategic process improvements that maximize value to customers and taxpayers.
- A management and organizational structure built around processes or how the work gets done in an organization.
- A strategy for managing the human aspects of changing from a static bureaucracy to a dynamic, improvement-driven organization.
- A common financial and managerial language for different parts of an organization and all of a government's agencies.

Activity-based costing approaches are ever evolving. Nearly every organization applying these approaches discovers new uses. They go far beyond ABC's original purpose of calculating accurate product costs, all the way to activity-based management, a comprehensive management approach. The case of the USPS's national credit card and debit card program provides an excellent example of how effective activity-based approaches can be in facilitating strategic process improvements that maximize value to customers while ensuring economic viability and cost effectiveness.

Terrell L. Carter is assistant treasurer, payment technologies, for the United States Postal Service. A 28-year career employee, Terry holds a B.S. degree in Computer Information Systems from Strayer College, Washington, D.C., and is an executive MBA fellow at Loyola College in Maryland. He is a member of the Treasury Management Association. He can be reached at (202) 268-2330.

Ali M. Sedaghat, CMA, DBA, KPMG Faculty Alumni Fellow, is an associate of accounting at Loyola College in Maryland. He earned his B.A. degree from Abadan Institute of Technology and MBA and DBA degrees from The George Washington University. He is a member of IMA's Baltimore Chapter, through which this article was submitted.

Thomas D. Williams is the financial management officer for the National Institute of Allergy and Infectious Diseases at the National Institutes of Health. A 15-year career employee of the federal government, Tom has extensive experience in domestic and international governmental budgeting, accounting, finance, and management. Tom is also an executive MBA fellow at Loyola College in Maryland.

Authors acknowledge valuable contributions by Julie Jack, Julie Moore, and Matthew Wong.

[1] "United States Postal Service Credit/ Debit Card Strategy—Final Report," Coopers & Lybrand L.L.P., Washington, D.C., April 19, 1994, p. 8.
[2] Ibid., page 37.
[3] Ibid., page 3.
[4] Ibid., page 12.
[5] Ibid., page 31.
[6] 6,000 "contract" stations would not be included in the two-year implementation.
[7] "Credit Debit Card Acceptance at the Retail Window," presentation to the Board of Governors, October 3, 1994.
[8] NaBanco is now First Data Merchant Services (FDMS).
[9] USPS window clerks must compensate the USPS for shortages, so errors in cash handling are costly to them.

ABC why it's TRIED and how it SUCCEEDS

BY KIP R. KRUMWIEDE, CMA, CPA

After a heated start for activity-based costing (ABC) in the early 1990s, some companies have cooled to this sophisticated costing technique. ABC can be more difficult to implement than early articles suggested, and not all organizations have achieved the success they had hoped for. Recent articles dwell more on the difficulties of implementing ABC and activity-based management (ABM), mostly from human and strategic perspectives. Yet, according to a recent survey conducted by the Cost Management Group of the Institute of Management Accountants (IMA), more than half of responding companies that have tried ABC (54%) are using it for decision making outside the accounting function. And of those companies using ABC, 89% say it was worth the implementation costs.

Interestingly, the factors most commonly associated with companies trying ABC were not the same factors most tied to its eventual success. Knowledge of these factors should be useful to those companies considering ABC as well as those trying to improve the success of an ABC system.

WHAT IS THE STATUS OF ABC?

Figure 1 illustrates the ABC adoption status of companies responding to the survey.[1] Adoption was defined for this study as the stage when companies decide to commit the necessary resources to ABC implementation. As shown, 49% of all responding firms have adopted ABC, which is up from 41% a year earlier. Of the nonadopting companies, 25% said they are considering it. Only 5% report they seriously considered ABC and then rejected it.

Adoption appears to be on the rise among nonmanufacturing companies or financial, nonprofit, utilities, and other service organizations. Of these companies, 61% reported ABC adoption, up from 42% last year. Adoption among manufacturers was 45%.

Figure 2 shows that for those companies that have adopted ABC, more than half (54%) have reached the stage at which ABC is used at least somewhat for decision making outside the accounting function. Another 14% report they are still in the analysis stage (that is, determining project objectives, analyzing activities, and collecting data). The 14% in the getting-acceptance stage are those companies that have finished analyzing activities and developing the ABC model but are trying to get organizational buy-in. Only 2% report that they implemented ABC and then abandoned it.

WHO TRIES ABC?

Our study set out to determine if adoption is associated with kinds of products and processes, quality and lean production practices, and information technologies. Factors that appeared to separate those who adopted ABC from those who didn't were: potential for cost distortions, decision usefulness of cost information, lack of system initiatives, and the size of the organization. (See Table 1.)

Figure 1. ABC ADOPTION STATUS

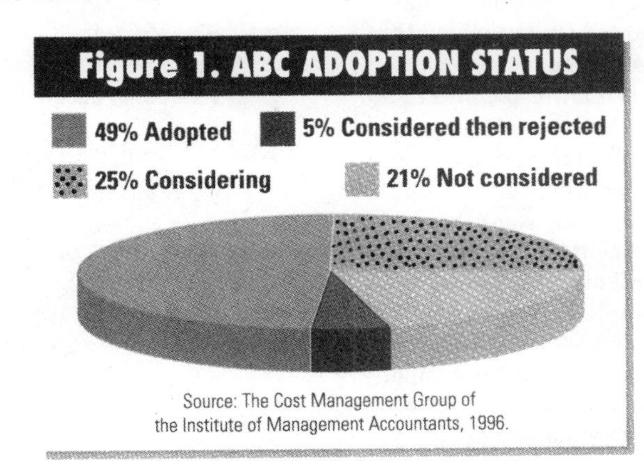

Source: The Cost Management Group of the Institute of Management Accountants, 1996.

Potential for cost distortions. The higher the potential for cost distortions, the more motivated an organization may be to adopt ABC.[2] Significant distortions may occur if only one overhead base is used. For example, allocating overhead based on direct labor hours to a product that needs relatively little direct labor might lead to under-costing the product. Because some products may require more direct labor hours than others, cost distortions could be caused by the number and diversity of products or services produced.

In the IMA study, the potential for cost distortions was a composite measure based on questions relating to the diversity of products, support departments, processes, and volumes. This distortion potential generally was much higher for ABC adopters than nonadopters. Many ABC adopters (71%) had above-average cost distortion potential versus only 39% of nonadopters. Another possible measure of potential for cost distortions is the percentage of overhead costs to total production costs. Table 1 shows that this percentage also differed between the two groups (32.8% vs. 28.7%, respectively).

Cost distortions can affect many decision areas including customer profitability analyses. Clete O'Dell, accounting manager with Diamant Boart, reports that management was shocked when ABC analysis showed that a major customer who contributed 6%-7% of total revenues was quite unprofitable when all of the special efforts for that customer were considered. The sales force, who are paid commissions on sales rather than profits, questioned the data at first. They did not realize all of the expensive services provided for the customer that were never charged for but which the ABC analysis surfaced.

When there is a lower potential for cost distortions, however, the benefits of ABC may be limited. For example, a cost accounting supervisor for a southeastern manufacturing company not using ABC commented, "We are almost a one-product plant. We don't believe our cost data would be substantially improved or refined with ABC/ABM." He did add, however, that his company would still benefit from doing activity analysis to identify nonvalue-added activities. Sixty-eight percent of nonadopters indicated they use departmental or multiple, plant-wide overhead rates as opposed to single, plant-wide overhead rates. The use of more detailed overhead allocation methods probably reduces the potential for cost distortions and might help explain why these firms do not feel strongly compelled to adopt ABC.

Decision usefulness of cost information. Even if ABC will reduce product cost distortions substantially, it probably will not be implemented unless a company can use the better cost information in its decision making. Based on questions relating to competition, cost-reduction efforts, and basis for pricing decisions, respondents ranked decision usefulness higher for adopting firms (65% scored above average).

Kirk Sherbine with Rockwood Manufacturing Company in Rockwood, Pa., says his company considered adopting ABC but rejected it. One of the key reasons was that the company has little control over the prices it can charge for its various lines of door hardware. Prices are dictated by the market, and highly reliable product costs are not that crucial. He explains further, "ABC looked a little complicated for our needs."

Edwin Poisson of Handleman Company reports that his company, a wholesaler of software products, music tapes, CDs, and videos, adopted ABC because of the highly competitive pricing in its industry. Major chains often sell music and video products at below cost to get customers to buy their stereo and computer equipment. Handleman plans to use ABC information in negotiations with suppliers and for cost reduction efforts.

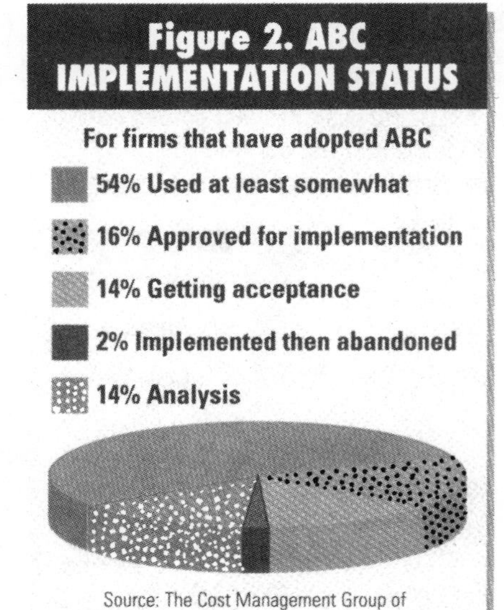

Source: The Cost Management Group of the Institute of Management Accountants, 1996.

Lack of system initiatives. Several survey respondents commented that their companies were in the midst of installing new information systems. In fact, 15% of all nonadopters reported that their company was in the midst of installing a new or upgraded information system. In contrast, only 7% of adopters reported a system initiative. Frequently, the plan is to implement, or at least consider implementing, ABC after the system upgrade is complete. For example, Hunter Douglas Fabrication reported its company is considering ABC but first must restructure the organization around its new integrated (SAP/R3) information system.

System initiatives can impede ABC adoption for at least two reasons. First, implementing ABC can take considerable time and effort. If the focus is on other important system enhancements, fewer resources are available for the ABC project. Second, ABC systems require more detailed information than traditional cost systems. Because of the increased information needed to implement ABC, many companies seem content to wait until supporting systems are improved or replaced.

A good example was provided by Robert Murphy, controller for Edwards Baking Company in Atlanta, Ga. He said that his company hopes to implement some form of ABC one day because overhead costs are not being allocated accurately. The two major product lines, baked products and cold sets, are quite diverse and require very different processes to manufacture. But for now, Edwards has focused on integrating its manufacturing system with a new user-friendly financial package. The company feels it has added tremendous value by providing real-time production and costing information with drill-down capability for sales and operating personnel. Of course, having real-time operations and costing data will facilitate the ABC implementation in the future.

Table 1. ABC ADOPTION FACTORS

Factor	Nonadopters	Adopters
Potential for cost distortions	39% had above-average potential	71% had above-average potential
Percentage of overhead costs to total production costs	28.7%	32.8%
Decision usefulness of cost information	54% had above-average usefulness	65% had above-average usefulness
Lack of system initiatives	15% report major system or software initiative occurring	7% report major system or software initiative occurring
Size of the organization	$51M-$100M (average)	$101M-$500M (average)

Source: The Cost Management Group of the Institute of Management Accountants, 1996.

Size of the organization. As shown in Table 1, ABC adopters tended to be somewhat larger on average than nonadopters. Although there was a wide variation, adopting firms had average sales in the $101-$500 million range versus $51-$100 million for nonadopters. Possible reasons for the size difference include availability of resources (people and dollars) and economies of scale in implementing ABC at multiple sites.

WHAT FACTORS AFFECT ABC'S SUCCESS?

The factors most related to ABC's implementation success were not the same as those affecting its adoption. Reaching the "success" stage, in which ABC is used for decision making outside the accounting function, had more to do with time, other major initiatives being implemented, existing information technology (IT) sophistication, top management support, integration of ABC into the financial system, and the use of ABC as part of the budgeting process. Table 2 illustrates the differentiating factors for users and nonusers.

Time. ABC often takes more time to implement than expected. Overall, usage-level companies first started implementing ABC an average of more than three years ago (versus only 1.3 years for nonusage companies). The amount of time necessary to reach the usage stage also appears to take longer as the size of the company increases. Companies with sales less than $100 million reported an average time of 2.3 years while larger firms reported an average time of 3.6 years. Time was found to be the most important factor in the study for differentiating usage and nonusage companies.

Table 2. FACTORS AFFECTING ABC USAGE

Factor		Nonusage Stage	Usage Stage
Time	Smaller companies (<$100M sales)	0.9 years	2.3 years
	Larger companies (>$100M sales)	1.7 years	3.6 years
	All companies	1.3 years	3.1 years
Other major initiatives reported		62% yes	48% yes
IT sophistication		46% above-average	61% above-average
Top management support		40% above-average	58% above-average
Integration into financial system		7% yes	47% yes
ABC part of budgeting process		24% yes	45% yes

Source: The Cost Management Group of the Institute of Management Accountants, 1996.

Other major initiatives. Sixty-two percent of the firms that have not reached the usage stage report other major initiatives being implemented. Several respondents commented that they were having trouble implementing ABC because of other priorities, such as entering new products or markets, implementing new information systems, and restructuring or reengineering projects. A director of cost systems lamented, "Everyone has three Number One priorities." Another director of finance for a northeastern manufacturer reported that his company is still in the analysis stage of ABC because of major initiative overload. Besides ABC, his company is implementing a division-wide information system, TQM, lean manufacturing, JIT, CIM, balanced scorecard, and MRP II. The company's CEO has set very aggressive cost-cutting and productivity goals. These initiatives have affected ABC implementation, but management generally feels that ABC/ABM will help support the other initiatives.

Information technology sophistication. Of the major initiatives being implemented, system or software improvements were mentioned by nonusage companies 22% of the time (only one usage-stage company mentioned a current system initiative). It would appear that improvements to the information system often precede both ABC adoption and reaching the usage level. A high level of IT sophistication appears to be an important factor in getting to the usage stage for the majority of companies. Of the usage-stage companies, 61% received an above-average IT score, compared to only 46% of the nonusage stage firms.[3] In general, companies will have an easier time implementing ABC if their IT system has the following characteristics: good subsystem (for example, sales system, manufacturing system, and so on) integration; user-friendly query capability; available sales, cost, and performance data going back 12 months; and real-time updates of all these types of data.

Dennis Jorgenson, finance manager with Tektronix, said that the IT system and MIS support are two of the biggest reasons for his company's success with ABC. An individual from the MIS department provides full-time support for the ABC module, which is fully linked to the manufacturing system. In

BASIC ABC IMPLEMENTATION TIPS

Focus on critical needs. Before implementing an expensive integrated information system or a more sophisticated costing system, decide what are the organization's most important issues or decisions and what types of information would help address those issues.

Get top management support. If you think ABC might be a useful tool in your organization, be sure to get top management's support first. With their help, identify critical information needs, and show how an activity cost approach could provide valuable information. Seek approval for small, relatively quick projects, such as a single process or a pilot plant. If these are successful, management will drive further implementation and help make it a priority for other areas.

The main cost system. If pilot projects are successful, try to incorporate ABC methods into your organization's financial reporting process. Successful implementers of ABC systems were more than six times as likely to have integrated ABC into their primary financial system and almost twice as likely to use ABC for budgeting.

Consider a separate model. If integrating ABC into the main cost reporting system is not feasible, consider developing a separate PC-based ABC system that can be used on an infrequent basis for strategic decision making. The model should be relatively simple and can be updated with data that already are available or easily collected. But even a relatively simple model can be far more accurate than many traditional cost allocation methods.

The existing information system. If you implement an ABC costing system, make sure that the input requirements can be easily supported by the existing information system. If not, either change the model or install a more sophisticated integrated system.

Smaller companies. Smaller companies need to be especially creative to find reasonable activity cost drivers from their often more limited data. Like one company using material cost as a proxy for its weight, look for available drivers that have some correlation with how resources are spent.

The implementation team. Make sure the people who will be actual users of the ABC information are represented on the implementation team. A common mistake is putting managers on the team and not getting enough input from the cost accountants or other analysts.

The right software. Several respondents reported purchasing expensive ABC software and having a fairly successful initial study, but then having to use spreadsheets to generate the specific reports that are needed. Complaints about maintaining ABC also were common. It's wise to start simple. Early studies should be high-level in order to get concepts across. Once you have created interest, there will be a "demand-pull" for more information. Use spreadsheets until you identify exactly what your needs are, and then buy the software that meets *your* needs.

general, the entire system is user-friendly, and users can get a lot of information on their own.

Although the capabilities of an information system generally are important to ABC's success, it is possible to succeed in a relatively poor IT environment. For instance, James W. Mays, vice president of cost management for First Tennessee Bank, which uses ABC extensively, applies the 80-20 rule. Banks are a specialized data processing situation with huge amounts of data, and access to that data is often limited. When starting out, his bank focused primarily on the core processes and gave up some precision for an understandable model of operations. "Our methods and systems are extremely simple," Mays concedes, "but the ABC information is getting used for strategic decisions because it is easily understood and 'close enough' for current needs."

Top management support. Survey results support the idea that ABC needs strong commitment from upper management if it is to be used outside the accounting function. As the table shows, 58% of the usage-level companies had a high level of top management support (versus 40% for the nonusage companies). Support was measured based on questions relating to the degree of top management's active support for ABC, adequacy of resources being provided, and ties to the competitive strategies of the business unit.

Mike Riggins, manager of Cost Management Field Support for Carolina Power & Light (CP&L), which uses ABC extensively, said that senior management went to ABC training seminars, required all employees (both salary and hourly) to fill out activity/time sheets, and made sure each operating area dedicated one full-time person to the ABC implementation team for at least one year. Because of this last requirement, the field operations always had a link to the project and system testing. CP&L top managers also have taken an active role in ABC usage. They review monthly ABC reports and now "ask the right kind of questions." As a result, Riggins reports, "Finance is seen as one of the most value-added functions in the organization."

For ABC to work, a certain time commitment is required from individuals across the organization. Clete O'Dell reports that the biggest barrier to implementing ABC was getting people to commit their time. There were all-day workshops and departmental activity interviews to attend while at the same time the workforce was being made as lean as possible. Support from the company's executive committee has been an important factor for success. But O'Dell would have liked to see Diamant Boart management require individuals to give more time to the project.

Integration into financial system. Using ABC cost information in financial reporting generally will lead to its use in decision making. Managers tend to pay attention to the information that is used for outside reporting. Of the usage stage companies, 47% say they have integrated ABC into their primary financial system. Only 7% of the nonusage companies say they have done so, although 50% of those that have not say they plan to.

Dennis Jorgenson related that upper management demanded that only one cost system be used. The prevailing feeling was that there were not enough resources for two systems. So ABC implementers had to develop a system that would provide costs for both marketing and manufacturing managers and still satisfy external reporting requirements. Auditors gave their OK to the system because it provided full absorption costing, although some fixed costs (for example, depreciation and other allocations) are pulled out for internal decision-making purposes.

Part of budgeting process. Using ABC information for budgeting purposes appears to be another good way to increase organizational usage. Of all

ABC users, 45% listed budgeting as one of the reasons for using it. By contrast, only 24% of the nonusers listed budgeting. This trend supports one manufacturing controller's recommendation to start ABC in budgeting and everything else "will happen naturally." Bruce Bingham of IFR Systems in Wichita, Kan., commented that his company plans to use ABC as part of the budgeting process. He said, "It has to be part of the budget because the budget should reflect what you expect to happen." As a general rule, companies should report actual costs using the same method that is used to develop the budget.

ABC WAS GENERALLY WORTH IT ...

As shown in Figure 2, 54% of the respondents who have tried ABC are using it at least somewhat for decision making. Eighty-nine percent of those companies using ABC said it was worth the implementation costs, and 42% rated their cost management system as good to excellent (versus 28% for all companies). The following examples illustrate how ABC can provide positive benefits.

Mike Riggins reports his organization has reaped substantial cost savings thanks to ABC, and he expects more in the future. One recent example involves security costs at one of CP&L's power plants. Based on ABC information, it was discovered that security costs at the site were significantly higher than at comparable facilities. The secured area was much larger than at other plants and larger than was required by law. The area was reduced, saving $1 million in contractor security costs. But Riggins reports that the real value of CP&L's ABC/ABM approach has been the increased awareness of costs throughout the organization. By using the concepts and philosophies of ABM, CP&L estimates it has saved approximately $40 million overall.

Other examples include a marketing research company that uses ABC for client costing. The manager of cost analysis says that ABC "gives us a clearer picture of the cost dynamics of our business." A cost manager for a Midwest machinery manufacturer that uses ABC extensively commented that ABC was worth implementing because it "was a huge improvement over the old system and added validity to problem areas that could not be quantified objectively before."

... BUT NOT ALWAYS.

Not all ABC implementations have proven beneficial, however. Of all the companies that adopted ABC, 31% reported it is still too early to tell whether ABC was worth implementing. Only 2% said that ABC was not worth it.

Many commented that ABC is not a single answer but merely one of many tools that can be used. For instance, a controller for a Midwest manufacturer felt there is "not enough emphasis that ABC will not reduce cost, it will only help you understand costs better to know what to correct." Others cited resource limitations as a major issue. A controller with a southeastern manufacturer that uses ABC somewhat commented that ABC was not worth implementing because it is "too costly to maintain, [and] we just don't have the manpower."

Quantifying the benefits of ABC also can be difficult. A manager of cost analysis for an information processing service company commented: "In our company, it is difficult to evaluate the value that ABC brings to the company, though we know how much the company has invested in this project."

Companies considering or already implementing ABC should realize that although certain product or market factors might make ABC potentially beneficial, those same factors might not lead to a successful implementation. Before implementing ABC, organizations should look at the factors for success suggested in this article. Other priorities, top management commitment, IT capabilities, and integration with financial and budgeting systems should be considered. And be patient. ABC takes time to implement.

Kip R. Krumwiede, CMA, CPA, Ph.D., is an assistant professor of accounting at Washington State University, Richland, Wash. Dr. Krumwiede is a member of the Washington Tri-Cities Chapter, through which this article was submitted. He can be reached at (509) 372-7246 or by e-mail at krumwied@tricity.wsu.edu.

[1] The data cited in this article come from two IMA surveys conducted by the Cost Management Group, one of the IMA's Member Interest Groups. Figures 1 and 2 are based on the most recent survey mailed in November 1996 (178 responses, 16% response rate). Tables 1 and 2 are based on another survey, which asked more questions. Results are based on 301 responses (28% response rate) to the survey which was mailed in November 1995 and January 1996.

[2] For more information on how to determine whether your company should consider ABC in light of the potential for cost distortions and decision usefulness of cost information, see "Is ABC Suitable for Your Company?" by T. L. Estrin, J. Kantor, and D. Albers, MANAGEMENT ACCOUNTING, April 1994, pp. 40-45.

[3] The "IT score" was based on responses to questions relating to system characteristics such as subsystem integration, query capability, available data, and frequency of updates.

MULTIDIMENSIONAL BREAK-EVEN ANALYSIS

We are all familiar with break-even analysis that takes a two-dimensional approach and determines the sales quantity at which total revenues equal total costs. In this article, Roger A. Camp *illustrates a "multidimensional" break-even approach used in profit analysis of his company's trucking operations. The author is the CFO of The Motor Convoy, Inc., a Georgia-based common carrier operating primarily in the southeastern United States.*

The chart below illustrates a typical break-even analysis at The Motor Convoy for a relevant range of trips—from about 100 to 450 miles. The rate and cost per pound are graphed along the Y axis, while the length of the trip (in miles) is charted along the X axis. The following curves are plotted:

- Motor Convoy's rate curve.
- A competitor's rate curve.
- Motor Convoy's cost curves at various volumes.

Graphing the rates charged by each competitor illustrates the competitive forces that the company must confront and the competitive constraints affecting analysis of profit margins. (Information for plotting this curve is obtained from the marketing department.)

Within the range of the chart, the fixed costs per unit increase or decrease while the variable costs per unit remain constant. The slope of the cost curves stays the same, producing a series of curves at different volumes parallel to each other. As volume increases, total costs per pound decrease by the reduction in fixed costs per unit.

In the chart the cost curve is plotted for volumes of 2,000, 2,500, 3,000 and 3,500 pounds. Motor Convoy's break-even points for the above volumes are trip lengths of approximately 190, 260, 320 and 410 miles, respectively.

The interrelationship of such factors as volume, trip length and competitors' rates are extremely important, requiring careful study so that strategies for increasing profits can be developed. To examine these interrelationships, let's discuss four cases at Motor Convoy, which are charted on the opposite page. In each case, volume is 2,000 pounds for the range of trips illustrated.

Case 1. The competitor's rate curve is parallel to Motor Convoy's cost curve and both rate curves cross at 110 miles. At this volume

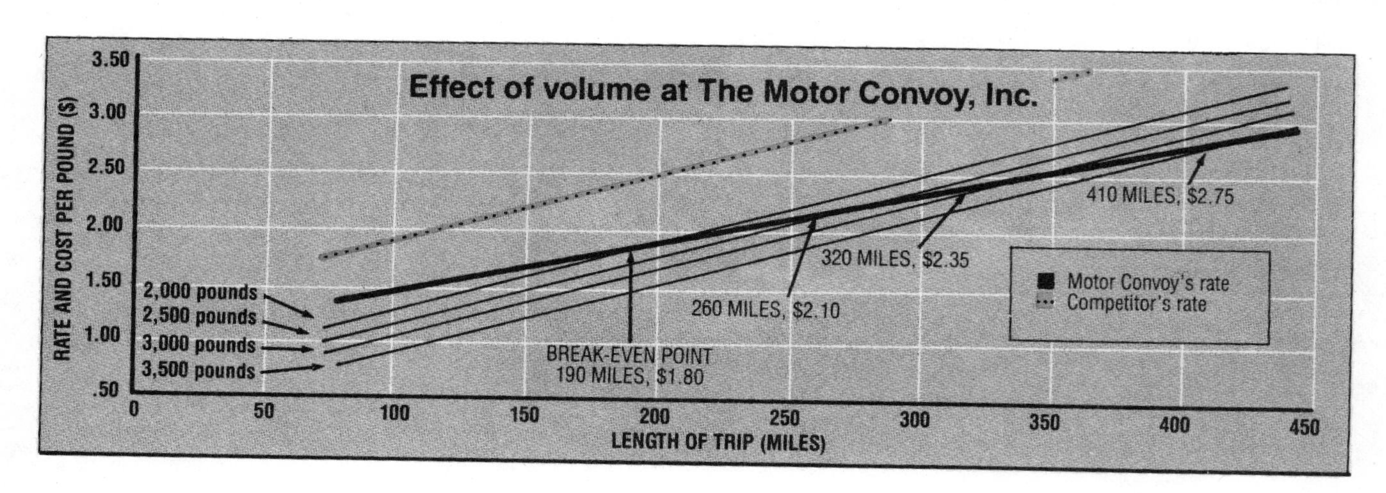

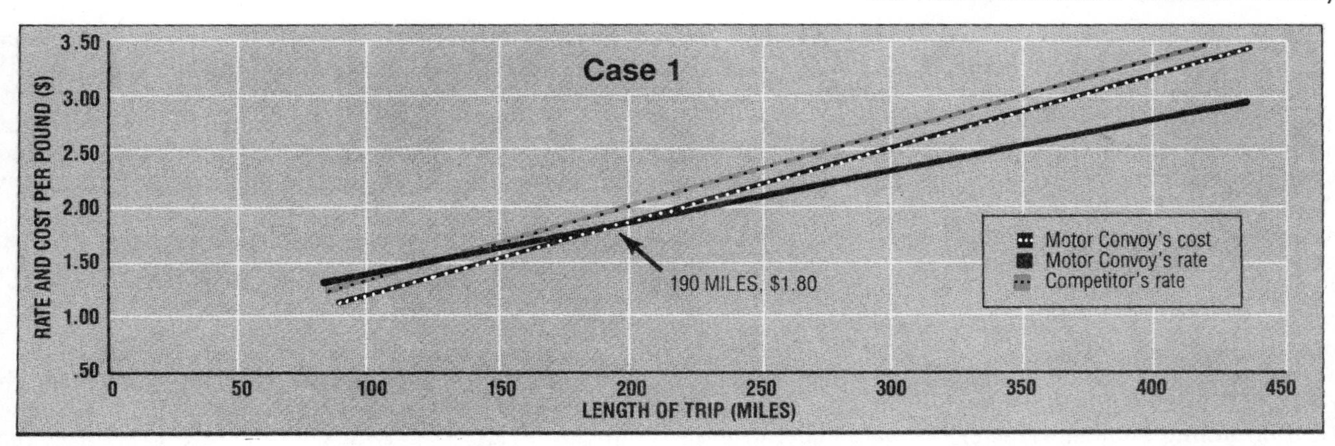
Case 1
RATE AND COST PER POUND ($)
3.50
3.00
2.50
2.00
1.50
1.00
.50
0
50
100
150
200
250
300
350
400
450
LENGTH OF TRIP (MILES)
190 MILES, $1.80
Motor Convoy's cost
Motor Convoy's rate
Competitor's rate

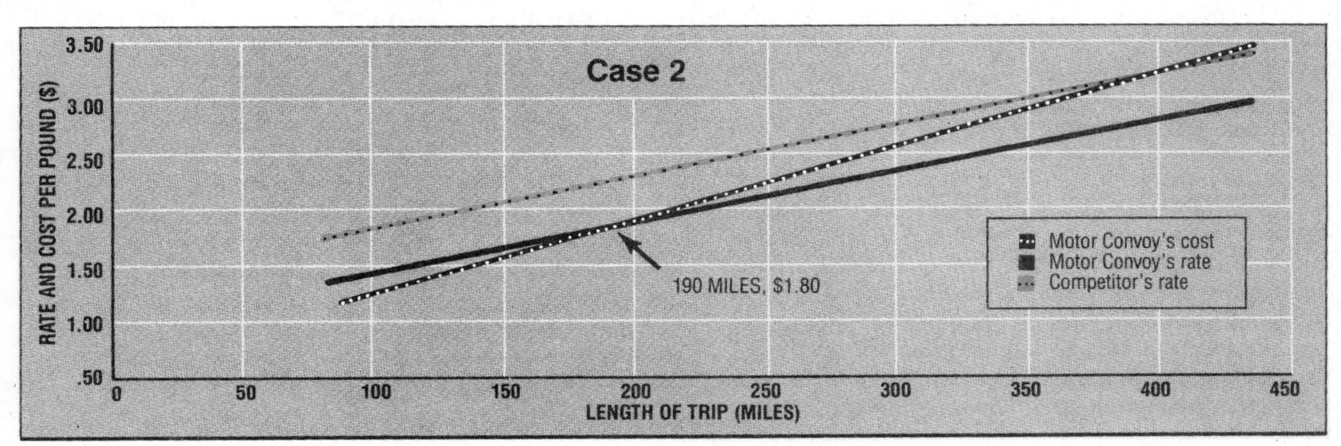
Case 2
RATE AND COST PER POUND ($)
3.50
3.00
2.50
2.00
1.50
1.00
.50
0
50
100
150
200
250
300
350
400
450
LENGTH OF TRIP (MILES)
190 MILES, $1.80
Motor Convoy's cost
Motor Convoy's rate
Competitor's rate

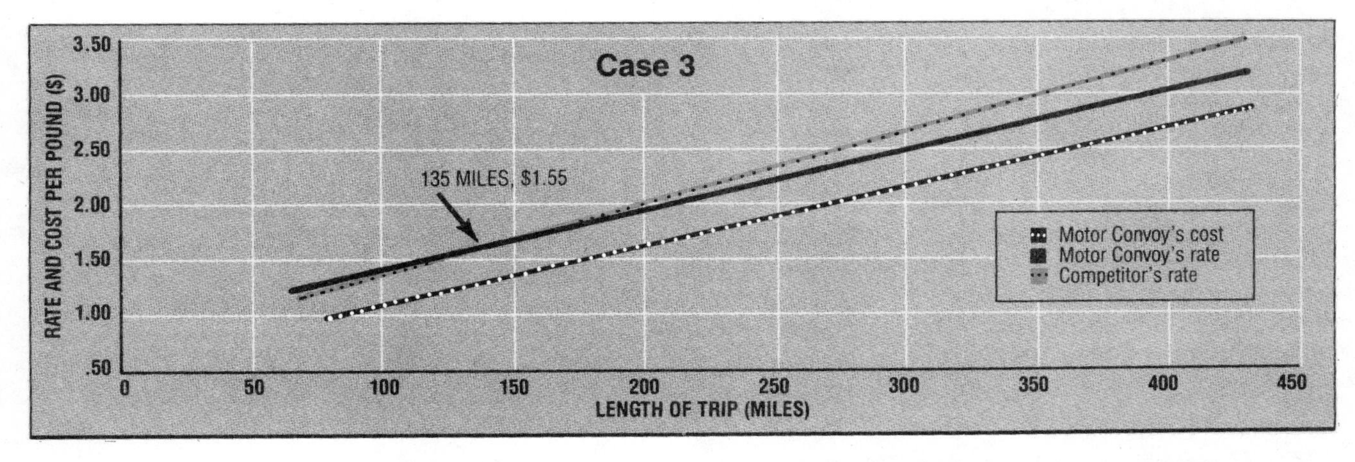
Case 3
RATE AND COST PER POUND ($)
3.50
3.00
2.50
2.00
1.50
1.00
.50
0
50
100
150
200
250
300
350
400
450
LENGTH OF TRIP (MILES)
135 MILES, $1.55
Motor Convoy's cost
Motor Convoy's rate
Competitor's rate

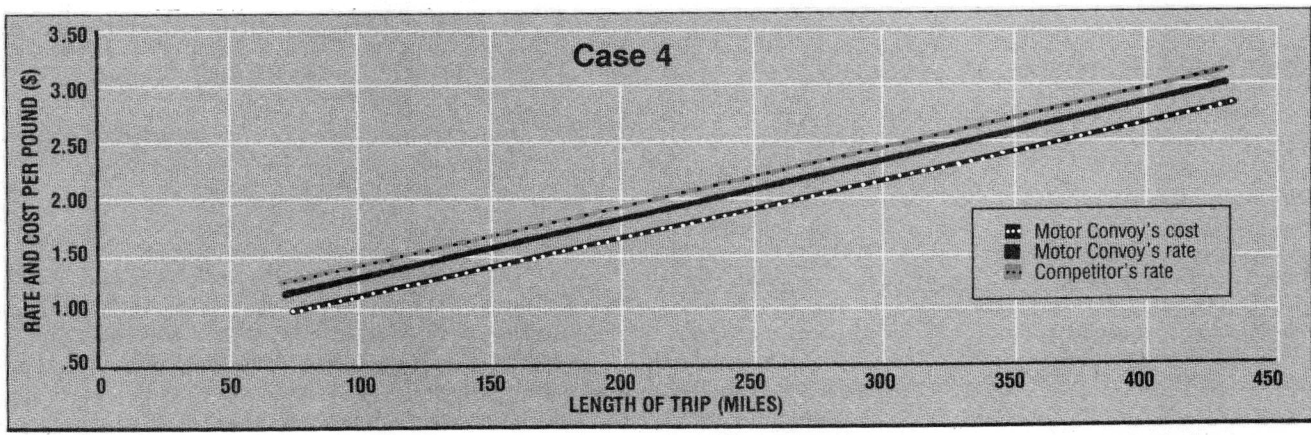
Case 4
RATE AND COST PER POUND ($)
3.50
3.00
2.50
2.00
1.50
1.00
.50
0
50
100
150
200
250
300
350
400
450
LENGTH OF TRIP (MILES)
Motor Convoy's cost
Motor Convoy's rate
Competitor's rate

Motor Convoy's business should be concentrated on trips between 110 and 190 miles. On shorter trips, the competition is cheaper than Motor Convoy, while on longer trips Motor Convoy is losing money.

Case 2. The competitor's rate curve is parallel to and above Motor Convoy's rate curve. Motor Convoy's cost curve crosses its rate curve at 190 miles (the break-even point at this volume). Although Motor Convoy is more competitive at all levels, it should direct its sales effort toward obtaining shorter trips of less than 190 miles, since it is unprofitable above this level.

Case 3. Motor Convoy's rate and cost curves are parallel. The competitor's rate curve crosses Motor Convoy's rate curve at 135 miles. Although Motor Convoy is profitable at all levels, it should probably place more effort on obtaining trips greater than 135 miles, since below that level the competition has lower rates.

Moreover, in this case, if Motor Convoy obtains its competitor's short business, it could probably eliminate that competition—not an unhappy scenario.

Case 4. Although highly unlikely, this is the ideal environment to operate in because the competitor's rate curve is parallel to and above Motor Convoy's rate and cost curves. There is no competition at any point and Motor Convoy is profitable at all levels.

In each of the above cases, volume changes and trip lengths outside the illustrated range could significantly alter strategies. Furthermore, such analysis can highlight those areas in which a company is not competitive and provide guidance for changing the company's rate structure to improve its performance and competitive position.

A MUST FOR SURVIVAL

Financial analysis of profit margins must take into consideration underlying cost and rate structures, competitors' rate structures, volume and patterns of business. This type of analysis is a must for survival because of the tight profit margins in most industries.

PLANNING FOR PROFIT

How much money do you really need to break even? Follow this simple formula to help your business thrive.

KEVIN D. THOMPSON

"Break-even point." Does the term ring a bell? It should. That's the magic number that tells you when your revenue will cover your expenses. Although entrepreneurs often fail to realize the significance of recognizing and reaching the break-even point in the financial cycle, understanding what it takes to break even is critical to making any business profitable.

Unfortunately, most small business owners fail to keep close tabs on their business. For many, financial reports are viewed as a necessary evil required only for tax purposes or assessing profits and losses. But unless you have an unlimited supply of operating capital, these reports could—and should—be used to monitor your company's fiscal health.

If your business is like most of the emerging companies that fill the pages of BLACK ENTERPRISE, then now is the time to understand how to make your business profitable. And the first step is to determine just how many units you must sell or the amount of sales you need to generate to reach that crucial break-even point.

"About 70% of the business owners I work with see me after they're in trouble," says Louis G. Hutt Jr., managing partner of Bennett, Hutt & Co., a Columbia, Md., accounting firm. Hutt, who has been using break-even analysis with small business owners for 12 years, laments that many entrepreneurs plan for their business in a vacuum.

Hutt, a certified public accountant, attorney and featured speaker at several BLACK ENTERPRISE Entrepreneurial Conferences, explains: "They look at their performance at the end of the year and then make judgments on what should be done the next year."

Failing to calculate your break-even point early in your business life is a grave mistake that could lead to an entrepreneurial nightmare. The Dun & Bradstreet Corp., a New York City business information marketer, reports that U.S. business failures increased 14.3% in the first nine months of 1992 to 74,715, from 65,368 in the same period in 1991. Poor financial planning is certainly a major culprit in the untimely demise of many of these businesses.

In fact, the National Federation of Independent Business Foundation, a Washington, D.C., small business research group, reports that in 1991, managing cash flow ranked third in the top five problems small business owners faced. Thirty percent called the problem "critical," compared with only 9% who didn't think it was a problem.

Incorporating accurate and thorough break-even analysis as a routine part of your financial planning will keep you abreast of how your business is really faring. Determining how much business is needed to keep the door open will help improve your cash-flow management and your bottom line. Bob and Armentha Cruise-Mills would definitely agree.

The Mills own and run Aspen Temporary Services Inc. (ATS), a 5-year-old Takoma Park, Md., temp agency, which grossed $1.2 million in revenue and posted a 6% profit margin in 1992. The couple's motto: Never spend more than you have to.

Says Armentha, ATS' president: "We've always been very cost-conscious. We've never had to borrow money, and about 75% of our sales go back into the business. We look at our expenses very closely to decide which projects we can take on."

The Mills credit Hutt, whom they met at a business finance seminar last October, with helping them identify company profit centers and unnecessary expenses.

"Break-even analysis made us realize that placing data entry operators is more profitable to the business than placing word processors," Bob Mills,

ATS' vice president, explains. "We were paying word processors $12 an hour and billing the customer $17 an hour (for a profit of $5 an hour). But with data entry operators, we paid them $8 an hour and billed $14 an hour (for a profit of $6 an hour)."

If break-even projections can help pump out more profits, then why don't more entrepreneurs do it? A major reason, say several small business consultants, is that many business owners don't buy into the necessity of keeping an accountant on retainer or using standard accounting practices. Despite the proliferation of easy-to-use computer and manual accounting systems, small business owners are famous for stuffing receipts and financial data in shoe boxes. But without carefully maintained balance sheets, calculating what it will take to make your business profitable is virtually impossible. Too often, entrepreneurs don't find out that they've been paying out more than they've been taking in until they are out of business.

How Break-Even Analysis Works

Break-even analysis isn't a novel concept. In fact, accountants have been using the formula for over 25 years. The analysis works best when you're selling one product or offering a single service. It gets messy, however, for multiservice or product line businesses.

To use Hutt's analysis, the break-even point can be determined by calculating your *fixed costs* (unvarying expenses), *variable costs* (fluctuating expenses) and your *contribution margin* (selling price per unit minus variable expenses per unit). (See worksheet, "How To Determine your Break-Even Point," for a step-by-step guide.)

After making your calculations, divide the total fixed costs by your average contribution margin per unit to determine your break-even point. Example: Let's say you own a small factory that manufactures belt buckles. You've estimated that your total fixed expenses for the year will be $200,000 (including rent, insurance and administrative salaries). Your variable costs (i.e., advertising or sales commission) on a per unit basis is $1, and your selling price to wholesalers will be $3. By subtracting your variable costs from your selling price you will make a contribution of $2 toward your fixed expenses. In this example, you would divide $200,000 (fixed expenses) by $2 (contribution margin). By this formula, you would need to sell 100,000 units to break even.

To determine the volume of sales you will need to break even, multiply the number of units you must sell by the selling price. Under this scenario, the needed sales volume is $300,000 (100,000 units x $3).

Doing an in-depth break-even analysis is critical for African American small business owners. Because most black businesses remain severely undercapitalized, African-American entrepreneurs have little or no margin for error. If they don't plan for profit early on, their chances of surviving three years are almost nil. After you've determined your break-even point, adds Hutt, "the profit factor can be built into your business."

Strategic financial planning can also help you answer such perplexing questions as: If my unit prices are reduced 5% and sales unit volume increases 15%, how is my operating profit affected? How will a reduction in my fixed costs affect my estimated net income and break-even point?

If you don't plan for profit, the chance that your business will survive is almost nil.

Measuring progress against a plan is paramount if you are to make your forecasted financial goals by your target dates. "Your analysis should be reexamined on a quarterly basis," suggests Hutt. "Be sure to compare actual to projected performance and adjust your plan if it is unrealistic."

While analyzing your progress, take a hard look at your operating expenses to identify where cost-cutting measures can be taken. For instance, if business is slow, you might consider cutting back on staffing, inventory or overhead. You may also have to restructure existing debt to lower monthly loan payments.

Becoming a Proactive Entrepreneur

Paulette J. Robinson, the self-employed president of PJ's Pen Inc., a 5-year-old McClean, Va., public relations consulting firm, says she probably wouldn't be in business today without break-even analysis. Every November, Robinson sits down with one of Hutt's tax planners to examine her firm's fiscal health. "Louis makes me do two spreadsheets, a receipts journal and a disbursements journal."

The former Cable News Network (CNN) producer and writer notes that break-even analysis also helped her make some tough decisions. In 1992,

HOW TO DETERMINE YOUR BREAK-EVEN POINT

To calculate the sales you must generate and the number of units you need to sell for your company to break even, do the following analysis. First, here are three terms you must know:

▼ Fixed expenses: Costs that remain constant regardless of sales. Examples include rent, insurance, taxes on property, general equipment maintenance, administrative salaries and interest on borrowed money.

▼ Variable expenses: Costs that vary as sales volume increases or decreases. Examples include direct labor costs and related payroll taxes, costs of goods sold, sales commissions and delivery expenses.

▼ Contribution margin: Your profit on sales.

Here's how the formula works:
Step 1: Subtract your variable expenses per unit from the selling price per unit. Example: If your selling price per unit is $30 and your variable cost per unit is $20, your contribution margin is $10.

Step 2: Divide your annual fixed costs per unit by your contribution margin. Example: If your annual fixed costs is $50,000, divide that by $10. Your break-even point in number of units is 5,000.

Step 3: To determine how much revenue you must make to break even, multiply your total break-even point in number of units (in this case it's 5,000) by your average selling price per unit ($30). Under this scenario, your total break-even point in sales dollars is $150,000.

BELOW IS A WORKING EXERCISE:

Company A sells standard computer chips used for manufacturing personal computers. Company A's annual fixed operating costs, including administrative salaries, office rent, utilities, travel, professional and other fixed expenses, are $425,000. Company A's normal selling price per chip is $30, and its estimated average cost of production per unit is $20.

CALCULATE COMPANY A'S

1. Break-even point in units ________

2. Break-even point in sales dollars ________

Remember, doing this kind of analysis doesn't guarantee that your company will make a profit. However, it does serve as an excellent planning tool. Once you determine the minimum level of sales needed to carry the business, you're better equipped to plan how your firm can operate in the black. Keep in mind that this formula works best with businesses that sell one product or offer one service. For businesses that offer multiple products or services, this formula would have to be modified to calculate the average cost and selling price.

ANSWERS 1. 42,500 2. $1,275,000

Robinson was running herself into the ground, working 20-hour days, seven days a week. She had two choices: Give up one of her contracts or drop from sheer exhaustion.

She explains: "I examined two of my contracts: CNN and Big Brothers of the National Capital Area and realized I couldn't handle both of them. I compared the $40,000 that I made from Big Brothers with the $50,000 from CNN. I also evaluated some of my outside contracts. I decided to cut Big Brothers and stick with the for-profit business where I made more money," explains Robinson, who broke even last year on $58,000 in revenues.

Adds Hutt: "We looked at each of those contracts as separate profit centers and calculated the break-even point for both. Based on the fees and expenses, we determined that the CNN contract would break even sooner than the Big Brother project."

Katherine G. Collier, owner of an 8-year-old dental practice, is another entrepreneur who profited from break-even analysis. Collier, whose Baltimore-based practice grossed $1.3 million last year, admits that when she started out she didn't know the difference between a debt and debenture.

When Collier wanted to purchase an additional office seven years after launching her business, she consulted Hutt. "We calculated the minimum volume of business that Katherine needed to break even," Hutt recalls. "In the end, she decided that it wouldn't be a wise financial move because the necessary volume of business wasn't there."

Business analysis separates the entrepreneurial contenders from the also-rans.

By using break-even analysis, Collier was able to make an objective decision based on hard numbers. Without it, she asserts, "I'd be so much less aware of how to run my business."

In the Final Analysis

The bottom line is that, especially for small businesses, the margins for error are much too narrow to make business decisions on gut instinct alone. Every idea, whether it is the introduction of a new product line, the opening of branch offices or the hiring of additional staff, must be tested through basic business analysis. If you don't have a business plan, or you haven't been reviewing it periodically, you're not likely to know how well your business is doing.

Crunching the numbers now—understanding basic financial statements, projecting future cash flow and determining your break-even point—could save you a lot of grief later. It's this kind of analysis, Hutt says, that separates the entrepreneurial contenders from the also-rans. He adds: "Successful business owners must establish goals, develop a plan and invest the time and resources the business needs to thrive."

Remember, the formula for break-even analysis is not designed to be 100% accurate. It's only one planning tool in an arsenal of financial help available to small business owners. But it can help you establish some parameters for operating performance.

"Business owners that do break-even analysis are searching for a methodology to produce and sustain profits for the long term," Hutt says. Without a doubt, these entrepreneurs are often my most successful clients."

IS IT TIME TO REPLACE TRADITIONAL BUDGETING?

A method to make a budget more useful to management is proposed.

by Jeffrey A. Schmidt

large company, frustrated by years of continual growth in real operating costs (despite severe margin pressures), decided to examine the effectiveness of its budgeting process. It was stunned by its findings:

■ Budgeting consumed the better part of the year and involved several hundred staff and line people.

■ Budgeting weakened strategic resolve. Staff became preoccupied with budgeting mechanics rather than with strategic issues. Senior management confessed it could not relate budgeted expenses to the strategic plan.

■ Participants tended to focus on incremental costs, taking for granted costs embedded in the previous year's budget.

■ The budget structure did not reflect changes in the company's organization and processes, and people were budgeting many costs largely under someone else's control.

■ Budgets were not credible.

Research done by my consulting firm supports this company's experience. In a study of 10 large energy, transportation and banking companies, we found that, on average, the equivalent of 5% of all staff employees were devoted full-time to budgeting activities.

JEFFREY A. SCHMIDT is a vice-president and a director of Towers Perrin, a management consulting firm, and region manager of the firm's general management division. He is a member of the committee on corporate development of the University of Chicago Graduate School of Business.

THE REAL COST OF BUDGETING

For a better idea of the real cost of budget preparation, consider this: At one of those 10 companies, which has a staff-support team of 3,000 employees, 160 employees devote time to some aspect of budgeting. At an average cost of approximately $105,000 per employee, the company's annual cost of budgeting is nearly $17 million—which does not include costs of services supporting the budgeting activity: computer operations, software maintenance and benefits administration for these employees. The full cost of budgeting may exceed $20 million a year.

For that kind of money, budgeting should yield accurate expense forecasts, provide effective support for decision making and control and employ efficient development and reporting processes. In fact, in most cases it fails to do those things.

Conventional budgeting fails to prevent the growth of uncompetitive cost structures in many companies. Evidence for that failure is sweeping corporate America—massive capital restructuring, organizational consolidations and staff cutbacks.

This article describes one way to achieve

effective resource allocation and control by replacing conventional budgeting processes. The technique is called multidimensional budgeting (MDB), which converts conventional budgets into formats that are more relevant to management. For the purposes of this article, that conversion is called a transformation, in which the data is reformatted into four separate but related budgets: an activity budget, a product budget, a customer budget and a strategic budget.

Properly applied, MDB yields tremendous insights into resource use effectiveness and enables management to align resources with corporate strategies and customer needs. MDB translates into higher profitability and an improved competitive position.

MDB can supplement conventional budgeting with a powerful new set of resource-allocation and decision-support tools. It focuses on the relationships between spending and the underlying value created, rather than on merely how budgeted funds are spent.

The outline for a typical multidimensional budget is illustrated in exhibit 1. As the reader will see, once the new budget is developed, management can assess resource allocations by working down from the strategic budget to the base conventional budget. At each level, management can test the correct alignment of resources against its priorities, and the budget can be adjusted, as necessary, until an optimal statement is achieved.

FIRST TRANSFORMATION: ACTIVITY BUDGET

The first step is to convert, or transform, the conventional budget into an activity budget, which discloses how much the company spends on specific tasks and the types of resources it devotes to them. An activity budget is created by mapping the line items in the conventional budget to a list of activities (responding to customer complaints, requisitioning new parts, etc.).

Mapping is easiest if costs are first divided into two categories: personnel costs and all others. Costs associated with personnel (including facility and personal computing expenses) should be allocated to activities on the basis of the ways employees actually spend their time.

To allocate personnel costs, the company usually needs to conduct an employee survey—to determine exactly what each person does. This adds a step to the budgeting process, but the survey is always enlightening. Most companies are surprised to learn, for example, how extensively line personnel are involved in such staff activities as budgeting, financial reporting and employee evaluation. Often, two-thirds of the costs associated with these processes are borne outside the departments that administer them. To reduce costs (and budgets) effectively, a company must cut overhead activities along with department manpower. Activity surveys, and the activity budget, address this problem directly.

Nonpersonnel costs such as mainframe computer costs should be allocated to activ-

EXECUTIVE SUMMARY

■ CONVENTIONAL BUDGETING techniques are proving to be wasteful and ineffective. One solution to this is to replace conventional budgeting with a technique called multidimensional budgeting (MDB), which is more relevant to management.

■ MDB YIELDS tremendous insights into current resource use effectiveness and enables management to align resources with corporate strategies and customer needs more effectively: That translates into higher profitability and an improved competitive position.

■ TRANSFORMING a conventional budget into an MDB requires the following steps:

1. Creating an activity budget, which enables management to look beyond the general ledger and probe the underlying work the organization performs.
2. Creating a product budget, which holds that each activity adds some value to a product—for either an internal or an external customer.
3. Creating a customer budget by matching products with their internal or external customers, which shows the total spending proposed for each customer or customer category served by budgeting entities.
4. Creating a strategy budget, which provides a basis for determining whether proposed expenditures are aligned correctly with corporate, business and supporting strategies.

ities after analyzing their cost drivers (activities or factors that generate work and—by association—cost). [For more on this subject, see "Improving Performance with Cost Drivers," by Frank Collins and Michael L. Werner, JofA, June90, page 131.]

If each mainframe application is tied to a specific activity, costs can be allocated on the basis of the computer time each application consumes. Alternatively, they can be allocated on the basis of the number of report pages generated to support each activity or according to the way people spend their time, as shown in the following example:

Workers using the computer for processing payables	23
÷	
Total workers using the computer	634
% of workers processing payables	3.6%
×	
Computer cost	$1,000,000
Computer costs allocated to processing payables	$36,000

Once created, the activity budget enables management to look beyond the general ledger and probe the underlying work the organization performs. Questions like the following now can be answered:

- How well do the processes and activities each unit performs conform to its mission?
- Could resources devoted to low-value processes or activities be scaled back or eliminated?
- Can the company reduce costs by reengineering processes or activities?
- Could some activities be performed more effectively or efficiently outside the company?

The insights developed in creating an activity budget also can help improve the accuracy of cost estimates and future budgets, especially for new programs.

SECOND TRANSFORMATION: PRODUCT BUDGET

The next step is to create a product budget. This budget holds that each activity adds some value to a product—for an internal or an external customer. More than one activity may be associated with a product.

The relationships between activities and products constitute the mapping procedures—typically called algorithms—for creating a product budget. But first the budget preparers must understand the supplier–customer networks that describe the business.

Business processes—such as product development, manufacturing and order taking—add value directly or indirectly in terms of a delivered product or customer service. Skills training is an example of an indirect business process. Support processes (employee benefits administration and strategic planning) don't add value to products but sustain the organization.

The activity budget then is aligned with products. Mapping of this kind calls for considerable ingenuity because it may not always be easy to identify activities with products. Also, if a logical allocation of some nonpersonnel costs cannot be found in creating the activity budget, an understanding of products and services might provide the necessary insights. For example, in a manufacturing environment, indirect product-support expenses such as engineering might vary, not by activity, but by product, batch or product line. Therefore, engineering expenses might be allocated using the appropriate cost driver.

Once this mapping is complete, the product budget has been created. Each budgeting entity can review its budget in terms of the accounting line items that form the original master budget as well as in terms of activities and products. The product budget helps address such questions as

- Does the resource allocation to business and support processes make sense?
- Should the manufacture or assembly of certain products or their parts and components be supplied by outsiders?
- How do customer support costs compare with those of peers and competitors?

THIRD TRANSFORMATION: CUSTOMER BUDGET

The third transformation produces a budget showing the total spending proposed for each customer or customer category served by budgeting entities. Products are matched with their internal or external customers. In some cases, fractions of a product may need to be attributed to individual customers or customer categories.

Any residual nonpersonnel costs also should be allocated to an appropriate customer or customer category. For example, certain types of marketing and promotion expenses might be assigned at this point.

The insights provided through this transformation help management ensure that resources are allocated properly with respect to customers' priorities. The latter are usually determined through a customer value survey. Any gaps between customer requirements and current performance then can be corrected.

The customer budget can be used to answer such questions as

- What is the true financial contribution of major customers or business segments?
- Does the proposed spending for each customer or customer category justify the returns it generates?
- What specific actions would reduce the cost of doing business with customer segments while maintaining or enhancing the value provided?
- How attractive is customer retention compared with customer acquisition?

FOURTH TRANSFORMATION: STRATEGY BUDGET

The final transformation re-sorts budget information by major strategy. This is done by describing the strategies associated with each business segment and then matching the strategies with major customers or customer categories. If the company does not have discrete business strategies for its major customer categories, the matching requires multiple steps. For example, end-use market strategies might be matched initially with distribution channels and then mapped from these channels to specific customers (see exhibit 2).

The process for creating this budget repeats the earlier steps. If a strategy applies to more than one customer or customer category, a description must be assigned to each. All remaining unallocated costs in the master budget—if any—must be assigned to their appropriate strategies.

The strategy budget provides a basis for determining whether proposed expenditures are aligned correctly with corporate, business and supporting strategies. Budgets misaligned with strategic priorities then can be adjusted. Obviously, any adjustments made to the strategy budget need to be carried down through the pre-

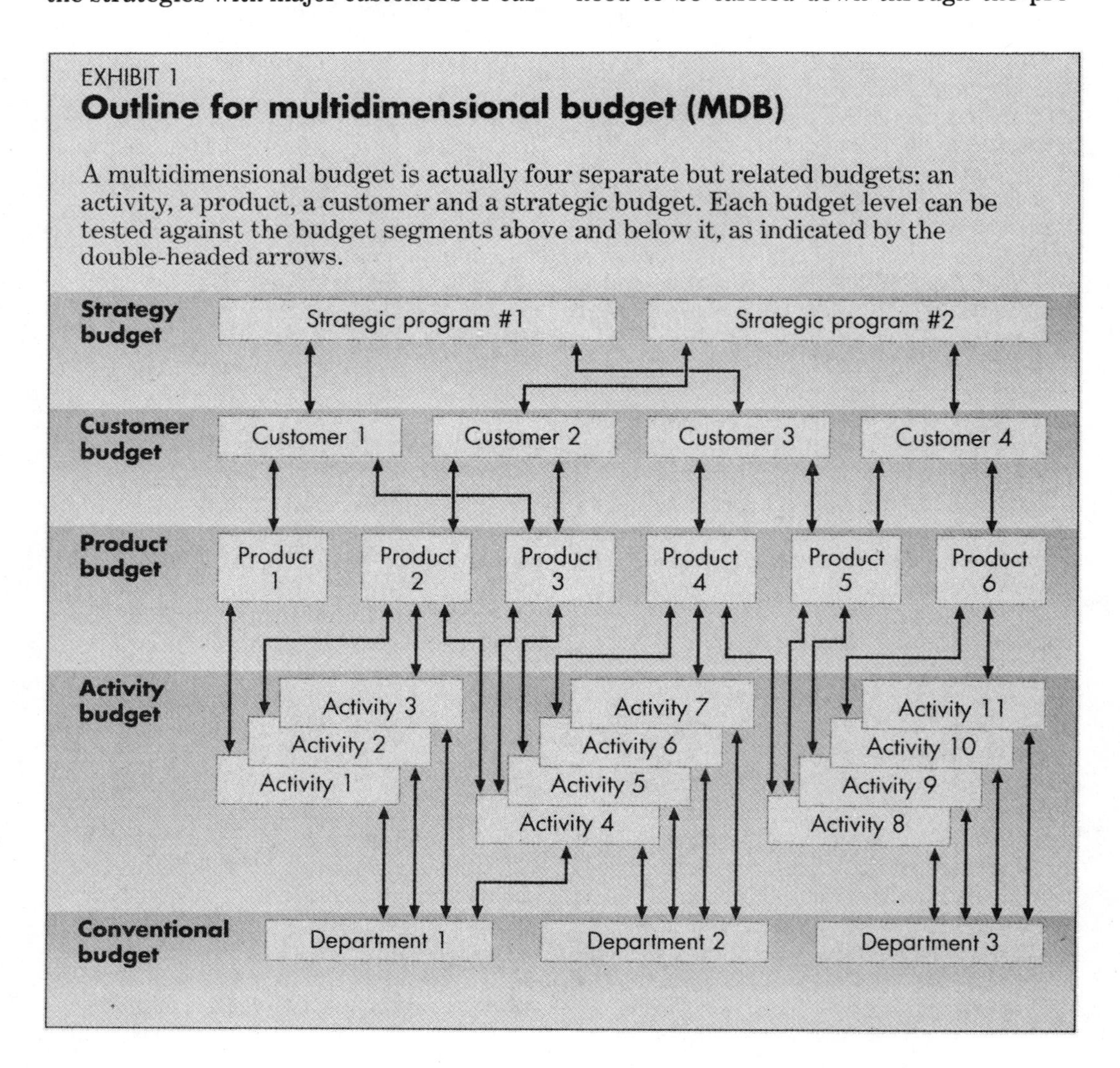

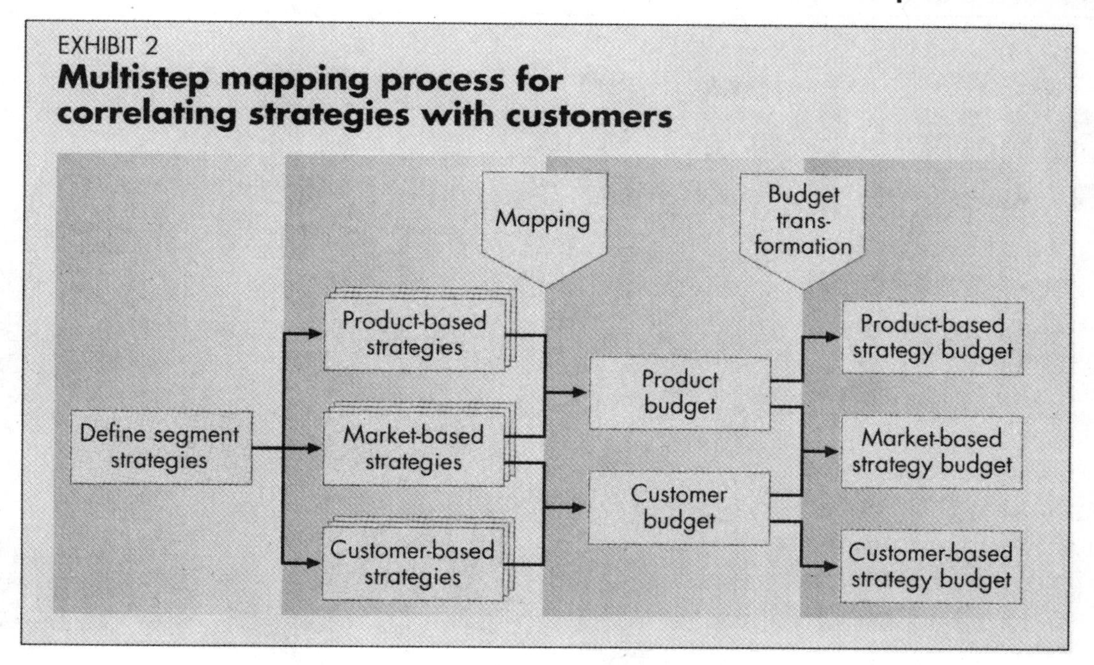

vious budget conversions. Exhibit 1 depicts this bottom-up development and top-down validation process.

FUTURE PROSPECTS

The most important advantage of multidimensional budgeting is that it offers a better way to direct and control resources. That translates into healthier growth and better operating margins. These benefits are possible because MDB

- Creates an explicit and clear relationship between budgets and the business strategies they fund.
- Permits comparisons of detailed expense information across organizations.
- Provides a powerful framework for measuring customer value, internally and externally.
- Helps a company understand the costs of operating its organization.
- Sets the stage for ongoing performance improvements by presenting managers with detailed budget information in formats that readily lend themselves to comparative analysis and that relate more directly to the logic of management decisions.
- Can be revised to reflect changes in the organization's strategy and structure.

What this adds up to is that multidimensional budgeting systems are a natural complement to computerized executive information systems. The power of such computerized executive information systems, especially when they contain MDB data, is that managers can analyze information from several different angles and ask any number of never-before-asked questions about performance.

As companies break with traditional accounting systems in favor of activity-based costing, MDB is likely to be adopted in some form by a steadily growing number of companies. The database and mapping technologies to create multidimensional budgets are available today, but there are, as yet, no large-scale MDB systems in operation. Once established, however, MDB will require neither more time than conventional budgeting nor major changes to normal accounting or control procedures.

An effective MDB system could be maintained today at a relatively low cost outside of a company's mainframe financial system. To avoid jeopardizing the current general ledger application used for accounting and budgeting, the MDB application could be established separately, either by downloading the general ledger or budget file to a personal computer or workstation or by creating a separate partition in the mainframe system. Today's database technology can provide the necessary support tools.

Whether multidimensional budgeting fulfills its promise will depend on the willingness of management to act on the insights it provides. For lack of such commitment, zero-based budgeting failed in numerous applications. The urgent threat of global competition, capital availability and inflation would seem to create an environment in which MDB can succeed.

How to Set Up a Budgeting and Planning System

BY ROBERT N. WEST, CPA, AND
AMY M. SNYDER, CPA

Two years ago, Penn Fuel Gas, Inc. (PFG) initiated its first annual and long-range operating budget process. PFG is a public utility holding company with consolidated revenues of $125 million and 550 employees. In addition to selling natural gas, the company provides natural gas storage and transportation services, provides merchandise services, and has a propane business. PFG's utility operations are split between two subsidiaries, each with a number of locations.

The motivation for budgeting came jointly from PFG's bankers, its board of directors, and its management. The information needs of all three users were fairly similar. All three were interested in cash flow projections and future earnings potential. The board was interested in improving PFG's return on equity (ROE), and it wanted to analyze the prospects of reinstituting a common stock dividend. In addition, management wanted segment P&Ls and improved departmental (cost center) expense and cash flow tracking. PFG's segments are regions, lines of business (utility, propane, and merchandise), and type of customer (commercial, industrial, residential).

WHERE TO START?

The first decision was whether to use existing in-house personnel, hire consultants, or hire a full-time budget manager. Consultants or a new hire would offer the benefit of an independent, fresh perspective with no biases. The disadvantage is that they wouldn't know the business as well as an insider. Penn Fuel Gas used consultants to set up its first budget and then hired a full-time, experienced professional to handle its budgeting. PFG wisely gave the position a manager title to assign appropriate status to the position. Once the staffing decision was resolved, the new budget director faced three primary tasks.

Learn the business. PFG hired a self-directed person (co-author Amy Snyder) who could understand the business quickly and get both long-range and operating budget processes up and running. Although the operations of PFG's business are relatively straightforward, the rules and regulations of the public utility industry are complex. PFG did two things to bring the budget manager up to speed. It sent her to a week-long technical program to learn the regulatory side of the business, and it extended her an open invitation to important meetings of operations vice presidents and top management so she could learn the operating side of the business.

Budgeting for natural gas and propane operations is difficult because a significant amount of demand for these products is dependent upon Mother Nature. Penn Fuel experienced two abnormal winters in its first two years of budgeting. In 1994, Pennsylvania had its coldest, iciest winter in history. In 1995, it had one of its warmest. But forecasting is difficult for many rapidly growing companies (one group for whom this article is intended). They must be flexible. For example, PFG budgets using the normal weather forecast, but it also provides sensitivity analyses and budget reprojections at least quarterly. Company and budget personnel realize that capital spending is partially a function of the winter season's revenues, which won't be known until the first quarter is over. The first quarter is particularly important in the utility and propane business as it represents 40% of total annual product delivered.

A medium-sized company shares its experiences and the lessons it learned.

Determine the users' information needs. Different users have different information needs, and users don't always know what information they "need." If managers or board members are not financially oriented, as is the case with many small businesses, they may need a little guidance. PFG's directors included several financially astute individuals who had a clear idea of what information they wanted. Costs were budgeted on both an accrual basis (for P&L reports) and cash basis (for cash flow reports).

Review and update the information system. All accounting information systems (AIS) face the daunting task of trying to provide the appropriate output for multiple sets of users. The reports needed from Penn Fuel's AIS included:

1. External financial reports (GAAP),
2. Tax reporting,
3. Internal management segment reports,
4. Cash flow reports, and
5. Reports for regulators.

The budget manager analyzed the AIS to determine whether data were classified and summarized in a manner useful for internal business plans and budget reports. Most accounting systems are geared toward external financial reports, and, in the case of regulated industries, for reports to regulators as well. Internal managers usually prefer information provided in a different format, such as results by division, product line, region, or customer group.

DECISIONS TO MAKE

PFG's budget manager faced some interesting information systems setups on which she had to make decisions when she started her work.

Different internal reporting systems. The Northern division, acquired several years ago, reported its results in different formats from the Southern division. Eventually a common reporting system will be attained, but the immediate task was to rearrange the data to assist with the consolidation and make the division data comparable. The underlying information systems differed as well. The two divisions used different accounting software, adding another challenge to the eventual merging of information systems.

Treatment of a different business segment. PFG's propane business segment seems similar to the natural gas business, but it has several key differences. Because it is unregulated, it has direct control over the pricing of its product. The utility's chart of accounts was not a perfect fit. PFG had to decide whether to maintain a uniform chart of accounts or create a separate general ledger account structure for its propane business segment. PFG adapted the propane business unit's account structure to the utility account structure. The tradeoff was ease of corporate reporting versus the individual business unit's desired view of the data. A slight edge was given to corporate reporting.

Management and the board of directors wanted segment information that was difficult to obtain. Total spending and spending by operating unit were easy to retrieve, but other views of the information had not been developed. For example, segregating operating expenses by business segment was provided partially by existing reports, but aggregation of all segments was tedious to reconcile to the general ledger due to corporate staff allocations. Most corporate personnel, from the president down to the fixed asset accountants, do not keep formal track of their time. Allocations were made to the various business segments on spreadsheets, requiring an audit trail and explanations to reconcile back to the results per the accounting records.

Review expense classifications. As a company grows, its chart of accounts should be reviewed periodically to determine if information is being captured in the most meaningful way. Introducing a budget system is an ideal time to modify the accounting system with a view toward future information needs. PFG's new budget manager reviewed the utility's accounting system with a fresh perspective and came up with a couple of suggestions to improve the precision of the accounting information system.

The first suggestion was to get rid of miscellaneous expense accounts with large balances. Most businesses prefer that almost nothing be recorded in miscellaneous accounts. PFG's state-mandated chart of accounts lent itself to this practice as the chart of accounts included many miscellaneous expense accounts. The challenge here was twofold:

1. Perform an account analysis to reclassify some of the charges to the miscellaneous expense account, and
2. Change the accounting system (add accounts and subaccounts) to ensure that future transactions are put into more descriptive accounts.

Lack of sufficient detail, such as the overuse of miscellaneous expense, is a common small business practice, so many new budget managers will face a housekeeping task similar to PFG's.

The next suggestion was to change the expense classification system. For example, the training & education account included charges for the training course fee, hotel, travel, meals, the salary charge for the time at the training session, and so on. This system actually was an activity-based costing system in which training included all costs driven by the decision to send an employee to a training program. While this classification of costs is perfectly acceptable, some accountants would record these items in separate accounts to maintain more detail. PFG has several hundred active general ledger accounts, so transaction classification is not a trivial task.

When initiating a budgeting and planning function, companies should review the chart of accounts, account classification, and the reporting system.

Most companies initiating a budgeting and planning function should review thoroughly the chart of accounts, account classification (particularly expenses), and the reporting system. In many cases, the accounting system will not have kept pace with the changes in the company (for example, expanded product lines or changes in customers and geographical regions served). It is best if the budget manager resolves information classification and reporting issues up front so that future budgets are comparable. It is difficult to change a system once it has been developed, and budget systems are no different from any other information system in that respect.

Difficulty reconciling amounts back to the ledger. Using the example of training costs cited above, some salary costs were included in accounts other than salary expense. Reconciling accounts such as salaries between the ledger and the payroll register can be difficult. Other accounts are difficult to reconcile as well. The budget manager decided to reclassify some data, but verifying the accuracy of reclassified data was, and still is, a challenge.

Information timeliness/availability. Budgeting brought the desire for better and faster information. PFG uses a minicomputer-based accounting package for general ledger, human resources, and payables. Yet portions of the accounting system still are manual, and monthly closings can take up to three weeks. PFG responded to some of its information needs by installing a new billing system that computerizes cash receipts and provides excellent summary information. PFG also is looking into a computerized project tracking system (for its many construction projects) and improving the computerized fixed assets system by adding a budget feature.

DELIVERABLES

Management wanted a one-year business plan prior to year-end as well as monthly updates (for example, budget vs. actual results). In addition, the board of directors wanted a long-range (three-year) plan each year. To meet these needs, the budget manager developed packets for the directors and management.

The board wanted the financial and operational data reported by segment—some reports segmented geographically, some by product line, and others by customer type.

The monthly financial packet. The monthly financial packet includes the following schedules:

A. P&L and cash flow (by region and in total)
   1. Current month
      a. Actual vs. budget
      b. Actual vs. same month in prior year
   2. Year-to-date (YTD)
      a. YTD actual vs. YTD budget
      b. Budget projections for remainder of year
      c. YTD actual vs. prior YTD actual
   3. Two full-year monthly bar charts
      a. Actual vs. budgeted cash flow
      b. Actual vs. budgeted net income
   4. Capital structure and ROE

B. Selected five-year comparative data
   1. Current month and YTD units of product delivered
      a. Residential
      b. Commercial
      c. Industrial
      d. Resale
      e. Detail provided for 10 largest customers
   2. Gas and propane stored
   3. Comparative YTD income statements

The annual business plan. The annual business plan contains data similar to the monthly package by region and in total. Full-year budget data are compared with the current year estimated (10 months' actual plus estimates for November and December) results and prior year actual results. These data are shown in tabular and graphical form. The annual plan also contains:

A. Budgeted income statements for all 12 months.
B. Budgeted cash flow statements for all 12 months.
C. Budgeted ROE schedule for all 12 months.
D. Capital expenditures forecasts, including brief written descriptions of the projects, by segment.
   1. New business (line extensions)
   2. Replacements/betterments
   3. Meters
   4. Tools & equipment
E. Personnel data including projected new hiring, replacement hiring, and workforce reductions.

Explanations of significant variances from prior year actual results are provided in both the annual and monthly packages. Second-stage variance analysis (breaking the variance into its price and quantity components) is provided as needed.

Formatting tips. After completing the first budgeting exercises, the budget manager came to the conclusion that some formatting tips might help those persons who were not familiar with the budgeting process. First, she suggests using graphs. Whoever is preparing a budget should consider displaying the information in graphical form rather than tables of numbers so it will appeal to all levels of readers.

Second, she suggests that a company consider the direct method for cash flow reports. PFG uses the direct method for its cash flow statement because it is more informative and is easier for readers to understand. The adjustments to net income with the indirect method are confusing and do not tell the reader where the money is coming from and to whom it is going. Reports for external parties still can use the indirect method if companies prefer. Table 1 contains a sample direct method cash flow statement.

THE BUDGET CALENDAR

What does the budget group do throughout the year? Table 2 shows the other functions performed by the budget manager each month. Notice that the annual budget data collection process begins five months before the packet is due to the board of directors. A four- to six-month lead time is fairly standard.

PFG decided to prepare its three-year forecast before doing the annual budget because the board wanted information on ROE and cash flow to analyze future earnings potential, for financing requirements, and for general business planning purposes. Once the three-year plan was reviewed, the first year's data were used as a guideline for the current year annual budget's operational and segment detail.

ONGOING CHALLENGES

We already highlighted the initial challenges faced by a new budget manager. Now let's look at some ongoing challenges.

Evolving mission. The budget function is formed with planning as its primary mission. In the early stages of its existence, however, it is expected to analyze company and segment performance. Variance analysis can be both interesting and challenging, challenging because no two years are ever the same. One obvious difference in the natural gas and propane business is the weather, which rarely is the same two years in a row. But other changes such as geographical growth, changes in product mix, and restructuring of divisions increase the challenge of reconciling operating results of two consecutive periods.

Gamesmanship. Budgeting also brings behavioral challenges such as lowballing revenues or padding expenses. PFG has experienced minimal budgeting gamesmanship for two reasons that are described next.

1. Budgets are developed with management, arriving at agreed-upon, reasonable expectations.
2. PFG has not used the budget as a "hammer" at year-end for employees or divisions who did not make budget.

Get people up to speed. The behavioral challenge at PFG has been to get people up to speed with budgeting. The budget manager came from a large company where budgeting was part of the culture. At PFG, she sent out schedules and written instructions on completing the budget requests the first time through. But not everyone understood how to complete the budget forms. Her goal the next year was to sit down with people and work through the forms with those who were unaccustomed to the budget process.

When formal budgeting is new to a company, the budget manager may end up doing the bulk of the budget preparation because people are new to the

Table 1. DIRECT METHOD CASH FLOW STATEMENT

	Current Month			Year-to-Date		
	Actual	Budget	Variance	Actual	Budget	Variance
Cash Inflows						
Utility						
Propane						
Merchandise						
Total Cash Inflow						
Cash Outflows						
Gas purchases						
Propane purchases						
Merchandise purchases						
Operating and maintenance expenses						
Labor and benefits						
Insurance						
Outside services						
Leases						
Storage						
Other						
Rate case preparation						
Other taxes						
Income taxes						
Interest on LTD						
Other interest						
Principal payments						
Common dividends						
Preferred dividends						
Total Cash Outflow						
Available funds						
Capital expenditures						
Net Change in Cash						

Table 2. THE BUDGET CALENDAR
PROCEDURES AND REPORTS DUE

Month	Procedures and Reports Due
December	Annual budget for coming year. Presentation to board of directors. Present current year results: 10 months of actual and projections for remaining two months (November's results would not be available at this point).
January	Issue approved budgets to managers and vice presidents. Set up monthly financial report for the new year.
February	Prepare actual P&Ls and cash flow by month for the prior year.
March	Clean-up work after year-end closing and audit.
April	1st quarter actual vs. budget to board of directors. Nine-month projections. Send out requests for long-range forecast.
May	Prepare long-range forecast.
June	Present long-range forecast to board of directors.
July	Requests for the upcoming year's capital spending, operating revenues, expenses, and cash flows sent to operating units and corporate departments. 2nd quarter actual vs. budget to board of directors. Six-month projections.
August	Follow up on July requests. Help employees unfamiliar with budget requests.
September	July budget requests due. Input, analyze, and summarize the data.
October	Top management reviews budgets. Have meetings, and negotiate final amounts with various vice presidents and managers. 3rd quarter actual vs. budget to board of directors. Three-month projections.
November	Prepare final budget.

process. One unfortunate byproduct that can occur is that managers then think it's the budget manager's budget. The budget manager has to impress upon them that it is their department and their budget. It is important to determine up front who is responsible and accountable.

Top management support. All new systems require top management's support. To make budgeting effective, management must communicate the importance of well-thought-out input from departments and operating units. If preparing a well-thought-out budget is not included in managers' goals and objectives for the year, employees may not make the time for the process. Resistance may result, not because employees feel threatened by the new budget system, but, rather, because they lack time.

BENEFITS FROM BUDGETING

Budgeting has improved communication throughout Penn Fuel Gas, Inc., and has improved teamwork toward a common goal. It has helped the board of directors to represent shareholders better and has provided support to management on major decisions. PFG expects even better planning in the future to result in operational improvements, improved management of resources, better cost control, earnings growth, and improved responsibility resulting from managers' active participation in the planning process.

Robert N. West, CPA, Ph.D., is an assistant professor at Villanova University. He is the author of several articles and the text, *Microcomputer Accounting Systems*. He is a member of the Valley Forge Chapter, through which this article was submitted, and can be reached at (610) 519-4359.

Amy M. Snyder, CPA, was manager of budgeting and planning at Penn Fuel Gas, Inc., when this article was written. Now she is controller of Espe America, Inc. She is a member of the Valley Forge Chapter and can be reached at (610) 277-3800.

Measuring the Costs of Quality

Cheaper is not necessarily better when you factor in the cost of quality.

BY KATHLEEN G. RUST

The cost of quality can be divided into two areas: the price of nonconformance and the price of conformance. The first measures all expenses incurred when things are done wrong, and the second measures the expenses needed to implement and maintain a system that strives to eliminate deficiencies.

These quality cost concepts were applied to a product purchased by BAC Engineering Plastics, a small midwestern firm that converts virgin plastic into reinforced thermoplastic.[1] A BAC raw material referred to as RM #033 was studied using a cost-benefit analysis approach to determine its quality costs.

The results show the quality costs of this raw material are high enough to justify terminating the use of RM #033 and searching for alternative materials or solutions.

QUALITY COSTS OF RM #033

Raw Material #033 is a byproduct of material produced by a BAC affiliate, XYZ Corporation. Rather than scrapping the unusable nylon, XYZ Corporation regrinds it and sells it to BAC for use in four different nylon products. These products, referred to as products A, B, C, and D, compose 4% of total sales in the nylon division of BAC. The quality of the final nylon products falls within customer specifications, so BAC continues to use RM #033 although other nylons can be substituted.

RM #033 is a nylon byproduct that comes to BAC sometimes loaded with various sized metal pieces. When the nylon is processed through the machines, everything melts down except the metal. The smaller particles of metal pass on into the final product, but the larger pieces get caught on the die plates. These plates have holes approximately 3/16 of an inch in diameter that the nylon must flow through to complete the process. When the plate becomes clogged, the machine must be shut down and the die plates removed and cleaned before the run can begin again. This downtime is about one hour in length and occurs, on average, twice in every six-hour material run. The downtime causes the machines to run behind schedule, possibly creating the need for overtime or late shipments to customers. The time (therefore money) spent correcting the problems caused by RM #033 could be spent better on revenue-generating activities.

The machines that process nylon were not designed to ac-

Molten plastic at BAC factory.

commodate metal impurities, so additional wear is created on the machine each time this raw material is used. RM #033 also has a byproduct, a gassy oil substance that is bothersome, and possibly dangerous, to some production workers.

Reports of the problems have come to the attention of upper management. They are investigating the causes and alternative solutions in this matter.

BENEFITS OF RM #033

According to the product manager of the nylon division, there never has been a customer complaint about any of the four products made using RM #033. These final products fall within the customer specifications. The price of RM #033 is very low at $0.50 per pound. The closest known substitute, referred to as regular nylon, would cost $0.99 per pound.

As mentioned earlier, this raw material is purchased from a BAC affiliate, XYZ Corporation. XYZ takes scrap material and regrinds it for use at BAC. Then it ships the material to the production plant. The costs associated with preparing and shipping RM #033 are unavailable, but it is safe to assume the time and money spent on performing these activities could be spent on activities that might generate higher profits.

The amount of XYZ quality costs may not be known, but the types of quality costs are the same types of costs buyers incur. They include the cost of inspecting outgoing RM #033, the costs of retransforming or scrapping rejected RM #033, and the possibility of incurring external failure costs due to rejection by BAC.

ALTERNATIVE SOLUTIONS TO QUALITY PROBLEM

There are various directions the management of BAC could take to deal with these circumstances. The first would be the base case—that is, make no changes. No customer complaints have been directed toward the use of RM #033, so the material may not be viewed as a problem. The BAC purchasing agent could discuss with XYZ the possibility of removing the larger particles of metal before shipment to BAC. He also could investigate the substitution of other materials that may cost less than the one known substitute.

As a second alternative, BAC could invest in new machinery that can remove most of the metal particles. Another option: The line of products using RM #033 could be discontinued without much loss because it contributes only 4% of total sales to the nylon division and only 0.4% of sales to the entire company.

The list of alternatives could be endless, but to analyze this situation fully the relevant factors need to be quantified. The costs of the base case need to be determined and compared to the costs of the alternatives. To make an accurate analysis, one must identify and measure all the relevant quality costs. As mentioned above, the hidden supplier costs cannot be quantified, but they are considered a part of the total quality costs and are relevant to this analysis.

PRODUCT CONTRIBUTION TO EXPENSES AND INCOME

Table 1 shows the average hourly contribution generated by the four products using RM #033. The standard cost information was obtained by the director of quality. The standard cost measure includes the total material cost, the cost of scrap at an average scrap rate of 10%, and the allocated fixed cost of the machine. The BAC controller was reluctant to provide detailed information concerning the accounting cost system. Therefore, the method of allocation could not be determined.

Table 1. PRODUCT CONTRIBUTION TO EXPENSES (LESS STANDARD COST)*

Product	Sales Revenue/lb.	Standard Cost/lb.	Contribution	Contribution/one hour**
A	$1.74	$0.89	$0.86	$ 431.50
B	2.84	0.95	1.89	946.00
C	1.71	0.96	0.75	375.00
D	$2.10	$0.91	$1.19	$ 596.00
	$8.39			$2,348.50
Average revenue/lb. $2.10		Packaging cost at a constant rate of $0.03/lb.		60.00
				$2,288.50
		Average Contrbution (rounded):		$ 572.00

*Standard cost includes: material cost, cost of scrap (at a 10% rate), fixed costs of the machine.

**Throughput rate of 500 lbs./hr. is typical.

As shown, the average contribution is $572 per hour of operation using RM #033, with an average sales revenue of $2.10 per pound.

The downtime cost can be measured by the amount of contribution that could have been generated if the hour were spent in full production plus the cost of direct labor incurred for that hour (See Table 2).

Additional costs arise when the downtime is due to problems with RM #033. A first-shift production supervisor estimates that he spends about four hours per month in additional inspection and analysis when RM #033 causes the machines to shut down. This cost can be expressed as 2.5% of his monthly wages, or approximately $9. This supervisor discusses the problems he encounters with at least three different people: the production manager, the director of quality, and another shift manager, costing the firm an estimated $36 per hour of downtime. Overtime charges due to failing to meet production requirements are approximately $54, based on three employees working at time-and-a-half. Therefore, the total cost of downtime per hour is $695.

Downtime of two hours is typical when running products

with RM #033. The total cost per run is doubled to $1,390. RM #033 constitutes, on average, 67.3% of total raw material in the four products. The cost per run comes to $1,010. The machines used are not equipped to process the metal pieces found in RM #033, so extra wear and gear damage is done to these machines. Maintenance costs increase, and the useful life of the machine is shortened. It was difficult to gather enough information to determine this cost, but we believe the figure of $360 per run is a good estimate. The total cost per run, less the cost of irrelevant material costs, comes to a whopping $2,760.

Table 2. AVERAGE HOURLY COST OF DOWNTIME

Average Hourly Cost of Downtime During GS Runs	
Average contribution	$ 572
Direct labor cost (2 x $12.00)	24
	$ 596
Average Cost of Downtime Due to Low-Quality RM #033	
Average cost of downtime	$ 596
Additional inspection and analysis (.25 x $2,880)	9
Time spent discussing problem (0.5 hour x $18 x 4)	$ 36
	$ 641
Overtime labor costs (3 x $12 x 1.5)	$ 54
Cost of one hour of downtime	$ 695
Total cost of downtime per run ($695 x 2 hours)	$1,390
Cost of raw material #033 (0.50 x 500lbs. x 6 hours x .673)	1,010
Cost of extra wear on machines (.12 x 500lbs. x 6 hours)	$ 360
Total cost of RM #033 per 6-hour run	$2,760

RM #033 COSTS COMPARED TO REGULAR NYLON

If regular nylon, an available substitute, were used in production, downtime due to poor quality would be near zero. The process would run continuously over the six hours. When the needed setup and cleanup hours are added, the total production time per batch is 12 hours. The shorter time span generates higher revenue per hour, about 18% more (Figure 1).

The differential costs include material costs, downtime costs, and extra machine wear. Other costs, such as labor, overhead charges, and other indirect expenses, are irrelevant to this analysis and, therefore, ignored.

The material cost per run reflects the 67.3% rate of usage in raw materials. As mentioned earlier, no other additional costs would be incurred by using regular nylon. The cost savings using a higher quality raw material is $760 per run.

Figure 1. AVERAGE 6-HOUR RUN*

Typical Run

Setup 3 hours —1—2— Downtime —3—4— Downtime —5—6— Cleanup 3 hours = 14 hours

Average revenue per hour = $445.46

Proposed Run

Setup 3 hours —1—2—3—4—5—6— Cleanup 3 hours = 12 hours

Average revenue per hour = $524.375

Differential Costs	Using RM #033	Using Reg Nylon	Difference
Material costs	(0.50/lb.) $1,010	(0.99/lb.) $2,000	($ 990)
Downtime cost (2 per run)	1,390	0	1,390
Extra machine wear costs	$ 360	$ 0	$ 360
Total	$2,760	$2,000	
Net differential cost			$ 760

*Process 3,000 lbs. of material. Average revenue per run (3,000 x $2.0975) = $6,292.50

STEPS TO A QUALITY COST SYSTEM AT BAC

The price of nonconformance has been estimated to be $760 per six-hour production run, plus some hidden quality costs incurred by the supplier. In order to arrive at a zero price of nonconformance, BAC needs to make some decisions about how to deal with this extra cost.

First, BAC should design and communicate more appropriate specifications that XYZ (or any other supplier) must follow. The suppliers need to know the quality expectations before improvements can be achieved. Once tighter specifications are developed, BAC can expect to suffer less downtime and lower inspection and overtime charges. This step will lower the overall cost of producing the four products that use RM #033 and result in an efficient production run.

Second, BAC needs to consider quality costs as part of the direct costs of products A, B, C, and D. The contribution margins

Definitions of Quality Applicable to BAC

Quality often is defined differently by producers and customers. For manufacturers or producers, quality usually refers to conformance to specifications. At BAC a tolerance is specified for critical dimensions for every product made. Products that fail to fall within the tolerances are either put through the process again and rechecked or are scrapped.

Customers typically define quality as value or how well the product serves its intended purpose at a price they are willing to pay. End users are concerned with fitness for use, or how well the product performs. At BAC the quality level desired is specified by each customer. The level of quality desired is affected by the end use of the finished product.

For BAC in particular, and businesses in general, success depends on the accuracy of management perceptions of customer expectations and how to determine if the operating capabilities of the firm can satisfy these expectations. Poor quality reduces a company's ability to compete in the marketplace and increases the costs of producing its product. By improving quality, firms like BAC potentially can increase market share as well as reduce product costs.

The costs of quality are the costs that would be eliminated if all workers were perfect in their jobs. Quality costs are important because every dollar and labor hour not used making scrap can be used for making better products on time or for improving the existing products or processes.

Most experts estimate that losses on gross sales due to poor quality range from 20% to 30%. Most executives underestimate these losses because they consider salient costs such as scrap and rework to be the only costs of quality.[2]

The price of conformance (POC) is the amount necessary to spend to achieve quality products. In most companies this represents 3% to 4% of sales. POC can be divided further into prevention costs and appraisal costs.

Prevention costs are associated with preventing defects before they happen. Examples include the cost of process design, product design, employee training, supplier programs, and quality improvement meetings and projects.[3] These costs are very low at BAC.

Appraisal costs include measuring, evaluating, or auditing products to assure conformance to quality standards and performance requirements. Specifically, the costs of incoming and source inspection/test of raw material, in-process and final inspection/test, quality audits, calibration of measuring and test equipment, and the costs of associated supplies and materials. At BAC the costs of incoming inspection are low, while the in-process and final inspection costs are high.[4]

The price of noncomformance is all the expenses incurred when operations go awry. Some estimate that these costs alone can be as high as 20% of sales.[5] These costs can be subdivided into internal failure and external failure costs. Internal failure costs occur before the product is shipped to the customer. Examples are the costs of scrap, rework, re-inspection, retesting, material review, and machine downtime. The internal failure costs associated with RM #033 are high at BAC.

External failure costs arise from product failure at the customer level. Some examples are the costs of processing customer complaints, customer returns, warranty claims, and product recalls. These costs are by far the highest at most companies. Defects found by the customer can cause the firm to loose market share and future profits because bad news travels fast. Dissatisfied customers tell others, they tell others, and so on. The intangible cost of lost future profits is difficult to measure, but undoubtedly poor quality reduces market share and profits.

Total quality costs are the sum of the above-mentioned costs. They represent the difference between the actual cost of the product and what the cost would be if there were no imperfections.

Quality cost systems. To aid the management of quality, a quality cost system needs to be implemented. The goal of this cost system should be to use quality improvement efforts that will lead to opportunities for cost reduction. This strategy involves four steps:

- Directly attack price of nonconformance causes, and attempt to drive them to zero;
- Invest in prevention measures to bring about improvement;
- Reduce appraisal costs according to results achieved; and
- Continue to evaluate and alter preventive efforts for further improvement.[6]

Before the quality costs can be tackled, they must be identified and quantified. Unfortunately, many quality costs are overlooked or unrecognized because the accounting cost system is not set up to identify them.

Quality cost bases. The effective evaluation of quality improvement requires accurate and reliable measures of the costs underlying quality-related activities. Companies fully committed to quality ask the controller to measure quality costs because accounting measures generally are perceived as objective. This practice keeps the cost of collecting information within practical limits and facilitates interaction between Accounting and Quality, the two departments seeking cost benefits for the company.

The base chosen should be sensitive to and represent the fluctuations in business activity. For long-range analysis, net sales is the base used most often for presentations to top management. Short-range bases, which are the bases used in this article, should be related directly to quality costs as they are incurred and reported. The best bases are those already used in production because the people who need to be concerned with quality are familiar with these measures. Examples of these bases include overall operating costs, total or direct labor costs, value-added costs, or costs per machine hour. Machine-hour costs were the main base used here.

Another view of BAC factory floor.

of the four products appear to be acceptable because they only measure the difference between the selling price and the standard costs. Other "indirect" costs, such as overtime, downtime, and maintenance, are allocated over many products and, in a sense, become hidden. These quality costs should be considered direct costs of the four nylon products. The BAC buyer, production manager, and controller need to be aware of and accountable for those costs.

We recommend that BAC managers consider the overall costs involved with the use of RM #033 and discuss the problems with the current supplier to see if the situation can be resolved. The purchasing agent would be the appropriate person to initiate the discussion. The alternative that is in the best interest of BAC Corporation should be pursued.

FUTURE CONSIDERATIONS

The improvements made with respect to RM #033 can be expanded throughout all BAC product lines. The measures used to identify the true costs of producing items need to be changed.

Moreover, the cost accounting system may need some adjustment to facilitate quality cost identification and control. The costs of poor quality, such as rework and scrap or excessive time spent on customer problems, need to be traced to the source before they can be eliminated.

Implementation of improved quality cost accounting will require interdepartmental cooperation. The accounting department will need input from purchasing, the director of quality, and the production manager, as well as the production line workers. In addition, the support of top management will be essential in defining the goals of the improved accounting system. Continuous efforts to identify and measure quality costs will lead to the reduction of many direct and indirect costs due to poor quality and, thus, satisfy customers while increasing profits.

MAKING A QUALITY CHANGE

Based on this team's interim report, the sales manager of the nylon division looked into the accounting methods and decided that something had to be changed. To summarize a portion of his memo dated October 29, 1993, "Therefore, I request that we change the [Bills of Material] that call for [RM #033] to our current prime nylon [raw material]. I realize that there will be a sizable increase in raw material price that will affect standard costs and profit margins negatively. But with all the hidden costs associated with dealing with a poor-quality raw material, we really don't know how negatively, if any, that will affect the company overall. I believe we will benefit in the long run."

Kathleen G. Rust is a doctoral student in organization studies at Southern Illinois University, Carbondale, Ill. This article was submitted through the Evansville Chapter.

1 The names of the company studied, its supplier, and all individuals working at either of the companies have been changed or deleted for reasons of confidentiality.

2 Philip B. Crosby, *Quality Without Tears*, McGraw-Hill Book Company, New York, N.Y., 1984.

3 Jack Campanella, ed., *Principles of Quality Cost*, ASQC Quality Press, Milwaukee, Wis., 1990.

4 Campanella, op cit.

5 Crosby, op cit.

6 Campanella, op cit.

We Need Better Financial

BY C. RICHARD ALDRIDGE, CPA, AND JANET L. COLBERT, CPA

During the past few years, successful businesses have become more customer and service oriented rather than product oriented. Entities are concentrating on human resources, information and data, and research and development as they adapt to rapid changes in technology and increased competition. The new focus replaces the traditional objective of managing and controlling raw materials, direct labor, and overhead.

Financial reporting, however, has not kept up with these advances. The traditional financial reporting model is grounded in historical costs and the reporting of economic events, so it needs to be broadened to make it more informative and useful to investors, creditors, and their advisors.

For users of business information and for financial markets, the stakes in an informative model of reporting are high. Capital allocation decisions are made based on information received from management, and accurate, timely information facilitates the flow of capital to the most appropriate business opportunities. In turn, capital allocation decisions and the liquidity of capital markets affect the competitiveness of the nation as a whole. Thus, it is critical for a business reporting model to encompass information needed by users.

The current model of financial reporting requires fairly consistent accounting principles and disclosures—with some limited range of choices—regardless of the company's industry or the particulars of the business. A more flexible model that emphasizes the usefulness of company-specific information is more appropriate in addressing the needs of users of business information.

BUSINESS REPORTING RECOMMENDATIONS

In 1994, the AICPA's Special Committee on Financial Reporting[1] issued a report titled *Improving Business Reporting—A Customer Focus* that called for significant changes to the current model of financial reporting. The recommendations are not binding on any standard-setting body or regulatory agency, but both the Financial Accounting Standards Board and the Securities & Exchange Commission continue to study the proposals and may choose to incorporate them into their own standards and releases. Because of the expanded focus, which includes not only financial reporting matters but also broader business issues in management's reports to users, it is important for management accountants and financial managers to understand the recommendations.

Business Reporting recommends changes in four areas:

- Extending the business information model,
- Enhancing financial statements,
- Improving auditing, and
- Facilitating change.

Extending the business information model. *Business Reporting* recommends improving the information provided to financial statement users by expanding the business information model to include nonfinancial as well as financial information and to provide forward-looking as well as historical information. These two elements are incorporated in the five categories of the extended business reporting model as shown in Table 1.

Traditionally, financial statements have been the primary means by which information about a company is communicated to users, yet they disclose financial information only. Today's users also demand nonfinancial or operating information. Nonfinancial information helps users understand the connections among ongoing events, the financial statements, and factors that produce long-term value and wealth for the company. Operating data can provide information to users before the effects of events are captured fully in the financial statements.

Although most of today's financial reporting focuses on the past, which may be useful when making predictions, users are more concerned with the future. Useful forward-looking information includes key

Reporting

The traditional model of financial reporting needs to add nonfinancial and operating information as well as financial data so users can get a clear picture of a company's performance.

trends and the disclosure of expected opportunities and risks resulting from those trends. Management's plans also should be disclosed along with factors critical to the plans' success. Finally, management should assess how actual business performance compares to previously disclosed opportunities, risks, and plans. To guard against unwarranted litigation risk, forward-looking information would be disclosed only with appropriate safe harbors. Safe harbors are specific requirements or standards that, when followed properly, preclude management from being held liable for its disclosure of forward-looking information.

Table 2 shows an annual report format a company might use in compliance with *Business Reporting*. Western Builders Supply, Inc., markets building materials to individual homeowners and small contractors. All stores house a retail unit as well as a contractor sales area. The annual report contains background and historical information on the company and both segments, management's analyses, information about management and shareholders, forward-looking information, and the auditor's report.

Enhancing financial statements. In addition to enlarging the reporting model, the Special Committee also recommends improving the financial statements within the model. Financial statement users say they are satisfied with the general framework of financial statements, but several areas could be enhanced. Here are some of the suggestions:

- Improved disclosure of segment information,
- Improved disclosure and accounting for innovative financial instruments,
- Improved disclosures of the opportunities and risks of off-balance-sheet financing,
- A clear separation of the effects of core and noncore activities and events,
- Improved disclosures about the uncertainty in measurements of certain assets and liabilities, and
- Improved quarterly reporting.

Segment data. Users note that multisegment companies often do not report enough segment information in their financial statements. In some cases, information is presented for too few or no segments, while, in other cases, insufficient detail about segments is provided. Because proper analysis of companies involved in diverse businesses is important, segment information is as significant as information about the company as a whole.

Business Reporting recommends defining segments consistently as companies do frequently when reporting internally to senior management. Geographic segment data also should be disclosed when they provide insight into the company's opportunities and risks. In addition, better information should be provided about unconsolidated investments and other affiliations.

Innovative financial instruments. The proliferation of complex innovative financial instruments such as swaps, compound options, and collars has not been followed by changes in financial reporting requirements. Disclosures are needed to address user questions such as: What risks have been transferred or taken on? What are management's objectives? What effects do these instruments have on the company's financial statements?

Off-balance-sheet items. Long-term leases, special purpose entities, joint ventures, long-term purchase agreements, and other similar transactions and events are not understood easily by users because they generally are not reflected in the financial statements. Disclosures and accounting requirements are needed to ensure that the risks, opportunities, resources, and obligations that result from these special arrangements are represented fairly in business reporting.

Core activities. Predictions of future earnings and cash flows can be made by examining historical data that exclude unusual and nonrecurring activities or events (noncore effects). Consequently, *Business Reporting* recommends that management should quantify and display separately the effects of core (usual and recurring) and noncore activities and events on the face of the income statement, balance sheet, and cash flow statement. Noncore events and activities and their effects also should be described clearly in notes to the statements. The Committee recommends that noncore assets and liabilities be measured at fair value because these assets and liabilities are not part of the ongoing business.

Table 1. ELEMENTS OF THE EXTENDED BUSINESS REPORTING MODEL

Background about the Company
■ Broad objectives and strategies ■ Scope and description of business and properties ■ Impact of industry structure on the company
Information about Management and Shareholders
■ Directors, management, compensation, major shareholders, and transactions and relationships among related parties
Historical Data
■ Financial statements and related disclosures ■ High-level operating and nonfinancial performance measures
Management's Analysis of Historical Data
■ An analysis of changes in the financial, operating, and performance-related data, including the identification and past effects of key trends
Forward-Looking Information
■ Opportunities and risks, including those resulting from key trends ■ Management's plans, including critical success factors ■ Comparison of actual business performance to previously disclosed forward-looking information

Adapted from *Improving Business Reporting: A Customer Focus*, p. 9.

Measurement uncertainties. Some assets and liabilities can be measured with great precision, while others require considerable estimation. For example, there should be no question about the cash balance at the balance sheet date. The accrued liability for environmental cleanup is much less certain. So users can understand the uncertainties inherent in some measurements, companies should identify in notes to the financial statements the specific types of assets and liabilities subject to significant measurement uncertainties. Management should disclose how these amounts were derived and explain the estimates, judgments, and assumptions used in making the measurement.

Quarterly reporting. Quarterly reports often give users the first indication of important trends or changes in a company's business. But some companies that report quarterly often do not report on the fourth quarter separately. Although users can derive fourth quarter data from the annual and prior quarterly reports, they would benefit from separate fourth quarter reporting including an analysis by management of fourth quarter activities and events. *Business Reporting* also recommends including more segment information in quarterly reports.

Improving auditing. The third component for better overall business reporting is improved auditing. At present, auditors report only on information derived from the accounting records. Under the expanded model, auditors will be called on to provide assurance on additional, more subjective information. Providing this assurance would require new skills and new auditing standards.

An auditor's involvement will vary from company to company and should be determined by the company and the users of the business reports. Some users might demand an audit, the highest level of assurance. Other users might find a review, which provides a much lower level of assurance, to be sufficient. The auditor's report must be tailored to meet a variety of assurance needs.

Facilitating change. The final recommendation in *Business Reporting* involves facilitating change. Business reporting must be responsive to changes in the business and economic climate, especially advances in technology and the rush toward a global marketplace.

To facilitate change, standard setters must focus more on users' needs by asking for users' direct involvement in the evaluation reporting process. Users also are encouraged to increase their direct involvement in the standard-setting process through participation on standard-setting boards, advisory councils, and task forces. Finally, if business reports are expanded to include forward-looking information, measures need to be implemented to discourage unwarranted litigation. Such measures could involve safe harbors and specific provisions relative to forward-looking information that enable companies to demonstrate their compliance with requirements.

OUT WITH THE OLD—IN WITH THE NEW

The present financial reporting model has not been altered significantly for decades. Concerns about the deteriorating relevance of financial reporting have been expressed for some time. When surveyed by the Special Committee on Financial Reporting, users indicated that not all their needs were met by traditional financial reporting. Although financial statements provide crucial information for investment and credit decisions, users have developed other sources for additional important information. But this information is less reliable than information prepared under GAAP and audited by CPAs. To meet users' needs, all relevant information should be included in a comprehensive, integrated business reporting format.

The recommendations offered by the Special Committee on Financial Reporting differ from current financial reporting in three ways. First, high-level operating data and performance measures would become an integral component of the reporting process. Current financial reporting requirements require no disclosure of operating information, yet performance measures used by management are important to users. The inclusion of operating data and other performance measures would allow users to understand management's perspective and the connection among ongoing events, the financial statements, and factors that create long-term value and wealth for the company.

Second, forward-looking information would be included in the reporting process because it would give users insight into management's vision and the opportunities and risks associated with an investment or a loan.

Third, segment reporting would be expanded and improved. Although under current financial reporting requirements some segment data must be disclosed, under the suggested recommendations segments would be defined in a manner that is consistent with internal reporting to senior management. Geographic segment data also would be required as companies with multiple segments operate diverse businesses that are subject to different opportunities and risks. Improved segment reporting provides additional insight about the opportunities and risks of each business activity and sharpens predictions.

Table 2. WESTERN BUILDERS SUPPLY, INC. ANNUAL REPORT FORMAT

Background about the Company and Its Segments

Overview

Retail Segment
- Broad objectives and strategies
- Scope and description of the business
- Impact of industry structure on the company

Contractor Sales Segment
- Broad objectives and strategies
- Scope and description of the business
- Impact of industry structure on the company

Information about Management and Shareholders
- Nonemployee directors
- Board organization and compensation
- Senior management
- Senior management compensation
- Criminal convictions of directors and senior management
- Major shareholders
- Transactions and relationships among related parties
- Disagreements with directors, independent accountants, bankers, and lead counsel

Historical Data (Financial and Nonfinancial)
- Five-year summary of business financial and nonfinancial data
- Financial statements for the years ended December 31, 1996, and 1995

Management's Analysis of Financial and Nonfinancial Data
- Retail Segment
- Contractor Sales Segment
- Corporate

Forward-Looking Information

Retail Segment
- Opportunities and risks including those resulting from key trends
- Management's plans including critical success factors
- Comparison of actual business performance to previously disclosed forward-looking information

Contractor Sales Segment
- Opportunities and risks including those resulting from key terms
- Management's plans including critical success factors
- Comparison of actual business performance to previously disclosed forward-looking information

Report of Independent Auditors

Adapted from *Improving Business Reporting: A Customer Focus*, p.9.

BENEFITS VS. COSTS

Increased competition and advances in technology have changed the way companies are organized and managed. The companies that are successful in today's marketplace focus on customer needs. Similarly, to foster efficient capital allocation among companies, financial reporting must focus on the needs of the customer—the user. As usual, there are both benefits and costs associated with supplying additional information.

Benefits. First, improved reporting should result in lower capital cost as investors' information risks are reduced. Second, more efficient trading should result in highly liquid markets as investors and creditors become better informed. Third, the new reporting model should meet the increased demand for more information by institutional investors and financial analysts and result in better relations with all users.

A fourth benefit to companies is the reduced cost of not having to maintain two sets of accounting records. The new reporting format would present information to external users in a manner that is consistent with the information management uses in making decisions. This uniformity of information for external and internal users also could reduce "window dressing" and suboptimal behavior by management. Fifth, an expanded, comprehensive business report reduces the potential for litigation when companies divulge information to some users (financial analysts) that has not been disseminated to all users. Finally, a comprehensive business report would reduce the cost and the potential for inconsistency of preparing the many reports that are required by various user groups.

Costs. Users may become "information junkies" because they do not bear the direct cost for the information they demand. But information contained in financial and business reports *does* have a cost. First, companies incur costs in preparing and disseminating information, which include the costs of collecting and processing data, the costs of refining the data to a quality level necessary for public disclosure, and the costs of auditing the data (if audited). Second, companies incur liability and litigation costs to defend against claims that the information is misleading. These costs are especially relevant given the recommendation that companies report forward-looking and other "soft" information. Third, in providing information to users, companies incur competitive costs. That is, Company A may provide information that Company B, a competitor, may find useful. If disclosure of the information is required by GAAP, no unfair advantage would result as Company A would have access to the same information about Company B. Competitive costs could be significant if the competitor is not subject to U.S. GAAP.

The Special Committee on Financial Reporting attempted to evaluate the benefits and costs of the proposed reporting model before making its recommendations. Although its analysis was more qualitative than quantitative, the Committee concluded that the benefits of the proposed general recommendations exceeded the costs. As standard setters attempt to implement the recommendations, however, they should assess the costs and benefits of specific standards.

THE CHANGE IS NECESSARY

Because businesses have changed so dramatically since traditional financial statements were developed, a corresponding change is needed in the way businesses report to investors and creditors. A broad reporting model that encompasses not only financial information, but also operating data, management's analyses, forward-looking information, facts concerning management and shareholders, and company background, is beneficial to users. Such company-specific information helps investors, creditors, and their advisors make appropriate capital allocation decisions. Although companies will incur costs to disseminate a wider spectrum of information to users, the benefits of lower costs of capital, more liquid markets, better investor relations, decreased preparation cost, reduced potential for litigation, and consistent information provide significant advantages to users.

RECENT DEVELOPMENTS

The AICPA continues to campaign for an expanded business reporting model. Earlier this year, its Special Committee on Assurance Services released a report detailing the results of research and recommendations related to the future of assurance services. The document strongly supports the Business Reporting model and urges the FASB to adopt its recommendations. The report also encourages the SEC to view positively the accounting profession's efforts to expand the business reporting model because enhanced decision-making information benefits decision makers and the economy.

C. Richard Aldridge, CPA, is professor of accounting at Western Kentucky University in Bowling Green, Ky. He is a member of IMA's South Central Kentucky Chapter and can be reached at (502) 745-3099.

Janet L. Colbert, CPA, CIA, is the Meany-Holland Professor of Accounting at Western Kentucky University. She can be reached at (502) 745-2971.

[1] American Institute of Certified Public Accountants, 1994. The Committee sometimes is referred to as the Jenkins Committee after its chair, Edmund Jenkins.

How Nonfinancial Performance Measures Are Used

Some companies waste resources when they measure nonfinancial performance factors but then don't use them, survey of U.S. and Canadian companies shows.

BY BONNIE P. STIVERS, CPA; TERESA JOYCE COVIN; NANCY GREEN HALL; AND STEVEN W. SMALT, CPA

Most executives agree that there is no magic formula—or one right measure—for evaluating business performance. Therefore, in an effort to capture the essence of business performance, many companies are creating new performance measurement systems that include a broad range of financial and nonfinancial measures.

Although we know much about the use of financial measures in companies, our knowledge of these new, nonfinancial performance measures is limited. To determine the scope of current practice, we surveyed top executives in U.S. Fortune 500 firms and in Canadian Post 300 companies. The study was sponsored by the Michael J. Coles College of Business at Kennesaw State University and funded by the Canadian Institute of Chartered Accountants. Study results indicate that top executives in both countries believe that nonfinancial measures are important. But the study also identifies two serious drawbacks: (1) Although nonfinancial factors are viewed as important, they may not be measured, and (2) Even when nonfinancial factors are measured, they may not be used. (For a description of the study design and survey sample, see sidebar.)

THE STUDY OF NONFINANCIAL PERFORMANCE MEASURES

Although much is being written about nonfinancial performance measures, very little is known about actual current practices. The objective of this study was to provide a comprehensive picture of the process of nonfinancial measurement. Specifically, the study examined the degree to which top executives in Fortune 500 and Post 300 firms identify particular nonfinancial performance factors as important, whether firms are measuring important nonfinancial factors, and whether or not companies actually are using nonfinancial performance factor information in their planning processes.

The questionnaire asked study participants to indicate, using a five-point scale, the importance of each of 21 nonfinancial performance factors in setting company goals. For discussion purposes, we have grouped the factors into five general categories: customer service, market performance, innovation, goal achievement, and employee involvement.

The five categories of nonfinancial performance measures are illustrated in Figure 1. For each individual performance measure, the figure shows of the 253 firms in the total sample: (1) number of firms identifying the factor as important, (2) number of firms actually measuring the factor, and (3) number of firms actually using the factor in the planning process.

An individual factor was identified as highly important if it received a rating of four or greater on the five-point scale of importance. Results of the study indicate that customer service factors are perceived to be the most important measures. Of the 253 responding firms, 235 (92.9%) rated "customer satisfaction" and "delivery performance/customer service" as highly important. "Product/process quality" was rated as highly important by 206 (81.4%) of the responding firms and "service quality" by 205 (81.0%) of the 253 firms (Figure 1).

Market performance and goal achievement also are perceived to be highly important categories. "Market share" in the market performance category was rated highly important by 200 (79.1%) of the responding firms, and "productivity" in the goal achievement category was rated highly important by 211 (83.4%) of the firms (Figure 1).

Reprinted with permission from *Management Accounting,* February 1998, pp. 44, 46-49.

Factors in the innovation and employee involvement categories were perceived to be less important in goal setting. Looking at the individual measures, we see that "R&D productivity" in the innovation category was rated as highly important by only 112 (44.3%) of the 253 firms, and "employee turnover" in the employee involvement category was rated as highly important by only 122 (48.2%) of the 253 firms.

The results of the study have important implications for those in the position of designing effective performance measurement systems. The first step is to get the right mix of key factors. If we were to develop a "hit" list of critical, nonfinancial factors to include in any performance measurement system by listening to Kaplan[1], Drucker[2], and Reichheld[3], we would include the following: market standing, innovation, productivity, customer service, and employee involvement. Although the responding executives in this study did identify market share, productivity, and customer service as highly important factors, they perceived innovation and employee involvement measures to be less important. This is clearly an area of concern if we believe what many business experts are saying about the increasing importance of innovation and human capital. It may well be that in the coming decade, intellectual capital will impact the bottom line more than booked, tangible assets. If this is the case, performance measurement systems must include leading indicators that tap human capital. This is one way managers will be able to manage and control knowledge.

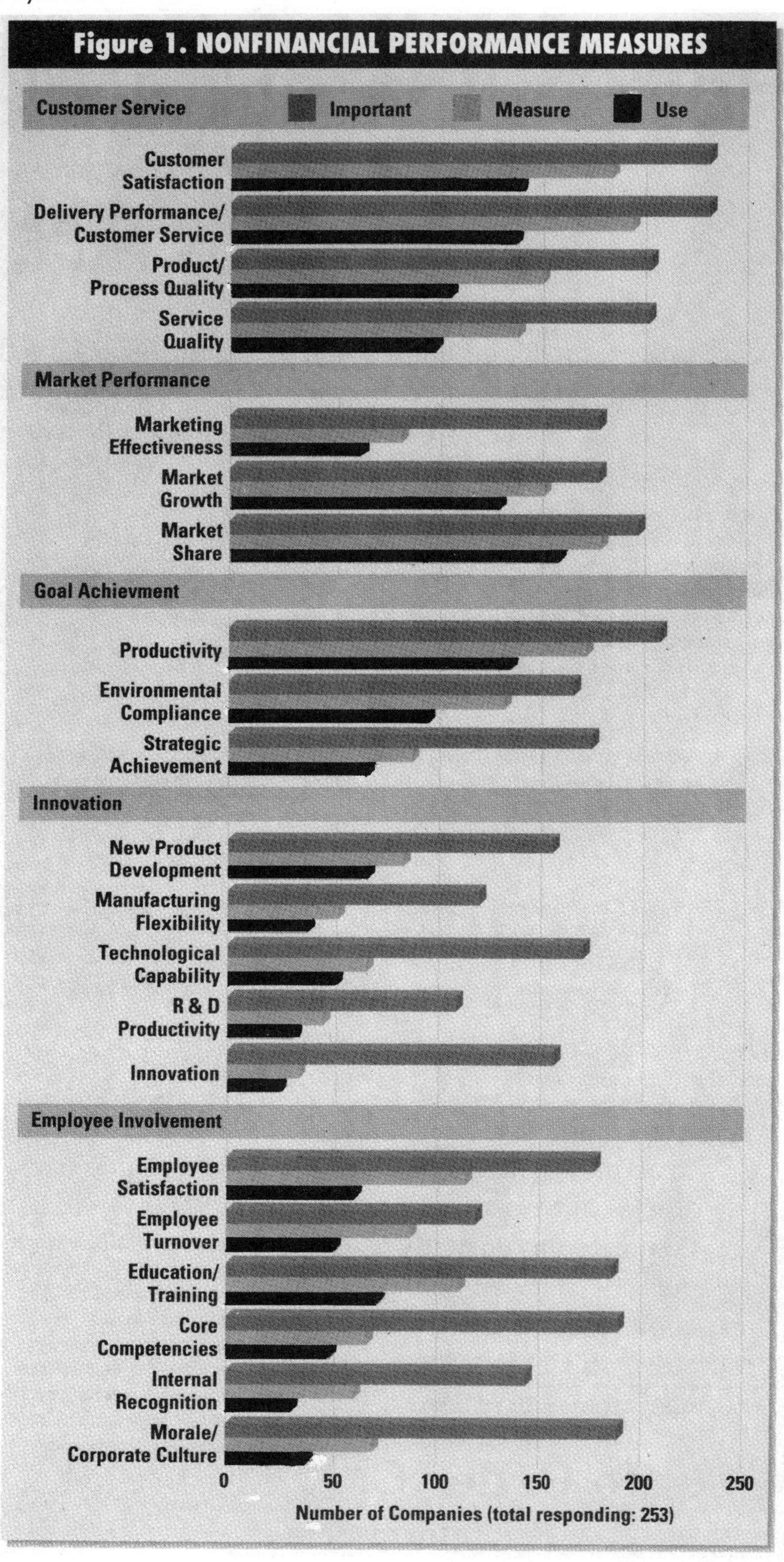

THE IMPORTANCE-MEASUREMENT GAP

Our results show a substantial importance-measurement gap. That is, many companies that view nonfinancial performance factors as important are not capturing data on these factors. As one would expect, the importance-measurement gap is greatest for factors that are perceived to be unmeasurable or at best difficult to measure. For example, in the employee involvement category, although 192 (75.9%) companies rated "morale and corporate culture" as highly important, only 72 (37.5%) are measuring this factor. There is a similar finding for "core competencies"—192 companies (75.9%) rated the factor as highly important, but only 69 (35.9%) are measuring this factor.

It is interesting to note that just as the categories of innovation and employee involvement received lower overall ratings of importance, responding firms indicated these two categories also have a low incidence of measurement. In particular, the nonfinancial performance factor least likely to be measured is "innovation." Although 160 firms (63.2%) rated the factor as highly important, only 35 firms (21.8%) are measuring this factor.

On the other hand, a number of other factors have a high rate of measurement. In the market performance category, 200 companies (79.1%) rated "market share" as highly important, and 182 firms (91.0%) are measuring this factor. "Market growth" was rated as highly important by 181 firms (71.5%), and 154 firms (85.1%) are measuring this factor. In the customer service category, "customer satisfaction" and "delivery performance/customer service" have measurement rates of 79.5% and 83.8%, respectively. In goal achievement, "productivity" has a measurement rate of 82.9%.

After a firm identifies the right mix of factors to include in the performance measurement system, it is critical that these factors get measured and reported. "What gets measured gets done" implies that the organization becomes what it measures. If you cannot measure something, you cannot control it, and control is essential. The results of this study show a substantial importance-measurement gap for a number of highly important factors, particularly in the categories of innovation and employee involvement. Many of these factors may be perceived to be unmeasurable or difficult to measure. However, the fact is that precise data collection may not be possible; a collection effort that provides even crude data can prove valuable. "What matters ... is not the absolute magnitude in any area but the trend ... that the measurements will give ... no matter how crude and approximate the individual readings are by themselves."[4] Companies may have to experiment with measuring and interpreting different factors. The objective is to provide action-oriented information to managers—not to report balance sheet figures.

THE MEASUREMENT-USE GAP

The final step in the performance measurement process is the use of measurements in developing and monitoring strategic plans. In this study, we found evidence that a large number of businesses are collecting data that are not being used to inform managers in the planning process. We call this the measurement-use gap. Of course, the underlying assumption is that if companies are collecting the data on important factors, they intend to use the data to make business decisions. To illustrate the measurement-use gap, look at "delivery performance/customer service" in the customer service category (Figure 1). While 197 (83.8%) of 235 study participants (who rated it highly important) indicated that their companies measure this factor, only 140 (71.1%) of 197 indicated that their firms actually use this information for planning purposes. In practical terms, this means that 28.9% of the firms are collecting information that serves no useful purpose in the planning process.

The measurement-use gap appears to be most pronounced in the category of employee involvement. Measures such as "employee satisfaction," "employee turnover," "internal recognition," and "morale and corporate culture" are not used in the planning process by more than 40% of the firms that collect data on these factors.

Study results show that the measurement-use gap is the smallest in the market performance category. For "market growth," 132 (85.7%) of 154 responding firms measuring the factor are using the factor. Results are similar for "market share" in that 161 (88.5%) of 182 responding firms measuring the factor report that they are also using the data. These are measures that have been around for a while; hence, managers are able to interpret the data and translate the information into action items.

The measurement-use gap appears to be moderate for the factors in the categories of customer service, innovation, and goal achievement. Roughly 25% of the companies who measure these factors do not use the results in their planning process.

The underlying assumption is valid—if companies collect data on important performance factors, they intend to use the data to make business decisions. Why would companies identify factors as important, collect measurements on these factors, and then not use the information in the planning process? Certainly, in the case of the employee involvement category, the measures are "softer" than in categories such as market performance. The measurements may be more difficult to understand, and, for this reason, managers may have trouble in translating the information into action items. If, for whatever reason, a firm finds that it is using resources to collect data but fails to use the resulting information, this is an inefficient use of resources that must be checked. Either the information is not relevant, in which case the factor should be deleted from the performance measurement system, or, if the information is perceived to be critical and managers do not know how to use it, every effort must be made to understand the significance of the information.

COMPARING U.S. AND CANADIAN RESPONSES

We also wanted to examine the extent to which perceptions of the importance, measurement, and use of nonfinancial performance measures were similar across U.S. and Canadian firms.

Both U.S. and Canadian respondents indicate that customer service and market performance categories are most important in setting company goals and that the other categories examined are at least moderately important. The only statistically significant difference between U.S. and Canadian firms is in their perception of the importance of the innovation category. U.S. respondents indicate that these measures are more important in the goal-setting process. U.S. and Canadian firms also show similar patterns in the measurement and use of nonfinancial performance factors.

For both U.S. and Canadian firms, market performance, customer service, and goal achievement are shown to be the most used and measured nonfinancial performance categories. However, consistent with U.S. firms' belief concerning the importance of the innovation category, the U.S. firms represented in this sample indicate that they are significantly more likely to both measure and use factors in the innovation category. Although there are several possible explanations for differences between U.S. and Canadian firms as they relate to innovation, it is likely that differences are due, at least in part, to competitive influences. Previous research has shown that competitive pressure often serves as a catalyst for innovation and forces firms to adopt creative internal structures to be responsive to changing markets.[5]

GETTING PAST THREE RED FLAGS TO A DYNAMIC SYSTEM

The performance measurement process involves: (1) the identification of important financial and nonfinancial factors, (2) measurement of these factors, and (3) use of factors in developing and monitoring strategic plans. The results of this study, based on responses from the top executives of Fortune 500 and Post 300 firms, provide a comprehensive picture of the process of nonfinancial performance measurement—and show that U.S. and Canadian firms face similar challenges. We believe that study results highlight three red flags.

First, measures of innovation and employee involvement were not perceived to be as important as customer service and market standing—this is a concern. If we believe the business experts who are telling us that human capital and other intangible assets classed as intellectual capital are becoming the basis of competitive advantage and wealth creation, then it is imperative that measures of innovation and employee involvement be included in the performance measurement systems—that is, identified, measured, and used to design and monitor strategic plans. Although results show that U.S. firms view measures of innovation as more important in the goal-setting process and are more likely to measure and use innovation factors, both U.S. and Canadian firms show substantial importance-measurement and measurement-use gaps.

Second, study results indicate a strong importance-measurement gap for certain factors. That is, although top executives believe that certain nonfinancial factors are highly important, a large number of firms are not capturing data on these measures. It is clear that some factors are more difficult to measure than others. But, even crude measurements on critical factors can provide valuable input to the control framework. To close the importance-measurement gap, companies may need to experiment with different measurement methodologies.

Third, results of the study suggest a substantial measurement-use gap. That is, a large number of companies are collecting data that are not being used by managers in the planning process. The reasons underlying the measurement-use gap should be investigated. If the firms are collecting data that are not useful, these factors should be deleted from the performance measurement system. If the data are on factors that are perceived to be critical, however, it may be that managers need help in learning how to use the information in the strategic planning process.

To develop a successful performance measurement system, managers must clearly understand the interests of the stakeholders (customers, employees, and investors), the strategic objectives of the company, and every aspect of the company's business processes. Only then can they be assured that the performance measurement system includes the right factors, both financial and nonfinancial. Long-term commitment to the system is required to assure that the factors are measured, understood, and used. The result can be a performance measurement system that is clearly linked to strategy, is dynamic, and is action-oriented.

HOW THE SURVEY WAS DESIGNED

Questionnaires were mailed to the top executives of Fortune 500 firms in the United States and Post 300 firms in Canada. The names and addresses of study participants were compiled from two databases: Compact Disclosure and CANCORP Canadian Financials. One hundred and two of the Fortune 500 U.S. firms and 151 of the Post 300 Canadian firms responded to the mail survey, providing an overall response rate of 31.625%. This response rate is significantly higher than might be expected given previous research on survey response rates for companies of this size.[1] Involvement by the Canadian Institute of Chartered Accountants may account for this higher than usual response rate; previous research has shown that endorsement by a well-known external party yields significantly higher response rates.[2] Respondents were chairmen of the board (70), chief executive officers (85), and chief financial officers (98). Based on 1993 Compact Disclosure and CANCORP Canadian Financials data, the average number of individuals employed by responding U.S. firms was 23,835, and the average number of employees in the Canadian responding firms was 7,689.

[1] Dennis H. Tootelian and Ralph M. Gaedeke, "Fortune 500 List Revisited 12 Years Later: Still an Endangered Species for Academic Research?" *Journal of Business Research*, Vol. 15, No.4, August 1987, pp. 359-363.

[2] Linda Rochford, "Surveying a Targeted Population Segment: The Effects of Endorsement on Mail Questionnaire Response Rate," *Journal of Marketing Theory & Practice*, Vol. 3, No. 2, Spring 1995, pp. 86-97.

Bonnie P. Stivers, Ph.D., CPA, is professor of accounting; Teresa Joyce Covin, Ph.D., is chair of the department of management and entrepreneurship and associate professor of management; Nancy Green Hall, Ph.D., is associate professor of decision sciences; and Steven W. Smalt, CPA, is assistant professor of accounting. All the authors are with the Michael J. Coles College of Business at Kennesaw State University. This article was submitted through the Atlanta Chapter of which Bonnie P. Stivers is a member. She can be contacted at bstivers@ksumail.kennesaw.edu.

[1]Robert S. Kaplan and David P. Norton, "The Balanced Scorecard—Measures that Drive Performance," *Harvard Business Review*, January-February, 1992, pp. 71-79; Norton (1993); "Putting the Balanced Scorecard to Work," *Harvard Business Review*, September-October 1993, pp. 134-147; "Using the Balanced Scorecard as a Strategic Management System," *Harvard Business Review*, January-February 1996, pp. 75-85.

[2]Peter F. Drucker, *Managing for the Future*, New York: Truman Talley Books/Dutton,1992; *Post-Capitalist Society*, Harper Business, New York, 1993; "The Age of Social Transformation," *The Atlantic Monthly*, November 1994, pp. 53-80.

[3]Frederick F. Reichheld, *The Loyalty Effect*, Harvard Business School Press, Boston, 1996.

[4]Drucker, *Managing for the Future*.

[5]Robert Simons, *Levers of Control: How Managers Use Innovative Control Systems to Drive Strategic Renewal*, Harvard Business School Press, Boston, 1995.

Arrivederci, Pacioli?

A New Accounting System Is Emerging

Technology is driving the creation of new event-driven accounting/business systems.

BY KENTON B. WALKER
AND ERIC L. DENNA

One of the greatest barriers to organizational change today is the way information technology is used. Managers are attempting to build 21st Century enterprises on the back of 20th Century architectures designed largely to automate manual information systems rather than improve the way work is accomplished. Modern information technology (IT), however, is able to support new relationships among the structure of organizations, business processes, and performance measures necessary to realize the benefits of reengineering. In order to bring about the transformation in business information systems (BIS) necessary to support reengineering efforts, assumptions and practices that have existed for decades must be reexamined in light of current capabilities.

The accounting system may be the biggest obstacle to significant advancements in BIS due to its role as the dominant business information source and the way it defines, organizes, and reports information. No other business information system has the ability to combine the performance of all functions of a business into one set of measures, which has led accounting to be known as the "language of business." This view is well supported by the use of accounting measures and reports for internal and external evaluations.

Double-entry bookkeeping, the cornerstone of the recording process in accounting, was developed by Luca Pacioli more than 500 years ago using "pencil-and-paper" technology. Today, the same basic ideas and procedures are still in use. Introduced this century, the computer has reduced processing time, dependence on manual and clerical efforts, and processing errors, and it has improved the timeliness of management reporting. At the same time, the computer and integrated financial systems have made information processing more complicated because of complex data and file structures, incompatible hardware and software products, and complex report writers.

The structure of accounting systems is dominated by financial accounting requirements to emphasize standards, conformity, and control. Unfortunately, systems development in recent years has focused on control so much that the products of the system are little more than reports showing how well we are under control (and about as interesting as reading a computer operating manual). In addition, much of our performance reporting is tied to the monthly financial cycle.

The accounting system has at least five primary weaknesses in its role as an organizational measuring stick. First, the accounting system focuses only on a subset of business events, those determined by the accountants to be "accounting transactions." There is an underlying assumption that the accounting "view" of the organization is able to satisfy many information customers. Unfortunately, the view of accountants that drives the classification scheme for storing data and determines which transactions are recorded is not satisfactory for many decision makers. Managers want information on quality, customer service, relationships with suppliers, and other important elements of business not captured by the accounting system.

Second, the system captures and processes data in an untimely manner, usually monthly, to conform with the preparation of periodic financial statements. Accountants are trained to think according to the financial cycle without considering that information customers often need reports on a more or less frequent basis depending on the organization's business cycle. Even if the outputs from the financial systems are delivered two weeks after the end of a month, which is quicker than average

Reprinted with permission from *Management Accounting,* July 1997, pp. 22-24, 26-30.

performance, some of the information will be at least six weeks old.

Third, accounting systems capture limited characteristics about accounting transactions (e.g., date, account, and amount in dollars). Not surprisingly, information customers want many different types of information about an organization. Interest in capturing multidimensional data is frequently limited and subordinated to recording financial transaction data.

Fourth, the system stores duplicate data in a highly summarized form (accounts), limiting alternative uses. Much of what is contained in the accounting system is generated by other sources, summarized, and reconstituted to conform with GAAP and the architecture supporting a general ledger chart of accounts. This format for information makes activity-based costing, compliance with international accounting standards, preparation of other non-GAAP financial reports, and reports providing other perspectives on business activities difficult to achieve.

Finally, the traditional accounting system architecture makes controlling business and information process risks defensive and expensive. The traditional system of internal controls, based largely on independent checks and separation of duties, focuses on providing the checks and balances to secure corporate assets and ensure compliance with management's directives. Meanwhile, controls for errors and irregularities are embedded in human information processing. Technology has been used largely to automate these very traditional safeguards that may be wholly inadequate for today's business environment.

During the five centuries since Pacioli we have acquired new information customers who want new services that provide them with new information (measurements), improved workflows (not just information processes), and better, less costly controls. Unfortunately, such fundamental changes in requirements do not seem to be reflected in automated accounting systems to date. Certainly the cost of accounting has been reduced, and the timeliness of financial and other reporting has been improved. But there is no change in the basic accounting data that are captured, how they are organized, or the way the data are presented to information customers. IT has benefited accounting and BIS primarily by automating 500-year-old pencil-and-paper systems instead of employing the unlimited potential of modern computer technology.

THE RISE OF THE VIEW-DRIVEN SYSTEMS ENVIRONMENT

There are multiple perspectives on business events, but no one system is able to satisfy the needs of all information users. A simple example illustrates different views of a business event. Assume that during December a company sells a machine to a customer for $300,000. In January of the following year, the purchaser is billed $320,000 after adjustments for features added during installation. Several accounting entries are made to the financial system, but others within the organization have different information requirements concerning the transaction:

- Manufacturing wants to know if the production and delivery schedules were met and the customer is satisfied.
- Marketing wants to know when the product was sold for the purpose of calculating commission payments to sales personnel.
- The corporate office wants to know when the cash was received and available for investment.

As a result of the inability of the accounting system to satisfy a diverse set of information requirements, functional customers demanded, and received, software applications to provide for their specific information needs. Some examples include production systems, personnel systems, sales and marketing systems, and executive information systems. But the problems inherent to the accounting system also are present in these systems because they capture and store information in limited dimensions and are not easily integrated with each other. Over time, the structure of business information systems has come to mirror the organization structures they serve.

This view-driven approach to business information systems has impeded the progress of businesses along a number of dimensions. First, it is a barrier to business process reengineering (BPR) efforts. BPR is directed at improving workflows and removing functional divisions. View-driven systems work counter to this effort. Companies that want to implement activity-based costing and management programs will encounter similar obstacles because of the limitations of accounting and other systems to provide information consistent with the perspectives on the organization embodied in these efforts. Information must be collected from a variety of sources to provide a complete picture of events and performance. Systems integration also is very difficult because managers want to see reports tailored to their view, but they cannot be provided from one system. Finally, the view-driven perspective is perpetuated by functional business education producing students lacking a broad business perspective.

The view-driven business information systems environment is in need of fundamental change if business information systems are to complement efforts to improve workflows and organizational performance. Two critical questions must be answered about the future of BIS:

- Can we provide better information, both financial and nonfinancial, for decision makers?
- Can we help organizations improve the way they work while also reducing their business, information, and process risks?

One alternative is to have BIS mirror the business process instead of the functional organization structure. The view-driven approach to BIS has produced function-specific applications programs, duplicate databases, and systems that do not communicate with each other. Instead of having enterprise-wide information customers, we have functional customers. Business processes are fragmented and ineffective. Unnecessary and burdensome organization structures arise because administrative structures are built around each system to input, maintain, and report the data. Despite all our systems development efforts, management still complains of inadequate and inflexible measurements. This situation largely has come about because IT developed faster than the ability of managers to adapt organizations and business processes. IT is an enabler of change, but people have not adjusted as quickly as technology permitted.

RETHINKING BUSINESS INFORMATION SYSTEMS

Unless we rethink our approach to BIS, we only will make marginal improvements to what we have. In order to make BIS support business processes, we need to have one set of business data that is able to satisfy all information customers, which requires a two-part prescription. The first half of the prescription is to adopt a different view of organizations and the information systems environment than the functional perspective. Second, we need a new IT application architecture that will support this viewpoint.

Common to both parts of the prescription is a need to take a different perspective on how to capture useful information and make it available for the majority of decision makers. Accounting information is characteristic of what is known as a "value" approach to providing information. This view assumes that the needs of information customers are well known and specified—that accounting (and other) information providers can furnish information that is immediately useful for input to decision models. Accountants accumulate data, transform data into information recorded in the general ledger, and give it to information customers for their use. In essence, value proponents say, "Let me give you summarized information about economic events, to which weights and values are already attached (based on accounting and other rules and conventions), and use this to make your decisions."

An alternative approach is based on organizing data and IT applications around business events. The event-driven approach assumes that the purpose of accounting (and other) information systems is to provide information about economic events that is useful in a variety of decision contexts. Events proponents say, "Let's collect raw business data that can be used by a variety of information customers, each with its own set of values and weights to assign to the data." It is the events view that provides an avenue to the next generation of business information systems.

BUSINESS PROCESSES, EVENTS, AND *REAL*

The need to rethink the organization of business enterprises around business

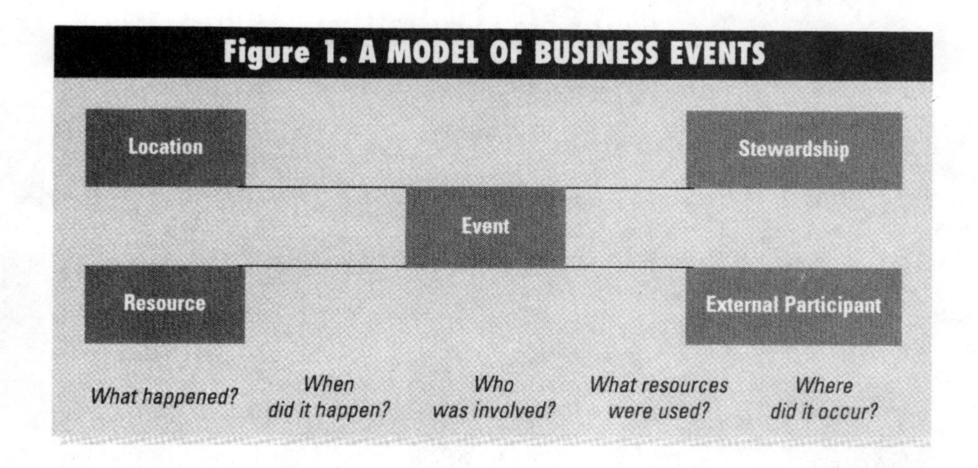
Figure 1. A MODEL OF BUSINESS EVENTS

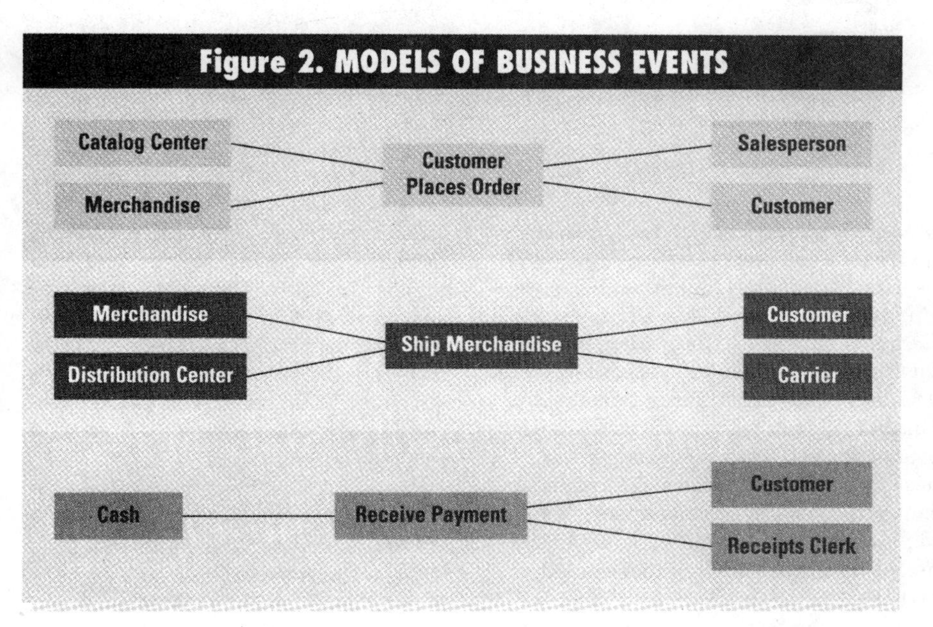
Figure 2. MODELS OF BUSINESS EVENTS

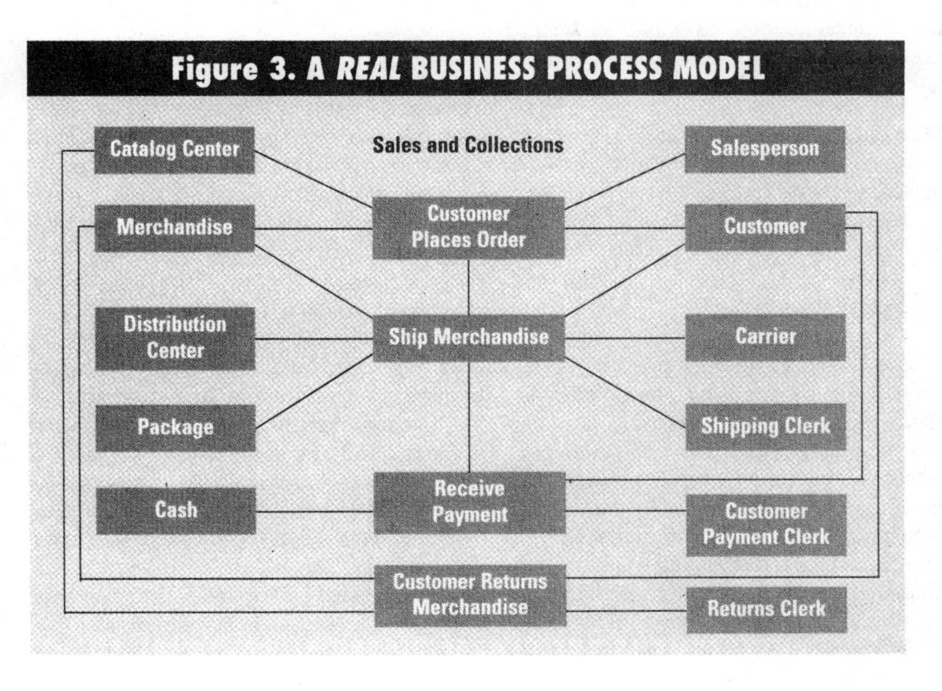
Figure 3. A *REAL* BUSINESS PROCESS MODEL

Figure 4. CURRENT INFORMATION SYSTEMS ENVIRONMENT

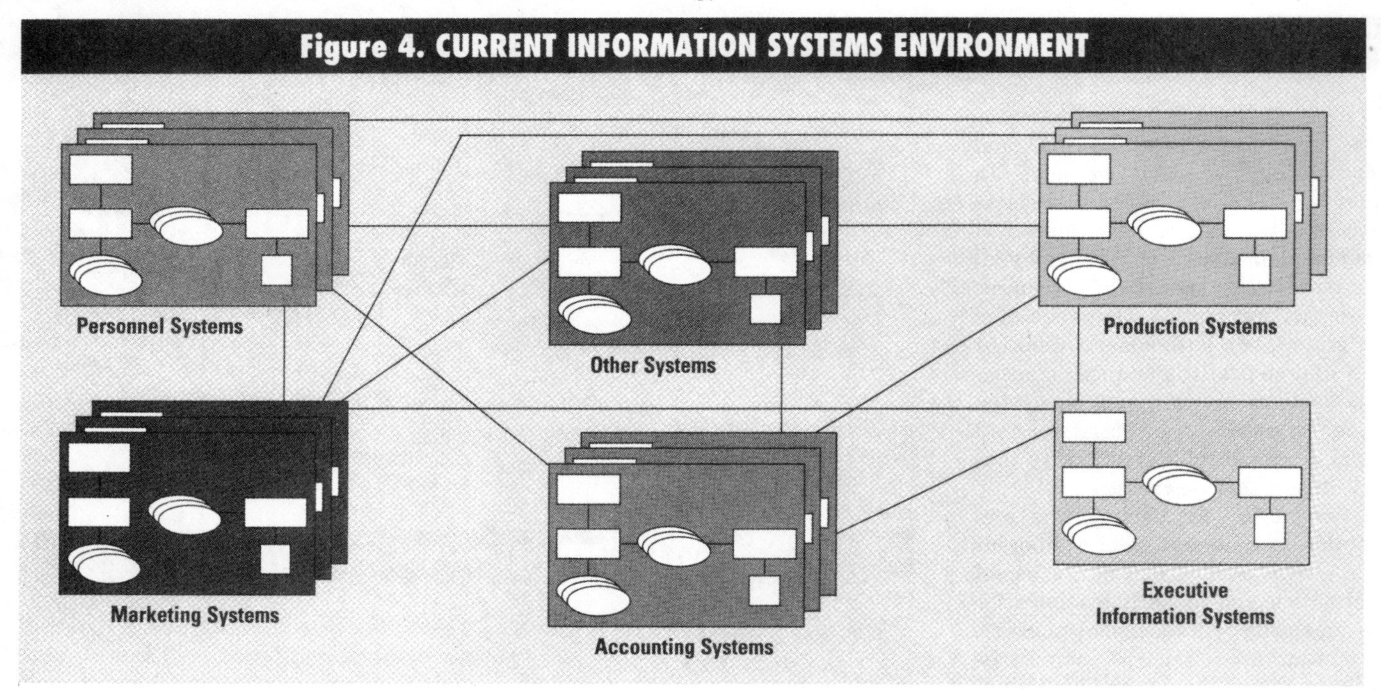

processes is well documented in books and articles on business process reengineering. Michael Hammer and James Champy in their best-selling book, *Reengineering the Corporation*, define business processes as collections of activities that take inputs and create outputs valued by a customer. Business events, the activities that compose business processes, are strategically significant activities that management wants to plan, control, or evaluate. Most businesses have what might be considered a rather limited number of business processes, sometimes fewer than 10 but rarely dozens. Some examples of business processes and associated events follow.

- Acquisition and payment (request a good, place an order, inspect, pay);
- Conversion (build, grow, educate, assemble, etc.);
- Sales and collection (receive an order, select a good, ..., deliver, receive payment).

The concepts of business processes and business events, combined with a modeling technique to provide a common language and representation of business processes, can provide the basis for evaluating workflows and the information system simultaneously. One such process modeling approach is REAL (resources, events, agents, and locations) Business Process Modeling. This approach is based on McCarthy (1982)[1] and was developed further by Denna, Cherrington, Andros, and Hollander (1993)[2]; Denna, Perry, and Jasperson (1995)[3]; and Hollander, Denna, and Cherrington (1996)[4]. REAL modeling considers that there are five questions that must be answered concerning any business event to capture relevant information:

- What happened?
- When did it happen?
- Who was involved?
- What resources were used?
- Where did the event occur?

In an effort to answer these five questions, REAL modeling focuses on identifying four modeling objectives: resources, events, agents, and locations. An example of a REAL model of business events appears in Figure 1. Figure 2 illustrates several models of related business events in the sales and collection process. Finally, Figure 3 shows how these models may be combined to create a REAL business process model of the entire sales and collection process. The amount of data collected for each box in the diagram will vary depending on the needs of information customers throughout the organization.

Besides providing a common language and representation of business processes, the REAL modeling system has several other advantages. This approach assumes all business solution components (those elements that must be incorporated into the solution to ensure its success) are important. The REAL models of business processes serve as a means of integrating the business solution components. The components include company strategy, stewardships and structure of the organization, performance measurements, and the information technology. The model is useful for aligning the solution components with the culture of the organization. Finally, the modeling system is flexible and provides for learning and adaptation in dynamic business environments; for example, changing information requirements is easy to accomplish as the business, environment, and management change.

A NEW IT APPLICATION ARCHITECTURE

Architecture refers to how data are organized and the nature of information processing. Historically, in accounting information systems, the application architecture was designed simply to automate the double-entry system and special journals to produce financial statements. As we explained earlier, other BIS evolved to satisfy the special requirements of functional management, thereby producing the fragmented, view-driven situation in which we currently find ourselves. In order to obtain a complete picture of organizational performance, decision makers

Table 1. AN EVENT-DRIVEN DATA REPOSITORY — SALES AND COLLECTION PROCESS

CATALOG-CENTER(Center#, Name, Address, Telephone, ...
MERCHANDISE(Item#, Item-Description, Color, Size, ..., Current-Cost, Current-Price, ..., QOH, ...
CUSTOMER-PLACES-ORDER(Order#, Time, [Center#], [SP#], [Customer#], [Shipment#], Ship-to-Instructions, Confirmation#, Tax, ...
SALESPERSON(Salesperson-ID, Name, Address, ..., Commission-Rate, Marital-Status, ...
CUSTOMER(Customer#, Name, Address, Phone, ...
SHIP-MERCHANDISE(Shipment#, Time, [Customer#], [Packer#], [Carrier#], [Ship-Clerk#], [Dist-Ctr#], [Pmt-Receipt#],
CARRIER(Carrier#, Name, Address, Rate, Performance-Score, ...
SHIPPING-CLERK(Ship-Clerk#, ...
DISTRIBUTION-CENTER(Dist-Ctr#, Name, Address, ...
PACKAGE(Package#, Weight, [Shipment#], Shipping-Cost
CASH(Acct#, Description, Balance, ...
RECEIVE-PAYMENT(Pmt-Receipt#, Time, [Customer#], [Cust-Pmt-Clrk#], [Acct#], Amount, ...
CUSTOMER-PAYMENT-CLERK(Cust-Pmt-Clerk#, ...
RETURN-MERCHANDISE(Return#, [Customer#], [Returns-Clrk#], [Center#], Time, ...
MERCHANDISE-ORDER([Item#],[Order#], Qty-Ordered, Order-Price, Order-Cost, ...
MERCHANDISE-SHIP([Item#], [Shipment#], Qty-Shipped, ...
MERCHANDISE-RETURN([Item#], [Return#], Qty-Returned, ...

must visit several sources, which often results in conflicting and confusing information. Figure 4 illustrates the current information systems environment.

We cannot be content to use IT to automate old thinking, however. The value of IT is in its ability to enable new thinking about how to provide useful information. REAL business process models provide a basis for defining a new type of business information system that is not limited by any one "view" of events in a business. An example of information collected in connection with the sales and collection business process applying events concepts appears in Table 1. Each of the capitalized items represents a table in a database followed by a series of fields capturing several important characteristics about the item of interest. The events approach to collecting event data provides for all information users and is done consistent with business processes—those individuals in the best position to collect data are responsible for doing so. The data in Table 1 can be used to compute accounts receivable and withdrawals from inventory, provide information for payroll, and produce a number of reports for sales and marketing as well as reports used by other functions in an organization. This approach can be applied to any business process, for example, operating a farm, building cars, selling services, or providing education. An event-driven information system architecture, based on the capture of event data in Table 1, is illustrated in Figure 5.

WHY COULDN'T WE DO THIS BEFORE?

The idea of an information system capturing detailed data about a variety of business events and providing an array of both financial and nonfinancial measures can be traced to the earliest days of managerial accounting in the 19th Century. The basic concepts behind REAL process modeling appeared in 1982. But the technology to enable implementation of an event-driven system was developed later in the form of database software. For many small to medium-sized businesses, almost any database software product can be used to build an event-driven system. But when data sets become very large—hundreds of millions of records or more—it becomes very time-consuming, if not impossible, to query the database.

Recently, high-performance data engines have overcome this obstacle. One such product is Geneva V/T™. This software was developed by Price Waterhouse and is designed for implementing event-based business applications with high-volume data requirements. This technology allows a wide array of information customers to develop a variety of views of a common set of business data.

WHAT ARE THE BENEFITS OF EVENT-DRIVEN SYSTEMS?

There are several significant benefits to adopting the REAL view of organizations and implementing event-driven business technology solutions. To begin with, data storage cost is lower because data are stored only once. Because data are not stored in multiple locations, data inconsistencies, a potential source of problems, also are avoided. Maintenance activities (adding, deleting, and updating records) are carried out more efficiently. Avoiding data redundancy also ensures that all applications use the same data structure.

Figure 5. EVENT-DRIVEN IT APPLICATION ARCHITECTURE

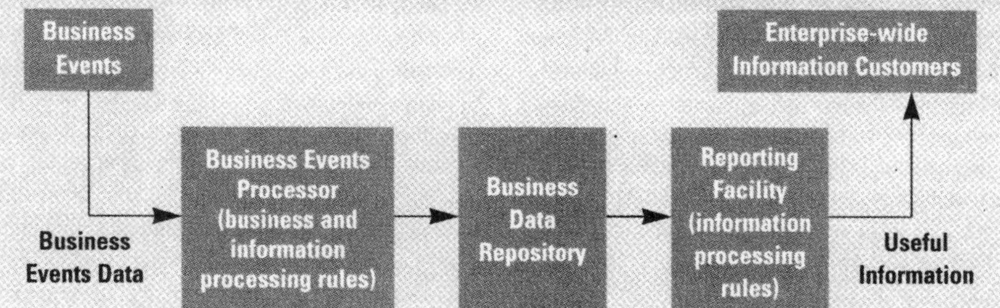

Organization structures based on business processes, instead of functional discipline, become readily apparent. The previous example of the functional organizations involved in the sales and collection process illustrates the problems associated with present organization structures—they do not parallel business processes. The REAL diagram of the sales and collection process in Figure 3 provides the basis for a new type of organization where business processes and information processes work in tandem.

The BIS is able to provide useful information for all customers—no longer is it view driven. Ad hoc query capabilities are almost unlimited because all information is built from underlying event data. The data elements can be mixed and matched to provide for any particular view of business events and to conduct a wide range of forecasting and planning activities. Cross-functional analysis is facilitated, modifying reports is simplified, and multiple users can access the database simultaneously.

Controls are enhanced. Consider a series of "event owners" (those responsible for entering business event data) in a business process. Management is able to assign responsibility for data entry functions to a person or group closest to the activity. Each event owner is responsible for entering certain information that subsequently will be used by many others during the course of the business process. Data are entered only once and in "read only" format—others interested in the data can use but not change the data. Controls over data are embedded in the tables as they are created, eliminating the need to program controls into every application. Controls are shifted away from applications to data entry.

The audit trail is shortened considerably because amounts appearing on a financial report are built directly from the underlying event data. There no longer is a need to search for information on events that resulted in a reported amount. In addition, many mundane, clerical activities to "tick-and-tie" amounts recorded on hard copy forms and documents in the audit function are no longer necessary.

A final advantage is the opportunity to develop a clear sense of business strategy. Information is collected for two primary purposes: legal or regulatory requirements and management decision making. The information requirements to satisfy the second purpose are far more difficult to satisfy than for the first purpose. Decisions made by managers should be consistent with strategy. Therefore, information collected should be considered in light of how it can be used to support strategic objectives.

OBSTACLES TO EVENT-DRIVEN SYSTEMS

There are several obstacles to implementing event-driven systems. Sometimes, the move toward an event-driven architecture requires new investment in hardware, software, and people to administer the system. For an event-driven system, where all information is controlled centrally, continuous operation of the system is important. If the system fails, data entry to the system stops for everyone. In addition, data entered incorrectly affect all users of those data. It is likely that disputes will need to be resolved over ownership of data. In addition, there may be incentives for event owners to expand data to enhance their positions.

Another obstacle is accountants' distrust of any system other than double entry. The substance of objections in this area is more perceived than real. There is a great deal of comfort attached to the system that has been in use for more than 500 years, but advances in IT now permit us to move beyond old thinking.

The most significant remaining obstacle to realizing the benefits of IT is the functional culture of business organizations. Consider how the present culture impacts the work and information flows in the sales and collection process. It is not unusual for at least four functional organizations to be involved in this one process: Sales to accept orders, Administration to determine credit terms, Logistics to handle delivery, and Finance to accept payment. Each of these groups will have its own information system and support structure. The involvement of separate groups, working for different administrative structures with their own agendas, contributes to duplication of information-gathering activities, communications problems, errors, and inevitable delays. This situation is detrimental to both internal and external customers. Contrast this culture with an alternative one based on business processes where all of these activities are combined in a "Sales and Collections Department" with a single administrative structure and responsibility for all information relating to this process. The result is a seamless process emphasizing customer service.

IMPACTS ON ACCOUNTING PRACTICE AND EDUCATION

Adapting to event-driven technology will be difficult for many accounting practitioners. The transition is filled with risks and rewards. Abandoning accounting conventions that have existed for centuries will be hard for some. Many of the mundane aspects of accounting largely disappear: data entry, account analysis, reconciliations, and some auditing procedures. In an event-driven system, data entry for accountants is limited to items that uniquely concern accountants. Account analysis as we know it no longer exists because there are no accounts to analyze. There are no reconciliations because information is entered only once into the system leaving nothing to reconcile to. The idea of period closings of financial systems has no meaning, and the process of preparing adjusting and accrual entries disappears because the database always is current.

On the other hand, the controller can evolve into the "Chief Business Information Officer." Event-driven business systems present an opportunity for the organization to have a single information source. Accountants are trained to analyze and report information and are well positioned to assume primary responsibility for information management. But accountants will need to adopt a broad view of the organization and information customer requirements to gain responsibility for administration of the database. Management will need help mixing, matching, and modeling the mass of data in an event-driven system to help reach the company's goals. Accountants must acquire a deep understanding of the business to prepare their own reports. The challenge to accounting professionals is to assist management in making the political and organizational changes necessary to implement 21st Century IT to support 21st Century organizations.

What Is Geneva V/T?

Geneva V/T™ is a high-performance data engine designed to handle large data sets (i.e., hundreds of millions of records) on mainframe computers. Geneva V/T™ is composed of a report writer and a transaction processor to capture, edit, and post data. The report writer, Geneva V/T™ ViewBuilder, is a unique tool that permits a user to create "views" of an organization's data and produce output in an efficient manner and in a variety of formats including hard copy, tape, fiche, online, and downloadable files compatible with Excel and Lotus spreadsheets.

Geneva V/T™ uses a proprietary search algorithm with lookup rates of 500,000 per CPU second (vs. 1,500-30,000 for conventional techniques) and extended memory to perform high-speed lookups and data joins. Geneva V/T™ is able to reduce input/output time by eliminating redundant retrieval of data and thereby reduce the cost of purchased processor time. Multiple user requests for data are consolidated, and Geneva V/T™ performs all processing in one pass of the data versus multiple passes with traditional software.

CAN BUSINESS AFFORD NOT TO ADOPT THIS APPROACH?

The bottom line for organizations that adopt event-driven systems and succeed in making the organizational changes necessary to realize their potential is higher profits. This goal is achieved through a combination of lower costs and ready access to information that was not previously available. Business processes are more efficient, and decision makers are able to make better decisions because they are likely to know more about the business from being able to easily combine previously separated information sources. Information is a source of competitive advantage as are the systems that provide the information.

The transition to event-driven technology already is under way. Corporations such as Sears Roebuck, Alcoa, IBM, and others are using event-based systems concepts. In addition, governmental organizations such as the U.S. Department of Health and Human Services, the state of Alaska, and the Oregon Department of Transportation are on this path. A variety of consulting firms including Price Waterhouse LLP, through its Geneva V/T™ product, The Hunter Group, and others are supporting development of these concepts and assisting clients in the transition to event-driven systems. Also, business solution software companies such as SAP, one of the most popular business information system products for major corporations, standardize information systems and data structures across an organization and capture the granular details that are part of transaction processing consistent with events concepts. It and similar BIS products, when coupled with high-performance data engines like Geneva V/T™, provide a set of powerful tools for reporting on current and longitudinal performance of business processes.

Figure 5 illustrates the clear choice of options in developing BIS. On one hand, we can continue with the present view-driven systems environment, or we can choose another path to a single information database that is capable of satisfying all of our information customers and that will support efforts of managers to reengineer the workplace successfully. The challenges to practitioners are to adapt to modern technology, facilitate its implementation, and make the organizational changes necessary to promote the future success of business enterprises.

Kenton B. Walker is associate professor of accounting, University of Wyoming, Laramie, Wyo. He is an IMA Member-at-Large.
Eric L. Denna is associate professor of accounting, Marriott School of Management, Brigham Young University, Provo, Utah.

[1]William E. McCarthy, "The REAL Accounting Model: A Generalized Framework for Accounting Systems in a Shared Data Environment," *The Accounting Review*, July 1992, pp. 554-578.
[2]Eric L. Denna, J. Owen Cherrington, David P. Andros, and Anita Sawyer Hollander, *Event-Driven Business Solutions: Today's Revolution in Business and Information Technology*, Irwin Business One, Burr Ridge, Ill., 1993.
[3]Eric L. Denna, Lee Tom Perry, and Sean Jasperson, "Reengineering and REAL Process Modeling," *Business Process Change: Reengineering Concepts, Methods and Technologies*, Varun Grover and Bill Kettinger, eds., Idea Group Publishing, Harrisburg, Pa., 1995.
[4]Anita Sawyer Hollander, Eric L. Denna, and J. Owen Cherrington, *Accounting, Information Technology, and Business Solutions*, Richard D. Irwin, Burr Ridge, Ill., 1996.

Does Your Accounting Software Pass the Year 2000 Compliance Test?

Evaluating your accounting software for Year 2000 compliance is a critical first step in assuring that January 1, 2000, will not be a disaster for your business.

BY WILLIAM H. MILLS

What year follows 1999? Of course you know, but there is a chance that your computer doesn't. Computers typically store year dates as two-digit fields. The year 1998 is 98, and the year 1999 is 99. That makes the year 2000 a confusing 00, and most computers think 00 means 1900.

All kinds of hardware and software are affected by the Year 2000 problem, but time-sensitive applications are especially vulnerable. That's why accounting and financial professionals are so concerned about the issue. If your word processing software stamps the wrong date on your document, it might be nothing more than inconvenient. However, if your accounting software uses the wrong date for invoices, payment notices, and depreciation schedules, the consequences can be staggering.

Many people are adopting a wait-and-see attitude, but experts agree that those who wait won't like what they see. The problem is real, it is serious, and time is running out. The federal government has efforts under way to solve the problem in its systems. According to one department head, "We started our conversion in 1987. I think we started early enough, but I'm still not sure." The estimated cost to companies in the United States alone will be at least $300 billion.

If you're like most corporations, you're only just getting started with your Year 2000 implementation. You still have time to complete the task, but don't delay. This is one project with a deadline that absolutely can't be moved!

HIDING PLACES FOR YEAR 2000 PROBLEMS

In order to locate problems in your computer system, you must first know where to look. Here are nine places where your Year 2000 problems can lurk.

Mini/mainframes. If you have an older minicomputer or mainframe, there's a good chance your system has a Year 2000 problem. These systems were developed many years ago and were designed with the space-saving, two-digit date field. Because you might be facing a significant upgrade or replacement, you should analyze your system right away.

PC hardware. Many PC systems have a BIOS (basic input/output system) problem that causes the internal clock to reset to 1980 when the 00 threshold is reached. In some cases, hardware is still shipping with this problem. If you have stand-alone or networked PCs, you should check every system for BIOS errors.

COBOL, FORTRAN, RPG3, or similar software. These older languages were not designed for Year 2000 certification and can be difficult to update. You may not be able to find programmers to help at a reasonable cost because many are now charging top dollar for Year 2000 updates.

Proprietary software. Perhaps you have a product that was created years ago exclusively for your company. A Year 2000 upgrade probably is not available, and it might be time to move to packaged software.

No source code. Regardless of the language in which your system is written, you will need access to the source code (original programming files) in order to make modifications. If your system has been in place for some years, the source code may be misplaced or unavailable. That will make changing your existing system difficult.

Data entry screens. Many input screens do not have the space or capacity to add digits to clarify the year. Also, you might not want to add digits because it slows data entry considerably. The industry standard solution is to interpret all two-digit dates higher than 50 as 20th Century years and all lower than 50 as 21st Century years. If your system is more than a few years old, it probably does not handle two-digit input properly. (Note that payroll systems must be updated to four-digit entry because birth dates prior to 1950 are still quite common.)

Output reports. Sort order of reports that include years after 1999 is likely to be flawed because 00 is far earlier than 97 if your computer has a Year 2000 problem. As a result, you might miss key comparison data in a year-by-year listing.

Human errors. Many data entry personnel routinely have used the years 00 or 99 as dummy fields so that test data or nonconforming data can be isolated from the rest of a report. As soon as you create a report with an actual 00 or 99 date, your data integrity is lost and might have to be recovered manually (if it can be recovered at all).

Business forms. As the Millennium approaches, all preprinted forms that include the year dates 19 will have to be replaced, overprinted, or crossed out manually.

APPROACHING THE YEAR 2000 PROBLEM AT YOUR COMPANY

As the financial manager at your company, you have an obligation to take the lead in resolving your Year 2000 issues. Although this is a "computer problem," which means that your MIS department will be responsible for updates and implementations, it is your company's financial systems that will be affected most directly by the problem. To find the best solution at the lowest price, you'll need to step up to the lead role.

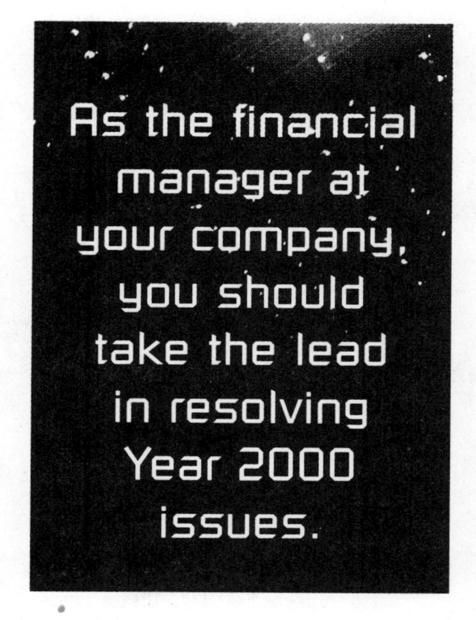

Although the finance department will take the lead role, it's important to communicate with key managers so that you gain cooperation within your organization. Moving up to a Year 2000 certified solution might require time and effort from people not in your department. Participation across functional groups will help you implement the best possible solution.

MIS department. These are the people who will manage the technical end of your update, upgrade, or new installation. They can help manage the testing process and identify technical issues that may not be related to finance.

System users and managers. System users are the ones who will have to shoulder much of the extra effort needed for thorough testing and implementation. They also are the people who will have to handle all of the exception processing if your system is not certified by the Millennium. Be sure to help them understand how their efforts now will save headaches later.

System customers. Customers can be found throughout the organization, in every department and at any level. These people rely on the reports and summaries generated by the system. They may not understand the fundamentals of accounting, but they know what they want the system to deliver. Including them in the process will help identify issues and support the testing and implementation effort.

Corporate management. These are the people who must give final approval to any funding for testing or new software. This group dislikes surprises, so it's best to provide detailed, accurate information about the Year 2000 problem as soon as possible.

TEST PROGRAM METHODOLOGY

Four steps outline a basic testing program for your accounting software:

1. Develop test data,
2. Test 1999 going forward,
3. Test 2000 going backward,
4. Year 2000 operation.

Before you can test your system, you will have to create a data set to use in the testing. Use transactions that represent the range of data normally used. Look ahead a few years, and make some educated guesses as to the kinds of transactions you'll be processing at that time.

For a starting point, set aside a test area on your network to house duplicate data. This procedure creates the least interruption to day-to-day business. Some software allows you to create a separate fictitious company, which is a good way to segregate the data. Document all procedures with a schedule for completing each task.

Step 1: Certified test data

The test data shown here are for illustration purposes. The data you use for testing should be different. The development of these test data should be documented, and the user department manager or accounting manager should sign each test data entry form certifying that the data represent the range of values to be tested.

All notes and working papers should be retained for five years or more. Auditors and managers might need them in the future to verify the scope of testing completed.

Step 2: Year 2000 dates entered in 1999

Transactions entered on a test date in this century include references to the next century. Set all dates (server, workstation, and accounting application dates) to your test date in 1999 (for example, 6/15/99).

Sample test data:

- Enter sales order on 6/15/99 with one line item required on 6/15/99 and another item required on 6/15/00.
- Enter invoice on 6/15/99 with payment terms of 12 months. (Due date 6/14/00.)
- Enter process manual and AP check for 12/31/99.

Sample results expected:

- Fields in accounting database entered with year 00 represented in date format for year 2000.
- Picking tickets print with correct required dates.
- Report sort by requirement date shows year 00 records ahead of 99.
- AR aging report shows items entered with due date of 6/14/00 as current.
- Manual and AP check entered for 12/31/99 should print for year 1999.

Step 3: 1999 dates entered in 2000

Transactions entered on the test date in this century include references to the next century. Set all dates (server, workstation, and accounting application dates) to your test date in 2000 (for example, 1/15/00).

Sample test data:

- Fields in accounting database entered with year 99 represented in date format for year 1999.
- General ledger journal entry for 6/15/99 period entered on 1/15/00.
- Vendor's invoice arrives late. Transaction entered on 1/15/00 for expense effective date of 6/15/99.

Sample results expected:

- General ledger journal entries for 6/15/99 show in period for 1999 date.
- AP vendor invoice (or voucher) posts to period for 1999 date.

Step 4: Year 2000 date operation sample tests

- Set all system clocks to 2/29/00 to verify that transactions can be entered for the leap day.
- Are two-digit years of 00 allowed (for faster data entry)?
- Are dates entered between 00 and 50 shown in accounting database as year 20nn?
- Are dates entered between 51 and 99 shown in accounting database as year 19nn?
- Birth dates for employees can be entered as 19nn and 20nn.
- All aging reports for AR, discounts, and payables handle combinations of 1999 and 2000 dates.
- User privileges (access to accounting menus, screens) work for dates in 2000.

Remember your test data will be different from the data shown here. Develop and certify your test data based on your normal transaction ranges. Be sure to document all errors. (See Figure 1.)

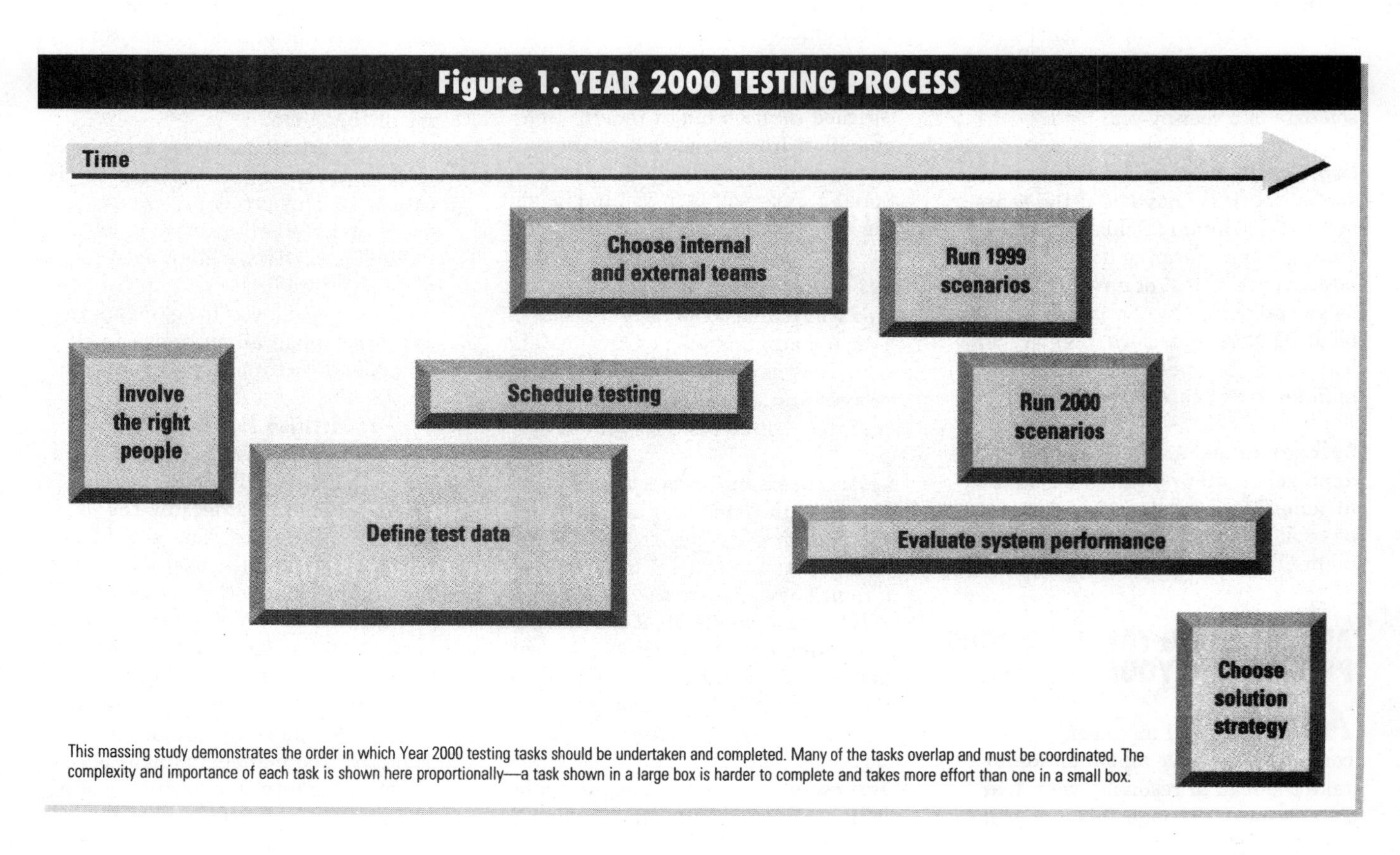

This massing study demonstrates the order in which Year 2000 testing tasks should be undertaken and completed. Many of the tasks overlap and must be coordinated. The complexity and importance of each task is shown here proportionally—a task shown in a large box is harder to complete and takes more effort than one in a small box.

WHAT IF YOU FIND PROBLEMS?

Let's assume your systems check reveals some problems with your current accounting software. Now you'll need to review your options and choose a direction for your company. You'll want to base your decision on the costs and benefits associated with either upgrading your existing system or replacing it with a new system. (See Figure 2.)

Updating means adding Year 2000 capabilities to your current system (usually through the help of a programmer/consultant). This option most likely will be pursued by users with older proprietary systems because there's no other way to get to Year 2000 certification. Before you update your system, however, compare the true cost of implementing a new system. You may find that moving up to current technology is a better strategy than trying to bring your old system forward.

Upgrading means staying with your current software supplier. You move up to a newer release of the same product. Naturally, your supplier will need to offer a Year 2000 certified upgrade to make this option viable. People often assume that upgrading is less costly than system replacement, but that's not always the case. You'll have to do some pricing homework to find out.

Figure 2. SOLUTION BENEFIT COMPARISON

	Update	Upgrade	Replace
Cost-effective	Maybe	Maybe	Maybe
New technology	No	Maybe	Yes
Prepares for future	No	Maybe	Yes
Can be capitalized	No	Yes	Yes
Provides choice	No	Maybe	Yes
Facilitates growth	Maybe	Yes	Yes
Minimum disruption	Maybe	Maybe	No

Replacing your system means implementing entirely new software from a new supplier. Maybe you already are considering this move. The Year 2000 is a good reason to stop waiting and start moving forward. Remember that according to Financial Accounting Standards Board rules, updating or fixing your current system must be expensed, while new system implementation can be capitalized.

Update your system if: *The software is relatively new.* You may have a proprietary system that's fairly new and that has not been fully capitalized. The cost of updating may be far less than the cost of a new system.

The system is working efficiently. Although it is unusual for older proprietary systems to function as efficiently as new technology, some actually are quite good. To evaluate and compare your system's efficiency, take a look at an up-to-date package currently on the market.

The system creator is on staff. Perhaps your system was built in-house, is running well, and the system builders are still available. They might be able to update the system cost effectively. Insist on a project specification and schedule. Be sure to weigh the cost of projects that won't be completed while the Year 2000 is added to your current software.

Upgrade your system if: *The upgrade is Year 2000 certified.* There's no point in upgrading unless the new product is tested for the Millennium. Don't accept promises of future deliveries; you need to make a move now. Ask questions about your supplier's testing and certification procedures.

Reports are what you need. If your system is delivering the kind of information you need, when you need it, you have good reason simply to upgrade to a new release of the same product.

Maintenance is reasonable. Older systems sometimes require so much tweaking and maintenance that you can't cost justify their existence, even if their output is worthwhile. If your maintenance expenses are high or growing, you may not want to upgrade.

The system is easy for your users. A system that's easy to use is a significant plus. Provided the upgrade has similar structure, look, and feel, you could save on training costs by sticking with your current system provider.

It offers an easy upgrade path. It's worth upgrading only if the product gives you an ongoing path for the future. Your software company should have a demonstrated history of new releases and a transition strategy that makes upgrading as easy as possible. Ask about data conversion tools.

The manufacturer is sound. Obviously, you want to purchase from a reliable software manufacturer that has a large installed base and a commitment to future product development.

Replace your system if: *You need new capabilities.* Stepping up to a new system takes longer than the typical upgrade, but it's a golden opportunity to retool for growth, better data management, and for future technology. The Year 2000 has proved to be a catalyst for many financial managers who had been planning to move up to a better system.

Your company plans to grow. If growth figures into your plans, there's a good chance you may outgrow your existing system anyway. Perhaps you can solve your Year 2000 issues while you invest in future expansion.

You plan to add new staff. If you're already planning to add staff in the finance department, your training costs for a new system will be no different than for an upgrade to the old system.

You need a new network or hardware. If you're making other infrastructure changes, a new accounting system can integrate easily into the process.

You face competitive challenges. Your decisions are only as good as the information used to make them. If your business faces competition, you need the best information possible. A new system can provide reports, data snapshots, and predictive indicators that can help you pull ahead in the marketplace.

Your technology is old. It's tough to breathe life into an old system. Even if you can update it for the Year 2000, you may be operating on borrowed time. If you already are thinking about a new, more capable system, don't spend on fixing what you have on hand. Invest in new software and move ahead.

There are a number of capabilities you should expect in a good accounting package. Make sure the new system can pass Year 2000 certification. The software should check clocks on the network and notify you of errors. It needs to integrate with your other applications and be easy to use. Almost every company has its own specific accounting needs, so look for modifiable source code to make sure you can make any changes. The report generator should allow you to produce most of the reports you need without extra programming. Make sure your software uses database fields to hold information so changes can be accommodated easily.

No matter how complete your accounting system, sooner or later you will want to transfer information to or from "foreign" programs. Many businesses use spreadsheets and databases for extensive sales analysis. Be certain your software uses formats that are easy to export and import. Finally, make sure your software is Internet enabled. Look for e-mail fields in customer and vendor information files so you can begin sending invoices, notifications, and confirmations electronically.

HOW COULD THIS HAVE HAPPENED?

Some software users are surprised to learn that Year 2000 updates are not an automatic part of hardware and software systems. "Why wasn't this solved years ago?" they wonder. The fact is, if computer manufacturers had designed Year 2000 capabilities, they never would have gotten off the ground. When computers first became available, memory was so expensive that all kinds of data shortcuts were used. The two-digit field is one of those shortcuts.

Once the applications were up and running, compatibility became an issue. It was tough for one vendor to make a change unless everyone else followed suit. As a result, manufacturers continued to use the two-digit date field. And customers definitely were not pressing for Year 2000 solutions. Remember how far away the Millennium seemed back in 1979? Also, there was the naïve assumption that the fix could be effected with just a few lines of code or with a little add-on program.

Responsible manufacturers now are providing upgrades for their customers that solve the problem. Implementation can be expensive, so most manufacturers provide more than just a Year 2000 upgrade. They include additional product features, new ease-of-use capabilities, or Internet capability as part of the Year 2000 upgrade. That way customers can cost justify a move forward.

William H. Mills is president and chief operating officer at SBT Accounting Systems. Prior to joining SBT, Mr. Mills was founder, president and CEO of PSI Systems, a leading accounting software consulting business in Atlanta, Ga. Mr. Mills can be reached at (415) 444-9900.

YEAR 2000 PROBLEM:

Is Your Company Exposed?

BY VITO C. PERAINO, ESQ.

Potential liability costs of the Millennium bug could surpass a predicted $300 billion-plus cost of fixing it.

Living in the bowels of many business computer systems is a bug that will come alive on January 1, 2000, and that may render many business computers useless. Known as the Year 2000 problem, this glitch is estimated to affect the majority of computer systems that are operating in the United States and, indeed, the world. Unless fixed, the Year 2000 problem will result in massive liability to industry and significant bottom-line impact to business.

The Year 2000 problem arises because of the logic computers use to read dates. In the early days of data processing, memory space was at a premium. It was limited, and it was expensive. To save space, programmers used only two fields to capture data relating to dates. So, for example, the year 1997 was represented by the numbers "97." The computer assumes that the first two digits are "19." In the Year 2000, computers will continue to read the last two digits "00" while still assuming that the first two digits are "19." Therefore, the computer incorrectly interprets the Year 2000 as the year 1900. This simple problem will cause significant chaos and will cost billions to fix. The chaos arises because the incorrect date field corrupts all date sensitive calculations. For a business this defect could undermine billing operations, interest calculations, inventory accounting, receivable tracking, debt instruments, and a host of other time sensitive calculations.

The problem should not be underestimated from a cost perspective, either. The Gartner Group, a leading computer consultancy, pegs worldwide cost for the Year 2000 problem at between $300 billion and $600 billion. These figures are exclusive of litigation and hardware costs. Capers Jones, another leading computer metric expert, includes these costs in his estimates at $1.5 trillion.

These costs arise because while the Year 2000 problem is simple to understand it is devilishly hard to fix simply. To correct the problem, one must identify all of the programs operating in an organization, scan tens to hundreds of millions of lines of computer code, find the problem code, fix the problem code, and test the corrected code to assure that the correction works and that no other operations are affected by the fix. Industry experts report that there already is a severe shortage of qualified computer programmers to address this problem and that it is anticipated that the problem will only worsen.

ACCOUNTING FOR YEAR 2000 COSTS

The Emerging Issues Task Force of the Financial Accounting Standards Board has reached a consensus with respect to Issue 94-14, "Accounting for the Costs Associated with Modifying Computer Software for the Year 2000." The EITF has stated that both the external and internal costs associated with modifying internal-use software for the Year 2000 should be charged as a current year expense. The EITF analogizes to repair and maintenance costs. But to the extent that a company purchases software or hardware to replace noncompliant software or hardware, those costs will be subjected to the company's normal policy for accounting for such costs.

Disclosure of Year 2000 costs also will be governed by Statement of Financial Accounting Standards No. 5, "Accounting for Contingencies." Loss contingencies that are reasonably possible, whether or not the amount can be calculated or estimated, need to be disclosed in the companies' notes to the financial statements. A company that determines that it is reasonably possible that it will not be Year 2000 compliant in time may be required under SFAS 5 to disclose this fact to the public.

Year 2000 consultants report that most organizations are behind where they need to be with respect to their Year 2000 conversion. Accordingly, most experts agree that the bulk of the Year 2000 costs that will be incurred by a typical organization will be backloaded to the 1998 and 1999 fiscal years. FASB's Year 2000 ruling, therefore, will have the effect of telescoping the cost of the Year 2000 problem into two fiscal years, with attendant bottom-line impact, and, for publicly traded companies, attendant stock price impact.

Table 1. SOME ESTIMATED COSTS FOR FIXING YEAR 2000 PROBLEM

Company	Projected Future Costs	Source
Air Products & Chemicals, Inc.	$10,000,000	10K (12/18/96)
Airline Industry	$2,000,000,000	*Airline Business* (December/96)
American Airlines	$75,000,000	*Airlines Financial News* (1/20/97)
Britain	$50,000,000,000	*The Daily Telegragh* (4/12/97)
Canada	$30,000,000,000	*The Financial Post* (7/5/97)
Electronic Data Systems Corp.	$144,000,000	*The Reuters Business Report* (5/28/97)
Federal Express	$500,000,000	*Broward Daily Business Review* (3/21/97)
Federal Government	$2,800,000,000	*C41 News* (7/17/97)
Hertz Corp.	$15,000,000	10K (3/25/97)
ITT Hartford	$20,000,000	*Datamation* (1/1/96)
Merrill Lynch & Co.	$200,000,000	*St. Louis Post-Dispatch* (6/25/97)
New York City	$100,000,000	*USA Today* (4/29/97
Prudential Insurance Company	$150,000,000	*Risk Management* (April 1997)
U.S. West	$40,000,000	*The Denver Post* (2/7/97)

DIRECTORS' AND OFFICERS' LIABILITY ISSUES

The potential for directors' and officers' liability associated with the Year 2000 problem is real and largely underreported. Quarterly and annual reports to the Securities & Exchange Commission require that the company include a section titled "Management's Discussion and Analysis of Financial Condition and Results of Operations" (MD&A). These requirements are set forth in Reg. S-K, Item 303. For companies facing a Year 2000 problem and possible noncompliance, disclosure may be mandated. Additionally, a company is obligated to disclose "material" facts in conjunction with the offer and sale of securities under the Securities Act of 1933 and the Securities Exchange Act of 1934. Given the costs of Year 2000 compliance, which for many companies range in the tens and hundreds of millions of dollars, disclosure will be required. Failure to disclose such information may well lead to director and officer liability.

Unfortunately, the problem may be deeper. A tour through any financial statement reveals myriad date sensitive calculations that compose the statement. Of course, these components are generated by the company's computer systems. To the extent that these calculations are undermined, companies may be facing auditors who refuse to issue unqualified auditors' opinions. The effect of failing to have an unqualified opinion could threaten the ability of a company to trade on a regulated exchange and certainly will undermine a company's credit rating.

CLASS ACTION EXPOSURES

The most daunting liabilities arise from the specter of companies that simply will not be able to open for business on January 1, 2000. These companies will face a host of potential liabilities arising from their customers and employees. Companies that fail to correct their Year 2000 problem certainly will face mass breach-of-contract actions and potentially mass tort actions. In some states, like California, companies may face consumer fraud actions as well, which carry with them the prospect of additional liabilities.

While the motivation to face and address the Year 2000 problem for companies would seem clear, many companies are continuing *not* to take this problem seriously. For those companies that are good corporate citizens and which do address their problem, however, potential liabilities nevertheless loom. To the extent that a company's trading partners fail because of a Year 2000 problem, another company's ability to open for business may be undermined and may result in liability. For example, if a company's bank cannot open for business, it won't be long before the ability of a bank's customer to operate will be undermined.

Prudent businesses are engaging their trading partners now in a conversation that addresses Year 2000 problems. Companies are canvassing their critical service providers and critical parts suppliers to ensure that they have addressed the Year 2000 problem and to ensure that the doors will stay open. Letters that request a status report on Year 2000 efforts are a good starting point for the inquiry. Many businesses are adopting a policy that if a company cannot certify that it will be Year 2000 compliant in time, they will seek a different service or parts provider.

MINIMIZING COST

Many companies also are taking a hard look at how they got into this problem in the first place. Companies may have rights of action against computer consultants and computer software providers for failing to install a system that is Year 2000 compliant. These issues will turn on the interpretation of the relevant contracts.

First, one must consider the applicability of any written warranty or written warranty disclaimer. If the product or services were warranted, the scope of the warranty may determine whether that warranty has been breached and whether there is a right of recovery against the provider of the good or service. With respect to the warranty disclaimers, companies should not readily assume that the existence of a warranty disclaimer necessarily precludes recovery. Warranty disclaimers are disfavored in the law and will be narrowly construed. In addition, many states have laws that limit the applicability of warranty limitations. Many states also have technical requirements for the wording, placement, and typeface of warranty disclaimers that might limit their application.

Second, one must consider the possibility that there may be an unwritten implied warranty that may address the performance of software goods or services. In particular, the implied warranty of fitness for a particular purpose may provide an avenue for redress of wrongs. While the outlines of the implied warranty vary from state to state, all states recognize such warranties in one form or another. This may be an active area for litigation arising from the Year 2000 problem.

PRODUCT LIABILITY

The Year 2000 problem is not limited to software, unfortunately. The Year 2000 problem also manifests itself in something called the "imbedded chip" issue. Imbedded chips are microchips that are incorporated into larger products and that perform a data function. In many products imbedded chips use a hard coded date logic that will not work at the turn of the century. There are reports that these chips have been found in elevator systems, security systems, heating and air conditioning systems, medical devices, and consumer home appliances. Should these chips fail, product liability issues will arise, and companies may face substantial liability. As a manufacturer of a defective product, or as a person in the chain of distribution, the potential for application of strict, joint, and several liability exists. These suits are expensive to defend and may be widespread as the full extent of the imbedded chip issue begins to surface.

TAKE ACTION NOW

The Year 2000 problem is real, it is expensive, and it is fraught with myriad potential liabilities. Prudent businesses are taking steps now to report the problem accurately and to take other steps that will help insulate them from liability. The best legal advice is to take action now and fix the problem. Time is *not* on your side.

Vito C. Peraino chairs the Year 2000 Working Group at Hancock Rothert & Bunshoft LLP. He is a frequent lecturer and writer on Year 2000 topics and has testified before Congress on the liability implications of the Year 2000 problem. E-mail: vperaino@hrblaw.com.

Unit 3

Unit Selections

Key Points to Consider

- Do you think that it is possible to improve financial management in the federal government? Why or why not?
- Prior to reading any of the articles in this unit, what was your perception of government's management of taxpayers' monies? Has your viewpoint changed? Why?
- What is your opinion of the 1990s legislation passed to improve governmental reporting? How will changes implemented under this new legislation affect the economy of the United States in the future?
- Following the 1997 first-ever audit of the consolidated statements of the federal government, what did the General Accounting Office report reveal? What can be done to improve the financial conditions of so many federal departments and agencies?

Links

www.dushkin.com/online/

28. **Bureau of Economic Analysis**
    http://www.bea.doc.gov/
29. **CCH Federal and State Tax News**
    http://www.cch.com/f_s_tax/master.htm
30. **Consumer Price Index (CPI)**
    http://www.stls.frb.org/fred/data/cpi.html
31. **FinanceNet**
    http://www.financenet.gov/
32. **FindLaw**
    http://findlaw.com/
33. **Government Auditor's Resource Page**
    http://www.trib.infi.net/~zsudiak/GARP.html
34. **Governmental Accounting Standards Board**
    http://www.rutgers.edu/Accounting/raw/gasb/gasbhome.html
35. **House of Representatives Internet Law Library**
    http://www.house.gov/
36. **Internal Review Service**
    http://www.irs.ustreas.gov/prod/cover.html
37. **SEC EDGAR Database**
    http://www.sec.gov/edgarhp.htm
38. **Tax Resources**
    http://www.taxresources.com/#contents/
39. **TaxWeb**
    http://www.taxweb.com/
40. **Thomas Legislative Information**
    http://thomas.loc.gov/

These sites are annotated on pages 4 and 5.

Accounting Issues of Government

Most people associate the word *tax* with accounting. While taxation is a specialty within the accounting discipline, generally only surface coverage (if any) is offered in introductory accounting courses. The area of taxation continues to be complex despite the 1986 Tax Reform Act and the Taxpayer Relief Act of 1997. Taxation affects all citizens, not just accounting majors, and therefore, it is appropriate that this topic be discussed in introductory accounting courses since most students will never have an opportunity to otherwise learn about the U.S. tax system.

Government in general receives negative press coverage whenever the issues of taxes and budgets are discussed. Waste and inefficiency are two words often connected to governmental organizations. The 1990 Chief Financial Officers (CFO) Act may be the catalyst that changes the way the Federal government operates and may offer hope for positive changes in the future.

The unit's three selections offer coverage of another accounting topic that affects all citizens of the United States. These articles can be treated separately or in conjunction with the area of budgeting.

"Federal Financial Management: Evolution, Challenges, and the Role of the Accounting Profession" offers background information on financial management in the federal government from the 1780s to the 1980s. The two articles that follow discuss the changes made to date as a result of 1990s legislation. The changes taking place are significant and exciting. For the first time the U.S. federal government has a comprehensive set of financial statements. After reading these selections, a more positive image of accounting in government should emerge.

FEDERAL FINANCIAL MANAGEMENT: EVOLUTION, CHALLENGES AND THE ROLE OF THE ACCOUNTING PROFESSION

BY CHARLES A. BOWSHER

OVER THE YEARS THE ACCOUNTING PROFESSION has worked closely with the federal government in solving some of the most complex problems of federal financial management, helping to put into place reforms that have influenced the way the federal government manages its fiscal affairs.

On this 100th anniversary year of the American Institute of CPAs, it is appropriate to review the evolution of our federal government's financial management structure and the role the accounting profession has played in that evolution. We would also like to highlight some of the significant financial management challenges facing the federal government today and the opportunities these challenges present for the continued involvement of the accounting profession in the last decade of the 20th century and beyond.

Alexander Hamilton was our first treasury secretary.

WHERE DID WE START?

As might be expected, the American colonies looked to Great Britain to provide our models for financial administration. From the principles of the Magna Charta the colonists learned to mistrust the idea of any individual's exercising sole power over public funds. Therefore, many of our original state constitutions guarded against a governor's excessive power by dividing control over finances among several different officials. The U.S. Constitution, reflecting this attitude, continued the British practice of legislative appropriations.

In 1789 one of the first things our Congress did after the states had ratified the Constitution was to pass the Treasury Act. Alexander Hamilton became our first secretary of the treasury and the creator of our early financial management systems. Hamilton believed in strong central control, which put him in conflict with others, such as Thomas Jefferson.

The key features of Hamilton's approach were detailed controls by the Treasury Department and an elaborate system of checks and balances designed to make the theft or misuse of funds impossible without massive collusion. However, this approach also made it very difficult to operate efficiently. Long de-

CHARLES A. BOWSHER, *CPA, MBA, is the comptroller general of the United States. The current chairman of the American Institute of CPAs centennial members in government committee and of the Railroad Accounting Principles Board, he is a member of the Financial Accounting Standards Advisory Council, the Governmental Accounting Standards Advisory Council and the U.S. Railway Association Board. He has served on the AICPA federal government executive committee and was assistant secretary of the navy for financial management from 1967 to 1971.*

From *Journal of Accountancy,* May 1987, pp. 208-284, 286-288, 290-294.

C. W. Haskins was on an 1894 committee investigating the Treasury Department.

The seal of the GAO.

lays in paying bills were common, and accounting and auditing became obstacles rather than instruments of public policy.

The complexity of Hamilton's system also made it difficult for lay people and part-time legislators to understand what was going on. It was partly in response to this problem that Jefferson made a statement in April 1802 that still rings loud and clear:

"I think it an object of great importance...to simplify our system of finance, and to bring it within the comprehension of every member of Congress.... The whole system [has been] involved in impenetrable fog.... There is a point .... on which I should wish to keep my eye... a simplification of the form of accounts... so as to bring everything to a single centre.... We might hope to see the finances of the Union as clear and intelligible as a merchant's books, so that every member of Congress, and every man of any mind in the Union, should be able to comprehend them to investigate abuses, and consequently to control them."

But Hamilton's approach won the day, and his philosophy of financial management has been a dominant force for most of our history.

Needless to say, the problems within Hamilton's approach were magnified under the pressure of war. It's interesting to note that, throughout the U.S. financial management history, we see a definite pattern—that is, major changes followed major wars.

After our Civil War Congress was faced with massive fraud and corruption and began a series of investigations into the Treasury Department. These culminated in the Dockery-Cockrell Commission in 1894. The commission, named after the congressman and senator who were its chairmen, hired three accountants from the private sector to aid in its deliberations. Two of them were Charles Waldo Haskins and Elijah Watt Sells, who later formed the firm of Haskins & Sells. The commission's efforts led to legislation in the 1890s that gave the Treasury comptroller the final authority to judge the legality of payments. And these final decisions were binding on the executive branch. Despite its problems, however, Hamilton's system of detailed central control survived.

At the turn of the century, financial management was in a state of change. Some of our city and state governments, such as those of New York State, were trying different approaches. These included such features as an independent auditor and an executive budget, formulated under the control of the governor.

These ideas quickly spread to the federal level and were debated extensively in the first decade of this century. Presidents commonly supported the notion of an executive budget but usually opposed taking the audit function out of the Treasury. The reasons are fairly obvious. Congressman James Good, a Republican from Iowa, summed them up in May 1921:

"I think it was under the administration of President Cleveland that the president desired to use a certain appropriation for a given purpose, and was told by his Comptroller of the Treasury, who happened to be a little independent of the system, that he could not do it. But the president insisted and finally said, 'I must have that fund, and if I cannot change the opinion of my Comptroller, I can change my Comptroller.' "

However, movement in the direction of a new model of financial management was interrupted by our involvement in World War I. At the same time, the problems we encountered in managing our government during that war and the enormous debt with which we emerged (at least it seemed enormous then, being $24 billion) opened the door for change.

Congressman Good was chairman of the House Committee on Appropriations. In 1919 he introduced a bill calling for a new budget bureau. The purpose of this bill was to prepare an executive budget and establish a separate accounting department under the Congress.

In 1920, the last year of President Wilson's second term, Congress passed Good's bill. Wilson was a reform-minded president and agreed with most of the bill's provisions. However, he could not accept the total independence of the auditor, so he vetoed the bill.

In 1921 Congress again passed the bill. President Harding signed it despite continuing debate about the position of the comptroller general as an independent auditor located in the legislative branch. Thus the General Accounting Office (GAO) was created.

From 1921 to World War II Hamilton's approach of highly centralized accounting and detailed auditing continued. The audit function had been moved to an independent agency, but the audit process changed only slightly, if at all. Yet, it was during this period that the seeds of change began to sprout.

Until this time the accounting profession had only sporadic involvement with the federal government. But in the 1930s the profession was in ferment. Simultaneously, and not by accident, CPAs began to make their mark in the government. With the revelations that flowed from investigations of the crash of 1929, both the public and the profession began to recognize the shortcomings of commercial accounting practices.

With this recognition came a realization of the need for accounting standards and independent audits of commercial financial statements. This led to the establishment of the Securities and Exchange Commission and provided an early substantive connection between the federal government and the accounting profession. (The advent of federal income taxes was another.) A significant feature of new federal legislation at that time was the requirement in the Securities Act of 1933 for independent audits of commercial entities issuing securities in interstate commerce.

Carman G. Blough, a CPA, was the first chief accountant of the SEC. Blough, who was later a partner in a major accounting firm, and for well over 16 years was research director of the AICPA, recommended that the public accounting profession—not the federal government—take the lead in eliminating and correcting the widespread differences in accounting practices followed by SEC registrants. The acceptance of Blough's recommendation by the SEC set the stage for the eventual development of accounting standards by the public accounting profession.

It was in the 1930s that CPAs first began participating in the federal government in a significant way. Eric L. Kohler, for example, a prolific writer and highly active member of the public accounting profession, served as controller of the Tennessee Valley Authority in its early years as well as in several other high-ranking government positions. Other prominent names in the profession were William W. Werntz, who succeeded Carman Blough as chief accountant at the SEC, and William A. Paton, an active member of the American Accounting Association and the Institute's committee on accounting procedure, who served for a time in the Bureau of Internal Revenue (now the Internal Revenue Service). However, by the late 1930s the state of the art of accounting in the federal sector lagged significantly behind the rapid changes in the sizes and types of government activities and the advancements made in the commercial sector. Federal sector accounting and auditing was preoccupied with activities such as detailed voucher examinations and other detailed verifications. Accounting expertise in the federal government left much to be desired.

World War II. This traditional, highly centralized system began to creak with the expansion of government functions during the Great Depression and, in the face of World War II, collapsed. The staff of the GAO had more than doubled during the Depression, reaching about 5,000; then it almost tripled during the war, to almost 15,000. Even so, by the end of the war, the GAO had a four-year backlog of unaudited transactions. Although the financial management structure had changed dramatically in the meantime, the sheer volume of transactions and the absolute necessity that contractors be paid produced a radical decentralization of the GAO's real financial management functions. Centralized auditing was impossible, and most of the accounting was done in the agencies.

In the face of World War II, our financial system began to collapse.

On the day after the surrender of Japan, U.S. Comptroller General Lindsay Warren told his staff that the GAO's number one priority from that day on was the improvement of accounting in government.

Warren decided that there was no going back to the traditional approach of centralized accounting and detailed auditing. In an action that is unique in our history, he joined with Secretary of the Treasury John Snyder and Bureau of the Budget Director James E. Webb, to map out a new strategy for financial management, replacing Hamilton's approach of the previous 150 years. From this cooperation emerged a new structure, one in which the operating agencies were to build and maintain their own financial systems. The GAO was to promulgate standards for those systems and then audit the systems, not the transactions.

Audits of government corporations. As the GAO began to move toward a more modern approach to auditing the operating agencies, it gained a special opportunity to test that approach in auditing government's business-type activities.

The Government Corporation Control Act of 1945 required financial transactions of government corporations to be audited by the

GAO "in accordance with principles and procedures applicable to commercial corporate transactions." As a result, the GAO established a Corporation Audits Division and staffed it with professional accountants experienced in public practice. Both the director and the deputy director were CPAs. By 1948 54 CPAs worked for the division compared with few, if any, in all of the GAO before 1945.

The establishment of the Corporation Audits Division marked a significant change in the relationship between the GAO and the public accounting profession. According to the Institute's committee on governmental accounting, in its 1947 annual report: "Prior to 1945, relations between the General Accounting Office and the certified public accountants of the United States, as represented by the Institute, were impaired by lack of mutual understanding and confidence." With the establishment of the new division, the GAO and the accounting profession had moved to an era of strong alliance and mutual benefit. In his report for the fiscal year ended June 30, 1945, Comptroller General Warren said: "A new Corporation Audits Division has been set up within the General Accounting Office, headed by a certified public accountant of long experience. The public accounting profession is cooperating splendidly in our efforts to build the finest aggregation of accounting talent within or without the government."

T. Coleman Andrews's AIA committee developed a plan for government accounting.

The effect of these changes on the GAO was astonishing. In less than 10 years

- The primary focus had changed from checking the accuracy and legality of individual transactions to establishing principles and reviewing accounting systems and management effectiveness.
- Staff had dropped from nearly 15,000 to around 5,000, while professional accountants increased from a few to almost 1,500.

The basic shape of the financial management structure created in that period by Lindsay Warren, John Snyder and Jim Webb continues today.

The Hoover commissions. These three government officials, however, were not alone in their efforts to improve accounting in government. By the end of the war, attention in federal financial management had turned to matters of management efficiency. Among the most significant events were two commissions established by President Herbert Hoover. Prewar criticism and dissatisfaction with accounting in the federal government played a part in prompting Congress in 1947 to set up the first Hoover commission. That commission, which was designed to study the organizations of government agencies, submitted its report to Congress in 1949. The second Hoover commission, created in 1953 to study policy questions relating to government operations, reported to Congress in 1955. Both commissions made recommendations on accounting and budgeting.

Again, the accounting profession was there to lend a helping hand. At Hoover's request, T. Coleman Andrews, who had resigned from the GAO after helping establish the Corporation Audits Division and been appointed chairman of the Institute's newly created committee on federal government accounting, had his committee undertake the development of an appropriate plan of accounting, auditing and financial reporting for the government.

In addition to testifying before Congress in support of commission recommendations, many CPAs served as members of Hoover commission task forces. For example, eight CPAs were members of or consultants to the second commission's Budget and Accounting Task Force, including the head of the task force. Another CPA chaired the task force on lending agencies.

The Hoover commissions made several significant recommendations, many of which were incorporated into law. The Budget and Accounting Procedures Act of 1950, which many praised at that time as one of the most important steps ever taken in improving federal financial management, included several provisions based on the first Hoover commission recommendations. By and large, the act was a statutory ratification of the structure developed by Warren, Snyder and Webb. It also had the effect of institutionalizing for many years the decentralized financial management structure that grew out of World War II. The act made the head of each executive agency responsible for establishing and maintaining an accounting system with internal controls, which has resulted in the hundreds of separately developed and incompatible agency accounting systems that exist in the federal government today.

Legislation in 1956 included provisions reflecting such Hoover commission recommen-

President Eisenhower appointed more CPAs to federal posts than any prior president.

dations as the use of cost-based budgeting; the maintenance of accounts on the accrual basis to show resources, liabilities and costs of operations of each agency; and the requirement for monetary property accounting records as an integral part of each agency's accounting system. The usefulness of formulating and administering budgets on a cost basis was recognized in a 1956 amendment to the Budget and Accounting Procedures Act of 1950; yet it continues to be largely ignored in practice.

The Eisenhower years. The 1950s saw the influx of increasing numbers of CPAs into important federal positions. Much of the momentum was attributed to President Dwight D. Eisenhower, who appointed CPAs such as Joseph Campbell as comptroller general and Maurice H. Stans as deputy postmaster general and, later, as director of the Bureau of the Budget. (Stans, who in 1954 was the president of the American Institute of Accountants, which became the AICPA, was later appointed by President Richard Nixon as secretary of commerce.)

Eisenhower had great respect for the profession and its contribution to the federal government. In 1960 he addressed the annual meeting of the AICPA with these words:

"One of the more statistically minded people in the government told me not long ago that I had appointed more certified public accountants to government positions than any prior President. I certainly did not do this because they are accountants. I have been for all these 8 years searching for talent—people of dedication, of training, of education, of capability—people who have a sense of civic responsibility. So, since I have appointed so many... persons who have been public accountants, I suppose it is a fair conclusion that your profession averages very high up among those that are so dedicated and so capable."

President Johnson set up the 1967 Commission on Budget Concepts.

It was during the late 1950s and early 1960s that the federal government and, in particular, Congress began to realize that many audits of governmental functions could be effectively and economically carried out by CPAs. Further, it was realized that the scope of public accounting services extended further than merely auditing financial statements. A survey in 1958 showed that there were only 10 federal agencies using outside public accountants to any significant extent. Ten years later there were thousands of engagements by public accountants involving 80 federal programs administered by 30 different agencies.

The Great Society and expansion of the federal government. The 1960s and 1970s were periods of growth in the federal government. President Lyndon B. Johnson put out his call for a Great Society in 1964 and, by the mid-1960s, the government, under Johnson's direction and with Congress's cooperation, had embarked on a course as challenging to American society as was the New Deal of the 1930s. This brought on a great expansion of government activities and federal expenditures, particularly in the domestic area. Expenditures for education, community development and housing, and health and welfare, for example—even discounting for inflation—tripled between 1965 and 1970. This expansion of federal activity, combined with the costs of escalation in the Vietnam War and a continuing trend toward decentralizing the responsibility for carrying out the programs, resulted in an unwieldy governmental structure that complicated the question of accountability and resulted in a surge of confusion over the costs of managing the federal government.

Several attempts were made to come to grips with the problem. One of the most noteworthy projects was the attempt to resolve problems resulting from the federal government's use, in 1966, of three separate budgets: the administrative budget, the consolidated cash budget and the national income accounts budget. The competing budgets were difficult to reconcile, and their concepts and terms were confusing to many. In 1967 President Johnson established the President's Commission on Budget Concepts to sort out the issues.

As with the Hoover commissions, the public accounting profession was well represented. Among the prominent members were Robert M. Trueblood, a past president of the AICPA. Elmer B. Staats, the vice-chairman of the commission, was beginning his distinguished 15-year term as U.S. comptroller general. The centerpiece of the commission's recommendations was that the three existing federal budgets be presented within the framework of a single unified budget. The recommendation was adopted, but there have been many exceptions since its implementation in 1969, with a fluctuating pattern of agencies and activities at various times being taken off and put back on the budget.

Recent incentives. The decade of the 1970s saw other major developments in financial management, particularly in the budgeting arena. For example, the Legislative Reorganization Act of 1970 and the Congressional Budget and Impoundment Act of 1974 altered the way in which Congress played its part in federal financial management.

The GAO helped take the initiative in several financial areas. In 1972 the GAO was a prime catalyst, working with the accounting profession, in developing and promulgating standards for audits of governmental organizations, programs, activities and functions—commonly known as the "yellow book." Updated in 1981, and with another update as of this year, the yellow book is required to be followed, by law, by most cabinet-level federal audit organizations and by CPAs who audit federal assistance programs. The standards, which provide for expanded scope auditing in government, help ensure full accountability and assist government officials and employees in carrying out their responsibilities. Several state and local audit organizations and several nations have adopted these standards.

In 1976, and each year thereafter, the GAO and other interested parties from the private and public sectors have assisted the Department of the Treasury in the development of prototype consolidated financial statements of the federal government. In 1986 the GAO and the auditor general of Canada jointly issued the *Federal Government Reporting Study.* This study resulted from a two-year research project designed to enhance the financial statements of the federal governments of both nations. The study identified the information needs of users of federal government financial information and resulted in illustrations of possible formats and disclosures for a summary-level financial report.

There have been numerous other initiatives aimed at improving federal financial management. Several of them, such as the Inspector General Act of 1978 and the Federal Managers' Financial Integrity Act of 1982, have brought about important improvements in federal financial management. Others, such as the Single Audit Act of 1984, hold promise of significant changes. In each of these initiatives, the profession played a key role in the development, enactment and implementation of the legislation.

Valuable as these efforts have been, each has attempted to deal with discrete problems in isolation rather than examining the systems as a whole. The decentralized structure which was created under the exigencies of World War II, formalized by the Warren-Snyder-Webb agreements and ratified in the 1950 act, remains in place.

Where We Are Now

The structure we now have—that is, the agency-based systems developed in the 1940s and 1950s—has deteriorated. These old systems, individually designed and poorly linked, provide a torrent of financial data, but little of the timely, reliable and consistent information needed for decision making as we face unprecedented budget deficits and the pressure to manage programs more efficiently.

Many new requirements have been added to the structure over the years, including the Planning, Programming, and Budgeting System; Management by Objectives; and Zero-Based Budgeting, with little consideration for the cumulative effects of incremental changes. The result is an unbelievably complex structure that simply does not meet our needs. For example, look at the problems in managing our recent defense buildup.

We believe it is very dangerous to wait for a crisis before taking action. The shortcomings of the present federal financial management systems are numerous and well documented. Some of the key problems are as follows:

■ Lack of cost information. Although federal government financial reports provide a flood of data, there is little information about the real resources used to carry out programs and projects. Unit cost data are rarely available and tend to be unreliable because they do not come from the accounting systems. Several problems result, such as a lack of data to make comparisons of similar activities and to establish performance measures for evaluating management's stewardship of resources.

■ Lack of reliable information on major weapon systems. The paucity of reliable and relevant cost information is especially acute and troublesome with respect to large capital projects involving private sector contractors. For defense contracts, current project reporting systems are not tied to the federal government accounting and budgeting systems. The reports all too often are incomplete, inconsis-

Elmer Staats served as U.S. comptroller general for 15 years.

Chief Staff Officers of the AICPA

CHENOK

OLSON

SAVOIE

CAREY

RICHARDSON

PHILIP B. CHENOK (1980-present)
Philip B. Chenok, CPA, president of the American Institute of CPAs since July 1, 1980, provides overall direction for AICPA operations. He serves as principal spokesman for the Institute in New York and Washington, D.C.

Previously he was director of auditing and chairman of the professional standards committee at KMG/Main Hurdman, where he had been admitted to partnership in 1967.

Long active in AICPA affairs, he was chairman of the auditing standards board and its predecessor, the auditing standards executive committee, from 1976 to 1979—a period of enormous challenge and transition for the accounting profession—and was a member of council at the time of his appointment as the Institute's chief staff officer. He has also served as a member of the accounting standards executive committee and was one of three U.S. delegates to the Accountants' International Study Group, which conducted studies of international accounting practices.

WALLACE E. OLSON (1972-80)
Wallace E. Olson, CPA, served as chief staff officer of the AICPA for eight years. First named executive vice-president by the board of directors in June 1972, Olson's title was changed to president two years later.

Olson was associated with Alexander Grant & Company for over 25 years and became its executive partner in 1967. He had been chairman of several ethics-related committees—the AICPA professional ethics executive committee and the code restatement committee—and had served on council and on the management services committee. In 1970 he was appointed to the study group on the establishment of accounting principles (the Wheat committee), whose report was adopted by council in May 1972. Olson's book *The Accounting Profession: Years of Trial 1969-1980* was published by the AICPA in 1982 after his retirement from the Institute.

LEONARD M. SAVOIE (1967-72)
Leonard M. Savoie, CPA, was selected by the Institute's executive committee in 1967 to fill the newly created post of executive vice-president. The first chief staff officer to hold a CPA certificate, he was responsible for all AICPA activities and acted as the Institute's spokesman. His objectivity and ability to explain timely accounting problems and issues vastly improved the Institute's relations with the financial writers and editors of the time. John L. Carey writes, "He was thoroughly familiar with the problems of the Institute in the technical areas, and his own professional reputation clothed him with a high degree of personal authority."

Before and during his term in office, Savoie was heavily involved in the work of the Accounting Principles Board. He also served on numerous AICPA committees—including the planning committee—both before and after his tenure as executive vice-president.

Prior to joining the Institute staff, he was partner in charge of accounting research and education at Price Waterhouse & Co., where he had been since 1946.

JOHN L. CAREY (1930-67)
John L. Carey had a long and distinguished career with the AICPA, serving as an officer of the Institute from 1925 until his retirement on May 1, 1969. He was also the author of a history of the Institute's first 82 years and a major contributor to the literature on accounting ethics.

A. P. RICHARDSON (1911-30)
A. P. Richardson was engaged as secretary of the American Association of Public Accountants (AAPA) on December 12, 1911, the organization's first full-time officer.

His first report at the 1912 annual meeting reflected his extensive duties: traveling frequently to Washington on federal legislative matters; editing the *Journal of Accountancy*; preparing the *Yearbook*; finding professional speakers for various programs; establishing a new headquarters office; visiting the state societies; and providing services to individual members.

He resigned his administrative position in 1930 but continued as editor of the *Journal* and other publications until his retirement in 1936. His 25 years of service to the Institute, according to John L. Carey, "had a large part in building [the] Institute to its current strength and stature."

tent and unreliable, with significant changes reported too late for remedial action.

■ Inadequate disclosure of costs and liabilities. The failure to reveal some costs is paralleled by the failure to disclose the accumulated liabilities for those costs. For example, major commitments of resources, such as the unfunded liabilities of Social Security and the federal employee retirement systems, are disclosed only in special reports, not in the government's primary financial documents.

■ Unstructured planning for capital investments. As with most national governments, ours plays a major role in determining the level of investment for public capital facilities and the priorities among various investment needs. Yet these decisions are made in an uncoordinated fashion. For example, the distinction between capital outlays and current operating expenses can be found only in the budget's schedules, not the summaries.

Deficiencies in federal financial management must be addressed.

■ Antiquated systems. Our government's basic approach to financial management is obsolete. The highly decentralized structure currently in use was designed to meet the needs of World War II. This decentralized structure and its obsolete computer systems, taken together, cannot provide the information needed by managers and policy officials.

ELEMENTS OF REFORM

Previous efforts to deal with the sampling of problems described above have been piecemeal and largely unsuccessful. Today's sophisticated management and technological environment suggests that it is imperative that a more integrated, comprehensive and systematic approach for addressing deficiencies in federal financial management be instituted.

In 1983 the GAO formed a task force to study the important financial management problems facing the federal government. The task force enlisted the aid of two CPA firms to help identify possible solutions to the problems found and to propose strategies for improvements. We believe the following four key elements of reform illustrate the breadth of the change needed.

1. Strengthened accounting, auditing and reporting. Effective financial management must start with complete, reliable, consistent and timely information. Therefore, government financial systems must be designed to produce routine and special reports that are timely, useful and readily understandable. The reliability of financial data must be assured through effective auditing procedures.

2. Improved planning and programming. As is true for other governments and large private organizations, the most pressing national issues can be adequately considered by using a modern financial management system that includes a structured process focusing attention on major issues and that identifies alternative courses of action and analyzes their probable future consequences.

3. Streamlined budget process. At the core of the difficulties faced by our government in creating its budget lies the lack of a political consensus, which can be resolved only by simplifying our very complex budget process.

4. Systematic measurement of performance. Effective management of resources requires examining the costs and the results of government activities. In order for this to be carried out, the government must institute financial management systems that provide consistent and reliable data on performance.

A CONCEPTUAL FRAMEWORK

The task force found that it was possible to begin building a new structure of federal financial management that embodies these four elements. The approach, or framework, for building this new structure has seven underlying concepts that are important for establishing a sound financial management foundation and serve as guides in financial management reform. These concepts, which represent a combination of existing legal prescription and sound management practices, follow:

1. Use a structured planning and programming process to evaluate and choose alternatives for achieving desired objectives. Such a process assists policymakers in focusing on what government should be doing, how best to accomplish those goals and how to measure performance based on expectations. This process provides an analytic framework for evaluating the benefits and costs of alternatives, and it facilitates choices among alternative goals, missions, strategies and programs.

2. Make resource allocation decisions within a unified budget. A unified budget focuses attention on total federal expenditure and revenue requirements and provides a context in which to deal with individual agency budget requests. Policymakers at all levels are aided in making informed resource allocation decisions when total requirements are known and deficits are fully disclosed.

3. Budget and account on the same basis. Timely variance detection aids corrective action. This can be effected when there is an integration of budget and accounting. This relationship between the two functions provides a common set of rules by which managers and policymakers can make valid comparisons between planned and actual results.

4. Use accounting principles that match the delivery of services with the cost of the services. Accrual principles provide policymakers and management with consistent information for comparing program–service costs between periods or agencies. Once interperiod distortions are minimized by the application of accounting and accrual principles, better-informed cost–benefit evaluations become possible.

Use accounting principles that match delivery of services with the cost.

5. Encourage financial accountability. A system of detailed and summary management reports serves these purposes: identifies costs and accomplishments by the managers and organizations responsible for controlling costs; provides accurate, comprehensive information on spending decisions; and aids in evaluation of these data for decision making.

6. Measure outputs as well as inputs. Incorporating performance measurements into the system of budget and management reporting provides policymakers with the capability to relate program–project costs with output and

CPAs Who Have Contributed to Federal Financial Management

Many CPAs have made valuable contributions in helping the federal government improve its financial management. Listed here are some of those who have attained high-ranking federal positions during their careers while contributing significantly to the work of the federal government.

John Abadessa, controller, Atomic Energy Commission.

Gregory J. Ahart, assistant comptroller general for human resources, General Accounting Office.

T. Coleman Andrews, commissioner of internal revenue.

Robert N. Anthony, assistant secretary of defense (controller).

Donald W. Bacon, assistant commissioner of internal revenue.

Andrew Barr, chief accountant, Securities and Exchange Commission.

Robert W. Beuley, inspector general, Department of Agriculture.

Herman W. Bevis, member, Cost Accounting Standards Board.

William A. Blakley, U.S. Senate.

Carman G. Blough, chief accountant, Securities and Exchange Commission.

Daniel Borth, deputy assistant secretary of defense.

Charles A. Bowsher, assistant secretary of the navy; comptroller general of the United States.

Karney A. Brasfield, assistant to the comptroller general of the United States; controller, Commodity Credit Corporation (Department of Agriculture); comptroller, Farm Credit Administration.

June Gibbs Brown, inspector general, National Aeronautics and Space Administration.

Percival F. Brundage, director, Bureau of the Budget.

John C. Burton, chief accountant, Securities and Exchange Commission.

Joseph Campbell, comptroller general of the United States.

Sheldon Cohen, commissioner of internal revenue.

Donald Cook, commissioner, Securities and Exchange Commission.

John Croxall, director of finance, Atomic Energy Commission.

Joseph J. DioGuardi, U.S. House of Representatives.

Roscoe L. Egger, commissioner of internal revenue.

Raymond Einhorn, director of audits, National Aeronautics and Space Administration.

(Continued on next page)

thereby to determine whether objectives are achieved at an acceptable cost. This analysis of how costs change in proportion to output assists future program planning.

7. Prepare consolidated reports. The consolidation of annually audited financial statements provides an overall picture of the federal government's financial condition. Disclosure of the cumulative financial effect of past decisions aids public and policy formulators in analyzing resources and commitments.

The overall financial management cycle will be strengthened if there is an integration of the budgeting and accounting functions. Resource allocation decision making must be based on the cost implications of these two areas. For example, the planning, programming and budgeting phases of the cycle will all have the consistent and reliable financial information necessary to help focus debate on policy and program issues. With the ability now to relate cost data to resource allocation decisions, management can better predict the future effects of current and past decisions and better estimate program costs. Thus, fiscal control is enhanced and better data provided for program and resource allocation decisions.

Also, the integration of budgeting and accounting provides a record of historical costs and performance data, which is the key to reliable future cost estimating. Budgeting decisions are likely to be more realistic if they are based on what actually happened in previous periods. In addition, a budget in which full costs are associated with the proposed decisions and strategies becomes a management

(Continued from previous page)

Henry Eschwege, assistant comptroller general for planning and reporting, General Accounting Office.

Mark W. Everson, executive associate commissioner, Immigration and Naturalization Service.

Ronnie G. Flippo, U.S. House of Representatives.

William B. Franke, assistant secretary of the navy (financial management); undersecretary of the navy; secretary of the navy.

Walter F. Frese, director, Accounting Systems Division, General Accounting Office.

Joseph Gerdes, assistant controller, Atomic Energy Commission.

John A. Grady, director of the Bureau of Accounts, Interstate Commerce Commission.

Paul Grady, member, first and second Hoover commissions.

Paul M. Green, controller, Atomic Energy Commission.

Richard Griffin, assistant controller, Atomic Energy Commission.

Neil Harlan, assistant secretary of the air force.

Russell C. Harrington, commissioner of internal revenue.

Leo Herbert, director of personnel management, General Accounting Office.

Warner Hord, chief accountant, Civil Aeronautics Board.

A. R. Jones, director, Tennessee Valley Authority.

Earle C. King, chief accountant, Securities and Exchange Commission.

Eric L. Kohler, controller, Tennessee Valley Authority.

Joseph Kratz, assistant controller, Atomic Energy Commission.

Arthur L. Litke, chief accountant, Federal Power Commission.

John J. Lordan, deputy associate director for financial management, Office of Management and Budget.

Bernard B. Lynn, director, Defense Contract Audit Agency.

Edward T. McCormick, commissioner, Securities and Exchange Commission.

Robert K. Mautz, member, Cost Accounting Standards Board.

David S. Monson, U.S. House of Representatives.

Ellsworth Morse, assistant comptroller general, General Accounting Office.

David Mosso, fiscal assistant secretary, Department of the Treasury.

Gerald Murphy, deputy fiscal assistant secretary, Department of the Treasury.

(Continued on next page)

tool for assessing results against plans. It also provides a more reliable basis for judging the cost of continuing or stopping projects and programs. If full costs are not associated with budget priorities and strategies, the budget is a less effective management tool.

At present, the link between program and budget choices and the use of funds and the results achieved often relies on ad hoc reporting and analyses. This ad hoc process is time-consuming, staff-intensive and, in many cases, unreliable. With the integration of budget and accounting, however, the critical link can be more easily made and the overall management cycle strengthened.

THE STATE AND LOCAL EXPERIENCE

Some may think that building a financial management structure along the lines outlined in the seven concepts is an impossible dream. However, they would be wrong. To prove the point, we need look no farther than our own states and localities.

In recent years many state and local governments have begun to build systems along the lines we believe are needed for the federal government. However, it took a crisis to motivate them. About 10 years ago, when lenders became concerned about their debt, some states and cities faced potentially higher interest rates and difficulty in obtaining financing.

For example, in 1975 New York City's financial markets refused to purchase securities issued by the city. Analysts had been expressing concern about its overextended position and rapidly growing short-term debt, but no one in

(Continued from previous page)

James A. Needham, commissioner, Securities and Exchange Commission.

Frederick Neuman, director, Defense Contract Audit Agency.

Fred J. Newton, deputy director, Defense Contract Audit Agency.

Lindsley Noble, controller, Atomic Energy Commission.

Ralph J. Olmo, comptroller, Department of Education.

Owen B. Pickett, U.S. House of Representatives.

Clerio P. Pin, assistant comptroller general for administration, General Accounting Office.

Joseph Pois, deputy assistant director, Bureau of the Budget.

Norris Poulson, U.S. House of Representatives.

John W. Queenan, member, President Nixon's Price Commission.

Percy Rappaport, assistant director, Bureau of the Budget.

William H. Reed, director, Defense Contract Audit Agency.

A. Clarence Sampson, chief accountant, Securities and Exchange Commission.

A. T. Samuelson, assistant comptroller general, General Accounting Office.

Frank S. Sato, inspector general, Veterans Administration.

Donald L. Scantlebury, director, Accounting and Financial Management Division, General Accounting Office.

Arthur Schoenhaut, executive secretary, Cost Accounting Standards Board.

L. William Seidman, chairman, Federal Deposit Insurance Corporation.

Nelson Shapiro, executive secretary, Cost Accounting Standards Board.

E. Clay Shaw, U.S. House of Representatives.

Gordon Shillinglaw, member, Cost Accounting Standards Board.

Maurice H. Stans, secretary of commerce; director, Bureau of the Budget; deputy postmaster general.

Harold I. Steinberg, associate director for management, Office of Management and Budget.

J. Harold Stewart, member, second Hoover commission.

James B. Thomas, inspector general, Department of Education.

Joseph Vigorito, U.S. House of Representatives.

William W. Werntz, chief accountant, Securities and Exchange Commission.

Frederick E. Wolf, director, Accounting and Financial Management Division, General Accounting Office.

the city government seemed to take the warnings very seriously. When the city was unable to refinance its debt, it faced the prospect of bankruptcy; when New York State tried to help out, the threat of bankruptcy spread there as well.

At the heart of the New York problem were the policies that led to excessive spending compared to revenues. However, underlying those policies was the fact that the governments of New York City and New York State did not have good pictures of their financial condition. After the crisis began, it took the state a year to find out how much debt it had. Although the city had a published financial report, not even the professional accountants could make sense of the numbers. City officials could not even reconcile the cash accounts for which the budget office and the comptroller's office carried different numbers.

Good financial management—once merely desirable—today is essential.

The New York fiscal crisis was to state and local governments what the 1929 stock market crash was to the national business sector. Many state and local governments, drawing on the lessons learned in New York, have since adopted more rigorous budgeting, accounting and reporting standards.

While state and local governments have made significant progress, they still have more to accomplish. An article on this subject in the September-October 1985 *Harvard Business Review* is entitled "Games Government Accountants Play." The author, Robert N. Anthony, points out that the business sector shifted to disciplined accounting practices focusing on performance only when the Great Depression of 1929 revealed the defects of old practices; the government sector did not make such a shift. Now, however, it is apparent that the government is considering changes. While many of the traditional government accounting practices persist and continue to be susceptible to manipulation and abuse, the recently established Governmental Accounting Standards Board is our best hope for overcoming these problems.

The time has come for our federal government to learn the lessons so recently recognized by our state and local governments: That is, the U.S. government, facing a $200 billion deficit and over $1.5 trillion of debt, is not immune from experiencing a crisis. It must put its financial house in order, which requires the adoption of policies that will permit us to live within our means. In addition, it means having the financial information needed to recognize and solve problems before such a crisis occurs.

A Call to the Profession

Clearly, the problems in federal financial management are far more complex now than at any other time in history. In these troubled times, the federal government can ill afford to operate with anything less than superior financial management of its resources. A company in the commercial sector cannot survive indefinitely without solid financial management. The federal government, under an obligation to more than 230 million American citizens who are the shareholders in the nation, cannot weather the storms ahead unless its resources are intelligently budgeted and accounted for. In the past, good financial management was certainly desirable. Today, it is even more essential and will remain so in the future.

Tremendous benefits can be achieved through a modern structure of federal financial management. Many of the benefits are already visible in integrated financial management systems of progressive state and local governments. But an improved structure for the federal government will not emerge by accident, nor will it result from the isolated efforts of a few agencies. Building the structure will require the design and installation of new systems over an extended period. Coordination of new and existing system development activities can yield major benefits at little additional cost. An equally important investment must be made in the people who implement the systems. They must be recruited more carefully, trained more thoroughly and offered a more attractive career path.

This kind of effort must continue if we are to realistically achieve improved financial management in the federal government. The public's demand for improved accountability can be met only if the profession and the federal government work together toward a common goal—an effective and efficient federal financial management structure.

In saluting the profession on its 100th anniversary, we urge its members to consider the past as only the starting point. Among the many challenges of the future is the problem we have laid out here. Together we can meet that challenge and make the second 100 years even more productive than the first.

Accounting's Last Frontier

Management accountants' challenge: Reinvent the government to make it more like a business.

BY STUART L. GRAFF, CMA

Certificate of Merit, 1994-95

Throughout U.S. history, financial transactions of all federal agencies have been recorded on a cash basis, and financial statements based on the books and records of federal agencies simply were not attempted. Other concerns with higher priorities always pushed any financial reporting initiative to the back burner. In effect, the federal government is the last frontier for generally accepted accounting principles (GAAP).[1]

Now the federal government wants to raise its level of fiscal accountability to the standards met by the most responsible publicly held corporations. Its stated goal is to conduct an audit of the entire executive branch by March 1, 1998.

Attaining this standard would presuppose that all accounting transactions would be recorded promptly and accurately in a general ledger system. This ledger system would be based on GAAP, using a uniform chart of accounts—the U.S. Standard General Ledger—and fully integrated accounting and financial management information systems. Also, for each fiscal year, financial statements would be prepared and audited at all 24 major federal agencies as well as for the entire federal government.

Once the federal government is able to operate in a businesslike manner, there will be complete accountability for expenditures of funds, collection of revenues, and net results of operations. Ideally, it also is expected that the products and services of federal agencies will be competitive in quality and price with those available from commercial enterprises. Perhaps most important of all, a state-of-the art accounting system will generate renewed public confidence in the government's effectiveness and efficiency.

A DIFFICULT JOURNEY

The federal government's journey toward its goal of running operations like a business is fraught with risk and unproven rewards. Many nonfinancial professionals believe that the federal government has unique financial management characteristics. Too big for its finances to be understood easily by any one person, it is the largest financial enterprise in the world with three major branches, scores of agencies, millions of employees, billions of dollars in suspected waste, and trillions of dollars of revenues, expenses, and cumulative deficit. The belief exists partly because the sovereign powers of the federal government include the authority to tax its citizens and to print money with which to pay federal debts.

Along with its size, the government is intrinsically complex. In the executive branch, there are 24 major agencies, including the 14 cabinet-level departments that are responsible for administering most federal programs. There are hundreds of accounting systems, most of which do not communicate with each other, and some transactions have not been automated yet on any system.

A cultural barrier also exists. Each group of federal employees sees itself as unique and separate from all other groups. This attitude of specialization is expressed strongly by federal program managers, accountants, and auditors.

Program managers are responsible for delivering services and products to government grant recipients and the public in general. In addition to making sure that program delivery systems are functioning properly, they also monitor and re-

No money shall be drawn from the Treasury, but in consequence of appropriations made by law; and a regular statement and account of the receipts and expenditures of all public money shall be published from time to time. — *The United States Constitution, Article 1, Section 9, Clause 7*

quest the use of budgeted resources. If there are cost overruns or reduced funding, they adjust program operations to keep within statutory budget constraints. Some program managers, however, are reluctant to assume any financial management responsibility for a program's performance once grant or loan funds are awarded.

Accountants are responsible for recording financial transactions on subsidiary and general ledger systems and reporting ledger activity and balances to Treasury, Office of Management and Budget (OMB), and others as required. Generally, accountants are not familiar with program operations. They often consult with program managers in drafting financial disclosure footnotes and the narrative financial entity overviews that accompany principal financial statements. (If government accountants were more familiar with their agency's programs, they could be more effective in developing performance measurement information, analyses of program costs and benefits, and other important management accounting functions.)

Auditors are drawn primarily from each agency's Office of Inspector General. Generally, these offices are concerned with the detection and investigation of suspected instances of

The Federal Accounting Standards Advisory Board

The Secretary of the Treasury, the Director of the Office of Management and Budget, and the Comptroller General of the United States established the Federal Accounting Standards Advisory Board (the FASAB or "the Board") in October 1990 to consider and recommend accounting principles for the U.S. government.

The Board develops its recommendations by considering the financial and budgetary information needs of Congress, executive branch agencies, and other users of federal financial information. The Board also considers comments from the public on its proposed recommendations, which it publishes for comment as "exposure drafts." The Board's sponsors, i.e., the officials who established the Board, then decide whether to adopt the recommendations. If they do, the standard is published by the OMB and the GAO and then becomes effective.

Additional background information is available from FASAB, including:

1. The "Memorandum of Understanding among the General Accounting Office, the Department of the Treasury, and the Office of Management and Budget, on Federal Government Accounting Standards and a Federal Accounting Standards Advisory Board."
2. The "Mission Statement of the Federal Accounting Standards Advisory Board."

The current Board includes Elmer B. Staats, chairman; James L. Blum; Donald H. Chapin; Martin Ives; Norwood Jackson; Gerald Murphy; James E. Reid; Cornelius E. Tierney; and Alvin Tucker.

Ronald S. Young is executive director of the FASAB and may be contacted at Federal Accounting Standards Advisory Board, 750 First Street, NE, Room 1001, Washington, DC 20002; phone, (202) 512-7350; fax, (202) 512-7366.

On January 24, 1995, he announced that the basic package of federal financial accounting and reporting standards would be issued by the fall. As of September 6, the basic package statements, with percentages of completion, are:

- 100%, Accounting for Selected Assets and Liabilities;
- 100%, Accounting for Direct Loans and Loan Guarantees;
- 100%, Accounting for Inventory and Related Property;
- 100%, Objectives of Federal Financial Reporting Concepts;
- 100%, Entity and Display Concepts;
- 100%, Standards and Concepts for Managerial Costing;
- 96%, Accounting for Liabilities of the Federal Government;
- 94%, Accounting for Plant, Property and Equipment;
- 90%, Accounting for Revenues and Other Financing Sources;
- 75%, Reporting on Federal Stewardship.

fraud, waste, and abuse with regard to the use of federal funding. Inspector General offices also have experience and expertise in performance auditing, which provides some assurance that appropriated and otherwise authorized funds are used for intended outcomes in an efficient manner. Most Inspector General personnel, however, have little experience in financial statement auditing. Therefore, many of these audits have to be conducted or assisted by the General Accounting Office (GAO) or by public accounting firms.

In addition, inspectors general hold a uniquely independent position within the agencies they serve. They report not only to their agency head but to the President of the United States and to Congress. Because of the need to preserve the appearance as well as the fact of independence, the Inspector General audit staff often is reluctant to provide suggestions and other assistance to the financial management planning process when new programs are developed and existing programs are being revised.

For most federal functions there has been no experience in preparing general purpose financial statements for external scrutiny. Automated accounting and financial management systems that enable large corporations to issue audited financial statements within a few weeks of fiscal year-end are not available yet at most federal agencies.

Related to the lack of experience in preparing auditable financial statements for federal organizations is the absence of a comprehensive set of accounting principles developed for the unique characteristics of the federal government. Only in the past three years has a body—the Federal Accounting Standards Advisory Board (FASAB)—existed to develop such accounting standards (see sidebar, previous page). During this period, three statements of federal financial accounting standards, two statements related to concepts, and one statement (on costing) combining standards and concepts have been issued. Also, there are two exposure drafts outstanding and two statements in the final approval process.

The pace is increasing for developing federal accounting principles. All 10 of the currently planned federal financial and cost accounting standards are expected to be issued as final statements by the end of 1995.

POISED FOR CHANGE

Some of the most significant financial management improvements realized over the past few years in the federal government have been initiated by new laws. These laws, summarized below, generally are being implemented on schedule even though none, as yet, are implemented fully.

The Chief Financial Officers Act of 1990 (CFO Act). The CFO Act designated the deputy director for management of OMB to be the chief financial officer of the United States. This law also provided that a controller would be appointed to direct the OMB Office of Federal Financial Management and that a CFO and deputy CFO, who are professionally qualified, would be designated at each of the 24 major executive agencies (the Social Security Administration is included because it recently became independent).

As part of the CFO Act, 10 agencies were designated as pilots to prepare agency-wide financial statements. The statements were to be audited by the agency inspector general, a public accounting firm under contract to the inspector general, or the General Accounting Office. The other executive agencies would be required to prepare financial statements for audit on their trust funds, revolving funds, and commercial-type activities only.

The chief financial officer of the United States also serves as the chair of the CFO Council. The Council comprises all agency CFOs and deputy CFOs and is an important forum for discussion and decision making as financial management laws are implemented (see Figure 1). The OMB oversees implementation through the Office of Federal Financial Management. This office provides guidance documents for various financial management laws. Of particular importance is OMB Bulletin 94-01, "Form and Content of Agency Financial Statements." This bulletin describes and illustrates the various parts of the financial statements that are required for each program and agency covered by the CFO Act.

The Federal Credit Reform Act of 1990 (FCRA). FCRA requires the government to recognize its full cost for the funding of credit programs. These costs include loan origination, service, and collection or write-offs for bad debts on defaulted

The Accounting Standardization Act

Sen. Hank Brown (R.–Colo.) has introduced S. 1130, The Accounting Standardization Act of 1995, "to provide for the establishment of uniform accounting systems, standards, and reporting systems in the Federal Government, and for other purposes."

The Act would:

1. Codify the generally accepted accounting standards for the federal government set up by the Federal accounting Standards Advisory Board (FASAB) and approved by the GAO, Treasury, and OMB. It also codifies the standard general ledger to ensure that all government entities account for similar activities in the same manner and consistency from one fiscal year to the next.
2. Implement the uniform accounting standards throughout the federal government beginning fiscal year 1997.
3. Impose penalties if any federal agency fails to implement the Accounting Standardization Act.
4. Require each federal agency to provide sufficient resources to implement FASAB accounting standards and allow federal agencies to work with private sector firms to develop basic accounting systems in accordance with this Act.

loans. The present value of all positive and negative cash flows for the life of each group of loans must be determined at the time they are committed. The result of following these procedures is that guaranteed loans (where private financial institutions make the loan with the commitment that defaults will be reimbursed by the federal government) will be put on an equal footing with direct loans (the federal government provides the loan). Also, loan programs are put on an equal footing with other forms of financial assistance, such as grants. Currently, these loans are administered by various federal agencies.

The Government Performance and Results Act of 1993 (GPRA). GPRA initiated a process for each executive agency to measure its annual financial and program performance against standard measures and to publish the results. The program performance indicators include measures of outcome, output, efficiency, and effectiveness.

An outcome measure provides an assessment of the results of a program compared to its intended purpose. Outcomes are difficult to measure because they require an assurance that the correct group of targeted people participated and that the program accomplished its mission. An example of an outcome measure for the Job Training Program (U.S. Department of Labor) is the percentage of welfare recipients who are employed within three months after job training.[2]

An output measures a tabulation, calculation, or record of activity or effort that can be expressed in a quantitative or qualitative manner. An example of an output measure for the Job Training Program is the number of welfare recipients to receive job training and job search assistance within two months of their initial receipt of welfare assistance.[3]

Efficiency measures the relationship between the inputs and outputs. The cost per unit to produce rounds of armor-piercing ammunition is an example of a production efficiency measure.[4]

Effectiveness measures the relationship between the inputs and outcomes. For example, initial medical treatment will be successful for 85% of all hospital admissions.[5]

By requiring the regular performance measurement of all federal programs, funding decisions can be made on the basis of a program's effectiveness rather than supposition. This information, in turn, provides executive branch and congressional decision makers the opportunity to make choices that result in the biggest bang per taxpayer buck.

The Government Management Reform Act of 1994 (GMRA). GMRA amends the CFO Act to extend the agency-wide audited financial statement requirement to all 24 executive agencies starting with fiscal year 1996. A consolidated financial statement for the entire executive branch is to be prepared by the Department of the Treasury and audited by the comptroller general of the United States, who also is head of the GAO. This provision, which becomes effective for fiscal year 1997, will come close to achieving the financial reporting objective of the Constitution in the year 1787.

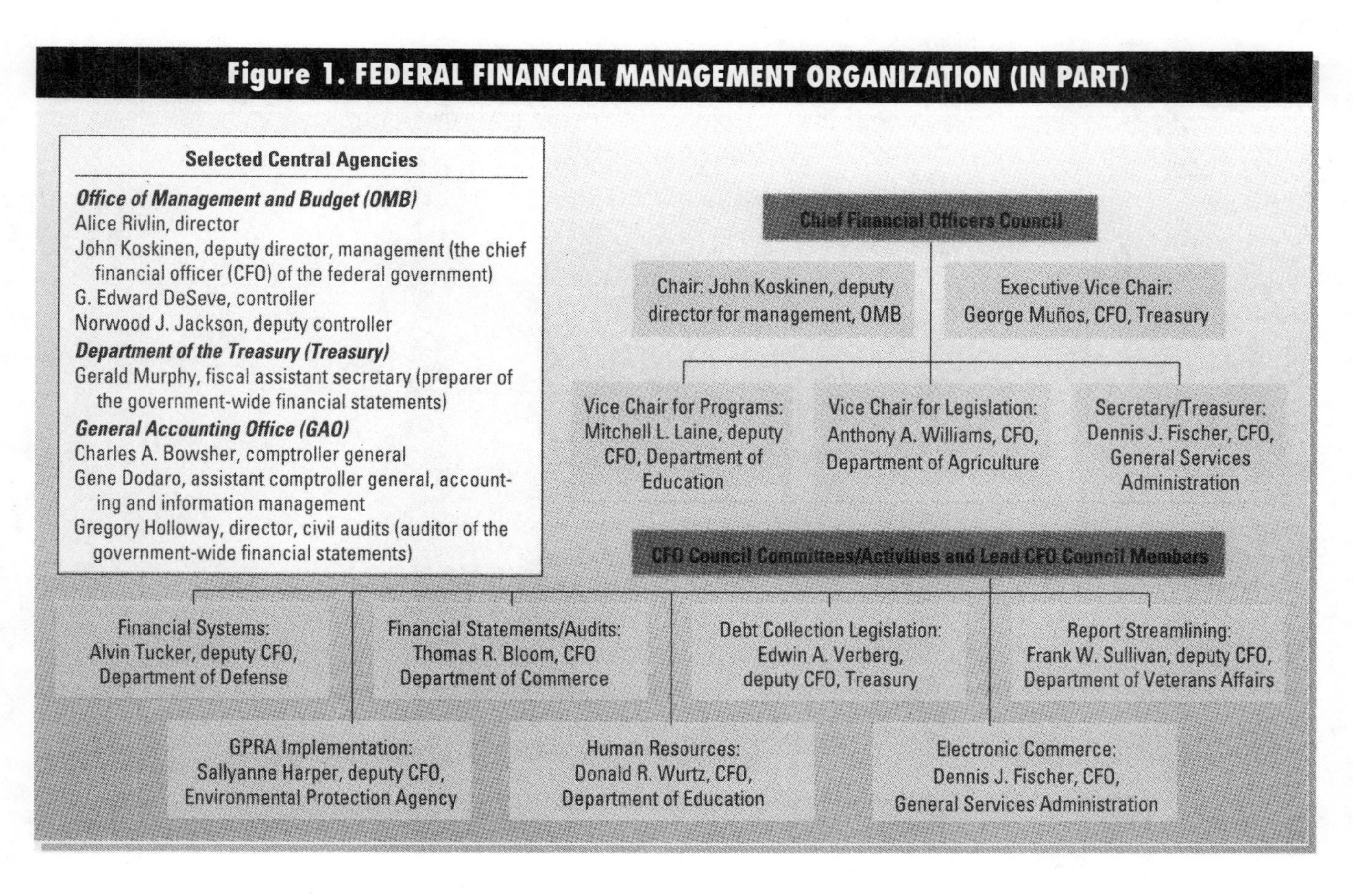

PUBLIC DEMANDS ACCOUNTABILITY

There are several reasons why a complete accountability of the federal government will be achieved, but the main reason is that the public is demanding it. Elected officials in the executive and legislative branches of government will have to respond positively or be voted out. In addition to these voter pressures for change, there is a positive trend toward more qualified—technically and professionally—agency CFOs, deputy CFOs, and financial management staffs. Prior to implementation of the CFO Act there had been concern that the CFO position would be filled by administrative assistant secretaries who would be appointed by their agency heads to assume the CFO role as additional duties. At the present time, however, many of the agency CFOs have recent experience in corporate finance, state and local government, financial management, and the public accounting profession.

Another reason that accountability will likely happen is the National Performance Review, an initiative spearheaded by Vice President Al Gore. That initiative, currently in its second wave, is intended to allow all federal agencies to determine their important functions and the efficient and effective way to fulfill them. This process will uncover those government functions that should be eliminated or privatized.

The government is a public service and a public trust. The public has many needs that it expects government to meet. Unfortunately, even with the power to levy taxes, the government does not have unlimited resources, so it must make decisions as to where to apply its limited resources.

The government's financial management initiatives of the past few years have far surpassed any that have been undertaken in any prior period. This last frontier of accounting is destined to lead us toward a government that is fully accountable and that provides quality goods and services. These are exciting times for the management accountants who work for the government. They welcome the challenge and are proud to be a part of the effort needed to make these initiatives succeed.

Stuart L. Graff, CMA, CGFM, CPA, is senior technical advisor of the Financial Reporting and Systems Operations Division, Office of the Chief Financial Officer of the U.S. Department of Education. (The Certified Government Financial Manager (CGFM) is a new professional recognition program.) Mr. Graff is immediate past president of the Washington Chapter, through which this article was submitted, and can be reached at (202) 205-0142.

[1]This article and the flowchart [see Figure 1] were written by the author in his private capacity. No official support or endorsement by the U.S. Department of Education is intended or should be inferred.

[2]Office of Management and Budget, memorandum from the Director to the Heads of Executive Departments and Agencies (M-95-04), Attachment E, *Primer on Performance Measurement,* March 3, 1995 p. E-4.

[3]*Ibid.*

[4]*Ibid.*, p. E-10.

[5]*Ibid.*, p. E-10.

Government Issues First Consolidated Financial Report—Results Are Poor

The federal government for the first time was subjected to the same fiscal discipline it imposes on private-sector businesses and state and local governments—and the results were not good.

The Treasury Department and Office of Management and Budget consolidated the financial statements of the federal government for fiscal year 1997. The General Accounting Office audited the consolidated statements and on April 1 submitted its audit report to Congress and the president.

According to the report, significant financial systems weaknesses, problems with fundamental recordkeeping, incomplete documentation and weak internal controls prevented the GAO from forming an opinion on the reliability of the financial statements. The GAO said such deficiencies impair the government's ability to safeguard assets, maintain proper records and ensure compliance with laws and regulations.

"Government requires effective and responsible management, vigorous leadership and accurate, timely information on its financial condition," said Congressman Stephen Horn (R-Calif.), chairman of the House Subcommittee on Government Management, Information and Technology." This first governmentwide audit demonstrates that we remain far short of these commonsense goals."

The FY 1997 Balance Sheet

The consolidated balance sheet of 24 federal departments and agencies

(In billions of dollars)

Total assets	$1,601.5
Total liabilities	6,604.5
Net position	–5,003.0
Total liabilities and net position	$1,601.5

Disclaimer of opinion: Because of the government's serious systems, recordkeeping, documentation and control deficiencies, amounts reported in the consolidated financial statements and related notes do not provide a reliable source of information for decision making by the government or the public.

Source: General Accounting Office Report

Bad grades

Twenty-four of the government's largest departments and agencies were required under the Chief Financial Officers Act of 1990 and the Government Management Reform Act of 1994 to each produce financial statements for the consolidated statements (see "Federal Audit Report Card"). Only two of the agencies—the Department of Energy and the National Aeronautics and Space Administration—had no material weaknesses, complied with all the laws and regulations material to the financial information in their statements and received clean audit opinions. Nine of the agencies did not submit their reports on time. "To be credible and useful, the information not only needs to be materially correct but also timely," said Horn.

According to the GAO report, the federal government could not properly account for billions of dollars worth of property, equipment, materials and supplies. The government also failed to

- Estimate the cost of most federal credit programs and related loans receivable and loan guarantee liabilities.
- Report material amounts of environmental and disposal liabilities and related costs.
- Accurately report major portions of the net costs of operations.
- Properly account for billions of dollars of basic transactions, especially between government entities.
- Ensure that all disbursements were properly recorded.

"This is the story of deficient financial systems, systems rife with problems and a general failure to comply with laws and regulations," said Horn. "The statements are riddled with gaps and filled with unreliable numbers."

In perspective—a good start

Nonetheless, Horn acknowledged that although it was common to compare the government with business, such a comparison was clearly inexact. G. Edward Deseve, OMB acting deputy director for management, told Horn's subcommittee the Clinton administration does not expect the governmentwide statements to receive a clean opinion until year 2000. "We knew it would take many years for several agencies to obtain an unqualified opinion, but we expect to see improvements each year in the accuracy, reliability and timeliness of agency financial statements."

Federal Audit Report Card

Twenty-four of the largest U.S. federal agencies and departments consolidated their financial statements in the first-ever audit of the federal government for fiscal year 1997. Unfortunately, most of the agencies received poor grades, and nine failed to turn in their financial statements on time.

Financial Management Report for Fiscal Year 1997

Departments and agencies	Reliable financial information	Effective internal control	Compliance with laws and regulations	Grade*
Department of Energy	Yes	Yes	Yes	A
National Aeronautics and Space Administration	Yes	Yes	Yes	A
National Science Foundation	Qualified	Yes	Yes	B+
Department of Labor	Yes	Yes	No	B-
General Services Administration	Yes	Yes	No	B-
Nuclear Regulatory Commission	Yes	Yes	No	B-
Social Security Administration	Yes	Yes	No	B-
Environmental Protection Agency	Yes	No	No	D+
Small Business Administration	Yes	No	No	D+
Department of Housing and Urban Development	Qualified	No	No	D-
Department of Treasury	Qualified	No	No	D-
Agency for International Development	No	No	No	F
Department of Defense	No	No	No	F
Department of Justice	No	No	No	F
Office of Personnel Management	No	No	No	F
Department of Agriculture	No report	No report	No report	INC
Department of Commerce	No report	No report	No report	INC
Department of Education	No report	No report	No report	INC
Department of the Interior	No report	No report	No report	INC
Department of State	No report	No report	No report	INC
Department of Transportation	No report	No report	No report	INC
Department of Veterans Affairs	No report	No report	No report	INC
Federal Emergency Management Agency	No report	No report	No report	INC
Health and Human Services	No report	No report	No report	INC

*Grades are based on the audited financial statements prepared under the Government Management Reform Act of 1994.

Source: House Subcommittee on Government Management, Information and Technology at www.house.gov/reform/gmit.htm.

Index

A

B

C

D

E

F

G

H

I

J

M

N

AE Article Review Form

We encourage you to photocopy and use this page as a tool to assess how the articles in ***Annual Editions*** expand on the information in your textbook. By reflecting on the articles you will gain enhanced text information. You can also access this useful form on our Web site at ***http://www.dushkin.com/online/***.

NAME: DATE:

TITLE AND NUMBER OF ARTICLE:

BRIEFLY STATE THE MAIN IDEA OF THIS ARTICLE:

LIST THREE IMPORTANT FACTS THAT THE AUTHOR USES TO SUPPORT THE MAIN IDEA:

WHAT INFORMATION OR IDEAS DISCUSSED IN THIS ARTICLE ARE ALSO DISCUSSED IN YOUR TEXTBOOK OR OTHER READINGS THAT YOU HAVE DONE? LIST THE TEXTBOOK CHAPTERS AND PAGE NUMBERS:

LIST ANY EXAMPLES OF BIAS OR FAULTY REASONING THAT YOU FOUND IN THE ARTICLE:

LIST ANY NEW TERMS/CONCEPTS THAT WERE DISCUSSED IN THE ARTICLE, AND WRITE A SHORT DEFINITION:

We Want Your Advice

ANNUAL EDITIONS revisions depend on two major opinion sources: one is our Advisory Board, listed in the front of this volume, which works with us in scanning the thousands of articles published in the public press each year; the other is you—the person actually using the book. Please help us and the users of the next edition by completing the prepaid article rating form on this page and returning it to us. Thank you for your help!

ANNUAL EDITIONS: Accounting 99/00

ARTICLE RATING FORM

Here is an opportunity for you to have direct input into the next revision of this volume. We would like you to rate each of the 48 articles listed below, using the following scale:

1. Excellent: should definitely be retained
2. Above average: should probably be retained
3. Below average: should probably be deleted
4. Poor: should definitely be deleted

Your ratings will play a vital part in the next revision. So please mail this prepaid form to us just as soon as you complete it. Thanks for your help!

RATING	ARTICLE
	1. The First Century of the CPA
	2. Are You Ready for New Assurance Services?
	3. A Prescription for Change
	4. How the Andersens Turned into the Bickersons
	5. FASB under Siege
	6. How Should the FASB Be Judged?
	7. Corporate America Is Fed Up with FASB
	8. Beresford Looks Forward
	9. Challenges to the Current Accounting Model
	10. Keeping in Step with the Competition
	11. 12 Tips to Make Financial Operations More Efficient
	12. Fraud Prevention and the Management Accountant
	13. Look Out for Cletus William
	14. Principles *Build* Profits
	15. High-Tech Sales: Now You See Them, Now You Don't?
	16. Numbers Game at Bausch & Lomb?
	17. First In, First Out
	18. Inventory Chicanery Tempts More Firms, Fools More Auditors
	19. Cash Flows, Ratio Analysis, and the W. T. Grant Company Bankruptcy
	20. Cash Flows: Another Approach to Ratio Analysis
	21. The Dangers of Creative Accounting
	22. New Accounting Standards and the Small Business
	23. Surviving Explosive Growth
	24. How Companies Report Income
	25. Understanding Global Standards
	26. The IAS Express Gains Steam

RATING	ARTICLE
	27. Finance's Futures: Challenge or Threat?
	28. It's Not Your Father's Management Accounting!
	29. Managerial Accounting Needs a Philosophical Base
	30. Cost/Management Accounting: The 21st Century Paradigm
	31. Updating Standard Cost Systems
	32. Are We Making Money Yet?
	33. Using ABC to Determine the Cost of Servicing Customers
	34. How ABC Changed the Post Office
	35. ABC: Why It's Tried and How It Succeeds
	36. Multidimensional Break-Even Analysis
	37. Planning for Profit
	38. Is It Time to Replace Traditional Budgeting?
	39. How to Set Up a Budgeting and Planning System
	40. Measuring the Costs of Quality
	41. We Need Better Financial Reporting
	42. How Nonfinancial Performance Measures Are Used
	43. A New Accounting System Is Emerging
	44. Does Your Accounting Software Pass the Year 2000 Compliance Test?
	45. Year 2000 Problem: Is Your Company Exposed?
	46. Federal Financial Management: Evolution, Challenges, and the Role of the Accounting Profession
	47. Accounting's Last Frontier
	48. Government Issues First Consolidated Financial Report—Results Are Poor

(Continued on next page)

ANNUAL EDITIONS: ACCOUNTING 99/00

BUSINESS REPLY MAIL
FIRST-CLASS MAIL PERMIT NO. 84 GUILFORD CT
POSTAGE WILL BE PAID BY ADDRESSEE

Dushkin/McGraw-Hill
Sluice Dock
Guilford, CT 06437-9989

ABOUT YOU

Name Date

Are you a teacher? ☐ A student? ☐
Your school's name

Department

Address City State Zip

School telephone #

YOUR COMMENTS ARE IMPORTANT TO US !

Please fill in the following information:
For which course did you use this book?

Did you use a text with this *ANNUAL EDITION*? ☐ yes ☐ no
What was the title of the text?

What are your general reactions to the *Annual Editions* concept?

Have you read any particular articles recently that you think should be included in the next edition?

Are there any articles you feel should be replaced in the next edition? Why?

Are there any World Wide Web sites you feel should be included in the next edition? Please annotate.

May we contact you for editorial input? ☐ yes ☐ no
May we quote your comments? ☐ yes ☐ no